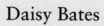

Daisy Bates

DAISY BATES

Civil Rights Crusader from Arkansas

Grif Stockley

UNIVERSITY PRESS OF MISSISSIPPI • JACKSON

Margaret Walker Alexander Series in African American Studies

www.upress.state.ms.us

The University Press of Mississippi is a member of the Association of
American University Presses.

First edition 2005
∞
Library of Congress Cataloging-in-Publication Data

Stockley, Grif.
    Daisy Bates : civil rights crusader from Arkansas / Grif Stockley.—1st ed.
        p. cm. (Margaret Walker Alexander series in African American
studies)
    Includes bibliographical references and index.
    ISBN 1-57806-801-0 (cloth : alk. paper)
    1. Bates, Daisy. 2. African American women civil rights workers—
Arkansas—Little Rock—Biography. 3. African Americans—Arkansas—
Little Rock—Biography. 4. Civil rights workers—Arkansas—Little
Rock—Biography. 5. Little Rock (Ark.)—Biography. 6. Civil rights
movements—Arkansas—Little Rock—History. 7. School integration—
Arkansas—Little Rock—History. 8. Central High School (Little Rock,
Ark.) 9. Little Rock (Ark.)—Race relations. 10. Arkansas—Race
relations. I. Title.
    F419.L7S76   2005
    323'.092—dc22   2005009959

British Library Cataloging-in-Publication Data available

To my granddaughter, Rachel Susan Tulk

CONTENTS

ACKNOWLEDGMENTS

During the research phase of this project, Roy Reed commented that his biography of Orval Faubus would have been a different book if he had written it after Faubus's death. I have no doubt his point applies here as well. Daisy Bates died in 1999. Most of my interviews were conducted in 2002. Yet no biography, no matter how candid the interviewees, can reduce a human life to the contents of a book. At the end, our lives remain a mystery, and perhaps that is why history fascinates: it is always a work in progress, always subject to revision as our perspective changes.

For the biographer or historian, one of the primary pleasures is the encounter with all the people who make your book possible. Though some will tell you that they are only doing their job in assisting you, for many it is their passion, their life's work. The only possible response is gratitude and humility.

From the very beginning, Johanna Miller Lewis at the University of Arkansas at Little Rock provided crucial assistance in ways too numerous to mention, including a close reading of the manuscript. I would also be remiss in not thanking her research assistant, Jessica Hayes. Tom Dillard and Jeannie Whayne (both now at the University of Arkansas in Fayetteville) read the manuscript and gave critical support. Cary Cox of the Butler Center for Arkansas Studies volunteered to read an early version and caught numerous errors. Elizabeth Jacoway, who has devoted decades to researching the era and events of the 1957 crisis, generously provided assistance in a number of areas. Her interview with Daisy Bates is indispensable to admirers and critics alike. Nor can I fail to mention the work and assistance of John A. Kirk, whose book and thesis on black leadership in Little Rock between 1940 and 1970 were invaluable, as evidenced by the number of references to them. To be fair to Kirk, I should note that we have some honest disagreements about Daisy Bates.

I would also be remiss in not thanking those people who were willing to be interviewed. In particular, I mention the assistance of Annie Abrams, a longtime community activist in Little Rock and friend of both L. C. and Daisy Bates. Unlike some, she wanted their story to be told and generously gave of her time and support.

There are some people who assist writers out of the sheer pleasure of finding information that seems otherwise unobtainable. The years Daisy Bates spent in New York writing her memoir, *The Long Shadow of Little Rock*, are still a bit of a mystery but less so because of the assistance of Barrie Olson, a delightful New Yorker who helped research this period. Helping to fill in the gaps of Bates's New York interlude, Audre Hanneman went far beyond the call of duty in providing both memories and perspective. I must also thank Lynn Pence for her endless help, support, and understanding.

Thanks also to Linda Pine and her staff at the University of Arkansas at Little Rock, Ottenheimer Library, Archives and Special Collections; Ethel Simpson and the staff at the University of Arkansas, Fayetteville, Mullins Library, Special Collections; Russell Baker and the staff at the Arkansas History Commission, particularly Carolyn Hervey; the Library of Congress; Tim Nutt and the staff at the Butler Center for Arkansas Studies in Little Rock; Harry Miller, archivist at the State Historical Society of Wisconsin; Ernie Dumas; Roy Reed; and Story Matkin-Rawn. I gratefully acknowledge the editorial assistance of Anne Stascavage and copy editor Robert Burchfield. Alas, any errors are mine. Finally, I wish to express my appreciation to the University Press of Mississippi and Seetha Srinivasan.

Daisy Bates

INTRODUCTION

The richness and complexity of the men, both black and white, who marched in opposing camps during the critical period of the civil rights movement during the 1950s and 1960s are only now being fully appreciated as scholars gain distance from that era.[1] One can almost hear the dead sighing in relief from their graves. Yet whatever their motives and the influences that shaped them, these men participated in a revolution such as the United States has never seen, before or since. In retrospect, their accomplishments were astonishing. In a matter of years, customs and laws that had endured for centuries simply vanished into history. Surely as important, the civil rights movement helped to spawn revolutions in the treatment of women, people with disabilities, juveniles, gays and lesbians, the environment, and a host of other concerns (such as the rights of criminal defendants) that are still being played out today. The fact that inevitable counterrevolutions have been launched in these areas only underscores the impact of the civil rights movement in this era.

Of course, men alone were not the only participants in the civil rights movement. Women, young people, and even children took to the streets and occasionally filled the jails in this era. But it is the role of women, and specifically the role of some of the black women, in the civil rights movement that concerns us in this introductory chapter about the life of one of them.

It is instructive to begin at the apex of the movement—the March on Washington on August 28, 1963, in which an estimated 200,000 to 500,000 people gathered on the Mall to hear and support their leaders as they demanded an end to racial apartheid in the United States.[2] Though now remembered primarily in popular culture for Martin Luther King Jr.'s "I have a dream" speech, the March on Washington and the program at the Lincoln Memorial that afternoon, beamed all over the world, were truly two of the high points in the civil rights movement. Immediately after the event, a number of the march's leaders, including King; Roy Wilkins, executive director of the National Association for the Advancement of Colored People (NAACP), and A. Philip Randolph, who conceived the march, walked over to the White House to discuss civil rights legislation with the president.[3]

Not one woman, black or white, was among this select group of civil rights leaders who met that evening for seventy-two minutes with President John F. Kennedy. Not only that, not a single woman had been scheduled to address the marchers at the afternoon program. In his authoritative *March on Washington: August 28, 1963*, Thomas Gentile writes that the march program by "mid-August called for Randolph to introduce five black women to the assembled crowd: Rosa Parks, Mrs. Medgar Evers, Daisy Bates, Cambridge, Maryland leader Gloria Richardson and SNCC's Diane Nash Bevell. None were to be given the opportunity to speak."[4] Though Anna Arnold Hedgmen, an organizer for the National Council of Churches and the only woman on the "administrative committee" for the march, found this absence "incredible" and protested, "no serious changes were made in the [afternoon] program" at the last meeting of the committee before the march. To add insult to injury, it wasn't only that no women were scheduled to be speakers, "without noticeable dissent, the planning committee barred Coretta King and the other wives of the male leaders from marching with their husbands."[5] Nor were the women who were to be introduced that afternoon allowed to march with the male leaders.

Why were these men so seemingly determined to risk alienating half of their supporters, including their own wives? The male black leadership planning the march, the so-called big ten, ran the gauntlet from militant John Lewis of the Student Nonviolent Coordinating Committee (SNCC), whose fiery speech would have to be toned down in order to be acceptable to the others, to Roy Wilkins, whose sophistication and political skills had grown the NAACP into a crucial cash cow for the movement and a nationwide organization that dwarfed the others present that afternoon. Surely one of these men could have stepped forward and brought the others to their senses. In fact, no one perceived the need to do so.

The answer to the question is that black women in 1963 were not ready to seriously challenge the unvarnished sexism displayed by black males, which mirrored the sexism in white society.[6] Granted, years later they would complain bitterly about their lack of meaningful participation at the afternoon program. In his biography of Rosa Parks, whose refusal to give up her seat on a city bus in 1956 sparked the historic Montgomery bus boycott, historian Douglas Brinkley has written that "Parks found the entire event, including King's soaring oratory, tainted by a male chauvinism every bit as ugly in its discrimination as Jim Crow."[7]

Perhaps. But Brinkley also has noted that while Parks became more "vocal for women's rights" after she returned to Detroit, where she had moved, "paradoxically," she continued to maintain "many old-school customs, such as always serving men their dinner first."[8]

Old habits are hard to break. Rosa Parks was hardly the only woman to find it difficult to confront the fact of male supremacy. In *I May Not Get There with You: The True Martin Luther King, Jr.*, historian Michael Eric Dyson, also an ordained Baptist minister, writes, "Coretta Scott King's relation to Martin Luther King, Jr., before and after his death, tells a powerful story of gender and race. It illuminates the sexist character of black culture and the movement in general, revealing the consequences of pursuing racial justice while leaving aside considerations of gender equity."[9]

Dyson reminds us that sexism was rampant in the movement, and it wasn't just King and the ministers of the Southern Christian Leadership Conference (SCLC) who gorged themselves on a steady diet of male chauvinism. "Despite the courage and vision shown by black female staffers, SNCC's gender politics were anything but democratic and just." Black women generally suffered in silence. It was two young white women in SNCC (Mary King and Casey Hayden) who complained in a paper that became "the opening salvo of the feminist movement of the 1960s."[10]

To be sure, black women were not insensitive about sexism, having endured white male supremacy as well as black; rather, they were understandably protective of black males and were still coping with the effects of black males' continuing emasculation by the white culture. In any event, the most obvious consequence of the chauvinism in the civil rights movement was that it severely hampered the development of female leaders. For example, while Rosa Parks was active in the NAACP, serving as secretary of both the state organization as well as secretary of the Montgomery chapter, she never became president of either organization. Similarly, Modjeska Simkins, a woman with ability and passion that often far outstripped her male counterparts in

South Carolina, never rose beyond the position of NAACP secretary in that state.[11] This was nothing new. During slavery, black women had displayed qualities of leadership (one thinks of Sojourner Truth and Harriet Tubman), but ultimately they almost all had to take a backseat to the men. Little changed through the decades during Reconstruction and Jim Crow and the civil rights movement itself. Within the movement, there was no better example of wasting human potential than the gifted Ella Baker, who Dyson (and others) has shown "was relegated to performing mundane chores as the ministers [of the SCLC] ignored her vast organizational skills and her talent for institutional building."[12]

One can only imagine how much more effective these organizations could have been had black women been allowed to rise to the top of them. On a local level in Arkansas, one thinks of the mother of the composer William Grant Still, Carrie Sheppherdson, who was given a national award by the NAACP in 1925 for her fund-raising activities. Women, as historian John Kirk has noted, in many ways had been the backbone of the NAACP in Arkansas, but they were always in supporting roles, raising money and organizing events. They sometimes had little respect for the men around them. Mrs. H. L. Porter, Little Rock branch secretary, summed up her feelings about the men: "The lawyers, doctors, preachers and businessmen . . . are just a bunch of egoistic discussers and not much on actual doings."[13]

Yet some women, despite all they endured, managed to assume major leadership roles in the movement. Diane Nash was a leader in the Nashville sit-ins in 1960 and went on to become one of SNCC's most valuable and influential members. Gloria Richardson Dandridge led a protracted struggle for equality in Cambridge, Maryland. Other women on the stage that day in Washington known for their leadership and support of civil rights included Dorothy Height of the National Council on Negro Women and Septima Clark, whose work at the Highlander School in Tennessee was legendary.

The minds of human beings prove repeatedly to be fragile instruments for remembering events precisely, especially when we have a point to make. The belief that there were no women speakers that afternoon at the Lincoln Memorial endures today. As recently as 2003, Dorothy Height told journalist Gwen Ifils that "despite all our efforts, and many women joined me, we were not able to have a woman speaker. The only female voice heard was that of a singer, Mahalia Jackson."[14]

In fact, there was one. Though a last-minute decision and a poorly handled sop to the women on the stage, according to Thomas Gentile, "ultimately Daisy Bates was permitted to say a few words."[15] Gentile does not tell us who made the decision to allow Bates to speak.[16] Her complete speech and the full text of what she and many others not as famous as Martin Luther King Jr. said have, according to Gentile, been locked away in the archives of the television networks and not allowed to be viewed or heard for research purposes. However, excerpts of some of their speeches can be heard at the National Civil Rights Museum in Memphis. Daisy Bates can be heard saying,

> The women of this country, Mr. Randolph, pledge to you, to Martin Luther King, Roy Wilkins and all of you, fighting for civil liberties, that we will join hands with you as women of this country. . . . We will walk until we are free, until we can walk to any school and take our children to any school in the United States. And we will sit in, and we will kneel in, and we will lie in if necessary until every Negro in America can vote. This we pledge as the women of America.[17]

Many Americans over a certain age will recall Daisy Bates at the center of the school integration crisis in Little Rock in September 1957. The attention of the world was suddenly riveted on this Upper South city of then 100,000 when, on Labor Day, September 2, Arkansas governor Orval E. Faubus ordered National Guard troops to Central High School to prevent black students from entering the next morning. Bates, president of the Arkansas NAACP and who would become the mentor to the black students known at the "Little Rock Nine," stood squarely at ground zero of the worst constitutional crisis the country had faced in the twentieth century. Regarded as the field general for the forces on the ground who were battling for school integration, Bates and the Nine would become known around the world for their dignity, bravery, and courage.

Though her speech at the Lincoln Memorial was short and unscheduled, the fact that Daisy Bates was chosen for this honor alerts us to her importance. It was not the first time that she had been thought of as a representative female leader in the civil rights movement by the men on the stage. On October 9, 1962, she had been invited to attend the American Negro Leadership Conference. The "conference callers included Martin Luther King, A. Philip Randolph,

Whitney Young and Roy Wilkins" and was held for the purpose of adopting a civil rights "policy" on sub-Sahara Africa. Bates had to decline because she instead would be addressing the Louisiana NAACP.[18] The timing of her appearance in New Orleans fit nicely with the October national release of her memoir, *The Long Shadow of Little Rock*, by the New York publisher David McKay Company. The book would go on to receive respectful reviews in the *New York Times* and *Washington Post* and several other national publications. Yet there has been no adult biography of her, as there has been, for example, of Rosa Parks and other women in the movement. Our own understanding of history is poorer if we leave unexplored the identity of this woman chosen by the Associated Press in 1957 as "Woman of the Year" in education.

Daisy Bates never fit the mold of the self-sacrificing black woman who patiently stayed in the back room feeding the mimeograph machine while the men planned the marches and commanded the headlines.[19] As a female civil rights leader, Bates confounds the expectations of those of both races who prefer their heroines modest and saintlike—in other words, like her friend Rosa Parks. As we shall see, Daisy Bates was marvelously human. Criticized as being "pushy," "ambitious," "aggressive," those qualities for which men in leadership roles are praised, her reputation probably suffers from the unconscious sexism that lingers in society today. A more serious question is whether, as some have charged, she was a windup doll for the movement, her every word fed by the better educated men around her. No one, not even her enemies, questions her unquenchable physical and emotional courage. Above all, Daisy Bates was cool under fire.

Though Daisy Bates had been president of the Arkansas NAACP since 1952, she did not become front-page news in the state until May 5, 1956, when she made the lead story in the *Arkansas Gazette*, then the largest statewide newspaper. The occasion was the case of *Aaron v. Cooper* during a pretrial deposition at the federal courthouse on Capitol Avenue in Little Rock. Almost two years to the month had elapsed since the U.S. Supreme Court in *Brown v. Board of Education* had announced its historic decision banning state-sanctioned segregation by race in the nation's public schools.

Aaron v. Cooper would provide the legal backdrop for the 1957 crisis in Little Rock. In deposing the local leaders of the NAACP, the school board lawyers attempted to show that the plaintiffs had been put up to the suit by the NAACP national office in New York, but the questioning wasn't going well. Earlier in the morning, Rev. J. C. Crenchaw, president of the Little Rock branch of the NAACP, had been vague about membership and contributions. Daisy Bates's answers were no better. A highly respected member of the Little Rock legal community, Leon Catlett, whose main client was the powerful Reynolds Aluminum Company, had no particular reputation as a race baiter; however, he was surely growing a bit frustrated with Bates, whom he continually referred to as Daisy. There was nothing unusual here. A time-honored control technique of white supremacy was to strip blacks of their dignity by calling them by their first names as though they were children. According to the *Arkansas Gazette,* "On one occasion, Mrs. Bates corrected Catlett on his pronunciation of Negro. It was a quick interjection and passed without comment, but Catlett changed his pronunciation of the word thereafter." In fact, though the paper didn't make it explicit, "during Catlett's questioning of Bates he occasionally referred to the NAACP's 'nigger' leaders."[20]

As the afternoon session got under way, Bates

leaned forward in her chair and said to Catlett: "You addressed me several times this morning by my first name. That is something that is reserved for my intimate friends and my husband. You will refrain from calling me Daisy."

Without hesitating, Catlett shot back, "I won't call you anything then."[21]

For a black person to confront a white person in 1956 in Little Rock publicly and in this manner was a shot across the bow of white supremacy in Arkansas and in the South. For centuries, an unwritten racial etiquette dictated that blacks in the South publicly assume an attitude of deference in their dealings with whites. For a black woman to insist on her dignity in so public a forum in the Jim Crow South— well, that took one's breath away. It was also news.

Ironically, Bates was able to come off so well in this exchange in part because of white male chauvinism. Had a black male confronted Catlett, he might well have been told, "Boy, I'll call you whatever I want to and don't you forget it," and then suffered an act of retribution. But again, as she often would do, Bates had used her femininity to advance her cause. It was a defining moment in her burgeoning career as a civil rights leader. Henceforth, blacks in Little Rock and throughout Arkansas, whether they liked it or not (and many would not), knew they had a leader who dared to confront whites face-to-face and as an equal. Little Rock whites reading their favorite newspaper the next morning knew their enemy was not just in the New York office of the NAACP or in the pages of the *Arkansas State Press*, the weekly civil rights newspaper published by Daisy Bates and her husband, L. C. Bates. Naturally, the *State Press* reported the exchange, adding that she had calmly responded to Catlett after his retort, "That'll be fine."[22]

By the time of Daisy Bates's death in 1999, obviously much had changed in Arkansas in the intervening almost half century. For roughly the last quarter century of her life, Bates's stature grew within the state, until at her death, her body lay in state at the Arkansas State Capitol.

To understand the life of Daisy Bates is to grasp the epochal psychological transformation that African Americans underwent in the middle years of the twentieth century that allowed them to challenge white supremacy and claim for themselves the dignity that is the essence of all human individuality. The manner in which she and others conducted this epic battle in Little Rock in the fall of 1957 transcended the actual results. The terms "segregation" and "Jim Crow" have never adequately described the experiences of either whites or blacks in the South. In fact, even today neither race has yet come to terms emotionally with the experience of white supremacy as practiced particularly in the states that once comprised the Confederacy.[23] To be sure, the experiences of both races had always been intertwined with a mutual quest for personal dignity: the upper-class whites of the Old South, with their obsession with a concept of honor that, among other things, claimed to sustain and give meaning to their subjugation of another people; blacks in their tortured effort to claim for themselves the respect whites have seldom given them. White supremacy presupposed a black hole of innate genetic inferiority that knew no bottom. This understanding was hardly a southern phenomenon. In a campaign speech against Stephen Douglas in 1858, Abraham Lincoln opined, "there is a physical difference between the white and black races which I believe will forever forbid the two races living together on terms of social and political equality. And inasmuch as they cannot so live, while they do remain together, there must be the position of superior and inferior, and I as much as any man am in favor of having the superior position assigned to the white race."[24] With the publication in 1994 of the highly controversial *The Bell Curve: Intelligence and Class Structure in American Life*, the debate over black intelligence burst into flame in the present era and lies today smoldering beneath the surface of public discussion. Thus more than 229 years after Thomas Jefferson, himself a slaveholder and father of slaves, penned his immortal words, "All men are created equal," most every black person in this country has had to live with the questions of whether he or she "was as good" as whites, as "intelligent," as "attractive," as "pretty," as "competent."

What has been underemphasized by some of the historians of and commentators on the 1957 school desegregation crisis in Little Rock is that everyone—white or black, southerner or northerner, liberal or conservative, integrationist or segregationist—who was involved in the crisis personally lived in the grip of white supremacy during those years. Until one can sense how totally the notions of Anglo-Saxon superiority had permeated the psyches of all of those who grew up in its hothouse atmosphere, those times cannot be fully understood or appreciated. It wasn't simply a "way of life," it *was* life, whether one was living in the Arkansas Delta, Little Rock, or even the White House.

The implications of living in such a world were profound. In a letter published in the *Nation* in 1933, John Gould Fletcher, still Arkansas's only Pulitzer Prize-winning poet, wrote from Little Rock, "But we are determined, whether rightly or wrongly, to treat him [the Negro] as a race largely dependent upon us and inferior to ours."[25] In the intervening years, continued pressure for change by blacks and their allies translated into a dim realization among some whites in Upper South states such as Arkansas that strict segregation by race could not endure forever. Yet by the mid-1950s nothing in Arkansas had occurred to alter the basic mindset that the principles of white supremacy would not endure. Naturally, whites would continue, when possible, to insist that they alone dictate the pace of any changes forced upon them. This psychological legacy of white supremacy in Arkansas wasn't merely rooted in a quaint custom called "segregation." It had been imprinted on both races through a daily living history of slavery, murder, rape, violence, intimidation, economic exploitation, discrimination, and humiliation of black citizens. Both blacks and whites coped with past and present race relations through the normal psychological defense mechanisms of denial, rationalization, and projection. The result was that race relations were "excellent"; Little Rock was a "moderate" city until blacks such as Daisy Bates insisted on forcing the pace of the inevitable changes to come. Certainly, in comparison to other southern cities such as Birmingham, Alabama, Little Rock would prove to be a much less violent city for blacks during the civil rights era, but this is only a matter of degree. For months on end, Daisy and L. C. Bates were subjected to endless harassment and their "dream home" repeatedly attacked. Only luck and the presence of armed guards prevented its destruction.

There has to be some irony in the fact that as much as Daisy Bates wanted to be written about, there is a good deal of her story that will not be told here and will have to await further exploration. Daisy and L. C. intentionally covered their early tracks too well, at least for this writer. It will become clear that this effort was a matter of close collaboration, but that will be part of their story. Finally, it must be said that a number of persons who knew Daisy and L. C. chose not to speak to me about them for a variety of reasons. Some of these reasons will become clear to the reader and will not be analyzed here.

The efforts of both black and white communities in Arkansas to perpetuate Daisy Bates's status as a legitimate heroine of the civil rights movement will not be diminished by an effort to understand and document her life. Like Martin Luther King Jr., Daisy Bates, as I have said, was marvelously human. And like the life of King, her life becomes only more remarkable as her humanity is revealed.

Chapter One

A LITTLE GIRL FROM HUTTIG

While mystery and controversy surround the early years of the life of Daisy Bates, the town of Huttig in extreme southern Arkansas had little mystery about it in 1913 for black people, the year Bates was born. In those days Huttig was no different from any other Arkansas town in its absolute commitment to white supremacy and the customs of Jim Crow. At the same time, it was a company town, owned by the Union Saw Mill Company, which started up in 1904 to harvest the shortleaf yellow pine timber that dominated the landscape of southern Arkansas and northern Louisiana. Named for C. H. Huttig, a principal investor from St. Louis, the Union County town was but four miles from the Louisiana border.[1]

The weekly *Huttig News* published during Bates's childhood reveals the same tight control and subjugation of the black population that characterized the era in the rest of the South. Superficially, as Bates notes in her memoir, the races were "cordial" to each other, but it was the type of cordiality that conformed to a strict step-by-step racial etiquette choreographed by whites first during slavery and then through decades of formal and informal domination. In Bates's Huttig period, the participants knew their parts so well they appeared to sleepwalk through them in what on the surface was an easy-going congeniality. Yet even the smallest gesture by blacks in their exchanges with whites was an act of deference, and each exchange between whites and blacks was monitored by both races to determine if the proper amount of respect had been given the other. The respect went all one way, to be sure. Like other newspapers in the South, the *Huttig News* was careful not to address blacks by "Mr." or "Mrs." In fact, African Americans did not appear on the front pages of the *Huttig News* unless they were involved in a criminal matter. Their doings were confined to a weekly column a few inches long called "Colored News," which listed their activities. Blacks were allowed to announce the meetings of their numerous fraternal organizations, such as the Royal Circle of Friends, Good Luck Lodge, and the Electric Light Court of Calanthe, as well as church services and occasionally social or other news. A typical entry reads: "The white gentlemen who are lecturing on profitable farming in Union County addressed our school Wednesday. The talks were fine and we were told the things we need to learn—raise what we need at home."

There were no such reports in the *Huttig News* of "colored gentlemen," which would have been a contradiction in terms. Instead, blacks were served up in the proverbial stereotype. "Why Sambo likes Lucinda: A Reading" and "Sambo & Old Mr. Moon" were offered along with more serious works of entertainment at a benefit put on by the white Huttig School Improvement Association in March 1915.[2]

In her memoir, Bates recounted an incident when she was a child in which her foster mother, who was ill, sent her to the meat market to buy pork chops for dinner. The butcher who eventually waited on Bates humiliated her when she showed signs of impatience. "Niggers have to wait 'til I wait on the white people," he said crossly. "Now take your meat and get out of here!" Bates reported she ran home crying.[3] In 2002 the white librarian in Huttig was quite certain that story wasn't true. She didn't know anything else about Daisy Bates, but, according to her, that didn't happen. A black child wouldn't have had to wait. "I don't think there was any discrimination," she, rather amazingly, insisted.[4]

This is not to say there were not exceptions to the racial etiquette. Up until a certain age children were exempt. Bates's memoir records her childhood friendship with a white girl named Beatrice with whom she shared her pennies to buy hard candy at the commissary. In private, the etiquette was sometimes suspended (sex has always been a great leveler as well as an instrument of power), but in public it was not. But what if the etiquette was transgressed publicly by black adults? What then? Indignant over her treatment, little Daisy had wanted her parents to stand up for her. "It's fat, Mother. Let's take it [the meat] back."[5]

Bates learned that night there was a line black people couldn't cross when her foster father, whom she adored, arrived home from his job at the mill. "He dropped to his knees in front of me, placed his hands on my shoulders, and began shaking me and shouting. 'Can't you understand what I've been saying?' he demanded. 'There's nothing I can do! If I went down to the market I would only cause trouble for my family.'"[6]

Prior to writing her memoir, Bates had told this story at least once earlier, in a 1957 interview, and it sounds plausible. Every southern black child learned the same lesson—that their parents were essentially helpless to deal with the injustices they faced. A more famous autobiographical description of this dilemma comes out of Arkansas in 1916 from Richard Wright. He was living in the Delta town of Elaine in Phillips County, less than a hundred miles to the northeast. When his uncle was murdered by white men for refusing to sell them his drinking establishment, Wright, then a child, writes, "Why had we not fought back, I asked my mother, and the fear that was in her made her slap me into silence."[7]

Arkansas, black children learned, was a dangerous place, like the rest of the South. Just three years later, hundreds of black sharecroppers were murdered in and near Elaine during a rampage by whites. Black sharecroppers in the area had organized a union to attempt to deal with the white planters who routinely cheated them at settlement time during the fall. It began when some of the black farmers resisted an attempt to break up their union meeting at a church in a hamlet called Hoop Spur three miles north of Elaine. One white man, a Missouri-Pacific Railroad security guard, was killed. Continued resistance sent the Delta whites into a panicked frenzy. A mob of between 600 and 1,000 armed whites from all over the Delta, including Mississippi and Tennessee, flooded the area on a "nigger hunt" the next day, October 1, 1919. Additionally, more than 500 soldiers from Camp Pike in Little Rock, armed with twelve machine guns (many of the soldiers battle-tested veterans of the Second Battle of the Marne), boarded a troop train at Union Station at midnight and arrived in Elaine on the morning of October 2. Though supposedly neutral, there is evidence that the troops also killed blacks indiscriminately. When the smoke cleared, five whites, including one soldier and three members of the Phillips County posse (all in pursuit of blacks), as well as hundreds of blacks (though the official total was twenty-five) were dead.

Arkansas governor Charles Hillman Brough, who had accompanied the troops, met with a self-chosen Committee of Seven in Helena on the afternoon of October 2 and declared himself satisfied that "no lynchings" had occurred. He then returned to Little Rock, where he held a press conference and eulogized the five dead whites by name. They had become instant martyrs in what whites in Phillips County termed an "insurrection" by blacks. No whites were arrested, but within a month twelve blacks were given show trials, which were over within two days (the locally appointed defense counsel didn't even interview their clients or call witnesses on their behalf). The Elaine Twelve, as they came to be known, were sentenced to die in the electric chair, and sixty-five others (many accepting twenty-one-year prison terms) entered into hasty plea bargains to avoid the same fate. Years of protracted litigation by the national NAACP and Little Rock local counsel, which included Scipio Africanus Jones, the leading black Arkansas attorney of his day, finally resulted in freedom for all of the convicted blacks by 1925.[8]

The lesson, however, was clear to blacks in Arkansas: when aroused, white Arkansans were as capable of racial violence as any group of people in the South. Reflecting the editorial policy that "no news is good news," the local weekly in Huttig didn't even mention the unpleasantness in the Elaine area. Of course, the news of the slaughter couldn't be kept quiet.[9] Within days, the national office of the NAACP had sent Walter White, its future executive director, to Elaine to investigate. White, who because of his light color was able to "pass," reported that a massacre in Elaine had occurred. Enraged by articles in national black publications—the *Crisis* (the national magazine of the NAACP) and the *Chicago Defender* both pointed out that there had been no attempted insurrection—Governor Brough futilely searched for a way to ban these publications from entering the state.[10]

Blacks in Huttig met with the same swift justice as occurred in Elaine. For example, the *Huttig News* in late October 1914 reported that a black man named Will Neely was arrested and charged with killing a white constable (Neely was originally said to have stolen a harness). He was removed from jail and hidden "for fear of mob violence." All within three weeks, the paper noted briefly, he was placed on trial, convicted, and sentenced to die in the electric chair.[11] No details of his trial were given.

Daisy Bates officially appears on the scene in Huttig in 1920, but as if out of nowhere. The census for that year lists her age as seven years old, her name, Daisy Lee Gatson, an "adopted" child, in the household of Orlee Smith. Because her name was not changed, it is unlikely she was formally adopted. Others at 75 A Avenue in Huttig included Orlee's wife, Susie; a seventeen-year-old stepdaughter; and two boarders.[12]

Who Bates's parents were has remained a matter of a fierce but unresolved debate. A delayed birth certificate obtained in 1962 by her husband, L. C. Bates, gives the names of her birth parents as John Gatson and Millie Riley, both of whom were said by him to be living in Huttig at the time Bates was born.[13] Thus far it has been impossible to confirm their identity or whether either was one of her biological parents.

In her book Bates states she was told as a child by a cousin that her birth mother was first raped, then killed by three white men, her body thrown into a millpond when Bates was still an infant. Her father had left her to be raised "by the people who have you now, his best friends. He left town. Nobody has heard from him since."[14] Bates wrote that she essentially confirmed this story with her foster father, who told her, "There was some talk about who they were, but no one knew for sure, and the sheriff's office did little to find out."[15]

After this conversation, her "life now had a secret goal—to find the men who had done this horrible thing to my mother." Then, one day while at the commissary, Bates, who was told all her life she was the spitting image of her mother, locked eyes with a young white man. By the way he stared at her, she knew he was one of her mother's killers. After this encounter, he was there often, now unemployed, drunk, sitting on the porch bench. Once in the commissary she overheard another white man explain his sodden state by saying, "You heard about that colored woman they found in the mill-pond a few years ago? I heard he was involved . . . leastwise, he started to drink about then, and he's been getting worse and worse ever since." She became obsessed by him and would invent reasons to come to the commissary to stare at him, as if her gaze could "make him pay for his sin." In the meantime, her own life had changed. She began to hate all things white. At one point in a drunken stupor, the man pleaded with her, "In the name of God, please leave me alone." Months passed, and then one day "Drunken Pig," the name she gave him, wasn't there any more. His body was found in an alley; he apparently drank himself to death out of guilt.[16]

The difficulty with this story is that the *Huttig News* contains no account of the violent death of a black woman named Riley between the years 1913 and 1920.[17] The paper does briefly mention a story in 1917 about the murder of a young black woman named Minnie Harris whose body was "thrown in the large storage pond" near the mill.[18] A neighbor was arrested, but the story was apparently not followed up. Yet the story that Bates's mother was raped and killed by white men is often repeated. Clifford Broughton was a nephew of Susie Smith's and in 2002 was the keeper of the Daisy Bates legend in

Huttig. Broughton said that he and his family lived with the Smiths and Daisy at one point in his life, which is confirmed by the 1930 census. According to the census, Broughton was only two at the time, and Daisy by then was seventeen and soon about to leave Huttig forever. His stories are thus secondhand from his aunt Susie. Broughton claims he was told that Daisy's mother was raped and killed by two men and her body thrown into a "forty-acre pond" near where the Smiths lived. However, an interview with Broughton's sister, Tommie, who was ten in 1930, did not confirm this account. She only remembered a story that Daisy's birth mother had drowned but did not recall being told she was murdered.[19]

Complicating the mystery of Bates's parents is the appearance in Little Rock in the 1980s of a family who claimed and still insist that they are related to Bates. Though they played a significant role in Bates's last years and in her affairs after her death (including her funeral), they have refused my attempts to confirm their identity. What weakens their claim is that, until Bates became famous, none of them are mentioned in her voluminous papers at the University of Arkansas or the State Historical Society of Wisconsin. If they are indeed related to her, it seems a bit strange that none of them appeared in her life at an earlier stage. Yet it is possible they are related, assuming Bates's father was a Gatson. The Huttig telephone book of 1917 listed a man named Jim Gatson. Gatsons, allegedly Daisy's half-brothers, lived in the general area of Huttig at the time efforts were made to confirm their stories. A note from the reference archivist at the State Historical Society of Wisconsin states that "several relatives of Daisy Bates, including her niece Melenda Gatson Hunter," appeared at the research room in Madison on June 28, 2001. The archivist related that Hunter described herself as the "family historian" and left copies of Bates's 1962 delayed birth certificate and a marriage license of "H. C. Gatson and Miss M. B. Boyett." Hunter "says that her research has established that Daisy's father was not John Gatson, but instead was H. C. (Hezekiah C.) Gatson."[20] The 1920 census mentions a Hezekiah Gatson, the son of a Demelleas Gatson, who lived in Union Parish, across the state line in Louisiana. The possible difficulty here is that Hezekiah Gatson would have been only about sixteen when Daisy was born. Efforts to reach Hunter through members of the Gatson family in Arkansas proved futile.

On the subject of Bates's birth father, Clifford Broughton volunteered, "I think her daddy may have been white." He also stated that

"Daisy didn't know who her people were."[21] Despite the unambiguous declaration in the 1920 census that her name was Daisy Lee Gatson, one wonders if he was correct on both counts. For her part, Bates writes in her memoir she was told by her cousin "Early B." that her "daddy was as light as a lot of white people."[22] Broughton confirmed Bates's account of her friendship with an "Early B. Broughton," who was his father's first cousin. What appears undeniable from Bates's chapter about her early life in Huttig is the influence of her foster father, Orlee, whom she loved without qualification. She wrote about her feelings for him as he was dying. "How I loved this strong man who all his life had not been able to use his strength in the way he wanted to. He was forced to suppress it and hold himself back, bow to the white yoke or be cut down. And now that his life was ebbing, he was trying to draw on that reservoir of unused strength to give me a lasting inheritance."[23]

What Bates's foster father had done for her was to take her seriously, and the boost to her self-esteem is obvious in the pages of her memoir. "I don't remember a time when this man I called my father didn't talk to me almost as if I were an adult," she recalled.[24] Lest one underestimate Orlee Smith's role in her formative years, Bates, in an early draft of *The Long Shadow of Little Rock*, admitted that her choice of a mate was influenced by him. "At times," she wrote, "looking back, I have questioned my reasons for marrying L. C., and his marrying me, for I must have seemed to him very immature. Maybe it was because he had so many of the qualities my father had."[25]

Bates painted a rather austere portrait of Susie Smith, the woman who raised her. Though she remembered her foster mother as "a tall, dark-brown woman with a kind face and big brown eyes that sparkled when she laughed," Bates included no anecdotes that showed this woman to be a kind and jolly caretaker of a high-spirited girl. On the contrary, Susie Smith appears in the memoir as a stern, churchgoing disciplinarian. "I was often clobbered, tanned, switched and made to stand in the corner. The floor in the corner was slightly worn from the shuffling of my feet."[26] Though Bates goes on at length about the death of Orlee Smith, a World War I veteran, she does not mention that she attended Susie Smith's funeral. Both Clifford Broughton and his sister recalled that she was not present. Clifford Broughton says that Bates and his aunt Susie had a falling out when Orlee died. Bates "smarted off" at the funeral that she was entitled to the American flag that Susie was given as Orlee's widow. She felt she had as much right to it as Susie. She didn't get it. Until that time, according to Broughton, Bates had gotten along well with her foster mother. Bates writes that Orlee Smith died when she was in her "teens." The 1930 census shows that he was head of the household in that year. Apparently, he died within the next two years.

Another Huttig resident, Ethel Smith, in her eighties, remembered Bates as a "young lady." She "looked almost like a white person to me but very, very pretty."[27] Bates was aware of her appearance. She wrote in *The Long Shadow of Little Rock* that her cousin Early B. told her that she looked like her mother, who was "very pretty, dark brown, with long black hair." As a young woman, Bates was stunningly lovely. In dark pants and a white blouse, she was captured by a studio photographer in an undated photograph in a rare moment of almost aching vulnerability.

For most young black women, no matter how beautiful, life in Huttig would have had its grim side. First, there was the matter of Bates's education. She would tell historian Elizabeth Jacoway that she completed high school.[28] Yet an entry in *The African-American Hall of Fame* states that "her education did not progress further than Huttig grade school."[29] Thanks to the inferior educational system provided to black children in Huttig, six or eight grades may be all the schooling she obtained. Education was not a priority in Arkansas for most children. It was not until 1915 that whites in Huttig approved a bond issue of $12,000 to erect "a suitable high school building" for their own use.[30] A year after Bates was born, in the "Colored News" section of the Huttig paper on May 16, the reporter mentions the closing for the year of the colored school, grades one through four. Eventually, there would be nine grades for black children in Huttig, who were later bussed to a black high school. With desegregation, the history of black education in Huttig (like much of rural black history throughout the state) has been lost.

Besides an inadequate educational system, Bates remembered that the Union Saw Mill Company homes in the black area of Huttig were of the "shotgun" variety and were either "rarely painted" or "drab red in color. On the other side of town where the whites resided, there were "white bungalows, white steepled churches and a white spacious school with a big lawn."[31] According to Clifford Broughton, Bates's home at 75 A Avenue in Huttig was destroyed by fire, but today one still can see some of the shotgun houses of her youth nearby.

Even had Bates been educated, the employment opportunities in Huttig for black women were limited primarily to domestic work that paid fifty cents a day. Bates, perhaps making a virtue out of necessity, paints an almost idyllic portrait, never mentioning she did a day's work in her entire time in Huttig. "The summers . . . for the most part, were spent on our farm in eastern Arkansas where my grandmother lived with a brown hound dog. . . . Occasionally we would take a trip to other states or I would be sent to visit friends or relatives of my parents."[32] Clifford Broughton indicated that his grandmother had a farm not in eastern Arkansas but outside of a town called New Edinburg, north of Huttig. He claims to remember visiting it in the summers with Bates.

However easy or hard Bates's life had been in Huttig, it would change dramatically after she met L. C. (Lucious Christopher) Bates. Her husband-to-be was twelve years older, much better educated, and a man of relatively broad experience. As she acknowledged, in the early years of the relationship he seemed very much a father figure to her. After moving to Little Rock in the late 1930s, both L. C. and Daisy would be understandably vague about their early life together, for there were a number of details that didn't fit their image.[33]

Chapter Two

A MUCH OLDER MAN

After Daisy had become famous, L. C. would tell the same sly, understated story, saying that when he had first met her, "She was nothing but a kid—I wasn't thinking about her. She later moved to Memphis. When she grew up and got a little older, she looked a little better."[1] It always got a laugh because of her obvious beauty and possibly because of his homely features. Though only five feet eleven and 140 pounds, he appeared taller because of his cadaverous physique. Never photographed in public without his black horned-rim glasses after he came to Little Rock, he also seemed older than his chronological age.

Compared to the mill workers and farmers around Huttig, L. C. would have seemed highly sophisticated to a young girl. Clearly, he saw himself as special and would claim at the end of his life he had been born with advantages the average African American in the South never knew. In an interview with a graduate student only a few months before he died in 1980, he told the story that though he had worked at a number of jobs doing manual labor, never once had he picked or chopped cotton. Indeed, his father, a farmer and later a carpenter and Baptist minister, had hoped he would become a doctor.[2] When asked about his upbringing, L. C. would respond with ironic humor that he had been born in Liberty, Mississippi. For historians of the civil rights movement, Liberty, the Amite County seat, would become known as the site where Bob Moses of SNCC tried to help blacks register to vote in 1961 and was arrested for his pains. As long as he wasn't trying to rock the boat, L. C., the only son of Laura and Morris Bates, reported that he had enjoyed something of a privileged upbringing. While L. C. was a boy, his father moved the family to Moorhead, Mississippi, and worked as manager of a farm for a wealthy white widow from New England (remembered only as Mrs. Pond), who used her money and influence to see to it that L. C. attended a private grammar school in which he was the only black student. He later attended a black school in Indianola.[3] It was not unusual at that time for black colleges to offer high school credit, and his father sent him to Alcorn College to get his secondary schooling.

His father then paid for him to attend Wilberforce College in Ohio, which was still famous as a school founded for the children of former slaves, but L. C. dropped out after a year, admitting his decision "broke" his father's heart.[4] He had always known what he wanted to do, and he didn't need a college degree to do it. As a youngster in Indianola, he had worked as a printer's devil, and he headed straight for the newspaper business. Coincidentally, his first job at the age of nineteen was in Helena, Arkansas, the county seat of Phillips County, site of the massacres in Elaine. He worked a year for the *Interstate Register*, which had a circulation of 3,500 and was published by a friend of his father's, H. W. Holloway. L. C.'s next job, at the *Kansas City Call*, was under Roy Wilkins, who would hire him again as a field secretary for the NAACP in 1960. In the same graduate student interview, L. C. made the startling admission that the next year, in his first venture at owning his own newspaper, he had "sold out" to the "underworld element, which really ran the city" of Pueblo, Colorado. He called his paper, which was still in business in 1923, the *Western Ideal*. He did not explain specifically what was involved in his dealings with the mob, perhaps endorsing their candidates in an election year with the thought he "would have influence in the administration" if the group he backed came to power. It did not, and the paper folded.[5]

After one more year of newspaper work in California, L. C. got out of it and sold "insurance and novelty advertising" in the "Mid-south" for a while. In 1924, while living in Omaha, Nebraska, he met and married Kassandra Crawford. Though Kassandra had a child by the name of Loretta, her father was not L. C.[6] The date is uncertain, but probably in the mid-1920s L. C. moved to Memphis and "travelled a nine-state area" as a salesman.[7] Daisy Bates wrote in *The Long Shadow of Little Rock* that she met L. C. when she was fifteen, which would have been 1928. He sold her father an insurance policy, and the two men became "fast friends." "For the next three years . . . [he] was a frequent visitor in our home." L. C. would bring gifts for the family, a hard-to-get newspaper for Orlee, candy for her mother, imitation pearls or a bracelet for her. Daisy recalled they began their courtship at the movie theater in Huttig when he held her hand. She knew then and there she would marry him. "Shortly after my father's death he proposed marriage and I readily accepted." A paragraph later, skipping over fifteen years, she writes, "After our marriage we settled in Little Rock."[8]

In fact, L. C. was still married to Kassandra and didn't marry Daisy until 1942, a year after they had begun the *State Press* in Little Rock. According to Clifford Broughton, Daisy left Huttig with L. C. before her father died. Daisy and L. C. came back to Huttig "one or two times a year" to visit. After her father's death and the falling out with her mother, Broughton remembered that she may have come back to Huttig perhaps once.[9]

Lottie Neely, L. C.'s first cousin, recalled more than one trip to Memphis to visit L. C. and Kassandra while she was a child. She did not became aware of Daisy until she moved to Little Rock in 1941 to work as a secretary for L. C. at the *State Press*. L. C.'s parents were also living in Memphis when Neely made these visits.[10] Though L. C. told the graduate student that he was divorced from Kassandra in 1930, an Arkansas State Police report said L. C. was known to be seeking a divorce in 1941.[11]

In lieu of more direct proof, the evidence that Daisy and L. C. had a long-running affair while he was still married is a matter of piecing together other bits of information. Memphis city directories show no listing for L. C. from 1930 to 1934, but he is included from 1935 to 1939. "Cassandra" is listed as L. C.'s spouse for each of these years. L. C.'s job was listed as "travelling salesman." In 1937 his occupation was given as "advertising manager."[12] The name of Daisy Bates or Daisy Gatson does not appear in the Memphis city directories during the 1930s; however, an incident in 1934 establishes that she was residing there, apparently under the name of Daisy Bates.

In 1934 Daisy and L. C. were stopped by the police in Monroe, Louisiana, an hour's drive from the Arkansas border. Daisy's Federal Bureau of Investigation (FBI) file contains the following report: "Nov. 16, 1934, Daisy Bates, A Negro female, 19, born Huttig, Ark, then residing at Memphis, Tenn., was arrested by the Monroe, Louisiana Police Department on a charge of 'investigation.'" (The Louisiana police had nothing more on him than the fact that he was carrying a pistol in his glove compartment.) The report bore the signature "Daisy Bates" and listed her occupation as "housewife."[13]

When in the 1950s the White Citizens Council and its allies were trying to destroy the couple and had obtained Daisy's arrest record,

Daisy brushed off the incident by saying the information was incorrect. She said she had been only fourteen and that her relatives had been with her in the car with L. C., who was a family friend. In fact, Daisy was nineteen in 1934. On the second page of a letter L. C. wrote to Daisy in 1962, he refers to the time when he "met you and brought you away." In the next paragraph he writes, "I knew I was not much and did not know much at that time. That was 1932."[14]

L. C.'s parents were also living in Memphis at this time. Did they know about Daisy during those years? Perhaps, but it would not have been welcome news. Piecing together Neely's comments, the contents of L. C.'s 1962 letter to Daisy, and the arrest record in 1934, one is left to conclude that between the years 1932 and 1941, Daisy was occupying what would have been the difficult role of L. C.'s long-term mistress. Like most affairs that run on for years, it could not have been a totally serene relationship and would have emotional repercussions throughout their lives. Annie Abrams, a black community activist in Little Rock and a longtime friend of each of them, has said both had a vested interest in maintaining a veil of secrecy about the early years of their relationship and related her own theory of the dynamics. According to Abrams, each believed there was cause for resentment against the other. From Daisy's perspective, L. C. had robbed the cradle. If Daisy had wanted to, she could "tell the world that this old man took me and exploited me." For his part, L. C. believed that "infidelity was nothing new to her," so in his mind he hadn't exploited her.[15] (Of course, as a married man, infidelity was nothing new to him either, but in the way of jealous lovers, that fact was not at issue.) As will become obvious, theirs was an extremely complicated relationship and would remain so as the power increasingly shifted to Daisy during the 1950s.

One might assume that Daisy was employed during those years since there were no children; however, L. C.'s 1962 letter to Daisy casts at least some doubt on whether she held a job. He wrote in part, "I did my best to do for you and give you the benefit of what little I did know and have. I did not know how bad I was until you told me recently. I do know it was not until 1945—thirteen years later before you made any attempt to help earn one dime. . . . Do not get me wrong—I did not want you to help me earn anything."[16]

These are the words of an angry and sad husband who may well have been referring only to those years after the *State Press* was up and running.[17] Yet at the same time he admits that he was happy for her not to contribute financially. As in Huttig, jobs for black women in

Memphis were mainly in the domestic service category, and L. C. possibly had no financial need to see his beautiful young mistress leaving the house each day to clean up a white woman's bathroom for the low wages she would have received.

The idea of coming to Little Rock and starting a newspaper must have seemed insane to Daisy. She readily admits she resisted it. "The decision was not made lightly. I held out, in fact, for several weeks against the venture, realizing that such a project required more money and effort than the two of us had to give," she wrote.[18] It would require much more than "money and effort" for the kind of newspaper L. C. had in mind. Not only would the paper be a hard-hitting advocate for civil rights, it would aspire to teach African Americans the habits and values they needed in order to live decent and respectable lives. In the last year of his life, L. C. remembered the incident that galvanized him to start his own newspaper. Selling promotional advertising displays in Alexandria, Louisiana, he arrived at the office of the white company president, who, not realizing L. C. was a salesman, inquired, "What do you want, boy?" L. C. could not recall the date of the incident, but he knew then that "I have to start my paper."[19] It was the final straw. If nothing else, the life of a black salesman, even if profitable, was a daily exercise in tact and humility he didn't have. L. C. had seen too much of the rest of the United States to pretend that he could ignore the humiliation of being an African American in the South. To cope, he tried to avoid the indignities of segregation, claiming to have ridden a bus "only one time" when he would have been forced to sit at the back. If he didn't have his own car, he took a taxi. But there was always the problem of where to eat and where to stay. Refusing to go to the back door of a white restaurant, L. C. loaded up his car with "cheese and bologna" and ate "out of cans."[20] He didn't tell his student interviewer where he slept, but it would have been a problem, too. No salesperson makes much of an impression if it looks like he or she slept in a car all night. L. C. solved the problem of where to stay by learning the names of blacks who rented out a room in their houses as a way of increasing their income.

No decision would be more momentous for either Daisy or L. C. than his decision to begin a newspaper. By the time the first issue rolled off the press in 1941, L. C. had lived precisely half of his life. Son of a preacher, he had something of the preacher in him, though for most of his life he had little use for the kind of black ministers of the Gospel that he saw in the South. The preachers he knew talked about heaven, forgiveness, acceptance. Even at the end of his life, he said his idol had been not his father but his grandfather in Mississippi, who had shot a white man who was about use a stick to hit two boys who were guarding his watermelon patch. After the shooting, his grandfather sent for the sheriff to come "pick up the son-of-a bitch" along with the message that he would "be in town on Saturday to see about it."[21] Apparently, his grandfather had lived to tell the story, and it was a much livelier tale than L. C. usually heard on Sundays. L. C. didn't believe in the Bible anyway. "I don't go to church, but I guess I am religious. I am a student of Bob Ingersoll and Thomas Paine. They were agnostics and didn't believe the Bible was the revelation of God. Neither do I. Now, there's got to be superior powers. . . . My belief is that every person is his own God because that person directs his own destiny. How you use your wisdom and knowledge is up to you."[22]

L. C. was a freethinker, but he knew he couldn't have it both ways. A newspaper editor who presumed to criticize as well as instruct both the black and white communities in the South in 1941 was going to have to accept at least some of the bourgeois notions of those communities in order to escape criticism, so on March 4, 1942, Daisy and L. C. slipped out of Little Rock and drove to the southern Arkansas town of Fordyce and married.[23] Daisy was twenty-nine years old and still at the start of an adventure that would briefly make her one of the most famous women in the world. All her life she naturally had a lighter touch than her husband (though she was angered more easily), which is not to say that she was necessarily less intelligent. Though heavily influenced by L. C., she simply didn't operate the way he did. He preferred to stay in the background, especially when she was around. After he became publisher of the *State Press*, he was quoted more than once as saying, "We can sacrifice a friend, but never compromise a principle."[24] Daisy didn't think in absolutes. Vivacious and friendly, she not only liked people, she had a way with them. Dr. Edith Irby Jones, who met Daisy on her first day of medical school in 1948 as the first black student at the University of Arkansas and who became a lifelong admirer of both L. C. and Daisy, said that Daisy "would come into a room and within half an hour she would know everybody in the room." If she didn't remember their names, she would know something about them. On the other hand, "Mr. Bates was always reserved . . . more mature."[25]

From the first issue of the *State Press* in 1941 until the last in 1959, L. C. almost always had one thing on his mind, and that was the paper. Though Daisy, as her fame grew, enjoyed the status of being referred to as copublisher, there should be no mistake that it was L. C.'s paper. L. C. wrote much of it, he edited it, and no matter what might happen, he saw that it came out on time, not an easy task for a small paper with few employees. He started off with "two printers, two secretaries, and one reporter."[26] In the words of Jones, "the paper was his." She also observed that Daisy didn't act "wifey" about her part in putting out the paper. "She did whatever was necessary. If it was cleaning and mopping the floor . . . if it was supervising . . . she acted like an employee."[27] Daisy may not have earned "one dime" until she became city editor four years after the paper was in operation, but her lack of a salary didn't mean she didn't work hard along with her husband to make it a success. And there was no guarantee that it would be. To raise the money to get the paper started, the house in Memphis was sold, netting half of the $12,000 that was needed.[28] Though there was a black press in Little Rock (the *Twin City Press*, *Arkansas Survey Journal*, *Southern Mediator Journal*, and religious publications), these publications had no intention of rocking the boat.[29] L. C. tried unsuccessfully to buy one of the small black papers in Little Rock, but when his offers were refused, he leased equipment from a local African Methodist Episcopal (AME) church, which had published a church newsletter called the *Twin City Press*.[30] The equipment was inadequate, and within two years the *State Press* moved its offices to 610 W. Ninth Street, and the paper was printed by Keith Printing Company, a white-owned company. After the owner objected to the content of an edition and refused to print it, L. C. moved the contract to the Bass Printing Company, which was also owned by whites.[31] At first they were financial partners, but by the late 1940s L. C. and Daisy bought out their investors and apparently at no time had these investors exercised any control over the paper's content.

Though she never admitted it (nor did L. C. ever put it this way), Daisy's real education was at the *State Press*; her husband was her tutor, and there was much to learn. Advocacy for desegregation wasn't yet on the civil rights agenda in 1941 (separate but equal still being the law and a notion largely accepted by blacks as well), but most everything else was. If L. C. was Daisy's tutor, he also had his own mentors. Black publications such as the *Chicago Defender* and the *Kansas City Call* had long taught him that blacks wanted to read about the struggle for civil rights but at the same time be entertained and be informed about gains being made by African Americans. The *State Press* seemed invariably to carry a picture on the front page of an attractive African American girl or woman, often local, who had won some honor. If black entertainers were coming to Little Rock, they made the front page as well. The *State Press* welcomed Lionel Hampton and his wife to the Club Aristocrat with a front-page picture. But L. C. wrote not only about how well certain blacks were doing; he also thought it was his responsibility to call attention to what he considered problems in the community. To build circulation, he ran for a time a column he wrote himself called "Mornin' Jedge," which was often taken from the pages of entries at the Little Rock Municipal Court. This column caused embarrassment and undoubtedly anger to those identified by name, but it was a source of intense interest as well. Later, he would admit to regret at having created "Mornin' Jedge" and would drop it, but the column sold papers. Besides local social news, the *State Press* was heavy on sports as well. From the beginning, L. C. intended to make the paper known in parts of the state where there were significant black populations, which meant the paper was distributed in towns such as Texarkana, Hot Springs, El Dorado, Pine Bluff, Jonesboro, Forrest City, Helena, and Fort Smith.

The *State Press* was always about advocacy journalism. Editorials and news articles shared the front page. If people wanted to get the white perspective in Arkansas, they could buy the daily *Arkansas Gazette* or the *Arkansas Democrat* or their own local paper. "NEGRO SOLDIERS GIVEN LESSON IN WHITE SUPREMACY IN SHERIDAN" blared the headlines. "GRAND JURY CAN'T MAKE IT RAPE WHEN RAPIST IS WHITE."[32] Each week it was in-your-face, tabloid-style journalism. Whatever the issue—blacks voting, police brutality and harassment, economic bias on the job, and other forms of discrimination—the *State Press* took it on in assertive language that, by definition, was inflammatory to Arkansas whites at the time.

L. C. argued consistently in the pages of the *State Press* that blacks should form their own labor organizations because they were being discriminated against by white workers. One such case was in the Delta at Helena in Phillips County, where members of the Carpenters and Joiners Union of America walked off the job at Pekin Wood Products and forced blacks to do the same. "Through intimidation and brutal treatment they [the 400 African Americans who comprised 60 percent of the labor force at the plant] were pulled off their jobs and made to stay off their jobs until . . . the white workers could get something better." Northern management had unilaterally given all workers a raise of three cents an hour. Giving blacks equal treatment angered the all-white union (an American Federation of Labor [AFL] union, which excluded blacks). The union demanded and got two cents an hour more for its own members. Instead of blacks trying to join the union, L. C. wrote: "We would say, 'Hell, no!! Stay Out.'" Blacks should remember that they were in the majority. "If you feel you should have an organization to bargain for you, why not choose your own."[33]

Civil disobedience was never a tactic in L. C.'s arsenal. A case in point was the hated streetcar laws in the South, the interpretation and enforcement of which required blacks, who were to sit in the back, to give up their seats to whites. As a salesman, L. C. could take a taxi or drive his own car and avoid the personal humiliation of public transportation. As a crusading journalist and editor, he couldn't avoid writing about it. "Get up, Nigger, and let that white woman sit down," a white had ordered a black youth riding a Missouri-Pacific bus returning to Little Rock from Pine Bluff in 1944. After the youth refused and a fight broke out, L. C. wrote, "We will not say the boy was right in taking the seat on the bus in violation of the laws . . . but what concerns us more, is why continue a law that always creates confusion."[34]

Behind L. C.'s rhetorical flourishes ran a deep streak of conservatism that never left him. The *State Press* was aimed not only at the conduct of whites but blacks as well. Though whites felt the sting of his words, blacks were not exempt either. In retrospect, the column "Mornin' Jedge" revealed L. C. as crotchety as an Old Testament prophet. Sober and extremely hardworking, he saw nothing good in the ways of a number of blacks. What others celebrated as African Americans' innate ability to live life at a given moment to the fullest, L. C. saw as frivolity. After having been to Robinson Auditorium in Little Rock and watching young African Americans dancing in delirious self-abandon, he wrote on August 27, 1943, "Nothing is imperative in the lives of the younger generation as frivolity."[35] These are the words of a man old before his time, but he was sensitive to the criticism that blacks were loud, uncouth, and boorish in their behavior. Before the 1940s were out, he began to run a cartoon that purported to instruct blacks on how to act in public; there was nothing subtle in his message. Each cartoon was accompanied by blunt text, such as "Don't Spit on the Street" or "Don't Be a Clown in Public."[36] To criticize the race publicly required not only courage but a strong and secure ego. L. C. never lacked a confident stubbornness in his beliefs, but it was masked by his quietness, especially in the presence of his wife.

L. C.'s attacks on black preachers were little short of astonishing in a culture where the clergy has always been highly regarded. He once called the sermons of a radio preacher "more offensive than the odor of a cesspool" and was successfully sued for libel.[37] The black clergy understood that it was L. C. who was their enemy since Daisy attended church and he did not. Still, his criticism of black ministers could not have made Daisy very comfortable, though there is no evidence she ever sought to restrain her husband in this or any other crusade he undertook.

Chapter Three

A NEWSPAPER ALL THEIR OWN

W hen L. C. and Daisy arrived in Little Rock, they were virtual strangers in a city of around 100,000 inhabitants, almost a quarter of whom were black. Every community of any size in the South has always had its black elites, and Little Rock was no exception. Two of these representatives were passing their last years in the capital city just as Daisy and L. C. were arriving on the scene. Both born slaves, Charlotte Stephens and Scipio Africanus Jones had not merely survived Jim Crow, they had mastered its intricacies and taken advantage of its possibilities. With the blood of their former masters coursing through their veins, both were hypersensitive to their place in black society and were at the same time guardians of the old etiquette of race relations. When interviewed for the Federal Writers' Project in 1937, Stephens, Little Rock's first black schoolteacher, noted in her formal, measured way that whites, even during slavery, had no monopoly on the right to define the social pecking order. In fact, Stephens, then eighty-three years old, remembered, "There was class distinction, perhaps to greater extent than among the white people." Understandably, Stephens had not identified with the 400,000 uneducated blacks in the state who toiled in the fields but rather with the house slaves of her owner, Chester Ashley, whose education, wealth, and status as a lawyer and landowner made him first among equals in the rough-and-ready frontier town of Little Rock. According to Stephens, the Ashley family had referred to her people not as slaves but as "servants." Her father, William Wallace Andrews, "brought up in the mansion, enjoying opportunities and privileges" with the Ashleys' two young sons, was regarded almost as a family member.[1] The irony, of course, was that Andrews and his little daughter, Lottie (like many members of the black elite in the South), were family members—Stephens's paternal grandfather was white. "On the subject of segregation," her biographer writes, "Mrs. Stephens during the last years of her life, was more of a conservative than a radical. At the root of her attitude in this matter there was personal pride and self-respect, the feeling that gentle folk do not intrude where they aren't wanted. . . . She thought some segregation was still natural. The time was not ripe for its entire abolition."[2]

A teacher in a segregated system all her life, Stephens and those like her in the black elite, including other teachers, college professors, doctors, lawyers, and certain members of the business community, readily accepted the notion of a black aristocracy based on education, skin color, or wealth, or any combination of these. Often given special privileges themselves (such as education) as a result of their partly white ancestry, they were less than enthusiastic about challenging Jim Crow. In the past few years, a number of historians writing about race in Arkansas have taken note of this phenomenon.[3] Most recently, in a study of Little Rock's black leadership between 1940 and 1970, historian John Kirk has written,

> Segregation provided black businesses and black professionals with an exclusive black clientele for their services that they remained reluctant to sacrifice in a push for social equality. Moreover, black leaders relied on their position as spokesmen for their race to gain status and prestige within the community, with their standing in part both defined and enhanced by their liaisons with influential whites for whom they often acted as go-betweens with the black community. Working to destroy segregation for black leaders ultimately meant undermining their own financial position, by abolishing their protected market, and community standing, by alienating influential whites.[4]

It goes without saying that blacks would have been at considerable personal risk in challenging the doctrine of white supremacy for much of the Jim Crow era. The history of the Old South, especially, is the history of white violence against African Americans. Any leaders too far ahead of their time risked their life and property.

The male analogue of Charlotte Stephens in Arkansas was Scipio Africanus Jones, born in 1861 or 1862 and son of a south Arkansas planter/physician and his house slave. The father saw that his son was educated at Philander Smith College and Shorter College in Little

Rock and arranged to have him study for the bar in the law offices of white men. At one point in his career, Jones, who had more than twenty appearances before the Arkansas Supreme Court in his lifetime, was driven around Little Rock in his own Cadillac by a chauffeur. As attorney for the Mosaic Templars (a fraternal organization and insurance company with offices in twenty-six states) and a busy private practice, perhaps no black man in Arkansas history studied the racial tea leaves more carefully than Jones or had more influence with the white power structure in order to help black people. His access was nothing short of phenomenal. If he wanted the ear of the governor, he got it.[5] Access was one thing; translating his reputation for getting things done into political success on a local level as a black Republican was much more of a struggle. Though he achieved a personal triumph by managing to get elected as a delegate to the Republican National Convention in 1928, the Republican Party in Arkansas had, for purely political reasons, long quit being sympathetic to black participation in party affairs, and his victory was more tokenism than a harbinger of things to come for blacks who once had flocked to the party of Lincoln.[6]

Within Little Rock's black community during the Jim Crow era, men and women with experiences similar to Stephens's and Jones's still set the tone for racial interaction when Daisy and L. C. arrived to open their newspaper on Ninth Street. On Ninth Street, blacks could do everything: go to a doctor, dentist, lawyer, or barber; eat, shop for groceries, drink, dance, and make arrangements for burial. Just blocks west of the Mosaic Templars building at Ninth and Broadway was college row: Arkansas Baptist College and Philander Smith College, the latter whose students would take part in the sit-ins in 1960. In this area south of the state capitol were the homes of the black elite of Little Rock, many of whose houses were built in the craftsman style and equaled their white counterparts north of the invisible line on Ninth Street that separated the races.

Along with black businesses and the black church, black fraternities and sororities, which required a college education for membership, were unique creations of a particular culture. At the same time, they were more lively mirrors of white Little Rock society with its own pecking order, starting at the top with membership in the Little Rock Country Club. Of course, the black elite comprised only 3 percent of Little Rock's black population. Nearly half of all blacks who had jobs were women employed in "domestic service"—a catch-all phrase that included women who worked as maids in whites' homes, dishwashers, cooks, waitresses, laundresses, and hotel workers. Besides working for whites as "yardboys," black men worked as "janitors, caretakers, labourers, waiters, bellboys, shoeshines, street cleaners, and garbage collectors."[7] Though a few blacks had managed to find jobs as carpenters, mechanics, and the like, the vast majority were in unskilled positions, earning subsistence wages. Thus both husband and wife often each worked two jobs to make ends meet.

As newcomers and without college degrees, Daisy and L. C. would always be outsiders in the upper crust of Little Rock black society. The class distinctions expressed by Charlotte Stephens very much applied to them. Though de facto members of the Little Rock black elite by virtue of their increasingly successful business venture, they would inevitably be viewed as arrivestes by a segment of that community.

Even if they had been charter members of the Little Rock black elite, they were both too critical of the status quo, too in-your-face to be fully acceptable. It was not that members of the black community and the black elite, especially, had never made efforts to resist Jim Crow. Before they disappeared from the Arkansas legislature, black legislators in 1891 had eloquently, if futilely, protested the passage of legislation mandating segregated railway cars. Anticipating the modern civil rights movement, blacks in Little Rock, Hot Springs, and Pine Bluff staged a brief boycott of the streetcar system in 1903 to protest legislation requiring separate seating by race.[8] In 1928 the newly formed Arkansas Negro Democratic Association, under the leadership of physician J. M. Robinson, sued to vote in the white primary. Despite a promising precedent out of Texas, the case ultimately went nowhere.[9]

When L. C. and Daisy moved to town, the Scipio Jones technique was still the preferred method in Little Rock of how to manage white folks, but change was already in the air. From the town of Stamps in south Arkansas appeared a young black man named Harold Flowers. His mother had been a role model and teacher for an impressionable black girl named Maya Angelou, who had to get out of Arkansas for her talents as a poet and writer to bloom. If Scipio Jones was a prototype of the old-style black leader, Harold Flowers, fiery and charismatic, represented a new type of advocate. Obtaining a law degree from Robert H. Teral Law School in Washington, D.C., Flowers came back to Arkansas and set up shop in Pine Bluff, thirty-nine miles southeast of Little Rock. His goal was to unite black people across class lines. No one, especially Scipio Jones, had seen anything like him in Arkansas. There is a sad but telling image of Jones as an old man at a meeting organized by Flowers in the 1940s reminding his black audience of how much money he had raised to support World War I. He wasn't exaggerating. Jones had almost single-handedly raised $100,000 (much of it through the Templars), but that wasn't what blacks in this new era wanted to hear. Granted, they would go to war again for democracy and hope to share in its benefits, but Flowers, the man they wanted most to see and hear, was telling them they must all come together to demand an end to the discrimination they had endured for decades. Initially unable to obtain help from the national NAACP (local Arkansas chapters of the organization were static to moribund), Flowers founded his own group, Committee on Negro Organizations (CNO), at a meeting of several hundred people at the Buchanan Baptist Church in Stamps. The purpose of the CNO was to bring blacks into one organization in order to fight for their rights, primarily at the ballot box as a political force. Flowers had high hopes for his group, which he said would "revolutionize the thinking of the people of Arkansas."[10] L. C. ran a picture and glowing article about Flowers in March 1942. The headline said it all: "He Founded A Movement."[11]

A warm personal friendship developed between Flowers and L. C. and Daisy. When Flowers came to Little Rock, he invariably would stop by the offices of the *State Press* or the home of its owners. Preston Toombs, a former employee, recalled, "Every Monday he would come in. He'd be there all day on Mondays. That was his headquarters."[12] L. C. and Daisy would have a major falling out with him toward the end of the decade, but in the early years Flowers fit perfectly the image of the black leader both L. C. and Daisy saw as necessary if blacks were going to achieve anything except what whites wanted to give them. The old way of going hat in hand to whites for crumbs was offensive to their growing consciousness that African Americans should not put themselves in the position of "begging" whites for anything. Political muscle could be gotten by exercising the ballot and closing ranks. Thus poll tax drives in various parts of the state were undertaken "under the direction of the CNO."[13] Flowers had no illusion about the ultimate outcome of any particular election, but blacks who voted could demand concessions from whites who needed their votes.

Though Daisy Bates would never become the mass movement leader that Harold Flowers was for a time in the 1940s, he surely influenced the direction she took. In his willingness to lay claim to the leadership of blacks in the state (he was president of the Arkansas

State Conference of Branches of the NAACP in 1948 and had single-handedly built the membership up in Pine Bluff to 4,382 members, almost a fifth of the population), he was a role model for Daisy in ways her husband simply was not.[14] In the first place, no leader who lectured his or her people on how to behave in public, as L. C. did on a weekly basis, could have expected to be held in universal esteem by his or her followers. In short, L. C. had neither the temperament nor ability to inspire a crowd with oratory. He felt more comfortable communicating through the printed word. Ironically, he was more inflammatory on paper than Harold Flowers was in person.

On March 22, 1942, an event took place that would highlight as nothing else could the growing influence of the *State Press*. The incident began as a low-voltage affair: a black soldier by the name of Albert Glover was arrested by two white military policemen on Ninth Street for being drunk and disorderly. A soldier, black or white, drinking while on leave was not a new phenomenon, and neither was the response of two white Little Rock policemen, Abner Hay and George Henson, who used their nightsticks on Glover's head until he was bleeding. All of Little Rock's much ballyhooed liberality as a southern city typically ended at the police station, and police brutality against blacks was a common occurrence.

Glover's beating naturally attracted a crowd, mostly black. They gathered outside a makeshift first-aid station, and their mood wasn't helped when a panicky Henson drew his weapon on them. It was an ugly moment but one that would have probably resolved itself had it not been for the stubborn persistence of Thomas Foster, a black sergeant, who insisted he had authority to investigate any situation involving men from his unit, the Ninety-second Engineers. Specifically, why were two white city policemen clubbing a black soldier? A stalemate developed immediately. Foster flatly refused to allow Glover to be taken back to Camp Robinson without an explanation of what had just occurred. For his trouble, he was arrested and dragged down Ninth Street by the two military policemen. Breaking loose, he ran into the alcove of a church and there stood his ground.

Once again, Hay insisted on showing how things were handled down South. He volunteered to bring Foster in if the others cleared him a path through the crowd. His offer accepted, he promptly attacked Foster but soon found the sergeant was more than he could handle. Foster's resistance brought out the nightsticks again from the accompanying officers. As Foster slid dazed to the ground, Hay drew his revolver and shot the unarmed man four times, missing a fifth shot at point-blank range. As if he had done nothing more than shoot a stray animal, Hays pulled out his pipe and lit it as he stood over the body and waited for the ambulance. Foster died within hours.[15]

Ninth Street was quickly shut down, and all black soldiers were whisked back to Camp Robinson. The response from the white power structure in Little Rock was predictable: a black man had been shot by the police in the line of duty. It was self-defense. Foster had grabbed Hay's nightstick and was about to hit him with it. Whites yawned and went back to sleep. Not so in the black community, due in no small part because of the way the *State Press* covered the story. Its headlines shrieked: "CITY PATROLMAN SHOOTS NEGRO SOLDIER, BODY RIDDLED WHILE LYING ON GROUND, WHITE MILITARY POLICE LOOK ON." One of the "most bestial murders in the annals of Little Rock tragedies," L. C. began his front-page story, "was witnessed Sunday afternoon at 5:45 o'clock at Ninth and Gaines streets, by hundreds of eyewitnesses."[16] His story was both an account and a call to action.

For the first time since the 1920s, when Little Rock's black elite had raised money to defend the Elaine Twelve, influential Little Rock blacks raised their hands to be counted in a civil rights matter of importance to their community and appointed themselves to a group charged with investigating Foster's death. Calling themselves the Negro Citizens Committee (NCC), they interviewed both blacks and whites who had witnessed the incident. Before a huge crowd on March 29 at the First Baptist Church, the NCC announced its findings that Hay had not been in any danger and that the shooting was unjustified. In Little Rock at this time (and elsewhere in the South), blacks did not charge whites with "bestial" murders, and one of the speakers, Rev. E. C. Dyer, reflecting the old way of dealing with trouble, pleaded that the solution was to keep black soldiers not only off Ninth Street but out of Arkansas altogether. Overwhelmingly, however, the group would have none of the old way of doing things. They called for blacks to be hired as policemen on Ninth Street, insisted that the city conduct a more comprehensive investigation of the shooting, and copied their report to federal authorities. Lest one be tempted to understate the importance of the *State Press*'s insistence on confronting both the black and white communities with police brutality, one need only compare the response of the black community to the massacres of blacks in Phillips County twenty-three years earlier. Then, a handpicked delegation of the Arkansas black elite had sat on their hands in silence at a biracial meeting at the state capitol as Governor Charles Hillman Brough extolled Phillips County whites as heroes who had averted a riot by blacks. Though the evidence of a massacre by white mobs was clear, the black community, out of fear and custom, went into complete denial and refused to challenge Brough. By printing the other side of the Foster picture in purple prose, L. C. challenged the way blacks in Little Rock and all over the state reacted to such acts of white supremacy. In an editorial on April 3, responding to a plea in a letter to the editor that the best response was to move on, L. C. roared: "The bestial murder of Sgt. Foster shall never be forgotten."[17]

Blacks might not always be aroused to take action, but no longer could they look the other way and try to pretend horrific things were not occurring in their community. That had been possible before. Now that the *State Press* was on the scene, it no longer was possible to do so.

Worried that the *State Press* was going to hurt business in downtown Little Rock, which was thriving because of all the soldiers coming into town and spending money, E. Hobson Lewis, manager of the Little Rock Chamber of Commerce, paid a call on L. C. "He told me he had been authorized to keep my paper full of ads. I asked him by whom. He said by the merchants of the city." It didn't matter whether he ran the ads or not.

"What's the catch?" L. C. said he asked, reprising this conversation for the public for the first time in 1972. "Soften your tone. Change your policy," Lewis told L. C.[18]

L. C. refused, and immediately white businesses that had taken out ads in the *State Press* began boycotting the paper. It was a body blow that staggered the paper. "We can't operate without advertisers," Daisy told her husband. "Let's quit now while we still have train fare."[19]

L. C. wasn't about to quit, but in order to survive, a new strategy was in order. Circulation was at 10,000. Energy that had gone into selling advertisements now went into increasing circulation. If blacks wanted a paper that supported them, they would have to support the *State Press*. It was war.

As expected, white officials did nothing but rubber stamp the prior investigation of the police chief, but the *State Press* kept the pressure on by demanding a federal investigation. Though not concerned about local problems of Little Rock blacks per se, the white power structure outside the state had to pay attention because of the war effort. Not only could the United States not afford a race war by its own troops, the

Germans were being handed a propaganda tool, since one of the Allies' most famous generals, Douglas MacArthur, was from Little Rock.[20]

The army completed its own investigation, and its findings differed greatly from those of the local officials. Doubtless, pressure from the Department of Defense was applied on the Department of Justice in Washington, D.C., to take more seriously what was going on in Arkansas. In June a federal grand jury was convened, but federal judges and federal juries in Little Rock were often as racist as their local and state counterparts. Judge Thomas C. Trimble instructed the jury to indict Hay only "if it would . . . serve some useful purpose."[21]

Given that excuse, the grand jury examined twenty-five witnesses but could not find enough evidence to bring charges against a white police officer who had practically emptied his gun into an unarmed man lying on the ground. Furious, L. C. continued his campaign of criticism, running editorial after editorial, and was finally rewarded in August. "NEGRO POLICE TO PATROL NINTH STREET," the *State Press* headline crowed on August 21. The city had caved in and agreed to hire eight black policemen. Their jurisdiction was circumscribed, and their arrest powers were limited, but it was a clear victory for the black community and a victory for the *State Press*. In a matter of months its circulation doubled. Off–Main Street advertisers began to support the paper. On July 8, 1945, the *State Press* had a new home on Ninth Street with a new printing press. Daisy recalled they celebrated with a bottle of champagne.[22]

The timing of the arrival of the *State Press* in Little Rock coincided not with just the movement spawned by Harold Flowers but also with the increased effectiveness of the NAACP itself, when its litigation efforts began to acquire a national focus. In the 1930s the time was not ripe to mount a direct challenge against segregated schools and over-turn the 1896 Supreme Court decision of *Plessy v. Ferguson*, which upheld the principle of segregation of the races so long as states pro-vided equal facilities for blacks. However, a young NAACP staff lawyer out of Howard University by the name of Thurgood Marshall, working with his mentor and former teacher, Charles Houston, had begun to attack school segregation indirectly by bringing and winning suits to equalize funding against southern school districts. The theory was that the South would abandon segregation because of the cost of maintain-ing equal school systems. Marshall and Houston began to have success with these cases around the country, and by 1942 Little Rock was ready for its own litigation, which of course did not occur in a vacuum.

Harold Flowers had helped raise the consciousness of black teachers in Little Rock by directly criticizing them for their elitism.

The national office of the NAACP could not help but take notice that something was stirring the pot in Arkansas when a brave black schoolteacher by the name of Sue Cowan Morris (later Williams) agreed to file suit against the Little Rock School District. Like every other district in the state and the South, the Little Rock School District paid white teachers more than black teachers. For almost two decades there had been no successful civil rights litigation in the state, and the case would be noteworthy for several reasons. First, it marked the passing of the guard. It would be Scipio Jones's swan song. As one of the local attorneys for the plaintiff class—the case was deemed important enough for Marshall to come to Little Rock to assist local attorneys in the litigation efforts–Jones died while the case was still being litigated. Despite its reputation as a "liberal" town, Little Rock fought the case every step of the way. The school district's attorneys called Annie Griffey, a white supervisor of primary teachers with thirty-one years of experience, who testified "regardless of college degrees and teaching experience no white teacher is inferior to the best Negro teacher"; thus the disparate wages were justified.[23] Using every racist argument they could, the school board's attorneys, whom Marshall called "top flight lawyers," were successful at the district court level. One of the most effective ways to deny justice is to delay a ruling, and federal district judge Trimble delayed deciding the case for over a year. Next came retaliation: Sue Cowan Morris did not have her contract renewed; the principal of all-black Dunbar High School, John Lewis, who testified for the plaintiffs, was forced out of his job; John H. Gibson, head of the black teachers association, also lost his job.

Although the Eighth Circuit Court of Appeals reversed the ruling, the victory was initially more symbolic than anything else. John Kirk notes that although some black teachers received raises, the Little Rock School District implemented a "merit" scale for teachers that continued to discriminate against blacks.[24] Still, victories of any kind were crucial, because incrementally, they tended to undermine the notion that dual school systems were equal. At the same time, these cases laid the groundwork for blacks' admission into the Arkansas law school and medical school. A number of these new graduates from the law school would become important to Daisy and L. C.

Finally, the case helped to put Arkansas back on the radar screen of the national NAACP. In 1940 there had been only 600 members of the

NAACP in the entire state of Arkansas.[25] It now seemed that there was all this energy being put forth in a state that had attracted little attention from the New York office since the Elaine massacres in 1919.

It seems likely that Daisy Bates would have met Thurgood Marshall during this time, since the *State Press* gave extensive coverage to the case. In 1992 Daisy, interviewed by an *Arkansas-Democrat* reporter for its Sunday High Profile section, listed Marshall as one of the persons she would invite for a fantasy dinner. She was not alone in her admiration. As Juan Williams notes, with the success of the *Brown* decision in 1954, Marshall would become known to blacks throughout America as "Mr. Civil Rights."[26] Before going on to become a federal appeals court judge, solicitor general, and the first black Supreme Court justice, this talented, complicated man with his own insecurities and demons would come to play a pivotal role in the 1957 Little Rock school desegregation crisis.

Chapter Four

TWO FOR THE PRICE OF ONE

One can see Daisy Bates maturing during the 1940s into a woman who was vitally interested in all that was going on around her and determined to be part of it. It wasn't always that way. In the beginning years of the *State Press*, there is reason to believe that Daisy saw herself as more of a privileged newspaper publisher's wife than as a working partner in the business. Lottie Neely, L. C.'s cousin and secretary at the newspaper who began work at the paper in 1941, remembered that Daisy "stayed in the bed until ten or eleven o'clock." L. C. would go home for brunch, which Daisy prepared. "She wasn't the best cook," Neely remembered. Daisy improved, but "they ate out quite a bit."[1]

Ninth Street was where the action was, and being a young woman who had put in a full day's work, Lottie Neely wanted to experience it. Daisy "taught me about clothes and how to dress. She loved to wear high heels, 3-inch heels. Everything was right—her hair, her nails, her clothes." Daisy made it into the office by "1:30 or 2:00." Neely remembered also that Daisy "didn't have a regular job with the paper at that time. She would come in and help out. She didn't write any articles in the paper."[2]

Over time, Daisy began to realize that life was much more interesting at the newspaper than alone in the house waiting for her husband to come home for brunch. Preston Toombs, who began work as a printer for the *State Press* in 1948 and stayed in that position until 1956, remembered that by then, Daisy got to the office by 10:00 or 11:00. She would call the office, and if L. C. was too busy, Toombs would be sent to pick her up, "and she would be in the place all day." She still did not have a "regular" job at the paper, although she did some of the bookkeeping, sent out the boys who sold the papers, and solicited money for ads. She also went out on stories with Earl Davy, who was the photographer for the *State Press* for a number of years. Toombs remembered going to Pine Bluff with her on *State Press* business. On the same trip, she stopped off to see Harold Flowers to talk about an NAACP matter. The "majority of [her] time," Toombs believed, was spent "doing NAACP business." Hampered by her lack of formal schooling and consequently insecure about her own writing skills, Daisy developed a lifelong habit of relying on secretaries, often allowing them to draft letters for her approval. "I don't believe she did too much writing," Toombs said. "No, I don't recall her writing anything. She mostly dictated to Jewel Porce and Ivy Wesley," the two secretaries at the *State Press*.[3] L. C. told an interviewer that Daisy wrote the social news in the paper, but the actual composition would have likely been left to others.

In *The Long Shadow of Little Rock*, Daisy wrote that she took courses at Shorter College in North Little Rock in "Business Administration, Public Relations, and other subjects related to the newspaper business" soon after the *State Press* started up. At one point she took flying lessons through Philander Smith College but dropped out just before obtaining her pilot's license because their insurance rates would have increased "astronomically."[4]

Though she rarely wrote for the paper, Daisy did have input into the editorials L. C. wrote. She "and Mr. Bates would discuss it, and Mr. Bates would write the editorial," said Toombs.[5] A rare editorial under Daisy's name ("Mrs. L. Christopher Bates") appeared in late November 1945. Headlined "The Public's View of Little Rock Leadership's Inconsistency," it was short on substance but reflected sensitivity to the lack of cohesiveness in the black community. After a conversation with a woman who voiced her discontent with the lack of progress under present black leaders in Little Rock, Daisy wrote, "As I sat listening to the lady while she emptied her soul with tension in every fiber of her being, what I saw in her face made me ashamed, ashamed, not for myself . . . but for those Negroes in positions of authority in the black community."[6]

In 1946 an event occurred that would have caused anyone to grow up in the newspaper business in a hurry. Daisy wrote in her memoir that L. C. took a vacation in March of that year and left her "temporarily as proud editor-in-chief." By then Daisy had the title of "city editor." Where L. C. went and how long he was gone are not known, but when he returned, Daisy had covered a story that was about to land them both in trouble. In a state that still favored informal peonage as its preferred method of relations with its agricultural workers, labor unions always had a hard row to hoe, and union activity in Little Rock was not received any better. In her memoir, Daisy wrote that she had just finished putting together a story about a strike by Congress of Industrial Organizations (CIO) members at the Southern Cotton Oil Mill "about a mile from the *State Press* office" when L. C. returned from his trip.[7] In traditional southern fashion, after a picket named Walter Campbell was killed by his replacement, three other pickets were arrested and found guilty of violating Arkansas's right-to-work law and sentenced to a year's imprisonment. Otha Williams, the replacement worker who had shot Campbell, was acquitted. How that could happen was the result of a provision of the right-to-work law. If any violence broke out on a picket line, everybody on the line could be found guilty of it.

In her story, Daisy pointed out the obvious: "Three strikers, who by all observations were guilty of no greater crime than walking on a picket line, were sentenced to one year in the penitentiary yesterday by a hand-picked jury, while a scab who killed a striker is free."[8] According to Daisy, L. C. wrote the headline for her story: "FTA STRIKERS SENTENCED TO PEN BY A HAND-PICKED JURY." Daisy had also written: "The prosecution was hard pressed to make a case until Judge Lawrence C. Auten instructed the jury that the pickets could be found guilty if they aided or assisted, or just stood idly by while violence occurred."[9]

Auten had a reputation for not liking any criticism, and the idea that a black newspaper would have the temerity to criticize him was obviously more than the judge could stand. He ordered L. C. and Daisy arrested for contempt of court. On April 29 Auten found them guilty, and he sentenced them to ten days in prison and imposed a $100 fine. He then invented some new jurisprudence, ruling they couldn't appeal, and he sent them to jail. Released seven hours later by order of the Arkansas Supreme Court, they posted bond of $500 and appealed the decision on the merits. Citing the First Amendment to the U.S. Constitution, Daisy and L. C., represented by white attorneys from the CIO, argued they could not be found guilty for merely expressing their opinion that the judge had erred in his application of the law. To its credit, the Arkansas Supreme Court agreed and reversed Auten. "We know of no rule of law permitting jail sentences and contempt fines merely because a newspaper thinks some judge mistakenly stated the law."[10]

Since neither Daisy nor L. C. obtained a college degree (which would have allowed them to participate fully as alumnae in the all-important black fraternities and sororities), nor were they tied into the Little Rock black community through the church (though Daisy went occasionally), they carved out their own niche. She and L. C. both became known as people one went to get to things accomplished, which was made easier by the business they were in.[11] The *State Press* gave them access to both the white and black communities in a way that social background alone never would have, and Daisy had the freedom (L. C. was often in the back in the print shop) and social skills to cultivate a wide variety of not just sources but resources in the community.

In 1948 a young, extremely attractive light-skinned black woman presented herself in the offices of the *State Press*. She told the woman behind the counter she was in her first day of medical school and had been advised that if she were ever in Little Rock and needed money, she should take the trolley downtown to the paper and ask for the Bateses. Daisy identified herself, "I'm Daisy Bates." She went into the back and returned with a can and counted out the $50 that Edith Irby (later Jones), the first black medical student in Arkansas, said she needed for lab fees.[12] It was the beginning of a lifelong friendship.

Daisy was impulsive, making snap judgments about people, but it was her spontaneity and warmth that drew them to her. And her help was ongoing. On a weekly basis, Daisy would drive to Irby's apartment in North Little Rock and present her with $25 or $30 that she had collected from "colored professionals." Why did she do this? "I'm going to see that you have money—all you do is study." Here was a young woman bucking the odds, and Daisy was going to see that they were shortened. But that wasn't all she did. Each weekend that first year Daisy and L. C. would come pick her up and take her with them. "They were always doing something," Dr. Jones recalled. "It might be a committee meeting of the NAACP or *State Press* business or just for fun. At the bottom of the social activity there was a purpose." The purpose in her case was to help a talented young woman go as far as she could. Daisy introduced her to the black professionals in Little Rock—Dr. Isch, Dr. Robinson, Dr. Obra White. But it wasn't just doctors. She met Harold Flowers, and once Daisy was responsible for her "meeting Thurgood Marshall on a train going to New Orleans."[13]

Perhaps Daisy saw a younger version of herself—the self she somehow might have become if L. C. had not made her his mistress. After all, people mistook them for sisters, which flattered both women. If Daisy thought that someone had potential, she was generous with her time and contacts. Theodosia Cooper, who was hired as one of the first black social workers in Pulaski County, remembers that Daisy "was always giving me resources." Working for the Center for Handicapped Children in Jacksonville, a suburb of Little Rock, Cooper remembered, too, that Daisy "always had her facts . . . she always did her homework. . . . She had a way with people, and it was not one where she lowered herself to get what she wanted."[14]

Yet even into the late 1940s Daisy's focus was extremely local, her knowledge of the bigger picture even in Arkansas surprisingly spotty. In an early draft of *The Long Shadow of Little Rock*, in which she re-created a conversation with L. C., she revealed astonishing gaps. "Remember how surprised you were with your nose for news when you discovered that Negroes were attending the Arkansas Law School"[15] One can't imagine L. C. not knowing such an important development. Though not in any sense an intellectual, he was intellectually curious. Daisy simply didn't process things the way he did, and vice versa.

From the beginning, her soft spot was young people. At various points in her life, a child lived with her and L. C. or with her alone. She "adopted" several children over the course of her life. She was never able to have children and must have rarely talked about the reason in Little Rock. The only explanation that this author ever discovered was provided by Audre Hanneman, a friend of Daisy's (and part-time secretary) when Daisy was living in New York between 1960 and 1963. Acknowledged in Bates's 1962 memoir, Hanneman wrote from her home in Kansas City, Missouri, in 2002, "I have to admit I thought I knew Daisy a lot better than I apparently did. She never spoke of problems in her marriage, or of L. C.'s first marriage. She told me that she once had a miscarriage when she was arguing with (I understood it to be with L. C.) and he pushed her and she struck the sharp corner of a table. And she couldn't have children after that."[16]

Whatever the cause of Daisy's inability to have children, they were increasingly precious to her. The relationships ranged from simple visits with friends' children in which Daisy acted in the role of any friendly adult who favors a particular child to long-term relationships in which the child came to live in her house and was treated like an actual family member. The media focused its attention on a child named Clyde, who was living with them during the 1957 school crisis until it became too dangerous, and he was sent away. The child's full name was Clyde Lee Cross, but who his family was has not been determined. Dr. Jones has memories of him as a "regular" child, "not special, not dull, not aggressive." Clyde was probably from a poor family that already had too many children to be able to support. In 1960 Daisy told the *Chicago Defender* that she and L. C. had known Clyde for nine years.[17] The decision to give him a home with them was probably not debated at any great length. Undoubtedly, Daisy proposed it, and L. C. went along with it, as he did with most things she wanted. Clyde would make his presence known again in 1962.

Daisy and L. C. It was always that way when they were together and other people were around. But not at the *State Press*. L. C. was the boss there. Preston Toombs revered him. "Mr. Bates was a genius. He was just smart, just smart."[18] To his printer, he may have seemed like one, but L. C. knew his limitations, and that was probably his genius. He allowed himself to be edited. A talented man named S. S. Taylor, who taught at the black colleges in town, went over L. C.'s editorials. As an employer, there was nothing heavy-handed or capricious about L. C. "He treated everybody the same," Toombs recalled fondly.[19]

It was a good atmosphere. Toombs remembered that Daisy "didn't really boss anybody. We was all there together. Everybody knew their duties. You know what to do and you did it. . . . He's in the back, she's in the front. What was in the back—the press. We made up all the paper. She was up in the front with the secretaries." There was always the crunch to get the paper out on time, but the rest of the week there wasn't the same kind of pressure. Once L. C. gave Toombs $3 (not an inconsequential sum in those days) and told him to take Edith Irby to breakfast. The printer taking out the future doctor who was both lovely and intelligent—he never forgot it.

Though L. C. could sound like a nag and a scold in the pages of the *State Press*, at work there was a camaraderie in the office, Toombs recalled. "They kid[ded] a lot. Everybody in the house be talking. We never had any arguments or say fighting. . . . I never knew them [Daisy and L. C.] to be mad at each other."[20] It was a good place to work—even a fun place to work with all the celebrities and important people coming in. Toombs met, among other musicians, Lionel Hampton and his wife, along with politicians, lawyers, and professional athletes. They all dropped by the *State Press* to get written about.

The years between 1941 and 1956–before the harassment and threats began, before Daisy became famous—were the best years in Daisy and L. C.'s marriage. Though they liked the work, there was play, too. There were the parties at the private homes of their friends. Christopher Mercer, who became Daisy's right-hand man for a time during the 1957 crisis, remembered Daisy and L. C. dancing with each other at parties when he came to Little Rock from Pine Bluff for what he characterized as "R and R." Daisy and L. C. "danced the swing." Mercer's first contact with them was purely social. The crusading editor and his beautiful, vibrant wife were, in Mercer's words, "high profile." The parties were in the homes of the black elite's doctors, lawyers, and business leaders. Daisy, he recalled, had "a great sense of humor." She displayed "no reservations about being on show," but "she was not gaudy, not suggestive. L. C. was content to let her have the limelight."[21]

Mercer saw no signs of jealousy on L. C.'s part, but Daisy didn't give him any cause. "Daisy didn't flirt with anybody . . . she danced with others."[22] One can imagine L. C. standing back, watching his younger wife having fun. Occasionally, they went to the clubs on Ninth Street; other times they stayed home to play poker with friends. In a curious incident in the early 1950s, they were actually arrested for gambling and fined $5. They complained, and it never happened again. But it would become part of Daisy's arrest record and used against her by the racists who hounded them.

When their new home was completed on Twenty-eighth Street, there would be parties in the basement, where there was a bar. A few whites would make an appearance, and occasionally the conversations would become intense. Fred Darragh, a successful businessman who qualified at the time as one of the few white liberals in the state on the issue of civil rights, said that the "greatest compliment" he ever received was from L. C., who, not more than "twelve inches" from him, talked about "Goddamn white people." L. C. had forgotten, or so Darragh believed, that he was a white man. "L. C. didn't like white people very well; he put up with them."[23]

Was this true? His printer, Preston Tombs, put it more diplomatically. "He didn't hate white people. . . . He wanted opportunities."[24] Given what he had experienced over his life, L. C. probably was not one to issue an invitation to his home to a white person. On the other hand, L. C. was probably not the kind of man who often expressed his deepest emotional self to anyone, including Daisy. It wasn't that L. C. didn't have his own charm. Many of those in the black community who were interviewed for this book emphatically said they liked him, but he didn't exude warmth the way his wife did. He had his own friends. He played poker with a male group in a backroom at Dubisson's Funeral Home and had the journalist's love for discussing politics and world events.

Historian John Kirk has portrayed Daisy Bates as basically an early feminist. In a chapter on her in *Gender in the Civil Rights Movement*, Kirk writes, "Although L. C. was the 'husband' in the marriage, his role in gender terms was more typically that traditionally assigned to a 'wife,' as a supporter from the sidelines." Part of his evidence for this assertion came from *The Long Shadow of Little Rock*. "Bates's own memoirs insist that she played an equal role in the founding and running of the *State Press*."[25]

It is true that Daisy Bates gave this impression after 1957, but it would not be an accurate characterization of how the *State Press* came to be or how it was run. Not one person of those interviewed who was familiar with the *State Press* mentioned or gave examples that Daisy was a co-equal in its management. Not only was L. C. the driving force behind the *State Press*, he was much more than the silent though supportive partner of a famous, strong-willed woman. Before 1957 and the fame that came with it, Daisy herself would have scoffed at the notion that she was an equal partner with her husband in the newspaper business. Too, she would have acknowledged the vital role L. C. played in the Little Rock chapter of the NAACP. Future events and the way the national media characterized them (as well as Daisy herself) would make it appear that L. C. was basically "second banana" to his notorious wife. Repeatedly, persons who knew them both agreed with Christopher Mercer's assessment that "L. C. was the brains behind the operation."[26] Mercer was referring to the couple's role in the 1957 crisis for which Daisy alone would become famous. However, while Mercer's comment suggests Daisy was something of a puppet, she most decidedly was not.

In any event, by the late 1940s Daisy was increasingly finding her voice, even when it seemed imitative of her husband's. L. C. had spent almost the entire decade complaining in editorial after editorial about the lack of leadership in the black community in Little Rock. It was not until the end of the decade that Daisy took pen in hand and addressed the issue in one of the few editorials for the *State Press* that she wrote. In substantive terms, she was dealing with a long-standing grievance— the lack of a park for blacks in Little Rock. The theme was nothing new. For years, editorials in the *State Press* had slammed the black leaders in the city for their inability to unite blacks behind a single proposal and pressure the white power structure to establish a recreational area, which had first been proposed in 1934. There was a catch: the site was not even in the city limits. At the time, the proposed location was out in the wilds, a ludicrous choice for a park if the white power structure had not been so serious about that particular location.

Finally, in February 1949 the city, under increasing pressure to act before it was sued to desegregate its parks, passed by a narrow margin a bond issue for a park for blacks in the rather astonishing sum of $359,000. The African American vote had proved decisive, but instead of uniting the black community, it had the opposite effect. Professing not to believe that the money would be used for its specifically stated purpose, Daisy wrote that the whole affair had been simply "a smart political scheme to garner Negro votes." Blacks should be smarter. From the city's point of view, it was damned if it did and damned if it didn't. Yet Daisy's skepticism was valid: the city was already embarking on a plan to box in its black population in east and south Little Rock. The city eventually used the bonds to attract federal funds for several other projects. As John Kirk has noted, "By building black recreational facilities at Gillam Park and tying them in with a proposed black housing project nearby, the city was consciously creating a segregated black district which would affect important decisions about where to build other amenities, for example schools, in the future. The authorities were thus engaged in a premeditated effort to shunt the black population out to the east of the city while encouraging whites to move westwards."[27] The process would accelerate dramatically in the 1950s.

In any event, one can see Daisy Bates making her own voice heard, one that was increasingly critical of her own people's choices. She saw the vote as an example of blacks still on their knees. Effective change in the black community "will have to be gained through the courts or the ballots and not through BEGGING."[28]

Though she mentioned no names, Bates was aiming her comments at blacks who were carving out their own bailiwicks as leaders in the community. Throughout the Little Rock area, Harry Bass, Charles Bussey, I. S. McClinton, and Jeffrey Hawkins all managed to form enclaves in which they created pockets of power and influence among blacks. Behind the scenes, Bates would lash out at blacks who seemed to be more interested in lining their pocketbooks than advancing the cause of civil rights. There was nothing new about these allegations. The theme of blacks selling out blacks for personal gain had been and would be a constant in the pages of the *State Press*. It had always been a problem, and according to Bates's early drafts of *The Long Shadow of Little Rock*, it would be a problem during the 1957 crisis as well.

Bates could be blunt in her comments about other blacks, even to whites. Edwin Dunaway, at one time perhaps her best white friend in Little Rock, asked her to join the board of the integrated but basically conservative Little Rock Urban League. She first turned him down by saying the executive board was "just a bunch of niggers who want to sit next to white folks once every two weeks."[29]

Despite this put-down, Bates was a joiner. Over the years she became a member of more than a score of organizations in Little Rock that had the general or specific purpose to benefit the community, including the Little Rock Urban League, the Arkansas Council on Human Relations, and the YWCA. "See, I was a newspaper person, and I went to all of these meetings I belonged to."[30] If she was there in part to get news for the *State Press*, she also attended meetings to advance the cause of civil rights and the NAACP, which would become her life's work.

Chapter Five

AN UNWAVERING COMMITMENT

Founded in New York by both blacks and whites in 1909, the NAACP was more than of symbolic importance to African Americans in the South during much of the Jim Crow era. The organization's significance to blacks can hardly be overestimated. Even in places like Arkansas where the organization had few branches, blacks like Daisy Bates's foster father counted themselves as members and sent in contributions to the national office.[1] Though in its initial years the NAACP had a reactive litigation strategy, that would change in the 1930s with the arrival of Charles Houston, an African American graduate of Harvard Law School.[2] Houston and his student Thurgood Marshall began to formulate and implement a plan of attack that was designed to force the South eventually into giving up segregated schools as well as the other vestiges of Jim Crow.[3]

Focusing the legal work merely highlighted the NAACP's need for further organizational growth in the South. The establishment of the Arkansas State Conference of Branches in the 1940s reflected a recognition by the NAACP's national office that from an organizational perspective, the state was moving forward, but soon thereafter, Walter White, now executive director, and his staff believed they had just opened a can of worms. The way the national office would handle the "mess in Arkansas" reflected its own uncertainty as to how militant an organization the NAACP should be, both on the national and local levels. It would be a problem that would surface again and again. In 1945 the national office gave the hard-charging Harold Flowers the job of "chief organizer of branches" but countenanced the election of Rev. Marcus Taylor, a far more conservative man, as president. By so doing, the national office was unwittingly inviting a fight over the direction of the NAACP in the state.

Taylor charged Flowers with "keeping half of the funds collected from . . . the branches for himself."[4] The national office confirmed that Flowers was slow sending in the money, but that was as far as it was willing to go after an investigation of the matter. For his part, Flowers contended that Taylor wanted to do nothing more than send dues collected from Arkansans to New York.[5] In 1948 Flowers went head to head with the older man and beat him.

Seeing that a new day in the organization was possible, that same year Bates tried an end run around the Little Rock branch (also headed by Rev. Taylor) by seeking to form a new NAACP branch in Pulaski County. Armed with "fifty membership subscriptions, plus the branch founding fee," she nominated herself as president. In her letter of December 9, 1949, she added a postscript: "Atty. Flowers State President is working with us."[6]

It was a battle the national office did not want. Gloster B. Current, who would come to know Bates well in future years as the director of branches, wrote her that Little Rock already had a chapter. "On checking the addresses of these members, we find that forty-two of them live in Little Rock."[7] New converts should join the existing organization.

Still, Current would have had to have been impressed with Bates's aggressiveness at the same time as he was charmed by her. As she would tell *Jet* in 1957, her father had raised her to be a lady, and her femininity was a part of her arsenal. In March 1949 she had appeared in a fashion show on the stage of the Dunbar High School auditorium. How this aspect of her psyche contributed to the growing recognition that she was a woman to be reckoned with in the larger world is straightforward enough. She radiated tastefulness and dignity. She was also married to a man who was constantly pointing out the inadequacy of black leadership but didn't have the personality or inclination to step forward and demand to be a leader himself. Given the incessant drumbeat of the *State Press* and her growing sense of herself as a person who was capable of holding her own in what was traditionally a man's domain, in retrospect, it seems inevitable that Daisy Bates would make the most of any opportunities that would come her way.

Meanwhile, the pot continued to be stirred by Flowers, who had persuaded more than 4,000 blacks to join the NAACP in his home base of Pine Bluff. Never happy with the national NAACP, Flowers allowed the dues owed the New York office to lapse and threatened to become independent of it. A showdown was unavoidable. The national office gave him fifteen days to resign.

L. C. and Daisy, always loyal to the NAACP, sided with New York in the dispute, thus temporarily ending a warm friendship with the man they had so ardently supported. Wiley Branton, who would work with Daisy and L. C. closely in the coming years, sided with Flowers and advocated withdrawal from the NAACP. The fight went all the way to the top brass. Walter White and Roy Wilkins, who would succeed White, entered the fray and pleaded with the Arkansas organization to get its house in order and not split off.

In the end Flowers resigned and was replaced by Dr. J. A. White, who was a throwback to the do-nothing leadership of Rev. Taylor. Hard feelings simmered through 1951 until Dr. White resigned, citing health problems. A woman from the Texas NAACP wrote Gloster Current in 1950, "no place in the country is there so much strife and division amongst Negroes as it is in Arkansas."[8] White was succeeded temporarily by W. L. Jarrett, a former Flowers operative.

Whether anyone realized it, a door was opening for Bates. Already she had become much more active politically. Earning the scrutiny of FBI informants, she and L. C. had worked hard in 1948 for the third-party candidacy for president of the United States of the left-leaning Henry Wallace against the incumbent Harry Truman. After a meeting at the Emmanuel Baptist Church, an informant reported that a small group of twenty-five "went to the home of Mr. and Mrs. L. C. Bates to attend a party."[9] L. C. and Daisy gave a check of $75 to the Progressive Party. At an earlier meeting, L. C. had reportedly said that "he could carry twenty thousand Negro votes . . . by supporting Wallace through his newspaper." Roosevelt's vice-presidential running mate in 1940, Wallace was no Communist, but he was too close for comfort for some, including Walter White, who was a friend of Truman's.[10] The *State Press* supported Wallace for the obvious reason that Wallace naturally appealed to blacks because he publicly and unreservedly advocated the end of Jim Crow, something no other major candidate dared do at that time. During this period, Daisy and L. C. once met Wallace for breakfast. The photograph of them along with two white males who were identified as members of the Communist Party would be used against them in 1957.[11] The fact that Daisy and L. C. both knew a handful of Communist Party members is meaningless in terms of indicating their capacity to be swayed by the party line. Since the Communist Party opposed racial discrimination, it attracted their attention, just as it did the attention of millions of people worldwide who had been appalled by the failures of capitalism and economic exploitation. The *State Press* subscribed to the *Daily Worker*, which naturally made Daisy and L. C. suspect in the eyes of the FBI, and there should be no mistake about the intentions of the Communist Party. An entry in Daisy's file reads: "Shaw advised that since the NAACP is a national organization the CP branches should get busy in it and not only belong to the organization, but endeavor to get on important committees and start it rolling."[12]

One could argue that Daisy (and L. C., too) may well have been naive about the Communist Party's intentions to infiltrate the leadership of the NAACP, but there is nothing to indicate that they were. In fact, her FBI file suggests a sophistication one might not have expected. During a conversation on November 21, 1950, "DAISY BATES inquired as to whether Communists were actually registering under the provisions of the Internal Security Act of 1950."[13] Clearly, she was no uninformed dupe.

What mattered to both Daisy and L. C. was a person's uncompromising stand against racism. As L. C.'s headline in the *State Press* on November 5, 1948, put it, "FOR THE FIRST TIME IN OUR LIVES WE FELT WE WERE VOTING FOR SOMETHING." Neither Daisy nor L. C. was ever remotely attracted to communism, but neither did they ever believe that their fight was being compromised by their association with members (or even former members) of the Communist Party. Was this naive and dangerous on their part? Daisy, along with other civil rights leaders, including Martin Luther King Jr., would later be faced by that very issue at the height of their leadership.

In state politics, the hopes of Arkansas blacks were raised by the election of Sid McMath, who became governor in 1948. Prior to McMath, the state had been governed by Ben Laney, whose commitment to white supremacy was so great that after leaving the governor's office he ran the campaign of Strom Thurmond, who bolted the national Democratic Party to run for president on what was appropriately called the "Dixiecrat" ticket. The Arkansas Democratic Party had successfully continued its policy of prohibiting blacks from running for office or voting in its primaries, and winning in the primary was tantamount to election in a one-party state, well after the Supreme Court had ruled the practice unconstitutional. As head of the Legal Redress Committee of the Little Rock NAACP in 1950, L. C. gave notice that the continuing practice of keeping blacks off the ballot would be fought in the courts.[14] A suit was filed by attorneys J. R. Booker and U. Simpson Tate on behalf of the NAACP. Faced with certain reversal if he ruled against the plaintiff, Rev. J. H. Gatlin, who wanted to run for city alderman, federal judge Thomas Trimble required the Democratic Party of Arkansas to place Gatlin's name on the ballot.[15]

No longer defensible legally, the term "white electors" was finally scrapped from the Democratic Party's constitution, thus opening the party to blacks in Arkansas. In contrast to Ben Laney, who had fought to keep blacks off the ballot, Governor McMath officially welcomed them into the Democratic Party. Though it might appear the death knell had been sounded for white supremacy in Arkansas, in the Arkansas Delta the contrary was true: the battle for a meaningful ballot was just beginning. As John Kirk (among other historians) has noted, "landowners in eastern Arkansas were able to coerce black sharecroppers and tenant farmers . . . into voting Democrat at a general election should any significant opposition ever arise. Often landlords paid the poll tax of their black tenants just in case they ever needed them to vote."[16]

While fighting battles for the right to vote, the Arkansas NAACP was involved in power struggles of its own. In *The Long Shadow of Little Rock*, Bates diplomatically omitted an account of the internecine conflict within the state organization and suggests that she was anointed for a leadership position by Rev. Marcus Taylor. "He came to my office at the *State Press* one day to discuss the association's growth in the state. He foresaw the oncoming struggles and believed they would require young, fresh leadership. At that time I was co-chairman of the State Conference Committee for Fair Employment Practices. . . . Mr. Taylor thought I should be the person to head the State Conference of NAACP branches."[17]

In actuality, she had opposed the do-nothing policies of Taylor and men like him for years. Both L. C. and Daisy ruffled the feathers of a number of very respected people in the black community. One of the most important blacks in Arkansas at the time was attorney J. R. Booker, who, now that Scipio Jones was dead, was dean of the black legal community in the state. In a letter to Gloster Current after Bates's election, U. Simpson Tate, southwest regional counsel, noted that L. C. and Daisy were "at sword's point with Bob Booker, who is the unquestioned leader of integrity in Arkansas, and will have nothing to do with anything in which the Bateses are involved."[18]

In the same letter, Tate, who obviously had some misgivings about Bates's ascension to the role of president, wrote that "Mrs. Bates tends to go off the deep end at times on various issues." Yet "there was no one else to be elected who offered any promise of doing any thing to further the work of NAACP in Arkansas. I am not certain that she was the proper person to be elected, but I am certain that she was the most likely person of those present at the Conference."[19]

By this point, Daisy Bates had come a long way from Huttig—and a long way from her first days at the *State Press* when she didn't make an appearance until the afternoon. Only thirty-nine years old and a woman, her ascendancy to the presidency of the State Conference of Branches was an astonishing feat in an organization dominated by older, conservative black males who were as sexist as their white counterparts. She had done it almost entirely by the force of her personality. After her death, some people who knew her well would describe her in terms that implied she was something of a lightweight. Daisy "had no skills. . . . [Her] greatest asset was PR," Christopher Mercer said in a typical interview in 2002.[20]

Saying Bates had no specific skills is accurate as far it goes, but it is like saying Lyndon Johnson was just a country school teacher. Beneath her lovely clothes and effusive manner she possessed a will of steel, energy to match, and an ego, as she became famous, that increasingly put herself at the center of the universe. Her ascent did not come without problems. A black women battling for civil rights had to take on both white supremacy and black and white sexism. In retrospect, it does not always make for a pretty story. Bates used what weapons she had: charm and a capacity for guile that might have even surprised her enemies. She was not like her friend Rosa Parks—humility was not Bates's long suit. Had it been, she would have been washed away as a historical footnote in the tidal wave of pressure of 1957. Due to a truly unique set of circumstances in that year, she would display a genius for public relations. The *State Press* would turn out to be the perfect background for her, for during the preceding decade she had absorbed the lesson that how one was perceived was more than half the battle for civil rights. Ever since blacks were brought into what became the state of Arkansas, by and large they had been viewed by whites in unthinking stereotypes. Daisy Bates would challenge that. Of course, all of this was five years in the future. Elected as president of the State Conference of Branches in 1952, Bates's official duties were generally limited to presiding at the state meeting once a year and remitting dues to the national office from a small group of NAACP chapters in a poor southern state. Being Daisy Bates, however, she would briefly come to embody the civil rights movement in the South at a crucial time in the nation's history.

The events that would eventually catapult Bates into the national limelight in 1957 had begun falling into place well before her election as state president. Not part of the Deep South, Arkansas was increasingly seen as a state where racial progress in education could be made. Indeed, in higher education the barriers were already falling. The state of Arkansas was unable to legally justify denying blacks admission to professional schools under the doctrine of separate but equal (and financially incapable of providing separate but truly equal facilities). By the late 1940s a handful of blacks had begun to be admitted to the Arkansas law school in Fayetteville and the medical school in Little Rock. Two graduates of the law school, Wiley Branton and Christopher Mercer, would be especially important to Bates.

Between 1952 and 1956, as president of the State Conference of Branches, Bates was undisputedly the driving force within the state organization of the NAACP; however, within the Little Rock branch, which was more active than all the rest of the state chapters combined, she and L. C. functioned merely as two members of a talented and busy executive committee. The head of the committee was, rather amazingly, a white Jewish professor at Philander Smith College. Dr. Georg C. Iggers was a German refugee who in 1939, at age twelve, had immigrated to the United States with his family. Brilliant and accustomed to a far more rigorous academic program, Iggers graduated from high school in Richmond, Virginia, at the age of fifteen. By the time he was seventeen, he had finished college at Richmond and entered the University of Chicago, where he completed his course work for a Ph.D. in 1950. At school, he met his wife, Wilma, who was also a refugee from Nazi persecution. She, too, would obtain her doctorate from the University of Chicago.[21] Committed as a couple to social justice issues, Georg Iggers got a teaching job at Philander Smith College in Little Rock, where he encountered the inability of his students to use materials at the public library. His successful effort to change this policy brought him to the attention of the Little Rock branch of the NAACP, which recruited him to its executive committee. At the time the "only active white person" in the Little Rock branch (and most likely the whole state), Iggers was elected chairman of the executive committee in 1952.[22] With his unsurpassed educational credentials, he was uniquely qualified to assist the local chapter in laying the groundwork for a challenge to Jim Crow policies in education. Though Bates does not mention his name in her memoir, Iggers was clearly an instrumental figure during his time in Little Rock.[23]

Through his written documentation of this period, he has become historians' single most important source of information about the internal activities around education of the Little Rock branch between 1952 and 1956. The officers of the Little Rock branch who assumed their duties on January 1, 1954, included the president, Rev. J. C. Crenchaw, who made the bulk of his living as a tailor. The real power, however, lay with the executive board, which was comprised of Daisy and L. C. and fifteen others, including a number of individuals whose names would become known in 1957 and thereafter: Dr. William H. Townsend, an optometrist, would go on to become the first black Arkansas state legislator in the twentieth century; Ozell Sutton, one of the principal founders of a black coalition that in the early 1960s negotiated an end to Jim Crow in downtown Little Rock; J. R. Booker; and Harry Bass, executive director of the Urban League.

Lee Lorch, another white male, also joined the executive committee in 1955. Lorch was already well known in NAACP circles (and to the FBI) by the time he came to Little Rock to join the Philander Smith faculty. A mathematician who had taught at Fisk University, a black college in Nashville, Tennessee, Lorch believed deeply in human rights and communist egalitarian principles. For his beliefs, he had been fired after refusing to answer questions he considered irrelevant before the witch-hunting House Un-American Activities Committee (HUAC). All he would admit to was that he once had been a member of the Communist Party. Charged with contempt of Congress, he fought the charge and won. An authentic hero in the civil rights community (he had fought housing discrimination in New York City in an earlier phase of his career), his activities were well documented in the *State Press* long before he set foot in Arkansas. His equally committed wife, Grace, would also be summoned to testify before HUAC in Memphis in 1957. She would also refuse to cooperate with the committee. Lee Lorch was a workhorse in the Little Rock NAACP. Unlike Georg and Wilma Iggers, he and Grace became personal friends with L. C. and Daisy, living in the same neighborhood and visiting in their home.[24]

The role of president of the State Conference of Branches was an unpaid position. Though in 1957–58 the Little Rock crisis consumed every waking moment of her time, in 1952 Bates had a life outside the NAACP. In the spring she was chosen to serve as a chaperone for a young woman selected as the "Spirit of Cotton," the African American counterpart to the Memphis-based "Maid of Cotton" extravaganza, an industry event that combined with social activities to promote the use of the fiber. Substituting for the regular chaperone, in April Bates embarked on a fifteen-city tour with Barbara Thompson, a native of Trinidad. If there was any irony in working hand-in-hand with an industry deeply associated with slavery and peonage, it was not noted by the black national press, which was entranced by Bates's personality and stylishness. The *Chicago Defender* gushed in March, "The new tour director is a dynamic figure in the civic and social life of Little Rock," noting she was "city editor" of the *State Press* and "vice-president of the NAACP."[25] During their four-day stay in Washington, D.C., at the start of the tour, Bates posed for a group photograph with Little Rock's congressman Brooks Hays, who would play an unhappy role five years later in the 1957 school desegregation crisis. Not yet forty in 1952, Bates was given her first sustained exposure to the broader African American society outside Little Rock and clearly relished the travel and attention. As she was to experience increasingly, in the world of black high society, there was a parallel universe to its white counterpart. For blacks who were willing not to rock the boat, it could be a good life. However, the boat was about to rock.

One of the difficulties of being an activist president of the Arkansas State Conference of Branches was that one could only do so much in an organization that was run out of New York and depended so heavily on national litigation strategies. That had frustrated Harold Flowers and had driven him to rebel against the national office. Bates never gave a thought to acting outside the structure of the national organization. To both Daisy and L. C. in those days, Jim Crow would survive or fall as a result of what the NAACP did. The organization was so wedded to litigation as a strategy that it would one day risk its relevance as a rallying point for black Americans because of its reluctance to embrace Martin Luther King Jr.'s vision that southerners (as well as the rest of the nation) had to be confronted on moral and religious principles.

Bates had ambitions to build the state organization in Arkansas. As president of the State Conference of Branches, each year she announced grandiose membership and fund-raising goals for each of the state's chapters and issued public statements declaring war on segregation throughout the state. For the 1953 State Conference of Branches meeting, she invited Walter White to speak. By this point, White was only a figurehead in the national office, having shocked and embarrassed many blacks throughout the country by divorcing his wife, Gladys, of twenty-seven years and marrying a "wealthy white socialite" from South Africa (of all places) by the name of Poppy Cannon. Additionally, White had written an article for *Look* magazine extolling the virtues of a skin whitener.[26] What the Arkansas rank and file thought about White's appearance in Arkansas is not known. Not then a national board member, Bates was surely not aware of all the infighting that was taking place within the national leadership as a result of White's actions. Roy Wilkins, L. C.'s former boss in Kansas City, and Thurgood Marshall would come out on top. Bates would hitch her star to Wilkins and, at the height of the 1957 crisis, he to her.

Though in 1957 and afterward it would almost appear as if she *were* the NAACP in Arkansas, Bates had always worked as a team player and dutifully complied with the wishes of the national office of the NAACP. These instances of her cooperation before 1957 shed light on the racial climate within the state of Arkansas, particularly in Little Rock, as well as on her own attitude. In 1952, before the 1954 *Brown* decision required schools to desegregate, the Little Rock branch of the NAACP, with its almost all-black membership, formed a coalition with two other interracial groups in Little Rock, the local Urban League and the Atlanta-based Southern Regional Council affiliate, which soon would become the Arkansas Council on Human Relations.[27] The coalition called itself the Little Rock Council on Schools and was headed by Lewis Deer, the white minister of the Pulaski Heights Christian Church. The group's mission was to try to convince the Little Rock School Board to allow a few blacks to use the print shop in the white high school.[28] At one point it appeared that three white members of the Little Rock School Board were willing to consider this proposal, but the meeting was scuttled when NAACP branch president, Thaddeus Williams, announced publicly the two sides were going to meet. This nonevent in 1952 reveals how white supremacy dominated the consciousness of both whites and blacks. The old strategy of using sympathetic white intermediaries to speak for blacks was still in evidence, however much Bates and others claimed a new day had arrived when blacks would speak for themselves. Though it has been argued that the fact that some whites in Little Rock were willing to talk to blacks about token desegregation was a display of "moderation," the real issue in all of these exchanges was whether the principles of white supremacy were at risk. The white power structure that held sway in Little Rock in 1952 was not threatened by such a modest proposal because its control of the situation was not challenged in the slightest. Nonetheless, such discussions might have been politically risky, since even tokenism would be subject to the sort of demagoguery exhibited five years later.

Georg Iggers reported that Daisy and L. C. were among the "militant" members of the Little Rock branch executive committee who wanted to sue the school district in 1952 to force integration.[29] The branch, however, desisted at the request of the NAACP's national office and the lawyers at the NAACP's Legal and Educational Defense Fund. Thurgood Marshall's lawyers had already put in place the litigation of the cases that would collectively become known as *Brown v. Board of Education*.[30]

Pursuing integration, not merely insisting upon equal funding, meant that blacks were prepared to confront whites at the most basic level of their relationship. The enormity of this undertaking was not minimized. Thus at that stage in Little Rock, even the most "militant" blacks, such as Daisy and L. C., and their white allies were prepared to accept initially the achievement of having a few black students being allowed to take courses at a white school and call it a victory. So long as the white power structure began the process of desegregation, the Little Rock School District would not be pressed too hard. It was one thing for the New York office of the NAACP to demand integration; it was quite another for southern blacks and white liberals in the South to do so. The most they hoped to accomplish in 1952 was to begin the process.

In his Pulitzer prize-winning *Parting the Waters*, Taylor Branch has shown that the negotiating committee for blacks in the Montgomery bus boycott in 1956 did not even demand an end to segregated seating—its primary demand was to end the system whereby blacks had to give their seats to whites.[31] It would take a lawsuit to end the system of Jim Crow on Montgomery buses. A movement to end Jim Crow in the South with Martin Luther King Jr. as its principal leader was being born with the Montgomery bus boycott, but it had to walk before it could run. Similarly, the informal coalition of the Little Rock NAACP and a handful of sympathetic whites in 1952 had limited expectations.[32] In 1952 the models for desegregation in Arkansas were the professional schools—law and medicine where the number of blacks enrolled could still be counted on one hand. As noted earlier, many blacks were content with segregation, and their lack of aggressiveness was continually a problem for Daisy Bates and the NAACP. When whites found an African American who would make a statement saying blacks preferred segregation—as occurred in 1954 in the case of Dr. J. B. Bryant, a black physician in Stuttgart, an hour's drive from

Little Rock—Daisy issued a statement in the *State Press*: "Negroes must make known to all Arkansans that they want no form of segregation, despite the recent wave of publicity being heaped upon Negroes in leadership positions. . . . Many Negroes are being unwittingly used to increase disunity on the segregation issue."

Without a doubt, in those rare cases where blacks were willing to stir the waters a bit, it was easier for an NAACP chapter to function in Little Rock than in the smaller towns of Arkansas, where intimidation was a routine matter. In most ways, the methods L. C. and Daisy used in the 1940s to attack Jim Crow were continued in the 1950s, but now it was formalized through the NAACP. When specific incidents of discrimination occurred, Daisy Bates's name invariably appeared as part of a self-appointed team that called attention to them and demanded action. For example, she was a member of a group from the Little Rock NAACP that investigated the refusal in January 1955 of the local airport to serve food to blacks. Typically, the policy of the airport manager was completely arbitrary. Black members of the armed forces passing through the airport's restaurant were served, but the president of the Dallas, Texas, NAACP was refused service. L. C. quoted Daisy in the pages of the *State Press* as asking the manager "if Negroes could eat while they were in uniform, why was it they lost their citizenship as soon as they are released from the Armed Services?" Though she got no answer, the mere fact that she was asking the question in such a pointed manner was a sign of things to come. Blacks did not speak to whites in Arkansas this way. Doubtless, a number of black readers cringed when they read this story, but on some level they had to feel good that someone was standing up to whites in Arkansas.

L. C. spotlighted Daisy in the pages of the *State Press* in her capacity as president of the State Conference of Branches. Every official act of Daisy's became front-page news, as on March 18, 1955, "Mrs. L. C. Bates . . . to direct . . . public relations workshop" at the Southwest Regional Conference in Shreveport, and June 10, 1955, "Mrs. L. C. Bates called a meeting of the Executive Committee to work out a policy for desegregating Arkansas Schools."[33] This would continue in issue after issue until Daisy left Arkansas in 1959 for the bright lights of New York.

Chapter Six

THE BOMBSHELL OF
BROWN v. BOARD OF EDUCATION

On May 17, 1954, the date of the U.S. Supreme Court decision in *Brown v. Board of Education*, it was likely that not a single black person in Little Rock occupied a position of authority over a white adult. White supremacy was an unquestioned fact of daily existence. This does not mean that cracks weren't beginning to appear in the practice of segregation. To be sure, in places like Little Rock, where the population was mostly white, certain minor adjustments in the color line were already being made. Besides limited use of the public library, small numbers of blacks were permitted on a prearranged, case-by-case basis to enter the public parks; the zoo was opened to blacks on Thursdays. Drinking fountain signs for "colored" and "white" began to disappear in some downtown stores, but woe to any African American who needed to use a public bathroom.[1] As long as blacks approached sympathetic whites in Little Rock in the time-honored way, that is, as grateful and respectful supplicants, racial progress was deemed more than a possibility in Little Rock. Though historian David Chappell and others have strongly challenged the stereotype of the unyielding white southerner who opposed any change in the color line, white supremacy remains the indispensable psychological filter through which all observations on this period must pass if we are to understand Daisy Bates and her role in 1957. What was occurring in Little Rock in the early 1950s was no more than a continuation of the paternalism that had always guided race relations in the South. Whites, and whites alone, would decide what exceptions to segregation were appropriate or a necessary accommodation to any pressure for change.

As a way of ordering race relations in Little Rock, white supremacy, of course, would not disappear in Little Rock with the announcement of the *Brown* decision in 1954. Its message would have to be internalized, and that would require time, but like the effect of the destruction of the World Trade Center towers on the United States, nothing in the South after the decision in *Brown* would ever be quite the same. From the moment the first black people had been brought to this country in chains, the core belief in their innate and utter inferiority had justified their treatment as a separate caste. Ratified by the Supreme Court in *Plessy v. Ferguson* in 1896, the creation and maintenance of a legally sanctioned caste system based on race in the United States doomed most black Arkansans to lives of poverty and extreme, if often unconscious, caution. They adjusted their lives accordingly and avoided humiliation as best they could through the normal defense mechanism of denial. To a remarkable degree, Bates had risen to the top of her caste. But the rationale for the caste system and its justification basically remained in place in 1954—until *Brown.*

In an opinion remarkably free of legalese and obviously written for the layperson and lawyer alike, the decision was rooted in morality and psychology as much as law. Speaking for a unanimous Supreme Court, Chief Justice Earl Warren found that "segregation on the basis of race had caused Negro children to carry within themselves a sense of inferiority that was harmful to their ability to learn." By accepting expert testimony that racial segregation in and of itself was destructive of the black child's ability to learn, the Court, without saying so directly, lay the blame for this situation at the feet of white America. The Court had relied in part on studies by the psychologist Kenneth Clark, who would come to know Bates and play a minor role in the 1957 school desegregation crisis at Central High. The way to begin to correct for the past was to open the same schoolhouse door to all. In its opinion, the Court emphasized the importance of schooling to obtain the American Dream. Thus educational "opportunity, where the state has undertaken to provide it, is a right that must be made available to all on equal terms."[2] This was a paradigm shift of epic proportions and, again, essentially moral in nature.

Though its opinion was not unexpected, the Court was far ahead of white Americans (including the president of the United States) and not an insignificant number of African Americans as well. The question would be how the rest of the nation would choose to follow *Brown* and the lengths the Court would go to enforce its decision if it met with significant resistance. That debate is still going on today.

As far-reaching as *Brown* was, the opinion had ended abruptly with instructions to the lawyers to argue further the point of how soon the decision should be implemented. It would not be until May 1955 that the Court addressed this issue in a decision that came to be known as *Brown II.*

On May 21, 1954, four days after the decision, L. C.'s editorial page contained some of his bluntest words about how blacks should react to *Brown*: "We feel that the proper approach would be for the leaders among the Negro race—not clabber mouths, Uncle Toms, or grinning appeasers to get together and counsel with the school heads."[3] Though his invective seemed aimed at blacks who would sell out the legal promises in *Brown* for a pat on the head, his approach to the white community was quite revolutionary for its time: he was daring to approach whites as an equal with his suggestion that whites and blacks "counsel" together. He could have saved his breath. Immediately after the editorial ran, Virgil Blossom, the superintendent for the Little Rock schools, assembled a group of blacks to inform them of the school board's intention before he announced it to the public.

In his book on the Little Rock crisis, *It HAS Happened Here*, Blossom remembered that L. C. was present. "As I talked, I observed that my audience, which had arrived in high spirits, was rapidly losing its enthusiasm." He remembered L. C. asking:

"Then the Board does not intend to integrate the schools in 1954?"

"No," I replied, "it must be done slowly. For instance, we must complete the additional school buildings that are now being started."

Bates turned abruptly and walked out of the meeting, and later his newspaper was critical of the Board's statement.[4]

Doubtless, part of the reason for the *State Press*'s reaction was that both Daisy and L. C. knew the rest of Blossom's statement was not true. Included were the words: "The Board of Education of Little Rock School District has been working for a number of years at the job of providing a program of separate but equal educational opportunities for all children in the city."[5] Just two years earlier, the Little Rock School Board had been presented with a chapter and verse account of the vast inequities between Central High School and Dunbar by the interracial coalition that included the Little Rock NAACP.

Written to justify his actions on behalf of the Little Rock School Board and his dealings with Orval Faubus, Blossom's book is unintentionally a primer of southern white male supremacy at the time.[6] Without a trace of awareness of the arrogance with which his dealings with the black community were invested, Blossom recalled he told the remaining blacks that the board "would not delay for delay's sake but in order to do the job right." Though the board (and Blossom) would soon delay precisely for delay's sake, Blossom made an important point. He went on to write that "in the long struggle ahead we had the co-operation of probably 95 per cent of the Negro citizens."[7]

While the word "cooperation" implies some kind of reciprocity and is an inaccurate characterization of the average African American's position in 1954, it is true that only a tiny minority actively opposed the board's position. Accustomed to generations of subservience and the conscious and unconscious fear that accompanied it, most blacks in Little Rock mutely accepted Blossom's word that the board would proceed in good faith. Not Daisy and L. C., and not the Little Rock branch of the NAACP. Actually, Blossom's initial plan seemed designed to produce quite a bit more desegregation of the Little Rock public schools than what eventually took place at Central High School. The original figure was that some 200 to 300 black students would attend desegregated schools in Little Rock, instead of the nine who eventually entered in 1957. There would come a time when the Little Rock NAACP would have gladly settled for Blossom's original plan.

In the next year Daisy Bates would bird dog Blossom as he spoke to groups all over the city, pitching his "plan" of school integration. Recalling that time, Bates said, "He made a speech at the YWCA; I was there. He made a speech in Pleasant Valley, I was there. And this burned him up. . . . And it tickled me to death. . . . He knew I was there, see, because he had been saying one thing to whites . . . and one thing to Negroes."[8]

In 1954 southern blacks simply did not confront white authority figures in public. Daisy Bates would. Blossom would walk into the meeting, and Bates would be there "and all the speech would go out of him." During "the question-and-answer period, . . . I'd say, 'When you spoke for the group at the YWCA,' or wherever it was—he spoke all over town—I said, 'Did you say that this?' " " 'I didn't say *that*.' "[9] Though Bates injected a certain degree of bravado in retelling these stories twenty years later, in 1954–55 she knew she was walking a fine line in any exchange with whites. Like all persons of color in that era, she knew exactly how far to go and what tone she could take. Impeccably dressed, courteous, and never directly contradicting them, she understood she could confront certain white males in authority and get away with it, so long as she did it with an air of innocence and the mask of a smile. In those years, no black male could have pulled it off without risking violence. The threat to the southern white male ego of that era, with the history of retribution toward blacks, made it extremely difficult, if not impossible, for black males to confront white males. It was not that, as Bates claimed, she had lost her fear of whites by 1954; it was that she knew how to handle them and refused to be intimidated by them. This intuitive grasp of how far she could go and make her point in a racial setting was an ability she displayed time and time again. Short of litigation (and that would come in 1956), making her point was all she could do. As Roy Reed has pointed out in his book on Orval Faubus, "The Blossom Plan was as simple as it was cynical. . . . Any significant integration would be put off for years, maybe generations." A member of the school board was quoted as saying, "The plan was developed to provide as little integration as possible for as long as possible legally."[10] As some said in bitter jest, the Blossom plan was a plan of continued segregation, not integration. If Bates caught Blossom telling two different stories about his plan for integration of the Little Rock School District, whites themselves took note of it. Elizabeth Jacoway has written, "Several white leaders, who have asked not to be identified, have corroborated this charge" of "Blossom's duplicity."[11]

The Blossom plan may have seemed like an old-fashioned shell game to Bates, but the details of "delay for delay's sake" school integration were really in the fine print. In his book, Blossom admitted as such: though the plan he announced in September 1955 to approximately 800 employees for the public schools in Little Rock called for gradual integration of the public schools beginning with grades ten through twelve, the board's intention was just the opposite. The mentality of the day was such that Blossom could write in his book: "In addition to this public statement, a long memorandum was prepared to clarify procedure, particularly in regard to the manner in which pupil transfers would be permitted. *The Board's purpose in regard to transfers was to lessen the impact of integration on local cultural patterns by a system of voluntary transfers allowing both white and colored students to maintain, as far as possible, the system of segregated education.*"[12] This kind of pretense seemed absolutely necessary to Blossom and the school board. As discussed in the next chapter, pressure was building on them to have no plan at all. Yet at the same time, the Supreme Court had spoken twice on the subject. In retrospect, the actions of Blossom and the school board seem transparent. While Reed's *Faubus* states that the Blossom plan was cynical in its intentions from the outset, some historians have painted a picture that portrays Blossom and the Little Rock School Board as, in the very beginning, acting in good faith to comply with dictates of *Brown* and developing a plan that would gradually integrate its schools.[13] Whether one accepts this interpretation or not, it is beyond dispute that unlike what occurred at Hoxie in northeast Arkansas (to be discussed), the board (and Blossom) would soon capitulate to the pressure of its white patrons and their leaders to "delay for delay's sake" and, as members of the school board admitted, only seem to have a plan. Blossom may not have been a southerner by birth, but he had perfected the old-fashioned southerner's time-tested ability to believe his or her own words about race without any conscious sense of hypocrisy, as well as the typical southerner's capacity to feel outrage when confronted with evidence of that hypocrisy.

Cooperation implies reciprocity. In fact, Blossom and the Little Rock School Board simply dictated to blacks during this time period. There was no negotiation, no back-and-forth, no effort to solicit comments or suggestions from the black community about how desegregation should proceed. Racial cooperation in Blossom's mind meant that no blacks complained too loudly, and just as Blossom's behavior was determined by decade upon decade of white supremacy, so, too, initially was the careful behavior of blacks themselves, including Bates and the Little Rock NAACP. The last time the federal government had forcefully intervened on the behalf of blacks had been during Reconstruction. Who was going to protect a black person who decided to take on the white power structure? Doubtless, many African Americans rightly feared the risks that accompanied a militant attitude. Too, those whites in Little Rock who, for example, joined the Urban League or the Council for Human Relations and who counted themselves as supporters of rights for blacks rarely spoke above a whisper. In their own way, they and their black colleagues were just as much captives of the regimen of white supremacy as anyone else.

Fervently committed to integration of the schools in the face of the opposition of nearly all the whites and not an insubstantial number of blacks, by the end of 1954 both Daisy and L. C. thought they had no choice but to put the most positive spin on the events of that year. As L. C. told the black-owned *Pittsburgh Courier* in December, "We consider

Arkansas Southern, but we also consider it the most liberal Southern state. The worst section in Arkansas is better than the best section in Mississippi." In the same article Daisy beat the drum for her organization. "Success of integration in Arkansas depends on the NAACP."

Certainly, there were positive aspects to emphasize: Governor Francis Cherry had promised that Arkansas would obey federal law. The Democratic challenger who had beaten him and was to assume office in January 1955, Orval Eugene Faubus, had not made a race an issue in the campaign, despite having said initially that it was. Additionally, a handful of school districts had announced they would comply with *Brown*. As far as the school districts' announcement that schools would be integrated, none of the schools were in the Arkansas Delta where most blacks lived, and of the few school districts that announced they would comply, in all but one instance simple pragmatism was primarily their motivation. The same economic factors that had led to the desegregation of professional schools in Arkansas came into play at the secondary level. The school board of the town of Fayetteville, home to the University of Arkansas in the northwest corner of the state, voted four days after the *Brown* decision to bring into the white schools their nine black students who previously had been bussed across the mountain to Fort Smith at a cost of $5,000 per year. Wayne Schoot, the superintendent, admitted that "segregation was a luxury we could not longer afford."[14] Nor was it any longer the law. School boards in Charleston and Bentonville, also virtually all-white towns, followed suit. Virgil Blossom would continue to speak to groups throughout Little Rock and became so well known that he was selected in a reader's poll in the *Arkansas Democrat* as the city's "Man of the Year" in 1955 for his efforts to publicize his plan.

Given the deeply imbedded nature of the white South's hostility to black equality, the question naturally comes to mind, why was there any acceptance of the *Brown* decision in Little Rock or elsewhere in the South? As has been pointed out by a number of historians, at the time of the Civil War the southerner's only regular contact with the federal government was the U.S. Postal Service. In many ways, the South was like a foreign country. A hideous civil war didn't alter that fact. But ultimately Franklin Roosevelt and the Depression changed all of that. Historian Ben F. Johnson III has brilliantly traced the transformation of the relationship between Arkansas and the federal government during this era.[15] Though white supremacy was still the order of the day in the 1950s, like their counterparts in the rest of the South, the white males who ran the city of Little Rock had become used to the increased control exercised by the federal government as a result of federal programs dealing with everything from Social Security for the city's elderly and people with disabilities to the welfare checks that went out to its poorest citizens. The Tennessee Valley Authority (TVA), which brought electricity to the rural South, and the federal highway program were welcomed, but most federal programs did not come without strings attached. Even in the 1950s the federal octopus was seductive, handing out money with one tentacle and wrapping another around its recipient to make sure it didn't get up and walk away with the government's cash. Though the Supreme Court swept away part of Roosevelt's expansion of federal power, southerners accepted the seeming inevitability of the steady march into their lives by the federal government. Lured by low wages, industry was coming, too, which meant growth, the mother's milk of capitalism, and the businessmen who ran Little Rock were getting their share.[16] For a while the white male power structure in the South had enjoyed what it considered the best of both worlds: federal largesse and a hands-off policy toward its treatment of its African American population. As a member of the "Solid South," Arkansas's only obligation was to vote Democratic. However, participation by Arkansans in the country's two world wars and the bloody Korean War had cemented the notion that they were an integral part of the most powerful nation on earth. Thus it did not come as a shock when Arkansas governor Francis Cherry, engaged in a hot run-off campaign with an upstart from the hills of Madison County named Orval Faubus, announced immediately after the *Brown* decision that "Arkansas will obey the law."[17] In *A Stone of Hope*, historian David Chappell has shown that as important as the maintenance of Jim Crow was to southerners, other concerns were more important.

Some commentators on the Little Rock crisis (including Daisy Bates) have viewed the willingness of the handful of school districts mostly in northern and western Arkansas to integrate their school districts as a sign of the moderate nature of race relations outside the Arkansas Delta.[18] In fact, white supremacy was as alive and well in the mountainous regions as anywhere in the state. Two episodes of "ethnic cleansing" in Harrison in northwest Arkansas in 1905 and 1909 reduced the black population from 115 to 1.[19] Though the violence had ceased by the 1950s, blacks knew half a century later they were not welcome in most of the hill counties of Arkansas. More than one

Arkansan of a certain age can still remember seeing at least one sign in the Ozarks warning blacks not to let the sun set on their heads. White supremacy ruled from border to border inside the state of Arkansas and was hardly threatened by a handful of blacks being admitted to a few schools in the northern part of the state. The reaction was totally different in the Delta and southern Arkansas, where blacks either out-numbered whites or where there were substantial black populations. None of the school boards in the Delta announced any intention to comply with *Brown* and would not until they were hauled kicking and screaming into court more than a decade later.

The NAACP's hope (both nationally and in Arkansas) was that the Supreme Court would announce when it decided *Brown II* that integration of the schools must proceed quickly. It was not to be. On May 31, 1955, the Court announced its decision that the federal district courts would superintend integration of the public schools "on a racially nondiscriminatory basis with all deliberate speed." The fine print in *Brown II* contained escape clauses for school districts uninterested in compliance, such as "varied local problems," "practical flexibility," and "adjusting and reconciling public and private needs." Though the Court's intention was presumably otherwise, the opinion left the door wide open for even the feeblest southern lawyers to argue that local conditions dictated that school integration proceed as slowly as possible. More important, the decision created the conditions for southern demagogues to exert maximum pressure on local school boards, which soon occurred in Arkansas.

It was evident that the Supreme Court had lost its nerve or, depending on one's view, had come to its senses. If there was ever a time for a president to exert moral leadership in the country, this was it, but Dwight D. Eisenhower, whose main contribution (and not an insignificant one) as a two-term president (1952–60) was that he kept the country from going to war, had no particular sympathy for blacks. As Taylor Branch has pointed out, "Forty years in a segregated Army conditioned Eisenhower to think of Negroes as inherently subordinate. His condescension was so natural and paternal as to seem nearly well-meaning. Only his private secretary winced with embarrassment when he passed along the latest 'nigger' jokes from his friends at the Bobby Jones golf course in Augusta." On a personal level, the gulf between the president of the United States and blacks was as wide as the Grand Canyon. Branch has written that Eisenhower "bridled at the company of Negroes."[20] Despite the ferment in the judicial system percolating throughout the country, Eisenhower waited until he had had been president five years before he received an African American delegation in the White House even to discuss civil rights legislation. Had Eisenhower used his office as a bully pulpit for compliance with the intent of *Brown*, he might well have saved himself and the country from the constitutional crisis that would occur in Little Rock in 1957 and then be replicated in other parts of the South. Whatever might have been, L. C.'s page-one headline in the *State Press* on June 3, 1955, lamented the Court's decision in his usual breezy way: "HI COURT FAVORS DIXIE." It was actually one of the few occasions when one of L. C.'s headlines was understated.

After *Brown II* was announced, a directive from the national NAACP office went out to all the branches in the South instructing them to pin down their local school boards about their plans to comply with the decision. "If no plans are announced or no steps towards desegregation taken by the time school begins this fall, 1955, the time for a law suit has arrived," the memo said in part.[21] As an activist president of the State Conference of Branches, Daisy Bates was fully committed to pressing for school desegregation throughout the state, not just in Little Rock. This, of course, was a hit-or-miss proposition, as it depended primarily on local leadership in the individual branches of the NAACP. Though a major part of Bates's written plan as State Conference of Branches president for 1954–55 was to assist local branches in getting enforcement of the *Brown* decisions under way in their communities, it was much easier said than done. Nearly all blacks worked for whites or were beholden to them for their jobs. Sometimes all it took was a letter from a black official of a branch chapter and a little publicity after *Brown II* to have a bad result. "The newspaper article which appeared in the West Memphis *Daily Sun* resulted in [board] president B. J. Yarbrough losing his job at the Eden Pontiac Company and receiving numerous threats," wrote Wiley Branton to the West Memphis School Board on September 30, 1955.[22] In his letter, Branton noted that Yarbrough had tried to negotiate with the school board without the intervention of lawyers. For another decade, it would make no difference whether black school patrons in the Delta had attorneys to represent them or not, so easily were they ignored.

Blacks in Arkansas did not immediately feel the negative consequences of *Brown II* due to a unique occurrence in the town of Hoxie. During the summer of 1955, Bates and the other participants in the

1957 Central High crisis were given a preview of the kind of pressure that would be brought against them by what transpired in the small community of Hoxie in the northeast part of the state. With only twenty-five black students in its consolidated school of 1,000 students, the Hoxie School Board followed *Brown II* by announcing through its superintendent, Howard Kunkel, that it would integrate its schools. For the first and perhaps only time, a white school superintendent in Arkansas acknowledged the question of morality that was the foundation of the Supreme Court's decision in *Brown I*. The Hoxie School Board had voted to integrate because to do so was "right in the sight of God"; it was "the law"; and lastly it was "cheaper."[23] Because Hoxie schools were on a split term (to allow students to pick cotton in the fall, school started in July) and, suddenly, thanks to *Life* magazine, which massively covered the story, Hoxie became a national phenomenon—a small-town southern school board president on the edge of the Mississippi Delta somehow doing what no other white leaders in the South could bring themselves to do—implicitly admitting that segregation by race in schools was wrong. The banner headline on the front page of the *State Press* on July 15 ran: "HOXIE PROVES DEMOCRACY CAN WORK IN ARKANSAS."

Thus, instead of disappearing into history as one of the handful of Arkansas school districts that had voted to abandon its dual school system, Hoxie immediately became a battleground in which the white supremacist instincts of Arkansans were roused to fever pitch by a number of people and groups who saw the Hoxie situation as an opportunity to defend what they considered their southern birthright and enhance their political standing as well. At issue was white supremacy itself. Local farmer Herbert Brewer organized a meeting on August 3 in Hoxie that attracted 200 whites. The point of the meeting was to force the school board to reverse its decision. The pressure would become intense. Foreshadowing the future, the Hoxie situation attracted the attention of outsiders, who made their way to this small rural community. Of all the white Arkansans who appeared as self-appointed defenders of the white supremacist message, no one delivered it more effectively than Jim Johnson, director of the White Citizens Council in Arkansas. The White Citizens Council primarily began to replace the Ku Klux Klan (though it hardly disappeared) as the organizing base for those whites who were willing to publicly express their outrage over school integration. From Crossett near the Louisiana border, Johnson, a lawyer, was handsome, lean, and a spellbinding speaker if one was inclined to follow his bombastic message. Johnson wanted to be governor, and he saw race as a way to the state capitol, but it wasn't opportunism that drove him. He was a true believer. Even in a documentary in 2003 about Hoxie's racial crisis, he was unapologetic for his stand.[24]

There was nothing remotely subtle about Johnson's approach: he went for the jugular of whomever was standing in his way. Johnson, with his sidekick, Curt Copeland, put out a magazine in 1956 called *Arkansas Faith*, which was drenched in the demagogic ranting of the era. A typical editorial began: "The National Association for the Agitation of Colored People (NAACP), also referred to as the National Association for the Advancement of the Communist Party, has been screaming 40 years for race-mixing in the South. They have clamored for mixed schools, mixed churches, mixed marriages, mixed children, etc."[25] *Arkansas Faith* pushed all the buttons of its readers—the age-old self-pity of white southerners that built quickly into resentment and racial hatred. It was potent stuff—white supremacy tartar with male testosterone a palpable presence on its pages. With its constant references to race mixing, *Arkansas Faith* was a psychologist's textbook case of classic projection, for after all, it had been southern white males who had gone into the slave quarters and taken whichever black women suited their fancy, producing a mulatto population of sizable proportion in Arkansas.[26] Johnson was not the only stalwart of white supremacy in Hoxie. Also making an appearance was another lawyer, Amis Guthridge, executive secretary of White America, Inc. From Little Rock, he would become a leading figure in the Little Rock crisis of 1957.[27] Both fanned the flames of white supremacy in Hoxie, and soon intimidation against both black parents and members of the school board followed the rhetoric.

In light of the favorable publicity given to Hoxie by *Life*, the fight was joined by the NAACP national office in New York, which saw the Hoxie situation as crucial to demonstrating to the nation that school integration could work in the South. Thus it sent a young black staffer named Mildred Bond to bolster the resolve of the black parents to continue to send their children to school. Bond recalled getting to know Daisy Bates. When in Little Rock, Bond stayed with a relative but would go over to Daisy and L. C.'s small duplex on Bishop Street to type her reports for the national office. It seemed to her that "Daisy was as poor as I was." The summer was very hot, and Bond recalled "window fans blowing over water," which affected her sinuses. Daisy, who had no direct involvement with what was occurring in Hoxie, impressed her. Bond found Bates to be "very articulate, well-spoken," and she had "good stage presence." Yet Bates knew she was far from a polished speaker. Bond noticed she pronounced certain words "funny," as she tried to get rid of her southern accent. To Bond, as it seemed to others, Daisy and L. C. "worked as a team." L. C. "was the editor . . . no question he did most of the work," but Daisy had input into what went into the paper. Daisy had a "sense of humor, would laugh at herself," but Bond also noticed that Daisy was "very deliberate." She remembered seeing her become "vocal and aggressive," but "she controlled her actions and reactions." Clearly, Bates, now a mature woman at the age of forty-two in 1955, had evolved into a formidable presence. Bond, a young woman in her twenties when she met Bates, felt "she knew her very well. . . . I think she considered me a friend. I don't think she had many confidantes. . . . L. C. fulfilled that role for her." One wonders if Bates bared her soul to anyone in this period of her life. Whatever her life had been before moving to Little Rock, she and L. C. kept their earlier life secret. It no doubt would not have mattered at all to their friends, but Daisy and L. C. remained sensitive to their image. Daisy had a "public persona and she lived the public persona." "Who she was in her other life," Bond said, referring to Daisy's stay in New York, she didn't know.[28]

Instead of caving into pressure, the Hoxie School Board, through the excellent and courageous work of its young white lawyer, Bill Penix from Jonesboro, went into federal court and with the help of the Justice Department, which filed a friend of the court brief, sought and got an injunction enjoining the harassment and interference by the White Citizens Council.[29] Despite numerous appeals, the injunction was upheld. It was an extraordinary example of how federal authority could be employed to protect a southern school board that acted in good faith to comply with the intent of the original *Brown* decision. It was a lesson that would go unheeded by the Little Rock School Board two years later.

With the events at Hoxie having a good outcome, the fall of 1955 was a heady time for Bates. With the new house now completed at 1207 W. Twenty-eighth, she showed it off for gatherings of the NAACP officials, both state and national. Before the State Conference of Branches met at the Dunbar Community Center in Little Rock the last weekend in October, the *State Press* announced a "get-together" for delegates "at the home of Mrs. L. C. Bates." In December the southwest region executive committee of the NAACP held its meeting there. The next year the violence would start, turning the house into an armed camp, but when Daisy and L. C. moved in, it was a time of genuine fulfillment and understandable pride. The house symbolized their success. Daisy wrote proudly, "When the house was finally built, over five hundred of our friends came to wish us well." Her minister, Rufus Young, offered a blessing that day. "God bless this home and may peace and happiness forever dwell within it."[30]

The house represented a stunning achievement for a couple who had made their living noisily going against the grain of both the white and black power structures. They had chosen not to remain in the Philander Smith–Arkansas Baptist College corridor, where upper-class blacks traditionally had lived for decades, in order to build their own home in a white area. Bates would come to know at least some of her white neighbors, though precisely who they were, she did not disclose. Described as "classic 1950s ranch-style," the house sat on a full acre of land. On the main floor, the interior was comprised of front and back bedrooms, a bath, a living room with a large picture window and fireplace, a dining room, and a kitchen furnished with modern appliances. A finished room downstairs was used for social activities and a utility and storage space. The room downstairs included a bar and at least one easy chair that had a vibrating mechanism, making it a place where Bates would, during the worst of the crisis in 1957, feel safe to sit late at night and try to unwind with a shot of scotch before taking a sleeping pill.[31] Off the kitchen was a carport. Though the total cost of the house was about $25,000, it is not certain which financial institution originally financed the loan. In an interview with Elizabeth Jacoway in 1976, Bates hinted that had it not been for a Federal Housing Authority (FHA) loan officer, their loan would not have gone through. In any event, Bates was delighted with the final product.

Originally, the man who was doing the plans died, and Daisy and L. C. had to start all over. Daisy said they had saved $10,000 and still needed "$14,000 or $15,000." They had not been able to afford a contractor and instead dealt with a lumber dealer who promised to help them if they bought their material through him. They developed the new plans themselves and got someone to draw up a set of blueprints. Their lumber dealer found them two "builders." Bates remembered, "This was the dream house; we worked on it together, and the builders made it a kind of community thing; they built that fireplace and he didn't charge me anything."[32]

L. C. may well have been involved in the layout of the house, but it was Daisy who decorated it. In October 1957, at the height of the crisis, a reporter from the Baltimore paper the *Afro-American* described the inside of the house as strictly reflecting Daisy's tastes and wrote approvingly,

> There are plants and vines in just the right places. The kitchen has a canary yellow refrigerator and wall range. Copper, the latest word in kitchen utensils for the ladies to hang on walls, is in just the right place. The draperies are filmy, full and fine at her large picture window and the carpets are well chosen in the den and the dining area and living room. The door bell plays a soft tune when rung and a blue parakeet fusses at his reflection in a mirror within his cage. . . . Mrs. Bates wore soft Italian slippers, a house dress of a soft print, and she petted the dog, named Skippy.

The dog accompanied her to the door to get the mail and barked at the mailman. "As she answered the phone, she thumbed a telephone book covered with blue felt upon which blue sequins had been sewn. Little fussy things women like were scattered on the many book cases against the paneled walls. A huge driftwood lamp was placed just right beside a large semi-circular couch."[33]

In watching their house being built and then moving in and showing it off to friends and admirers, Daisy and L. C. truly were living the American Dream. By anyone's measure, they were at the pinnacle of success. Of course, it was all local—occurring in a poor southern state that most people outside the South knew little about. In two years time everybody in the world who had access to a newspaper, radio, or television would, however briefly, learn about Daisy Bates.

The intervention by the federal government at Hoxie surely helped convince the Little Rock NAACP to sue the Little Rock School District. Except in a few isolated instances, school boards throughout Arkansas had dug in their heels. Ominously, a carefully planned NAACP lawsuit in August 1955 by Thurgood Marshall against the Van Buren Independent School District in the northwest corner of the state went absolutely nowhere. Federal judge John E. Miller refused to order any timetable to enroll twenty-four blacks to desegregate the school. A shrewd politician and judge who knew how to write an opinion without getting himself reversed by the Eighth Circuit Court of Appeals (Miller had been an obstructionist senator during the New Deal until

Roosevelt got him to resign by making him a federal judge), Miller was no friend of blacks. He had been their zealous prosecutor during the Elaine massacres. Later, writing a report for Governor Thomas McRae, who was deliberating whether to spare the Elaine Twelve from the death penalty, Miller had claimed that none of the blacks had been beaten to make them confess. A man with a talent for trying to get on the right side of history, Miller, almost fifty-five years later in an oral history interview in 1976 (in which he would slip and refer to African Americans as "niggers"), admitted that blacks had been tortured to give confessions and portrayed himself as their defender. (He spoke of dismissing charges against black defendants after he told a defendant to raise his shirt and show the scars.)[34]

No matter which federal judge would be assigned to hear the case, by the summer of 1955 a majority of the Little Rock NAACP executive committee believed that litigation was now their only option. "We aren't trying to put pressure or make threats," Bates told reporters in September after Blossom had once again refined his plan—this time to allow white students to "opt out" if they had been assigned to all-black Horace Mann. "We just want to know what the plans are—officially."[35]

Her statement was disingenuous, because plans were already under way to raise money for a lawsuit. Besides holding the hands of black parents at Hoxie, Mildred Bond also found time to help write fundraising letters for the lawsuit in August 1955.[36] Bond's involvement meant that the NAACP's national office had already agreed to participate in a suit once local counsel had been obtained and financial arrangements had been made. It was determined that the case would not be filed until after the new school semester began in 1956 and students officially registered for classes.

Meanwhile, Bates's stock with the national NAACP continued to rise. In December the New York office hired Arkansas's first permanent field secretary, who was charged with recruiting members and funds on a statewide basis. Frank W. Smith, who had been executive director of the black Arkansas Teachers Association, was sent to New York in January for ten days of orientation. It also meant hiring a secretary and renting office space. Near the end of January, Bates wrote Gloster Current, the director of branches, "We held our board meeting January 21. The board was grateful to the national office for its consideration in hiring Mr. Smith. We secured an office and I advanced a month's rent. The office has been cleared and painted and is ready for occupancy. . . . As soon as we receive the allotted amount from the national office, we will complete purchase of furniture and other equipment."[37] Bates's enthusiasm and energy once again raised New York's hopes that Arkansas would regain the membership base that it had enjoyed when Harold Flowers had been president of the State Conference of Branches. Under Flowers's leadership, NAACP membership in Arkansas had attained a high of almost 9,000 members in 1948, but after his resignation the number had fallen to less than a fourth of that during the acrimonious period when he had been forced to resign. Since then, it had remained flat, with no more than 2,187 members in 1954.

It was the upcoming lawsuit against the Little Rock School Board, however, that occupied most of the attention of the Little Rock branch of the NAACP. In December 1955 Lee Lorch, as a member of the executive committee, had written to attorney U. Simpson Tate at the NAACP regional office about strategy concerning the proposed suit against the Little Rock School District. Despite the plans for litigation, there was still discussion within the Little Rock branch and with the national office whether a suit in Little Rock was even a good idea. Why not concentrate on suing those districts that had not even offered a plan to desegregate? If the case in Little Rock was lost, would it not hurt the cause elsewhere? The national office was not at all certain that a case needed to be brought in Little Rock since at least there was a desegregation plan, however shifting and increasingly ephemeral. Another issue was how to frame the suit—should the plaintiffs simply act as if Little Rock had no plan and sue for immediate integration? Or should they seek the more limited goal of requesting relief incorporating elements of the original Blossom plan, which, after all, could be interpreted to require a meaningful start on integration?

Meanwhile, the Lorches and Bateses were becoming more than simple acquaintances who shared membership in the Little Rock branch of the NAACP. "We lived right across the street. They visited in our home. We became friends socially," Lee Lorch recalled in an interview in 2002. Georg Iggers confirmed the friendship between the two couples, remembering that "the Lorches, particularly Lee, were much closer to the Bateses" than he and his wife. Barely two years later, the relationship would be put to the test. Lee Lorch's respect for Daisy was evident. When told that others had said that L. C. "was the brains behind the operation," he responded that this was "not a characterization I would make or find favor with. She was no dummy. . . . I regarded her as having a considerable amount of ability."[38]

Bates continued to see her role as still very much part of a group effort. According to Georg Iggers, Bates's involvement in the preparation for the litigation against the Little Rock School District that became known as *Aaron v. Cooper* was significant. In order to bring suit, parents had to be found who would agree to have their children request to go to white schools. Thus eight Little Rock NAACP branch members formed teams of two and went from house to house recruiting parents and their children. Iggers recalled Bates as a member of one of the teams, though L. C. was not. She "roll[ed] up her sleeves and knocked on doors."[39]

On January 23, 1956, twenty-seven students tried to register for second-semester classes and were turned away from both of Little Rock's high schools.[40] They were directed to the superintendent's office. Accompanied by Bates and Frank Smith, they arrived about 9:30 that morning. Blossom would later brag in his book that he had been tipped off at 5:00 that morning about the NAACP's plan. At this point, all present knew that Blossom would deny the students' requests, but it was necessary to go through the motions to set up the lawsuit. "We're here to register the children," Bates told Blossom. "Negro children appearing at white schools today live in adjacent neighborhoods— some within six blocks." Surrounded by media, Blossom replied, "I want to be as kind as I can. . . . But I'll have to deny your request. This is in line with the policy outlined to you many times before and made public long ago."[41] Bates, who had brought along Earl Davy, the photographer for the *State Press*, asked Blossom if a picture might be made in his office to record the moment, and Blossom agreed. The photograph, which was run in the *State Press*, shows the face Bates always gave whites in these situations. She is smiling.

Chapter Seven

A FOOT IN THE SCHOOLHOUSE DOOR

Speaking to reporters outside of Virgil Blossom's office, Daisy Bates said, "I think the next step is obvious. We've tried everything short of a court suit."[1] The case was filed on February 8, 1956, in federal district court in Little Rock. Attorneys listed on the complaint for the plaintiffs were Wiley Branton, local counsel, and U. Simpson Tate, regional counsel of the NAACP, whose office was in Dallas, Texas. Robert L. Carter and Thurgood Marshall, who would later argue the case before the Eighth Circuit Court of Appeals, were also listed as counsel. The class action suit was brought in alphabetical order in the names of and on behalf of thirty-three black minors, ranging from grades one through twelve, and by twelve adults, including L. C. Bates. Hoping they would shield the NAACP from scrutiny, the attorneys did not include the organization as a plaintiff in the suit, nor was Daisy Bates's name listed as a "next friend" on behalf of the children. No case filed in Little Rock would have a greater impact on the lives of its citizens or, indeed, a longer life. Though in 2002 federal judge Bill Wilson relinquished jurisdiction over most of the case, he still retained monitoring authority over part of it (though under a different case name). Local counsel was crucial, because the staff attorneys in the national office were stretched to the breaking point. In the Upper South alone, sixty-five other school suits with national NAACP participation were being litigated simultaneously.[2]

Though from Jefferson County, almost forty miles from Little Rock, Wiley Branton, head of the Legal Redress Committee of the State Conference of Branches, agreed to serve as local counsel in the case "for a minimum retainer, basically a mere guarantee of his expenses," remembered Georg Iggers.[3] His memory was correct. Other, more experienced African American attorneys on the Legal

Redress Committee, such as J. R. Booker and Thaddeus Williams, had set their fees too high, a typical way of declining to take the case. Branton, whose family was well known and respected in Pine Bluff in both the black and white communities, would go on to an illustrious civil rights career before becoming dean of Howard Law School. For the time being, however, he was cheap and available, and he believed the suit needed to be brought. He agreed to start the case for $250, only $150 of which was paid up front. The other $100 was not paid until April. "We understand that we are to pay the additional fee of fifty dollars ($50.00) per day [for services while in court]," J. C. Crenchaw wrote Branton in a letter confirming the agreement.[4] In an interview at Howard Law School, Branton recalled that "I thought the day I filed that suit it would be just a routine case. . . . And from the last week of August '57, I think I was in court or in the courthouse on conferences, including Saturdays and Sundays, darn near around the clock for almost the next forty days, and couldn't devote any time to my private law practice or my personal business." Branton was finally told by Thurgood Marshall that he could get paid by the NAACP's separately organized Legal and Educational Defense Fund.[5]

Funds to get the litigation started were hard to come by. Georg Iggers remembered that he and his wife had written their friends, asking for contributions. However much money the Iggerses raised, it was a mark of the difficulty of the task that the Little Rock NAACP had to go outside Arkansas for funds to begin the suit. Yet for the next four years, until the student protests began in 1960, the case would be practically the only viable weapon blacks in Arkansas had to battle discrimination. It would be taken very seriously by the white power structure, which assembled a high-powered team of lawyers to meet it.

Though she had been president of the Arkansas NAACP since the fall of 1952, it was not until the spring of 1956, during the litigation of *Aaron v. Cooper*, that Daisy Bates truly came into her own as a civil rights leader. Until the suit was filed, the NAACP in the state had been seen as primarily an irritant, not as an organization that had much impact or credibility. In fact, the early strategy of Archie House, the senior member of the attorneys who represented the Little Rock School District, was to attempt to show that the idea for the suit had come not from blacks in Little Rock but from New York. Thus, before the actual trial of the case, arrangements were made to take the depositions of both Rev. Crenchaw, the president of the Little Rock branch, and of Bates, in her capacity as president of the State Conference of Branches, in part for the purpose of showing how little support the suit had among local blacks. Unfortunately for the Little Rock NAACP, the case was assigned to Judge John Miller because of the resignation of the federal judge who would have normally heard the case. Historian Tony Freyer has shown that Archie House believed the Little Rock School District could gain sympathy from Judge Miller if it could demonstrate the national NAACP was seeking to control the pace of integration rather than the local black community. In a trial memorandum, House wrote, "It seems to me . . . that when [the] NAACP comes into a community like Little Rock and starts dictating what is a reasonable time to accomplish integration, it may be opening itself to criticism."[6]

As stated earlier, in her exchanges with school board attorney Leon Catlett, Bates asserted herself in a way she had not done previously. She knew what she had accomplished by her confrontation with Catlett from the mail she received. L. C. occasionally ran the letters in the paper under the caption, "From the Files of Mrs. L. C. Bates." A typical letter after her exchange with Catlett (always signed) read, "I thank God for Mrs. L. C. Bates. She is doing good work by the help of God. Every Negro in Arkansas should cooperate with her."[7] This feature in the *State Press* should not be understood as the shameless vanity of a proud husband. L. C. saw his wife as the best hope for the kind of leadership he had been advocating ever since he started the paper in 1941. For her part, Daisy obviously did not object to this effusive adulation being publicized. The point of it was not simply to laud her but to convince Arkansas blacks that she was not the kind of leader who would sell them out. Both L. C. and Daisy believed that for a price, other so-called leaders could be had, and the *State Press* was not shy about saying so. On the front page of the July 20, 1956, issue, L. C. wrote, "No public explanation has been made of the alleged funds being paid to Negro preachers and a high church official. But it is a fact that the church men are carrying the flag for Faubus's re-election."[8]

Daisy Bates's bold actions in Arkansas were bringing her more attention from the NAACP's national office in New York, and she made sure no one was going to forget her when she had the opportunity to mingle with the leaders at the national conventions. At the week-long annual meeting in July at the Statler Hotel in San Francisco, Bates was photographed as she presented two dozen red roses to Mrs. Roy Wilkins in the Gold Room during the "Freedom Fund" dinner. Though the top guns dominated the events (Thurgood Marshall warned of "southern politicians" who were "using state legislatures and the state courts either to outlaw the NAACP or to make it difficult to continue") it was Martin Luther King Jr., a rival and at the same time an ally of the national NAACP, who captivated the delegates with his oratory. The *State Press* ran a picture of him being congratulated on his speech by Roy Wilkins and called him "a youthful and dynamic leader."[9]

The filing of lawsuits to enforce the *Brown* decision in places like Little Rock sounded a continuing alarm throughout the bastions of white supremacy in the South, and an overwhelming number of their leaders in Congress responded in the spring of 1956 by signing a document known as "The Southern Manifesto," which "challenged the legitimacy of the Supreme Court's decision [in *Brown*]." As one legal scholar noted, it was "a calculated declaration of political war against the Court's decision."[10] Feeling the heat of their white constituents, the entire Arkansas delegation signed off on it. Three southern senators, including Lyndon Johnson, did not sign it. The other two were Tennessee's Albert Gore, father of the future vice president, and Estes Kefauver, also from Tennessee.

Another Arkansas politician was feeling the heat, too, in the summer of 1956. Jim Johnson's racial rhetoric had Orval Faubus, who was running for a second term, breaking out in sweat, the clammy kind that had its genesis in fear. Johnson was coming after him. Son of a bona fide socialist from the hill country of Madison County in northwest Arkansas, Faubus's views on race were complicated. He was populist enough to understand and appreciate the aspirations of African Americans. After *Brown I*, he was quoted at a private meeting as having said, "If I had been on the Court, I would have voted that way myself."[11] Despite this capacity to empathize with the downtrodden, Faubus was not immune to the South's continued insistence that blacks were inferior to whites and not deserving of social equality. His biographer, Roy Reed, noted the contradictions. Growing up in the Ozarks, Faubus would have had but occasional contacts with the few blacks who found their way to the region. A group of black workers from time to time appeared in the town of Combs to "load railroad ties." There was "the little band of black folk at Wharton Creek," but it was in the army that Faubus would have first encountered black males in any significant numbers. "He found that he resented black servicemen's dating white girls."[12]

Yet this prejudice by a white American during the Second World War was hardly a southern phenomenon, and as a politician (much to L. C.'s continued consternation in the pages of the *State Press*), Faubus successfully courted the vote of blacks, appointing blacks to the State

Democratic Committee and helping to "integrate the state Democratic party." Despite his initial statement in his first campaign for governor that the state was not ready for "a complete and sudden mixing of the races in the public schools" (a position L. C. never let his readers forget), Faubus had kept out of the brouhaha at Hoxie and generally took the stand that school integration was a local matter.[13] Daisy Bates's view of Faubus was complicated by the fact that, in some ways, the two foes were alike. Whatever they felt, in public and even in private, they would be courteous to each other. Both had deep resentments, one based on race, the other emanating from class. Both understood how important it was to their identity to be treated with at least superficial dignity and respect, and neither forgot it when they were not.

By June 1956, each time the governor looked over his shoulder in his bid for another two-year term, all he could see was Jim Johnson waving his arms and stirring up the racial issue. Johnson was a master of the politics of resentment: the federal government was the enemy—that Dixiecrat lament, which, if traced far enough back, ended up at Lee's surrender to Grant at Appomattox. Now it came with an ugly new wrinkle—the Communists were behind all the turmoil blacks like Daisy Bates were causing.

Johnson was making hay out of his proposed state constitutional amendment, to be submitted to the voters in November 1956, which would somehow interpose the authority of the state to thwart federal authority. The fact that such an amendment, if passed, was a nullity in terms of giving the state of Arkansas any actual authority to do such a thing counted for nothing. Faubus knew it, too. "Everyone knows that no state law supercedes a federal law," he would say in 1957.[14] But that was before he began to get worried about the election. If enacted and used as a reason to defy the federal government, it meant another civil war. Johnson was not acting in a vacuum, nor was he particularly original. Other southern states were passing various measures aimed at thwarting federal authority. Their public officials, like those in Arkansas, would ultimately settle for trying to drive the NAACP out of business and setting up private schools, but the rhetoric of the two candidates trying to "outseg" each other proved irresistible. Faubus held a press conference and thundered, "No school district would be forced to integrate" so long as he was governor.[15]

Meanwhile Virgil Blossom was steadily refining the Little Rock School District's plan, telling the Pulaski County Bar Association that no black teachers would teach white children. Any white student in the minority could transfer. This meant the burden to integrate the schools would fall exclusively on blacks, which of course was critical for those who considered themselves "moderate" whites. When these moderate members of the white power structure talked about "obeying the law," it was explicitly understood by one and all that that they would remain in control of the process of integration. This fact was not lost on Daisy or L. C. In response to a Blossom speech at the Sertoma Club, L. C. editorialized that good race relations in Little Rock meant "the power to keep the Negro meek and humble where he will not exert any action that is contrary to the white man's will."[16]

On August 15, 1956, the case of *Aaron v. Cooper* began in Judge Miller's court, and from the beginning it had disaster written all over it for the black plaintiffs. The night before the trial, the NAACP's national attorney, U. Simpson Tate, would not even meet with the plaintiffs and Wiley Branton to discuss strategy, claiming he was tired and needed his rest. In fact, as mentioned earlier, there was a dispute over the immediate goals of the litigation between the Arkansas affiliate and the national NAACP. For tactical reasons only, the Little Rock NAACP wanted Tate to argue during the trial that the plaintiffs were merely seeking the limited goals of the original Blossom plan, which, had it been implemented, would have resulted in more integration than the later revised version.[17] However, the national office insisted on an all-or-nothing approach, and Tate argued the case on general constitutional principles.[18] Thus in a way, Archie House had been correct. The Little Rock NAACP was willing to accept something less than total and immediate integration in 1956. Actually, it was much ado about nothing. In hindsight, it did not matter what the strategy or tactics were: Judge Miller was not about to write an opinion that threatened southern white supremacy in the slightest. Additionally, in the post–*Brown II* environment, no federal appeals court was going to reverse him so long as he paid lip service to the principles set out in *Brown I*. In his opinion, Miller wrote, "The testimony of the defendant Superintendent of schools, Mr. Virgil Blossom, is convincing in that not only he but the other defendants have acted in the utmost good faith."[19] Daisy Bates's reaction to the defeat was dead-on. The Little Rock School Board wasn't acting in good faith; it was simply employing "delaying tactics."[20]

Though the opposite of what had been intended by the original decision by the Supreme Court, *Brown II* was tailor made for federal judges like Miller, who had no intention of forcing school boards to act in good faith. He ruled that the school board could proceed as it wished—it had said all along that 1957 would be the year school desegregation would begin, and he would not disturb its decision. The subtext was that white supremacy was not to be disturbed, despite the obvious signs that the "plan" was already well on its way to mere tokenism.

The defeat in court was difficult, but Bates had other problems as well. She once had high hopes for Frank Smith, the first NAACP field secretary hired exclusively for Arkansas, but the man was not working out. On September 25, 1956, Bates wrote a letter on *State Press* stationery to Roy Wilkins bluntly criticizing Smith. "I don't think our field secretary is very good at fundraising, or of obtaining memberships. Our statewide membership is now lower than ever. He has not raised one nickel towards our obligation to the National Office, or anything else." Since increasing the membership and fund-raising were his precise duties, it was blunt criticism, but it would not be until the end of 1957 that the national office finally took action to deal with the matter. Instead, Bates began to take an active role in fund-raising herself. She wrote Wilkins that she had been out soliciting money. "Last night I met with the Beauticians of Greater Little Rock. They reported 130 shops."[21]

There are different ways to look at the violence and harassment that inevitably followed against Daisy and L. C., as she was increasingly identified as *the* black civil rights leader in Arkansas. One can compare it to what occurred in Birmingham, Alabama (also known as "Bombingham"), and conclude that it was mild. After all, their home was never successfully burned or dynamited. Too, they both survived. In neighboring Mississippi, NAACP field secretary Medgar Evers was murdered outside his home in 1963. No children were blown to bits in a church as occurred in Birmingham. Arkansas, as historians and others (Daisy and L. C. among them) have repeatedly stressed, was not the Deep South. One can understand all of this but still miss the point. From a personal perspective, beginning in October 1956 when the first cross was burned on their lawn, the cost was emotionally incalculable. For the next four and a half years until Daisy effectively moved to New York in the spring of 1960, she would never feel secure a single night in her own house. Clyde Lee Cross, the twelve-year-old child Daisy and L. C. had taken in, would have to be given up a year later because of the fear he might be harmed or killed. Due to the boycott of advertisers and the intimidation of their newspaper distributors,

Daisy and L. C. would lose their business and livelihood in 1959. In truth, their lives would become hellish, and in private, after the second cross was burned at the end of October, Daisy admitted how the incidents affected her. "It is rough here now," she wrote Roy Wilkins on November 8, 1956. "Two car loads visited us last Saturday night. They saw the guards, and left without doing anything. Since that time we have been guarding the house each night, with the help of friends. However, if the intimidations keep up, we will have to have a regular guard. We have appealed to the city police, and they are patrolling the area a little closer. We have also been able to hire off-duty police to guard the house on special occasions with the permission of the police chief."[22] There would be several close calls. They were constantly worried about their new house being burned to the ground, and it would have been destroyed had it not been for the vigilance of their neighbors. Even though neighbors, friends, and supporters would often stand guard at night outside the home, the cost of security was a continuing drain, not always covered by the NAACP. It was in the November letter that Bates first began to mention to Wilkins the loss of revenue to the paper. The *State Press* in the last week "had lost over $300 in advertising contracts."[23] Years earlier the *State Press* had weathered a boycott by advertisers. Reporting on the slow demise of the paper would become a regular theme.

Publicly, neither Daisy nor L. C. ever showed the slightest fear. After the first cross burning, Daisy went ahead with the State Conference of Branches meeting in October and held registration and the board meeting in her home. As if to taunt their adversaries, the article in the *State Press* announcing the gathering gave out their home address in Little Rock. None of the key players was deterred from coming. Wiley Branton led an afternoon workshop on combating discrimination. Chris Mercer, Clarence Laws from the national NAACP office, Lee Lorch, Georg Iggers, and George Howard Jr., who would later succeed Bates as president of the State Conference of Branches and become Arkansas's first black federal judge, were listed as "resource persons" for the meeting. A well-placed bomb could have wiped out the civil rights movement in Arkansas that very afternoon.

L. C. headlined each incident on the front page of the *State Press*. "SECOND CROSS BURNED ON BATES LAWN" the banner ran on November 2. As if it had happened to someone else, he related the account in the third person, even though he had been the only one at home when a neighbor knocked on his door to alert him. It was this kind of grace under fire that won Daisy the admiration of so many people outside of Arkansas. But L. C. never flinched either. At night they took turns guarding the house, and then L. C. would get up to go to the office at the *State Press* without much sleep.

As with any incident in the South by this time, the news of cross burnings was frankly money in the bank to the national office of the NAACP as well as points scored in the halls of Congress. As Wilkins wrote to Bates on November 19, "I am convinced, however, that these cross-burnings are a help to us in the overall battle." And then in a final sentence that doubtlessly pleased her, he added, "I just pray no one as valuable as you gets hurt in the mean time [sic]."[24]

The voters of Arkansas formalized their continuing commitment to white supremacy in November by passing, with healthy majorities, three measures that appeared on the ballot: an amendment to the state constitution purporting to nullify *Brown I* and *II*, a resolution interposing the authority of the state against the federal government, and a measure allowing school districts to assign children to schools on factors other than race. Bates sent copies of these measures to Wilkins as well, for whom this information was routine. Everything presented to the voters copied proposals from other southern states. The only difference was the sponsor. The governor had campaigned for his pupil placement act in order to keep pace with Jim Johnson's promise that a simple amendment to the state constitution would enable whites to maintain their authority over blacks and avoid integration. The governor was easily elected in November over his Republican challenger, but with a glaring lack of support in Little Rock. The business leaders in the Heights, the upper-class section in Little Rock, did not much like Faubus. In truth, he was far too liberal for most of them. Now that he had won reelection by a comfortable margin, the governor could show his true colors. He was for the little man and woman and wanted a tax increase (sales, income, and severance) from the legislature that was about to convene early in 1957 so he could raise teachers' salaries, increase welfare payments, and give Arkansas a modern state hospital that would replace the dungeon for the mentally ill. The business community preferred one of their own at the state capitol, someone who would keep the lid on things. They did not know then how good a politician Faubus was, how effective he was at the art of getting things done. None of that had been apparent during his first term, but then he hadn't had a mandate from the voters. Passing legislation meant getting your hands dirty—making compromises, patronage, rewarding friends, and knowing what everyone required to get his or her vote. He loved it.

As Roy Reed wrote in the introduction to his book on Faubus, he "was one of the last Americans to perceive politics as a grand game. He was always a little surprised that other people did not understand that."[25] The November ballot items were just a warm-up for the real game played when the legislature came to town in the winter of 1957.

Chapter Eight

TWO STEPS BACK

The *State Press* greeted the new year of 1957 with grim determination, noting that in the state, "anti-Negro forces are organized and are gaining momentum by the day and are urged on by Arkansas's executive head, and some of the state's news media, and enjoy the sneaking cooperation of many of modern 'Uncle Toms.' "[1] There would be no letup against Daisy and L. C. In a telegram dated January 7 to Roy Wilkins, Daisy reported that on Saturday night a crude incendiary bomb was thrown in the carport but that the wind had blown it out before it caused any damage.

Aside from the Civil War, 1957–59 was to become the ugliest period in Little Rock's history. Tyranny begins with the suppression of minorities or those who hold unpopular positions, but it spreads quickly. Indeed, as Virgil Blossom wrote in his book, quoting an unnamed leading citizen of the Little Rock power structure in 1958, "You had all just as well recognize that we are living in a police state."[2] It would hardly be Iraq under Saddam Hussein, but it would be quite uncomfortable for people who were used to being in control. From the gallery of the House of Representatives at the state capitol in the winter of 1957, Bates watched the process begin to unfold as she took notes for the *State Press*. House Bill 322 created the State Sovereignty Commission, which authorized the state to resist the federal government's school integration efforts and gave it wide investigatory powers. Witch hunts were in fashion nationally as well. In February the country's most famous playwright, Arthur Miller, and Dr. Otto Nathan, Albert Einstein's literary executor, were indicted on charges of contempt of Congress for refusing to cooperate with HUAC. In one of life's strange twists, Nathan and Daisy Bates would live in the same hotel and become friends in New York. As great a threat to civil liberties was

House Bill 324, which would require the NAACP to report its finances and membership. Another bill permitted school districts to use their funds to defend integration cases. House Bill 323 exempted compulsory school attendance in integrated schools.

In an editorial on February 15, 1957, L. C. correctly identified the sponsors of the bills as "opponents of constitutional government" whose purpose was to "introduce legislation aimed at killing the NAACP."[3] Those hardy souls who testified against the passage of these bills made an impression on Daisy, who covered a meeting of the Senate Constitutional Amendment Committee for the *State Press* on February 18. The interest in these bills was such that the committee met in the chamber of the House of Representatives. Bates sat in the packed gallery "listening to speakers representing church groups and organized labor as they made fervent pleas against passage of these bills."[4] The president of the Arkansas State Federation of Labor, Odell Smith, pointed out that the bills were "more in harmony with the principles of Communist and Fascist governments than with democratic government." The Reverend W. L. Miller Jr., head of the Arkansas State Convention of Christian Churches, warned that the "bills would set up a secret police with undefined powers and that could only mean the loss of our freedom."[5]

Rabbi Ira E. Sanders of Temple B'Nai Israel correctly foretold the future: "If they [the four bills] are adopted, it will mean a loss of industry and this would be morally just opprobrium for the State."[6] After the public hearing, Bates sent NAACP members to plead with their representatives and senators to oppose the bill. She herself "was a member of a Pulaski County delegation of business and professional people who visited the Governor in an attempt to get him to use his influence to help defeat the bills." It was her "first formal meeting" with Faubus. She recalled that "he was very gracious" but brushed aside their concerns.[7] The four bills passed with overwhelming support.

Only a handful of white Arkansans displayed any recognition that the actions in the legislature resembled some of the measures of the people who had allowed Hitler to take over Germany, but the parallel was too obvious to miss. In an editorial, L. C. quoted Msgr. James E. O'Connell, rector of St. John's Seminary in Little Rock, who had testified at the hearing that "the dominant principle of Nazism was its subscription to segregation and the cardinal principle of the master race." The master race in Arkansas (with certain exceptions) looked in the mirror each morning, but instead of being shocked by the reflection of the face of nascent totalitarianism, interpreted the image staring back as that of a victim of a federal government intent on destroying their way of life.

It was classic, vintage projection—whites were not the aggressors, the NAACP was the aggressor, and whites were only defending themselves. With the passage of these bills, white Arkansans were replicating a pattern of psychological projection that itself could be traced back to slavery. White men hadn't raped their black "property"; it was white women who had been at risk of an untamable black lust. Whites hadn't used violence to suppress blacks; it was the primal rage of blacks that had to be curbed. In the present, the same psychological mechanism of behavior prevailed. White Arkansans were not depriving blacks of their constitutional rights; instead, the U.S. Supreme Court was depriving white Arkansans of their constitutional rights to live in a sovereign state. Given the way the brain is hard-wired to resort to psychological defense mechanisms through which reality is filtered, Blossom, speaking for the vast majority of whites, wrote without a conscious trace of hypocrisy: "Little Rock was proud, too, of its reputation as a city of excellent race relations."[8] Of course, implicit in this assertion was the condition that blacks accept the status quo. Indeed, until the *State Press* and the local NAACP began rattling their chains, blacks in Little Rock had, for the most part, accepted the status quo.

In a reply to Bates on February 25, Wilkins said the NAACP lawyers were "tied up" at the moment dealing with the same types of laws passed by the Virginia legislature. The strategy was obvious: "These states are trying hard to keep us so busy defending the Association and spending our money that we will have no time or resources left to push the program. Also, they are trying to frighten our people. So far, nobody has been frightened in the other states. We shall see what we shall see in Arkansas."[9]

In March Bates attended a regional NAACP conference in St. Louis, where she continued to impress the national office. Roy Wilkins was the principal speaker at the Freedom Fund Dinner in St. Louis, and Bates was asked to report on the situation in Arkansas. Already, she was enjoying the attention and travel, volunteering for a speaking tour in the spring involving NAACP state presidents, but with events heating up in the South, the tour never took place. She continued to complain about Frank Smith. "I do hope some definite steps will be taken soon, regarding our state office. Incidentally, I think there is a possibility of employing Attorney C. C. Mercer."[10] Mercer, who briefly worked for the newly formed biracial Arkansas Council of Human Relations, would not come to work for Bates until the fall.

Despite the noise coming from the Arkansas legislature, the power to decide how much integration would occur was in the hands of the federal courts. The success of the "Anti-Negro" forces was taken seriously. In early March Bates presided over a statewide NAACP meeting at the Phyllis Wheatley YMCA in Little Rock to discuss the passage of the bills. Representatives from forty-two chapters were in attendance. The act allowing local authorities to force local chapters to open up their books was a major threat to the NAACP's existence, but at this point all Bates could do was to assure the group that the national office would assist in challenging the statute when it was enforced. Calling the work of the legislature "unAmerican and unChristian," she saved some of her harshest comments for "modern day Uncle Toms" who fed off hand-outs from the whites to do their dirty work. She urged her audience "to expose them in their communities for what they are."[11] Though there was a line she couldn't cross when speaking to whites, neither she nor L. C. exercised such restraint when it came to dealing with blacks. A month later, while trying to drum up enthusiasm for a membership campaign, the *State Press* singled out black teachers and ministers for not belonging to the NAACP, calling teachers "indifferent" to their own self-interest.[12] In the next two years Bates would be disappointed by both whites and blacks, but she would claim it was the response of blacks that pained her the most.

The *State Press* had noted approvingly the results in March of two school board races in Little Rock and one in North Little Rock. "JIM CROW GROUP FAILS TO GET HOLD OF LOCAL SCHOOLS" ran L. C.'s headline. It would be the last real defeat until 1959 for the group called the Capital Citizens Council, which pledged to "use every legal means to prevent integration in the public schools."[13] Though its membership was never more than about 500, this group would reflect the feelings of the overwhelming majority of white residents of Little Rock and, indeed, white Arkansans generally.

As spring turned to summer, the concerns of the Capital Citizens Council would find their way into print and bring maximum pressure on Blossom and the Little Rock School Board, but before the crisis at Central High reached full boil, the Eighth Circuit Court of Appeals had to render its decision. Finally, in early April the court upheld the Little Rock School Board's "plan" to desegregate the schools in *Aaron v. Cooper*, and Virgil Blossom lost no time in deciding how he would go about implementing it. As a result of the court's decision, Blossom was given carte blanche to proceed as he wished. Bates learned immediately through the Little Rock NAACP Youth Council that Blossom was soliciting applications from black students who were interested in attending Central, and she asked for a meeting with him. After Blossom agreed, she appointed a group from the Little Rock branch executive committee to go see him. L. C. was most likely a part of the delegation.

Now sustained by two court decisions in the school district's favor, Blossom conducted the meeting in his typical dictatorial fashion. He would make the final decision himself as to who would attend Central that fall. "I know it is undemocratic, and I know it is wrong, but I'm doing it," Blossom stated.[14] As far as Bates and the group she took to see Blossom were concerned, it was vintage Blossom. According to a report of the meeting written by Frank Smith for the NAACP, Blossom was saying, on the one hand, "that any Negroes however ill-prepared could attend Central if they were living in that attendance zone," but also he said that he would make the final decisions about which black children would attend Central. John Kirk has written that "with the help and support of Daisy Bates, nine applicants, all members of the NAACP Youth Council in Little Rock with which Bates had a close affiliation, made it through the rigorous interviewing process and were given permission to attend Central High."[15] At least one of the Nine and her parents had not met Bates before September. Elizabeth Eckford, whose photograph of being hounded by the mob was flashed around the world, stated in an interview in 2002 that she "met Daisy and L. C. Bates on the night when I first attempted to get in school."[16] In a later interview, her father, Oscar Eckford, who worked for the railroad at night, explained, "We travelled in different circles. I wasn't travelling in their circle."[17] Daisy and L. C.'s circle was that small part of the black elite in Little Rock that supported civil rights. Though Oscar Eckford would become a fervent defender of Daisy, he was not yet a member of the NAACP.

As much as Daisy and L. C. would have preferred otherwise, the NAACP was not the only thing on blacks' minds in 1957. Oscar Eckford occasionally read the *State Press*, but "making a living," was his primary concern before his daughter became one of the Little Rock Nine. Though some of them were friends before entering Central in 1957, the children who were to make up the Little Rock Nine lived in that special world of adolescents everywhere, in which one's race was only one of life's problems. Melba Pattillo Beals, in her memoir of the period, presents an affecting picture of what it was like to be a typical black teenager of the time. For her, it was quite a bit like being a white teenager. White culture dominated. The slogan "black is beautiful" was almost a decade in the future, with its ramifications for American society.[18] For their Little Rock counterparts raised on a steady diet of white supremacy, it was a total impossibility for whites to imagine (much less acknowledge) the similarity of most black and white lives. To accept that simple but overwhelming fact would have required giving up the whole notion of white superiority. Instead, the white mind defaulted to whatever favorite stereotype served preconceived notions of what blacks were supposed to be like. As mentioned, Bates confounded whites (though impressing them at the same time) by dressing better than most of them and only letting her anger show when it served her purposes.

In her 1976 interview with Elizabeth Jacoway, Bates said that at one point Blossom was only going to admit "one of the Nine. . . . And she was as light as you are." Bates identified the student as Carlotta Walls. "And so if Carlotta got in, nobody would know if she was white or black."[19] Blossom wanted them invisible if possible. If not, looking white was the next best thing.

Whether that was ever in Blossom's mind or just a rumor, it was an indication that Bates understood how the game was to be played. Blossom wanted black children who would not rebel at white supremacy but accept its terms, which were prove yourself as good as whites, be as smart as whites, and be prepared for hostility. Terrence Roberts remembered he saw the challenge of being one of the Nine as a personal test. Asked if he wished he had been more aggressive in his responses to the harassment he encountered at Central, he replied, "I understood from the start that militant retribution, militant responses or retaliating in kind would not serve any real purpose—it might have satisfied a fleeting emotion but in order to really present to the universe that our cause was just—that we were in a righteous battle here . . . we had to demonstrate that the other side was truly evil and let them do their thing, you know, some sort of Gandhian [exercise] in a sense."[20]

White southerners, of course, never thought of themselves as "truly evil" or evil in any sense. In fact, the members of the Capital Citizens Council were ordinary white Arkansans who justifiably felt they were being ignored by the white power structure in Little Rock. White supremacy had been the order of the day in Arkansas throughout the state's history. No black children had ever been permitted to go to school with white children in Little Rock, and leaders from Faubus to Blossom and the Little Rock School Board were trying to fudge the issue. For them, it was Bates who was "truly evil" for stirring up trouble. As a college-educated white Arkansan remembered in 2002, "Daisy Bates was our Osama Bin Ladin."[21] As outrageous and grimly ludicrous as this comparison is, it captures the emotions of the white community at the time. For Bates and the students who became the Nine, there was no meaningful choice about their behavior. In 1957 whites were still in absolute control, and a person played by their rules or didn't play at all. Bates did what she could. She told Jacoway, "I got the names of kids that he [Blossom] had not interviewed, and I talked to them before [the interviews]. When they went down there, they knew what to say and what not to say."[22] Though Blossom made it seem that the black children who were in the Central attendance zone had a choice, the reality was they did not. Of the eighty who originally applied, all but thirty-two had been winnowed out, and Blossom "persuaded" all but sixteen of these not to attend Central. Understandable fear would cause all but nine to drop out at the last moment.

Through his total control of the application process, Virgil Blossom succeeded in marginalizing Bates's role. The NAACP had no input as to which students would be allowed to enroll at Central. There would come a time in September when he needed Bates in the worst way, but that was months in the future. Blossom presented the integration of Central High to both whites and blacks as primarily a privilege for blacks, not as a legal right, and at the time, it was a mindset that was not easily shed. NAACP field secretary Frank Smith wrote of the meeting with Blossom that there was some protest. "The committee advised the superintendent that it felt that . . . the procedure used in selecting students seemed only to instill a feeling of inferiority, fear and intimidation, and that the procedure should be discontinued."[23]

Given what the courts had already said, it would have been futile for the plaintiffs in *Aaron v. Henry* to return to Judge Miller and ask him to intervene in the selection process to allow students to be admitted based on a strict attendance zone admittance policy.[24] In fact, Bates and Blossom were in basic agreement about what kind of students should first be admitted to Central. It was obvious to her and members of the committee that the first black students admitted to Central would be under a microscope.[25] Smith's account of the meeting made it clear that Bates and her committee knew far in advance of the first day of school that only a few black students would be admitted to Central.[26]

By this time Virgil Blossom had a personal stake in how school desegregation was going to proceed in Little Rock, and no blacks were going to have a real say in it. If Roy Reed's account is correct, Blossom saw the successful integration of Central High as his ticket to the governorship of Arkansas.[27]

Meanwhile, Blossom's plan was leaving a bad taste in the mouths of the Capital Citizens Council, which was making its concerns heard. Besides white supremacy, there was the simmering matter of class conflict. No blacks would be going to Hall High School in the part of Little Rock where the rich folks lived. No one was speaking for the whites who were being expected to bear the burden of integration. Who was going to stand up for them? In Mansfield, Texas, Governor Allan Shivers had sent in the Texas Rangers after a federal district court had ordered school integration there, and the federal government had backed off. The Capital Citizens Council president publicly reminded Faubus of this fact, but the governor's reply was evasive. School integration was a local matter, he replied, contradicting himself yet again. As if to pour salt into an open wound, the governor "followed that a week later with a call for more Negroes on the state Democratic Party Central Committee. That strengthened the long-held opinion of many that their governor was an outright integrationist."[28]

The Capital Citizens Council continued to be outraged by Faubus. It took an ad out in the *Arkansas Recorder* calling on citizens to write Faubus. Many did.[29] The governor was not the only one to feel the heat. The Little Rock School Board meetings became a battleground. The council wanted separate schools for those whites who did not want to attend school with blacks. Getting at the heart of the matter, Rev. Wesley Pruden demanded to know how the board was going to handle the day-to-day interaction between whites and blacks in Central. What about school dances? What about black girls taking showers with white girls after P.E.? Stalling for time, the board suggested that these concerns be put in writing. The council had found the school district's weak spot and immediately published an ad, posing its questions in an open letter. Its thrust was simple: "WHEN YOU START RACE MIXING—WHERE ARE YOU GOING TO STOP?" This one advertisement got to the core of the issue. Addressed to Blossom and the school board, it asked, if integration occurs in September at Central High, "will the negro boys and girls be permitted to attend the school sponsored dances? Would the negro boys be permitted to solicit the white girls for dances? Or would discrimination be permitted here?" On and on the ad ran. What about school-sponsored trips? "Will they stay in the same motels?" "Because of the high venereal disease rate among negroes, the Public is wondering if the white children will be forced to use the same rest rooms and toilet facilities with negroes?" The questions all ended with a final query: "Or will discrimination be permitted here?"[30]

Half a century later, the questions posed in the advertisement seem crude relics of the South's racist past, but in Little Rock in 1957 they touched the rawest nerve in the white southerner's body. Forget the polite racial etiquette that governed public dialogue. All the past bubbled up in one explosive open letter that was published for all to see. Though there was nothing new in its sentiments (except the fact that it was public), it was a public relations masterpiece, because white southerners had long ago mentally converted their history of rape and oppression of black people into a scenario in which white southern children were now to be the innocent victims of black fantasies. The image of a filthy, slobbering black man leering at the flower of southern womanhood had been imprinted for centuries. With one advertisement, the racial genie was truly out of the bottle. It was tailor made for the hysteria that followed.[31]

Whites on both sides dug in their heels, and there was anger and resentment igniting in both camps. Despite their own segregationist sentiments, the Little Rock School Board and its supporters, the white power structure, believed they had no choice but to comply in a minimal way with a federal district court order (when given the chance, however, they would engage in the most dilatory tactics possible to keep token desegregation in place). For their part, people like Amis Guthridge (who had been active in Hoxie) and Wesley Pruden in Little Rock had lost their patience with the people whom they believed were selling them out. Guthridge was quoted as saying, "Little Rock schools would never be integrated," and if they were, there would be "hell on the border."[32] It was a phrase that would be remembered.

Meanwhile, the divisions in the black community continued to appear in print. Before the Eighth Circuit Court of Appeals ruled in April in the Little Rock school case, there was talk of a boycott by blacks against downtown department stores in Little Rock to protest their practices (for example, blacks were often not allowed to try on clothes before making a purchase). C. H. Jones, publisher of the *State Press*'s rival, the *Southern Mediator Journal*, argued against it, writing, "I know you can't change customs overnight." His sympathy for a go-slow policy on ending segregation was a little more than convenient. His paper was full of ads from white-owned businesses. The Bateses were incensed, and L. C. took Jones to task in an editorial. "If you enjoy segregation, discrimination and second-class citizenship, that is entirely your business . . . when you call Negroes stupid, that makes them mad."[33] At the same time, Roland Smith, pastor of the First Baptist Church (whom Bates mentions in her memoir as the sole black who spoke during the legislative hearings in February), advised blacks in Arkansas not to go to Washington, D.C., for a national civil rights march. Speaking for a local ministers' group in Little Rock, he said that "by staying away from Washington, the Negro could make more friends that could help him."

"Let's go to Washington," the *State Press* encouraged its readers. Doubtless, Daisy (and possibly L. C.) went there for the rally on May 17, 1957, which drew 27,000 marchers, who heard Martin Luther King Jr. and other national figures address the crowd.

As usual, the South was in the spotlight at the national NAACP convention in Detroit during the last week in June and the first few days of July. Besides Daisy Bates and Rev. J. C. Crenchaw, still president of the Little Rock branch, lawyers Wiley Branton and George Howard went to Detroit for the meetings to discuss the legal ramifications of the law forcing the NAACP chapters to disclose their membership lists. The bill requiring the NAACP to open its books had passed its ninety-day waiting period and was now the law. It is doubtful that Bates or anyone could have anticipated the legal onslaught the NAACP was about to face in Arkansas. Though Bates and the Little Rock Nine would be mostly remembered, it was the lawyers—the NAACP staff counsel together with local attorneys such as Branton and Howard—who filed and would eventually win the cases.

In August it was as if the people of Little Rock found themselves trapped inside an old-fashioned pressure cooker. With each passing moment, the lid seemed about to blow off the pot as the days wound down to the opening of school. The voices of whites who wanted the school board to defy the federal courts were now being heard in ways that could not be ignored. With each meeting and rally of the White Citizens Council and Mothers League of Central High School (a newly formed group that worked hand-in-glove with the council), the rhetoric grew more ominous. As Arkansas historians and writers have pointed out, in its frontier days Arkansans had routinely resorted to violence in resolving disputes, and now the old ways seemed about to reappear.

"Hell on the border" no longer seemed like an idle threat, and the Little Rock School Board and Blossom were caught in the middle. They could deal with Bates and the NAACP, indeed had beaten them in court twice in a row, but now they could not satisfy the whites who no longer trusted them. In desperation, the Little Rock School Board dropped the pretense of acting in good faith. The school board's attorneys wrote Guthridge and made sure the letter appeared in the newspapers: "The plan was developed to give as little integration as possible over as long a period of time as it is legally possible to have."[34] Nothing could have been clearer. The white power structure, the White Citizens Council, and the Mothers League were on the same side. But it no longer mattered what Blossom or his attorneys said. The smell of blood was in the air. "A nigger in your school is a potential Communist in your school," W. R. Hughes of Dallas, the head of the executive committee of the Association of White Citizens Councils of Texas, told the Mothers League. Not only that, "Communism was behind every effort of the NAACP."[35]

On August 22, around eleven o'clock that night, a large rock came crashing through Daisy and L. C.'s living-room picture window. L. C. was apparently asleep, but she was awake, reading a newspaper. Seated on the divan and thinking it was a gunshot, she threw herself to the floor and was immediately covered with glass. A note was wrapped around the rock. "Stone this time. Dynamite next." Within days another cross was burned on the lawn, accompanied by a note that read "Go Back to Africa—KKK." The catalyst for the rock being thrown through the window was most likely the appearance of Georgia governor Marvin Griffin and racial firebrand Roy V. Harris at a Capital Citizens Council's dinner held at the Marion Hotel in downtown Little Rock. The atmosphere had been electric. Here was a southern governor who was calling upon white people to resist the federal government's efforts to cram integration down their throats. In Georgia, they had set up legal machinery to close the schools. But there was much more. Harris spoke to the group's pride. "Our way of life is constitutional, American, Christian and scientific." Whose fault was it that anyone might question that? Communists, of course. "For twenty years the Communists and Reds have conducted a brainwashing campaign through the churches, the two political parties and national organizations, and have been so successful."[36]

It was the kind of red meat the crowd wanted. Rebel yells and cries of "Amen!" punctuated the remarks of the Georgians. The speeches were credited with turning the tide in favor of the Capital Citizens

Council and its insistence that "our way of life" was worth fighting for. As Roy Reed has written, "Griffin's appearance quite suddenly convinced large numbers of people that the entire integration problem could be solved quickly and simply."[37]

Daisy and L. C. were lucky they only had a window broken that night. Yet their anger publicly over these incidents was directed more at the black community than at whites. Using the pseudonym of A. M. Judge, L. C. quoted Daisy as saying that she wasn't "concerned with attacks but 'with the people who say they want first class citizenship, equality in education, but when her organization makes these things possible, they are too cowardly to take advantage of them.' " These were strong words, but on the verge of school opening, the number of black children willing to go to Central was understandably dropping. It would soon be down to nine. To her attackers she merely said, "Their aim is damned poor. Their luck might run out before mine does."[38]

Where was the governor of Arkansas during all of this? Faubus now seemed to be in no mood to help the very people who had elected him. He had not even bothered to appoint anyone to the State Sovereignty Commission until mounting criticism by his opponents forced his hand. Though he did not say so, he had only gone along with the eastern Arkansas crowd that wanted the bills in order to get their support for a tax increase. He was furious with Blossom, the Little Rock School Board, and the Little Rock silk-stocking crowd that lived in Pulaski Heights. They had complicated everything by instituting a plan that favored themselves (omitting Hall High School from the integration plan), and now they wanted him to risk his political skin by saying he would make sure Central High School would open without any trouble.

Faubus, as always, was keeping his options open. He had his friend Jimmy Karam meet with Guthridge and Pruden. If the governor blocked the integration of Central, could he count on their support for a third term? Oddly naive that Faubus was concerned about his political future, Guthridge was startled by the question. The answer, of course, was yes. As a result, Faubus met with Guthridge, Pruden, and others on the upper floor of Karam's store and, according to Guthridge "indicated . . . very strongly that he was going to stop it, the integration of Central High School."[39] It was not the only secret meeting. Faubus met with others, sometimes in private, sometimes not. From Crossett, Jim Johnson kept the telephone wires humming. "We were dedicated to hustling him," he told Roy Reed years later. "Orval hid out, but our people in Little Rock got through to him."[40]

Two Steps Back

One of the persons who met with Faubus was Virgil Blossom, who was horrified by what he was hearing. Hell was indeed coming to the border if Blossom went ahead with his plan. No one burned a cross in his yard, but he received enough harassing phone calls that he considered sending his own children to school in Jonesboro, then a good three-hour drive from Little Rock. His hands-on approach was going up in smoke. "We had Blossom climbing the wall," Jim Johnson recalled later, obviously not without satisfaction. In his own meetings with the governor, Blossom asked Faubus to throw the weight of his office behind a law-and-order position. By Faubus declaring himself forcefully on the issue, the tension would soon dissipate. Blossom then asked the governor for a public statement that Faubus "would not tolerate any violence." Faubus's "replies can best be described as evasive," Blossom later wrote.[41]

Doubtless, his replies were vague. Faubus was first and last a politician. Why make himself a martyr when he had not created the problem in the first place? The federal government had started the crisis, why should he fall on his sword for others? Tony Freyer and Roy Reed have detailed the failure of the Little Rock School Board, Judge John Miller, and the Department of Justice as far back as June 1957 to deal firmly with the threats of violence that were now routinely coming from those determined to resist the integration of Central High. Miller had several off-the-record conversations about the case pending before him. Each person involved in the conversations wanted the others to be the human lightning rods and absorb the wrath of their fellow southerners. The Little Rock School Board could have directed its attorneys to seek the aid of the federal court in resisting the intimidation that was now occurring in Little Rock. This tactic had worked in Hoxie, but Little Rock School Board members had no stomach for such action, knowing the reaction of their fellow white citizens if they appeared to side with federal authority. As a federal judge, Miller had lifetime tenure, a wrinkle in the Constitution devised by the nation's founders for the purpose of insulating the judiciary from the politics of just this kind of situation. But Miller had been a politician long before he had been a judge and acted accordingly. He was not about to take it upon himself to enforce his own orders or even formally ask the Justice Department to undertake an investigation. On the other hand, he might respond by tying the case up for months, though he might have to rule the "anti-integration statutes" unconstitutional if others initiated the appropriate legal action. On August 13 Little Rock

School Board member Wayne Upton, an attorney, approached Miller after appearing before him in another matter. Judges and lawyers are ethically forbidden from discussing substantive matters in a case without all the lawyers being present. However, according to Tony Freyer, Upton told Judge Miller "he believed a suit would be filed in state court requesting a delay in the desegregation of Central until the constitutionality of the 1957 segregation legislation was determined. Miller replied that if such a case did develop, the school board should return to his court and he would consider ordering a stay until the constitutional question was settled."[42]

But southerners were not alone in trying to pass the buck to each other. Why didn't President Eisenhower demonstrate the kind of leadership that had helped win World War II? The short answer is that white supremacy had long ago so thoroughly permeated the nation's soul that it would take a televised reign of terror against African Americans in the South before the rest of the nation's conscience would be pricked enough to make any sustained and lasting moves on behalf of civil rights.

When Upton returned to Little Rock, he discussed his visit with Judge Miller with Blossom. They approached Faubus, who initially tried to do what nearly all politicians do—he tried to make the problem go away by putting it off while at the same time creating some political cover for himself. Though it was not clear to the general public at the time, as Upton predicted, Faubus arranged for a lawsuit to be filed in state court that would delay the integration of Central. A week earlier he had tried to get the Little Rock School Board to petition the federal court for a delay, but Archie House, the school board's attorney, "squelched the idea," persuading Blossom and board members that they ran the risk of being held in contempt of court if they initiated a delay. Faubus had phoned the Justice Department to find out what its plans were in case there was violence. The response was that the Justice Department would send someone to talk with the governor.[43]

According to later interviews, Blossom and at least one member of the school board, Wayne Upton, joined Faubus in initiating the lawsuit. Blossom, of course, denied it.[44] The case was brought in Chancellor Murray Reed's court in Little Rock. The nominal plaintiff was Mrs. Clyde Thompson, a member of the Mothers League, but the star witness was the governor himself. In an early draft of *The Long Shadow of Little Rock*, Bates wrote that she attended the hearing. One can imagine Bates impeccably dressed, her smile in place as she listened to Faubus testify that he had reason to know that "knives and pistols were being sold in huge numbers; caravans of armed men were preparing to advance on the capital; there well may be bloodshed."[45] A later investigation by the FBI would conclude there was no evidence that members of the public were arming themselves. After an exhaustive investigation, its report stated: "Not a single individual had any knowledge of any act of violence or actual threats of violence prior to the time the Governor called out the Guard on September 2, 1957."[46] Blossom appeared to double-cross Faubus by testifying at the hearing in Reed's court that he had "no reason to anticipate violence when school opened."[47] According to Blossom, "House had told Faubus in a meeting the day before the suit was filed, 'Under no circumstances will the Board enter into collusion with a state agency to counteract the federal order. And if a court suit is brought we will have to fight it and you must understand that it will not be a token fight.' "[48] Though unwilling to seek the federal court's intervention, House knew a trumped-up state court suit to halt integration was not only doomed but improper. It is not clear why, if Blossom was involved in secretly seeking the suit, he testified as he did. One explanation is that he had been warned of the consequences of colluding with Faubus to bring such a suit. Ironically, Bates, too, would publicly minimize the possibility of violence because she saw it as the one excuse that would jeopardize the attempt to integrate Central. She never wavered from the mission to get the children in school and keep them there.

Bates recalled the "celebration" after Murray Reed issued the requested order delaying integration at Central High because of the alleged threat of violence. That night whites "drove by our home, blowing their horns and yelling, 'Daisy! Daisy! Did you hear the news? The coons won't be going to Central!' "[49]

All involved knew the NAACP would not allow the matter to rest in state court, but then Judge Miller, who would have heard the NAACP's challenge to the state court order in federal court, threw a monkey wrench in Faubus's plans by temporarily recusing himself from the case. Judges are not required to explain the reasons for their recusal, and Miller never offered one. Roy Reed speculated that Miller simply did not want to have to deal with a difficult case that would make him unpopular in his native South. Another explanation might well be that his frequent ex parte communications with the defendants and their attorneys made him vulnerable to the allegation of unethical conduct. Thus, to avoid that charge, he briefly stepped down. Even after all this time, it has never been determined who was and who was not telling the truth. Faubus and Blossom, now deceased, each had his own version of what was said and what was promised. Each felt betrayed by the other.[50]

Bates had her own view of the class warfare breaking out in front of her. Roy Reed has written that Bates told Edwin E. Dunaway, perhaps her closest white confidante and supporter, "He's [Faubus] against you and the people in the Heights, and I'm going to have to pay for it."[51]

When speaking of "the people in the Heights," Bates was referring to the old money crowd in Little Rock. Once basically a subdivision connected by trolley car to downtown Little Rock, Pulaski Heights sits up above the city and originally attracted residents because it was thought to be more healthful than the downtown area. Home to the Little Rock Country Club and expensive real estate values, Pulaski Heights was more a state of mind in the sense that the white power structure lived (and still do) in different parts of town but generally in an area of Little Rock north of Markham, overlooking the Arkansas River.

For ease of classification, I shall refer to Bates's "people in the Heights" as that group who became known as "Southern Moderates." At one end of the Southern Moderate spectrum was, for example, William F. "Billy" Rector, a wealthy real estate developer and relative of a Civil War Arkansas governor. Rector, whose focus was business, originally supported Faubus, then broke with him when it became clear that industry had quit locating in Little Rock. Once on the school board, Rector barely paid lip service to the federal court's decree to integrate.

At the other end of the spectrum of Southern Moderates were men such as Harry Ashmore and Edwin Dunaway, who both would shortly come to Bates's aid. A journalist and writer, Ashmore came to Little Rock via the Carolinas to edit the *Arkansas Gazette* and had supported the liberal administration of Governor Sid McMath. By 1954 he and Dunaway (along with later federal judge Henry Woods), outraged by the red-baiting tactics of Governor Francis Cherry in the Democratic primary campaign, set about helping Faubus get elected. In late August 1957 the rumors were rampant that Faubus was about to capitulate to the desires of Jim Johnson. On the Sunday before Labor Day, Ashmore and *Arkansas Gazette* publisher Hugh Patterson went to the office of Patterson's father-in-law, J. N. Heiskell, owner of the paper, to tell him what was coming. "The position you have to take is to support the school board but I can't make that decision. It's your newspaper and it's costing you money, Ashmore told me."[52]

Heiskell was then eighty-five years old. His family had owned a con-trolling interest in the paper since 1902. Early in his career Heiskell had "justified lynching of blacks on the theory that some plantations were so remote that nothing else would deter their savage behavior."[53] He later opposed lynching as "uncivilized." During his ownership, the *Gazette* had once favored the repeal of the Fifteenth Amendment allowing blacks to vote. He had favored the swift execution of the twelve blacks convicted of murder following the Elaine race massacres in 1919, but he had been appalled by the rioting in Little Rock in 1927 during the city's last lynching. Twenty-five years later he still believed ardently in white supremacy, but not the way Faubus was going about it. After listening to Ashmore and Patterson, Heiskell was reported to have said, "I won't let people like that take over my town."[54] The price would be steep.

In his 1958 book, *Epitaph for Dixie*, Ashmore argued passionately for preserving the separate but equal doctrine. After the *Brown* deci-sion, he recognized change must come as blacks upgraded themselves, but "time in this instance must be measured in generations." Whites would dictate the pace of change in the South, and they could best do so without sermonizing from the North. "The key to today's dilemma does not lie in attempting to change the white attitude by moral per-suasion, but in re-ordering our institutions to accommodate the legiti-mate demands of the minority group."[55]

Blacks would prove unable to wait generations for meaningful change. Martin Luther King Jr. would have other ideas about "moral persuasion" and would ultimately make religion and morality the cen-ter of the battle over segregation. But in Little Rock in 1957, Harry Ashmore was, in Bates's view, "at that time about the most liberal [white]."[56] Bates told Jacoway in 1976 that "Harry Ashmore . . . said, 'Daisy, you keep fighting for the Nine. If you get one or two in there this year, one or two.' I said, 'Harry, what the hell is going to happen to the rest of the kids?' "[57] "One or two" was the extent of southern lib-eralism in the fall of 1957, and Bates knew it. Yet she could not afford to turn down any southern white who was in a position to help her.

Edwin Dunaway was not your average white southerner either. According to Reed, Dunaway "was one of the few white leaders in Little Rock who had personal friends in the black community."[58] An accomplished attorney who had served as a law professor, prosecuting attorney, and Arkansas Supreme Court justice, Dunaway had a family history of sympathy for the plight of Arkansas blacks. His father was a member of the firm Murphy, Dunaway, and McHaney that had helped defend the Elaine Twelve. In 1921 Dunaway's father had helped represent Emmanuel West, a black man accused of raping a white woman in Little Rock, and had gotten a hung jury in the first trial, an absolute rarity in those days.[59] Dunaway, the son, was actively involved in organizations like the Urban League.

Although Ashmore and Dunaway surreptitiously assisted Bates, the white southerner who helped her the most during the 1957–58 school year was J. O. Powell, the assistant vice principal of Central. In an early draft of her memoir, Bates wrote that Powell changed from a man "who had been completely indifferent" to the plight of the Little Rock Nine to a man who was "obsessed" with their fair treatment at Central. "Powell helped me enormously because he would identify the troublemakers. . . . He used to sneak over to see us in the middle of the night to bring information dressed in old fishing clothes. . . . We could never have kept the children in school without his help."[60] Powell's wife, Velma, had identified herself as a supporter even before her husband had done so. Bates remembered her coming into the office of the *State Press* and offering her assistance. Not knowing who she was, Bates received her coolly that day but soon came to find out that she was one of the few whites in Little Rock who openly advocated school integration. Later, when Bates told Velma Powell of her initial reaction, Powell laughed and admitted, "You made me feel like a little puppy."[61] Though they were not mentioned in the final version of *The Long Shadow of Little Rock*, the Powells would stay in contact with Daisy and L. C. for many years afterward. Daisy was moved by J. O. Powell's personal moral transformation. What some white southerners would experience upon watching Police Chief Eugene "Bull" Connors's dogs in 1963 attack black children, Powell felt on a daily basis watching the Little Rock Nine go through the school year under siege. A few other whites displayed varying degrees of sympathy and support for the Nine, but as Bates noted bitterly more than once, it would be increasingly rare as the atmosphere in Little Rock changed to that of a police state. In her interview with Jacoway, Bates remarked, "Of course, all of my friends stopped coming, because they were afraid."[62]

Like many people whose lives become defined by a cause, Bates tended to judge others based on how useful they were to her as she went about serving that cause. Thus, for the most part, she eventually discounted the contribution of the Southern Moderates. But as historian

David L. Chappell has pointed out, it was white "moderates" who made integration in the South possible. "Without any moral commitment, [they] found themselves compelled to break with the segregationists in order to restore social peace, a good business climate, or the good name of their city in the national headlines."[63] In analyzing the history of this era, he and other historians have compellingly argued that to focus purely on the ethical and religious issues of the civil rights movement is basically to turn the era into a satisfying morality play, an analysis that ignores the central fact that the impetus of movement leaders such as Martin Luther King Jr. to force the South to abandon Jim Crow was as much about pragmatism and politics as it was about ethics and religion. In 1957 white moderates were not emotionally ready to confront the moral issues involved in segregation, but so long as the question was presented to them in terms of law and order, they were in a position to deal with it. Coming at them from the perspective of law and order, as an NAACP stalwart, Bates could engage them. And in the 1950s, she and others did exactly that.

Chapter Nine

FRONT AND CENTER

With Judge John Miller no longer exercising authority over the proceedings in the case of *Aaron v. Cooper*, Orval Faubus's victory in state court would be short-lived. Wiley Branton immediately filed a petition in federal court on behalf of the NAACP to overturn the decision, and the case was quickly assigned to Judge Ronald Davies of Fargo, North Dakota, who issued a stay and scheduled a hearing for Friday afternoon at 3:30. By the end of the day on Friday, he had issued an order enjoining interference of the plan by all involved. Finally, a federal judge had acted with sufficient resolve to enforce federal law.

In writing to Robert Carter, NAACP counsel in New York, on August 31, 1957, summarizing the events of the week, Bates ended her letter presciently with the phrase, "in spite of it all, some Negroes will enter or be found trying come Tuesday, September 2." She began the letter by saying, "We have been in a legal dither here in Arkansas for the last few days."[1] Legal dither, indeed. Suits were being lobbed into court with the regularity of mortar fire. In addition to a suit filed by developer William F. Rector as a stalking horse for Faubus, Eva Wilbun filed suit to set up segregated schools for white children. On August 26, the Arkansas attorney general sued the NAACP for more than $5,000 for failing to pay corporate franchise taxes in the previous seven years. A suit had also just been filed by ten black ministers, supported by the Little Rock NAACP, challenging the "four segregation acts" passed by the Arkansas legislature.[2] At a meeting of the Legal Redress Committee on the August 30, George Howard Jr. was selected as local counsel to defend the franchise tax suit against the NAACP.[3]

In her letter to Carter, Bates added, "As of now I hold the world's record for crosses burned on lawns of houses. The third one-Sunday,

August 25, 8 feet tall was set ablaze on my lawn and Wednesday, 1:A.M. August 28, a bottle was thrown through my plate glass picture window. We now have flood lighted the place and placed guards around the house at night."[4] Bates sent copies to Roy Wilkins, Thurgood Marshall, and Gloster Current.

If August was hectic for Bates, nothing in her life would compare with September, for Faubus was about to make his fateful decision to surround Central High with the Arkansas National Guard and prevent the Little Rock Nine from entering. In her letter to Carter, Bates referred to the testimony given by Faubus and others in Murray Reed's court as "trumped up." Certainly, that was to be the view of not just Daisy and L. C. but of those who opposed the governor in the coming months. The governor's enemies were not necessarily Bates's friends, though there were some whites she would come to like and admire and with whom she would maintain contact for much of her life. Generally, as suggested in the previous chapter, Bates would not be able to trust white moderates, for they would prove only too willing to follow Faubus and the Capital Citizens Council down the path to continued segregation when it appeared he might somehow be successful.

Now that the governor of the state had testified under oath about Little Rock citizens arming themselves, the number of children willing to enter Central High on Tuesday after the Labor Day holiday dropped from sixteen to nine. As late as Saturday, August 31, Blossom had been expecting "fifteen or sixteen" students to show up on Tuesday.

It seems likely that Bates spent the weekend trying to keep parents and students from changing their minds. She and L. C. were now used to harassment, and though it had to bother her, there is no indication at this point she expected it to escalate into violence against the children and their parents. In his interview about the period before the events at Central High, Oscar Eckford could have been speaking for Bates as well when he said that when a white man in authority told you something, you knew he had the power to make it happen. Thus if the white power structure decided that a few blacks were going to enter Central High, it was something you could count on. Bates most feared individual acts of terror—someone driving by and shooting into the house or setting it on fire. She knew that if whites wanted to organize violence against blacks, nothing would stop them. The Capital Citizens Council had always maintained that it would use every lawful means to resist integration, and it had stayed peaceful though noisy.

In the final version of her memoir's account of the three-day weekend before Faubus made his infamous Labor Day evening announcement, Bates only mentions Jefferson Thomas of those who would become the Little Rock Nine. She says that he had stopped by the house for a brief visit when a radio news bulletin in the middle of the Labor Day afternoon announced that Faubus would address the state that night. In *The Long Shadow of Little Rock*, she created a conversation in which Thomas asks her if anyone could block them from entering Central High the next day. "I don't think so," she replied.[5]

The children and their parents generally shared one thing in common: they were stable, hardworking citizens of Little Rock. They were willing to take advantage of what they perceived to be opportunities offered by a system that was being forced to open itself to them. This did not make the parents (or children) militant civil rights advocates. They could not afford to be; directly or indirectly, their livelihoods depended on whites. As a Pullman car cleaner who worked the night shift for the Missouri-Pacific Railroad, Oscar Eckford was typical of the parents. As he said, he was busy trying to make a living. His wife, Birdie, taught black children at the segregated state school for children who were deaf and the blind how to wash and iron for themselves. There were no doctors' or lawyers' children among the Little Rock Nine.

A segment of an early draft of *The Long Shadow of Little Rock* in diary form captures a portion of that Labor Day holiday in 1957 much better than what finally appeared in the book, and incidentally reveals her hobby along with her spelling difficulties.

MONDAY, LABOR DAY MORNING. Talked with most of the children that morning . . . swimming, picnics with families. . . . Bates' slept late. That afternoon got out moulds, started to pour greenware, preparation for ceramics class of adults that she taught during the school year in her home. MID-AFTERNOON. Tv station interuppted the program. Not really listening. "We interuupt to bring you a special announcement. Governor Faubus will address the citizens of LR tonight in a special address. . . ." Immediately, phone began ringing.[6]

A number of people have written that Bates had a detached view of Orval Faubus. In fact, it was not at all detached. She was rarely detached about anything. Anger boiled up in her repeatedly. In public, she controlled her anger like a baseball pitcher who can throw a ninety-five-mile-an-hour fastball to any corner of the plate. She told an interviewer in 1992 that when she became angry in a situation, "I am very calm."[7] In speech after speech to NAACP supporters outside Arkansas, she would blister "Awful" Faubus in a takeoff on his name. Then, to his face, she would bare her teeth in a smile that wasn't far from a grimace. What people were observing was that she didn't have any personal malice toward Faubus, for Faubus was not disrespectful. He treated blacks in public as he did all people. She saw the governor simply as a political opportunist with whom she had to deal.

Daisy and L. C. (who were still very much a team at this point) had their fingers firmly on the racial pulse of Little Rock, and they understood white people, or thought they did. As governor, Faubus seemed too cautious and shrewd to do anything so radical as to defy federal authority, which now was being exercised in such a firm manner. If integration of the Little Rock schools had been whittled down to a few token figures, it was hard to imagine that Faubus would do anything now to try to stop it. He had made the scene-stealing gesture by testifying in state court, and now he could blame a federal judge for making whites do what they claimed to most hate.

After hearing around 7:00 in the evening from a reporter that National Guard troops were congregating at Central High, Bates's early draft of her memoir continues:

> Jumped into the car. A friend had come to help guard. LC gave him the shotgun. Took off for Central (1950 Chrysler (black) Parked, a block away. Could see soldiers unloading, taking their places. Saw reporters going, trying to talk, soldiers wouldn't talk. Car radio. Flashed over. Natnl Guards around school. Nobody knew what meant. Governor to speak. Brown uniforms. Helmets. Full combat, boots. Canopied trucks. Just the regular thing, just like a war.[8]

Like people in the rest of the state who received the television station reports from Little Rock, Bates watched Faubus announce that he had called out the National Guard to surround Central High School the next morning. In *The Long Shadow of Little Rock*, Bates wrote that she "didn't remember all the details of what Governor Faubus said that night. But his words electrified Little Rock. By morning they shocked the United States. By noon the next day his message horrified the world."[9]

In fact, what shocked the nation and horrified the world was not what Faubus had said or done on television the night of September 2; it would be the faces of white Arkansans and their actions on September 4. Actually, much of the typewritten script of the governor's speech reads like a document drafted by the white power structure of Little Rock that Faubus was now opposing. Almost three pages of the ten-page speech are devoted to the progress blacks had made in Arkansas. "It is well known that Negroes are now in attendance and have been attending the University of Arkansas, a state institution, for a number of years. Last year, members of the Negro race were in attendance at the many state-supported colleges of Arkansas. Also, Negroes have been integrated into the public school systems of the state where it was acceptable to the majority and could be peaceably accomplished." On and on he went, pointing out that "Negroes serve on both the Republican and Democratic state central committees, and this is the only state in the South where this is true." He mentioned "that public transportation systems of the state have been peaceably integrated with no disorder and no untoward incidents except of a minor nature."[10]

All of this was true, and more, Faubus said, mentioning, too, that under his administration welfare grants and teachers' salaries had been raised, and "a medical aid program was set up for the medically indigent people of the state."[11] Blacks also were employed in a number of jobs in state government, and he took the trouble to enumerate some of them as if they were administrators instead of janitors and domestic service workers.

Faubus read the speech in a grave, earnest tone. No arm-waver, he did not pound the table or get red in the face. To Bates, Faubus often exhibited "a big man's easy congeniality" and "a folksy manner."[12] Others saw almost a painful hill country dignity that kept educated people at a personal distance. In fact, Bates and Faubus were much alike in that they both had a way of demanding and getting a grudging respect from people who considered themselves superior.

What Faubus did not say directly, and did not need to say, was that white supremacy still flew its flag proudly over the state. Despite some improvements, the overwhelming number of blacks were largely kept in a state of subservience and dependence; this suited most whites just fine and in fact was not objected to by most blacks, who, out of fear that had become habit and had existed for generations, remained too cowed to complain. Nor, of course, did he say that many of the "improvements" had been forced on the state by lawsuits or the threat of more federal intervention. Faubus pointed to the measures passed by the legislature and the constitutional amendments as expressing "the will of the people" and said as governor he was bound to observe them until they were declared unconstitutional.

Finally, he turned to the violence that he said was about to erupt in Little Rock if he did not act. "Now that a Federal Court has ruled that no further litigation is possible before the forcible integration of Negroes and whites in Central High School tomorrow, the evidence of discord, anger and resentment has come to me from so many sources as to become a deluge. There is evidence of disorder and threats of disorder which could have but one inevitable result—that is violence which can lead to injury and the doing of harm to persons and property."[13] Then, he enumerated for the television audience what he had testified to in court, as well as mentioning that he expected "caravans" to converge upon Central "to assemble peaceably." For those who could read between the lines, it was clear in retrospect that black students were not going to be permitted to enter. In the next-to-last paragraph, he said, "The inevitable conclusion therefore, must be that the schools in Pulaski County, for the time being, must be operated on the same basis as they have been operated in the past."[14]

Bates may have thought until that night that she understood Faubus, but she did not really understand the man. According to his biographer, she was hardly alone. Roy Reed wrote that after listening to him for hundreds of hours, looking him in the eye for many of those hours, and studying him for six years, he was

> forced to admit that Orval Eugene Faubus is more mysterious than when the process began. . . . It is not just that he was opaque. He appears still in my mind, even after his death, as an insoluble mixture of cynicism and compassion, of guile and grace, of wickedness and goodness. I have observed his life off and on for forty years, and I don't know whether he was good or evil, or even whether those are the choices. There was a time when I knew. But that was long ago, and I was young.[15]

What possessed Orval Faubus to defy the federal government? As mentioned, Bates, like a number of his Southern Moderate opponents in Little Rock, would regard him as a political opportunist of the worst kind. Indeed, there is a hardy band in Little Rock even today who will hear no other explanation. Sifting through the evidence, historians have been less than certain that Faubus was solely motivated by his desire for a third term. For example, Tony Freyer has pointed to his need to win support for his legislative program from east Arkansas politicians as a reason for his actions. Had Faubus done nothing to support those who cried out for him to oppose school integration beyond having arranged to file a lawsuit that got overturned before the week was out, his support would have withered in the fire-eating Delta. Additionally, Roy Reed has shown there were threats of violence (either manufactured or real) that had to be taken seriously. "Both Faubus and Blossom had in their possession evidence of impending violence—evidence that was either real or handcrafted by Jim Johnson's invisible army. The one man, while tumbling into a private panic, publicly denied knowing anything about it. The other grabbed the tale of alarm and ran with it."[16] Obviously, Faubus was furious with Blossom and the Little Rock School Board, and he virtually called Blossom a liar the day after his speech.[17]

The questions still remain: Did Faubus see the threats as his golden opportunity for a third term and act accordingly? Or did he think he could buy some time until the courts struck down the constitutional amendments and legislative measures and thus provide additional political cover for himself? As Reed points out, Faubus always claimed he would ultimately obey the federal courts, and eventually he did. But in a central way, the debate over whether Faubus was demonized misses the point. The real demon was the doctrine of white supremacy that Arkansas whites demanded that their leaders, whoever they were, maintain, despite its cost. As Faubus himself pointed out, if not him, who? Jim Johnson? Amis Guthridge? Whether the Southern Moderates liked it or not, Faubus's decision was overwhelmingly supported by white Arkansans. Had the governor somehow been able to keep Central segregated, he would have been supported by the Southern Moderates as well. Meanwhile, Bates's mission, supported by the national office of the NAACP, was to get however many children as she could in school and have them stay there and do well. It was a role that she willingly accepted. L. C. and Daisy Bates were true believers. By their unwavering persistence and determination, they knowingly put themselves and their business at risk and never once looked back. Their commitment to the cause was absolutely total.

The third of September was chaotic for Daisy, but it would mark the day when the parents of the Little Rock Nine began to see her as their link to whatever legal rights they now possessed. After Faubus's speech, the Little Rock School Board "requested" that the black students not try to enter on Wednesday "until this matter is legally solved." The only black to appear at Central High on the morning of September 3 was L. C., "who arrived at 9 A.M. and said he was a spectator."[18] Daisy told the *Arkansas Democrat* that "events have moved so fast we haven't had time to catch our breaths or formulate any statement."[19] She recalled in her memoir she was "in touch with their parents [of the students who would become the Little Rock Nine] all day." A crowd of 300 to 400 whites stood across from the school's main entrance. They had been there since before 6:00 in the morning. Capital Citizens Council members distributed leaflets to the group entitled "What Lincoln Said about Segregation." Actually, it was what Lincoln had said about white supremacy. At the bottom was a postscript that called for abolishing the public school system, if necessary.

The black parents contacting Bates were naturally terrified that their children would be guinea pigs for mob violence, Little Rock style. Typically, Bates downplayed the possibility. As she wrote, Faubus had pledged to protect "life and property" against violence. "No, it was inconceivable that troops, and responsible citizens, would stand by and let a mob attack children."[20] With no black students trying to enter, there was no violence at Central High, not on Wednesday.

But the showdown was coming, and the national media knew it. The *New York Times*, *Life*, NBC, and many others were already in place Wednesday morning to cover the opening day at Central High School. In New York, the full attention of the national headquarters of the NAACP was suddenly riveted on Little Rock. Bates, who as late as August 31 was communicating by mail with the NAACP's national office, the next day would be considered so important to its mission in Little Rock that Roy Wilkins ordered that her conversations with New York for the next few weeks be transcribed daily for his review. Ordinarily, a field secretary of the NAACP would have filled Bates's role, but Frank Smith, already ineffective at raising funds and increasing membership, would virtually disappear during this period. On Tuesday, Faubus had issued contradictory statements as to the role of the Arkansas National Guard. At one point in his press conference, he claimed the troops were not there to stop "integration" from occurring, but then said "I doubt it" when asked if they would allow black students to enter.[21]

Waiting for Faubus to back off, or at least to clarify his intentions, federal judge Ronald Davies waited until Tuesday night to hold a hearing. The Little Rock School Board's attorneys were already expecting

Davies to order them to go forward with their plan, so Blossom rounded up the children's parents and other blacks for an emergency meeting to tell them how he wanted to proceed the next day. Though Blossom omitted from his book, *It HAS Happened Here*, the fact that he did not invite Bates, she did not. Bates wrote in *The Long Shadow of Little Rock* that she was "not notified of the meeting," which included not only the parents but also included "leading Negro citizens." However, "the parents called me and asked me to be present." At the meeting, Blossom "instructed the parents *not* to accompany their children the next morning when they were scheduled to enter Central. 'If violence breaks out,' the Superintendent told them, 'it will be easier to protect the children if the adults aren't there.' "[22] This scenario went against the grain of every parent in the room. Typically, a measure of their powerlessness was that they almost all acquiesced without uttering a word of protest. It was the same old story. Blacks were being told to trust whites, and given the domination of whites at the time, once again they did. The difference was that now their children's lives were at stake, and they were told they could not be there to protect them. Bates wrote, "During the conference Superintendent Blossom had given us little assurance that the children would be adequately protected. As we left the building, I was aware how deeply worried the parents were, although they did not voice their fears."[23]

Bates had to be worried, too. She was placing her trust in a white man whom she had learned could not be trusted, one who most certainly had perjured himself in a court hearing hardly a week earlier by saying he did not know a thing about any potential violence. Blossom, it must be said, was a tortured soul during this period, if William J. Smith, an adviser to many governors, including Faubus, is to be believed. At one point, Blossom grabbed Smith "by the lapels and cried that the blood of children would be on his, Blossom's, hands if Smith did not help him stop integration."[24]

That afternoon, attorneys for the school board filed a motion with the court, asking that the members not be held in contempt of the judge's order, saying the board was caught in the middle between the troops and the court's order. In an interview with the Associated Press apparently before the hearing in federal court set for 7:30 that evening, Bates gave assurances that the students were not backing out. Bates said she had been in touch with some of them. "It would be a matter for the individual student and his or her parents to decide. I'm sure some of them will want to go, even if there is some risk."[25]

The hearing at the federal courthouse was anticlimactic, taking only five minutes. Attorneys for the Little Rock School Board told the judge they stood ready to comply with whatever order he made. Judge Davies tersely told the parties that he was going to take the governor's speech the previous evening at "full face value." Faubus had said the National Guard was in place to preserve the peace; Davies said he was proceeding on the assumption that the troops would protect the children. He ordered the school board to proceed with its plan forthwith and also ordered U.S. Attorney Osro Cobb to conduct an investigation of those persons who were interfering with his previous order.

A game of high-stakes chess was about to occur, with nine black children the sacrificial pawns, but in order to satisfy her lawyers, Bates knew she had no choice. Thurgood Marshall had asked her the night Faubus went on television what was the purpose of the troops at Central. Bates told Elizabeth Jacoway, "The first time I said, 'I don't know. . . . I don't know whether they're there to protect us or to deny us.' He said, 'I can't go into Court with 'I don't know, Daisy.' He said, 'The man has to say that "I am here to deny you, based on what the Governor told me."' "[26]

The parents had every reason to be worried, and Bates even more so, when a young white reporter whom she never named (he obviously demanded that she not reveal his identity) came to her house at ten o'clock that night to warn her the situation was spinning out of control. She re-created his urgency in *The Long Shadow of Little Rock*:

> "Look, Daisy," he said anxiously. "I know about the Superintendent's instructions. I know he said the children must go alone to Central in the morning. But let me tell you this is murder!" He knew how ugly the whites were going to be the next morning. "I heard those people today, I've never seen anything like it, people I've known all my life—they've gone mad. They're totally without reason. You must know you can't expect much protection—if any—from the city police. Besides, the city police are barred from the school grounds!"[27]

It was not just whites from Little Rock who had been out at Central High that morning. "New recruits are pouring into the city from outlying areas. Even from other states. By morning there could be several thousand."[28]

When her white reporter friend left, Bates wrote that she "sat huddled in her chair, dazed, trying to think, yet not knowing what to do."[29] It must have been a feeling like no other. No longer could she minimize the danger to the children, and clearly she had done that. It was one thing to risk her life, another entirely to know children might be injured or die. She had allowed herself to believe that the mob would not stoop so low as to attack children, but that was fast becoming an untenable notion. The question, which seemed unanswerable, was what could she do to see that the children had some protection? She and the rest of the black community had always depended on the white power structure for solutions, but now it was unbearably clear that she had been in denial about their willingness and ability to contain their worst elements. Others drifted by, including Rev. J. C. Crenchaw, president of the local branch. In *The Long Shadow of Little Rock*, Bates wrote that it was seeing Crenchaw that gave her an idea that, if it could be implemented at the eleventh hour, might restrain the mob. Crenchaw thought it was worth trying. Though she did not mention it in her book, a group of sixteen white ministers had issued a statement earlier in the evening protesting Faubus's actions and calling on "every citizen to pray for a 'right example' for every child in the community."[30]

It was a roll call of the white community's most prestigious churches. To name just a few, ministers from Second Presbyterian, Trinity Episcopal, Second Baptist, Immanuel Baptist, and Pulaski Heights Methodist signed the letter. Bates phoned one of the signers, Dunbar Ogden Jr., president of the newly formed Interracial Ministerial Alliance, who was minister of Little Rock's Central Presbyterian Church. For all of her contacts, she didn't know Ogden, but she asked him if he could get some ministers to walk with the children into the school.

Though polite, Ogden was understandably noncommittal. "You know, this is a new idea to me," he told her lamely, knowing it was one thing to sign a letter, another entirely to put his career and perhaps his life on the line. Bates wrote that she "said the idea was new to her, too."[31]

Ogden said he would make some calls and get the opinions of others and call her back. Though neither could have imagined it, their brief exchange was the start of a lifelong friendship. When he finally called her back, he sounded "apologetic." The ministers he had called had not been receptive. The black ministers had countered that Blossom had said no black adults should accompany the children. The white ministers had "questioned whether it was the thing to do." He would continue to try however, and "God willing, I'll be there."[32]

It was now 2:30 in the morning, and Bates still had more calls to make. The next one was to the police. She wanted a police car to be stationed at Twelfth and Park, where she would have the children wait to meet the ministers, assuming any of them came. Though she did not name the officer in charge, he agreed to have a car there at 8:00 but added that Central High was now out of their jurisdiction since it was occupied by the National Guard. For good reason, Bates would always be grateful in particular to policeman Eugene "Gene" Smith, who was in charge of providing security at Central that day and who soon became chief of police.

Finally, she called the parents to tell them to have their children at Twelfth and Park at 8:30 the next morning. There was one hitch. Elizabeth Eckford had no telephone. Her father worked at night at Union Station. Should Bates go there and look for him? In an early draft of her memoir, Bates admitted that by this time she was so exhausted and desperate for a little sleep she "took a sleeping pill and a bit of scotch."[33] In the final version, she wrote, "Tired in mind and body, I decided to handle the matter early in the morning. I stumbled into bed." Because of Bates's understandable negligence, Elizabeth Eckford would face the mob alone the next morning and become world famous.[34]

The next morning at ten minutes to 8:00, Gloster Current reached Daisy before she and L. C. left the house. Current told her he had gotten his information from the paper about what had happened the day earlier. In this brief call, Bates managed to raise a number of subjects, including the fact that litigation was already beginning to swamp the Little Rock NAACP. In fact, she was due in court at 2:00 in the afternoon for a hearing involving the franchise taxes that the Arkansas attorney general claimed the NAACP owed. She told Current she had been subpoenaed to bring the books and records of the NAACP. George Howard would be representing her and would seek and presumably be granted a continuance because of the day's more pressing events. She was not certain all nine children would show up at the school. It could be as few as five. She also referred to her own exhaustion, saying, "I haven't slept two hours." Her main focus naturally was on what was about to occur in the next hour. "If the children are admitted, I will call you and if they are not admitted I will call you. We will have to do something and do it quickly."[35]

Believing that the court's order would be followed, Current's main reason for calling was to offer encouragement. He told her, "Well, keep your chin up. Don't let this get you down. After the children get out of school this afternoon, call us back."[36]

Bates wanted to know what impact all this was having. She also wanted to know what impression *she* was making. "What about the publicity up there on tv? Did they carry the statement I made?" she asked, referring to an interview she had given to an Associated Press reporter.[37]

"There is nothing else in the paper except what you say," Current stroked her, having worked with her since she had been elected president five years earlier. Current concluded the conversation by telling her, "This is when the Daisy Bates personality is standing us in good stead. A lot of people couldn't stand up under this."[38] Implicit in his comment was the recognition that Bates rubbed some people the wrong way, but this was a time when a strong ego was essential. A shrinking violet was not what the national office needed, and no one ever accused Bates of being a wallflower.

In the car on the way to meet the students and the ministers at Twelfth and Park with L. C., Daisy heard the news on the radio, "A Negro girl is being mobbed at Central High." It was only then that Bates remembered that she had never contacted Elizabeth. It had to be one of the worst moments of her life. " 'Oh, my God!' I cried. 'It must be Elizabeth! I forgot to notify her where to meet us!' "[39]

L. C. got out of the car and ran to find Eckford. Daisy wrote that she went on to the meeting place at Twelfth and Park. In her memoir, Bates puts herself at the center of the events. She wrote that it was she, after the students were turned away by the National Guard, who suggested to Rev. Odgen that "the students should go immediately to the office of the Superintendent for further instructions."[40] Since he was out, Bates wrote that she went with the students to the office of U.S. Attorney Osro Cobb and then to the FBI's office. In the account given by the *Arkansas Gazette*, Bates is mentioned once: she came out of the FBI office "and said the students were giving statements to the F.B.I." The article also mentions that the parents of the students were present.[41] The sworn affidavits of the students and some of the ministers, given that same day to the FBI, and the newspaper accounts help flesh out what occurred that morning. Oddly, none of the affidavits actually mention Bates during this sequence of events. The ministers who were going to walk with the students had met earlier in the morning at the Dunbar Community Center. According to Rev. Harry Bass, those present were not only ministers, black and white, but also attorney

Thaddeus Williams and Lee Lorch, whose wife, Grace, would play a role in the drama.[42]

Bass told the FBI that four white men walked in front of the students and that he and Rev. Z. Z. Dryver were in back. In his affidavit, he indicated that the four men were "Rev. Ogden. Rev. Campbell, Rev. Chauncey, and another unknown individual." Will Campbell was an activist from the National Council of Churches in Nashville. George A. Chauncey was the minister of the First Presbyterian Church of Monticello, a small town in southern Arkansas. The individual unknown to Bass was David Ogden's twenty-one-year-old son. Of those men who accompanied the students, Bates failed to name George A. Chauncey in her memoir. Of the group who would become the Little Rock Nine, Jefferson Thomas, Carlotta Walls, Gloria Ray, Ernest Green, Thelma Mothershed, and Minnijean Brown attempted to enter the school, accompanied by the ministers. Melba Pattillo was not among those who attempted to enter the school that morning. Jane Hill was in the group accompanied by the ministers, but she did not enroll in Central.

The attempt of this group of seven students to enter Central was fortunately anticlimactic, compared to what Elizabeth Eckford experienced. In her memoir, Bates identifies Rev. Odgen as the leader of this small band, saying that a National Guard captain told him they could not pass through to the school. Ogden asked why and was told it "was by order of Governor Faubus."[43] Bates has Ogden returning with the students and ministers and reporting to her.

The other affidavits establish that Harry Bass and Ernest Green had exchanges with some members of the National Guard. The National Guard had orders not to let them pass. Bass recalled that when the students arrived at the southwest corner of Fourteenth and Park, a line of troops stopped them, and he heard a Col. Johnson say to the students, "This school is off limits to Negro students and Negro schools are off limits to white students." Bass established that they were acting upon orders of Governor Faubus.[44]

In every telling of Elizabeth Eckford's story, there is no mention of L. C. at one point sitting on the bench with her as she waited for a bus after being turned away by the National Guard. However, a photograph of L. C. sitting with Elizabeth establishes that he was there at least for a moment.[45] In her account, Daisy wrote that L. C. jumped out of the car to go find Elizabeth and told her later that he had seen her get on a bus. How long he sat there with her, what he said, and why he left have been lost to history. Strangely, L. C. never wrote about his experience that day for the *State Press* and did not mention it when he was interviewed by the FBI. Nor did Eckford mention him in her interview by the FBI. Eckford, probably almost in shock, said almost nothing in her interview to the FBI that day. However, there were two other adults who did give Eckford support while the mob raged at her that morning. Eckford had come to Central, but not finding the others at the spot she was supposed to meet them, somehow had the courage to proceed on her own. According to the reporter for the *Arkansas Gazette*, after being turned away twice from entering Central High School by the National Guard, Eckford spent thirty-five minutes at Park and Fourteenth streets enduring the taunts of the mob while she sat waiting for a bus. When they got too close, a National Guard officer told the mob to "move back from the bench."[46] For a few moments, Benjamin Fine, a reporter for the *New York Times*, also sat down by her and told her not to let them see her cry beneath her tinted sunglasses.[47]

The presence of the National Guard saved Elizabeth Eckford from attack that morning, but she also had another protector toward the end of her ordeal. Grace Lorch stood between the mob and Eckford as she sat on the bench, and then Lorch went across the street to a drugstore to ask that a taxi be sent for her. The employees refused. When a city bus finally arrived, Lorch got on the bus with her and intimidated a group of young toughs into silence.

Bates would write in her memoir that after the ministers came back to the car with the students, she told Ogden that "it was my feeling that the students should go immediately to the office of the Superintendent for further instructions."[48] She writes that she went with them, but that when Blossom failed to arrive after an hour, she "suggested that we speak to the United States Attorney, Osro Cobb, since Federal Judge Davies had ordered the Federal Bureau of Investigation, under the direction of the United States Attorney, to conduct a thorough investigation into who was responsible for the interference with the Court's integration order."[49] According to the affidavits of the students and black ministers, Rev. Harry Bass, along with Rev. Z. Z. Dryver, drove some of them down to Blossom's office. Minnijean Brown's stated, "I got into an automobile with Rev. Dryver. . . . When I arrived at Mr. Blossom's office I was told to wait outside by Rev. William Harry Bass while he went into Mr. Blossom's office." After "twenty minutes" he came out and said he "was going to take

me home as that is what he had been told to do."[50] Similarly, Carlotta
Walls told the FBI that it was Bass who took "a group of us to the
school board office." Once he emerged from someone's office, he
"instructed us to go home." But after she had arrived home, Bass
called Walls and said that "he would pick me up and take me to the
Federal Building," which he did. Bass told the FBI after they had been
turned away by the National Guard, he "left the group and went to a
telephone and placed a call to the office of Mr. Blossom."[51]

An addendum to Bass's affidavit states that he also told the agents that
after he and Dryver had taken the children home from Blossom's office,
he had called Bishop Odie L. Sherman of the AME Church to discuss
what to do next. Bishop Sherman suggested he call the U.S. Attorney's
office, which he did. According to Bass, Bishop Sherman called him to
meet with other ministers at the Dunbar Community Center that morning before going to the school to accompany the children.

Though Bates suggested she orchestrated the events that morning
("Mr. Cobb looked surprised when we entered his office"), at least
according to the affidavits given to the FBI by the students and ministers, the trip downtown appears to have been much more of a collaborative effort than she sets out in her memoir.[52] According to the
affidavit of Rev. Colbert S. Cartwright, the white minister of Pulaski
Heights Christian Church who had been present at the school in the
capacity of an observer, Bates spoke to him by telephone. She told him
the students had been referred to the FBI and suggested that "since
I had been close to the Negro students when they were turned away
from the high school, and that since the F.B.I. was trying to get as complete a picture as possible of what happened that I go to the F.B.I. and
tell what I had witnessed."[53]

In her talks around the country and throughout *The Long Shadow
of Little Rock*, Bates for the most part did not emphasize the role of
the black ministry or other local NAACP officials in supporting the
Little Rock Nine and their families that day, but in retrospect, it is
clear, as the FBI affidavits suggest, others were vitally involved.[54]
Perhaps it is not surprising that Bates made it seem that it was she and
not Harry Bass who was more involved with the students on this
historic day. Though in writing *The Long Shadow of Little Rock* she
could not deny that he was one of the ministers who had the courage
to walk with the students, she might well have wanted to minimize his
role. Before the school year was out, they would have a fight over
who spoke for the Little Rock Nine. For his part, Bass had his own

resentments. The *State Press* had headlined his troubles on page one: he had resigned under pressure as executive director from the Urban League and was indicted, though not convicted, on running a gambling operation. At the same time, it is important not to overstate the rivalries both Daisy and L. C. had with other blacks throughout their lives. Harry Bass was often mentioned as a friend, especially of L. C.'s, and if they fell out with each other as both L. C. and Daisy did with others, it was usually temporary.

As that famous September day in 1957 further receded into history, Bates would continue to place herself at the center of events. In her 1976 interview with Elizabeth Jacoway, Bates stated that she had walked with the students when they tried to enter the school on September 4.

E.J.: You walked up to the National Guards.
Bates: We walked up to them.
E.J.: And you were in the group that walked up to the National Guards.
Bates: Walked to the guards.[55]

Though Bates did not walk with the students that day, she doubtless received instructions from Thurgood Marshall, as she claimed in her interview with Jacoway, to ensure that the students would be able to testify that the National Guard, acting on the orders of Faubus, had prevented them from entering Central High.

E.J.: You made them say that?
Bates: That's right. But I had Thurgood's advice to get them to tell us that.[56]

The working title of Bates's memoir was "The Little Rock Story." In much of her correspondence, it is referred to as "The Daisy Bates Story." Putting one's self at the center of major events is par for the course for memoir writing, and, as we shall see, she had professional help.

In retrospect, Bates's idea of using ministers to walk with the children was her most inspired contribution to the events on September 4, and it was an important one. None of these students experienced the vicious intimidation that was meted out to Elizabeth Eckford. Blossom's insistence that the parents not accompany the children may have saved all of them from beatings. Though Bates would exaggerate her role in the events on September 4, her lack of direct participation would have no effect on the parents themselves and their willingness to rely on her. Ordinarily, parents and the media in this situation would have been in regular contact with the lawyers involved in the case. However, it was far easier for Wiley Branton, as local counsel, to communicate with his clients through Bates, since he lived in Pine Bluff and had no office in Little Rock. The media, too, found it easier to contact her for information. They wanted someone who could let them know the collective intentions of the children and their parents, and though she had no specific authority to speak for them, as president of the State Conference of Branches, she immediately began to assume that role.

On September 5 Bates told the *Arkansas Democrat* she "advised" the students against returning to Central High. "We wouldn't send those kids out there again in that situation."[57] The "we," of course, was the NAACP, but when one broke it down, the NAACP had no legal authority to make any decisions for the parents or their children. However, with the governor of the state now opposing them, they were more than willing to have the NAACP to turn to for direction. There was no one else. None of the parents had been plaintiffs in the suit brought back in the winter of 1956, but since they resided in the Little Rock School District, they were "class members" of the suit. If they wanted to attend Central, there was no other group backing them. And Bates had no qualms about speaking for them. As Blossom observed in his book, "Mrs. Bates . . . was a woman of great energy with an aggressive, crusading spirit. She was an efficient organizer and enjoyed her role as a leading figure in the state's NAACP."[58]

With her background at the *State Press* and her position as president of the Arkansas NAACP, it was logical that Bates would become the spokesperson in general for the parents and their children, but it was not inevitable. Others, including some of the more aggressive parents, could have filled that role. What is significant is that no longer were blacks using whites to speak on their behalf. The Little Rock NAACP was to come under pressure to keep Lee Lorch away from the attention of the press as much as possible. Moving on to Fayetteville to teach at the University of Arkansas in 1956, Georg Iggers and his wife, Wilma, stopped by Daisy and L. C.'s home on Labor Day in 1957 to say good-bye before moving to New Orleans to another teaching job.[59] But even had both Georg Iggers and Lee Lorch remained in active roles, Bates had already become the acknowledged spokesperson on behalf of the black community on the issue of school integration. It was a truly empowering event, similar to what was occurring all over the South as blacks began to claim responsibility for their own destinies.

Chapter Ten

WHO IS THAT WOMAN IN
LITTLE ROCK?

A s stressful as September 4 had been for the children and their parents, the national office of the NAACP in New York knew that what was going on in Arkansas was worth a king's ransom in favorable publicity for the organization. No longer a dry legal battle that bored supporters even as they were implored to reach for their wallets to send in a check, the photograph of the mob hounding Elizabeth Eckford had seared into the consciousness of the outside world what the NAACP was fighting for and against.

Though Daisy Bates was proving herself to be an ideal spokesperson, as well as the center of gravity for all that was occurring from the African American side in Arkansas, she would soon realize she needed help. In a conversation with Gloster Current on September 6, she was told that local field secretary Frank Smith had not been heard from in this crisis. It was no news to Bates. "What is he doing?" Current asked. Bates answered, "Nothing."[1]

Though almost half a century later one marvels at how well Bates and the local NAACP branch worked together with the national office, it was never that simple. Each decision represented a solution to a problem no one had ever faced. Bates told Current that "yesterday it had been recommended that the nine children make an attempt to get into the school, every day." Given what the children had endured the previous day, that idea was ludicrous, but the fact that it was even considered showed that there was no automatic response to the roadblock Faubus had placed before the NAACP. That idea had been rejected as far too dangerous. Bates told Current that there had been a mob of "about 700 in front of the school," referring to the previous day. "One of the newspaper reporters said it looked like an angry situation."[2]

Angry, indeed. There was a coolness about Bates, an absolute refusal to panic, which was one of her best qualities. With each interview Bates gave, Roy Wilkins and his staff knew they had a star in the making. The press was coming to her door every day. Instead of attorneys pontificating about constitutional rights, there was an attractive, well-dressed black woman from the South who, despite great pressure, was perfectly calm, perfectly in control of herself. From all her years in working at the *State Press*, Bates was completely attuned to the needs of the media. Instead of a terse "no comment" or "talk to our attorneys," Bates humanized what was basically a continuing legal and political battle. Instead of plaintiffs, they were "kids."

Yet it would be very much a collective effort. Both Chris Mercer and Frank Smith's daughter, Carutha Braden (then Carutha Davis), who served as the office secretary, remember that Bates did not compose the statements that she gave to the press.[3] They were written for her by L. C., by Clarence Laws, and by them. Similarly, her speeches would be written by others, including L. C. and Frank Smith. Did this make her a windup doll who could not function without a script? Hardly. She would give too many interviews for this to be true. Others around her had skills and information she did not possess, and she knew it. The tragedy was that she never publicly acknowledged how much a joint enterprise it all had been.

But it was first and foremost a legal battle. Wiley Branton knew he needed help and called Thurgood Marshall. As a result of the pressure and turmoil, the Little Rock School Board was now seeking a delay of the federal court order to proceed with its integration plans. When Marshall arrived in Little Rock over the weekend of September 8–9 to prepare for the hearing scheduled for Monday on the school board's request, he stayed at the Bates's home. He found it an armed camp. In his biography of Marshall, Juan Williams writes that "Branton escorted him into the guest bedroom, which they would be sharing. Branton had his suitcase on the bed farthest from the window—and a safe distance from any rock that marauding segregationists might heave. Marshall joked with the nervous people in the house that he planned to sneak back when Branton was not paying attention and remove his roommates' gear to the bed near the window." In teaming up with Wiley Branton, Marshall was in for a pleasant surprise. "I just figured he was a normal, local lawyer," Marshall said much later. "And I would say to my surprise he was one of the most competent guys I ever ran across.

They had crosses burning on his lawn and everything. But he was a really tough guy. Any kind of jam you got in, you'd call Wiley."[4]

Marshall told reporters that the Little Rock School Board's position was unacceptable, and on Monday morning Judge Davies agreed. "The testimony and arguments this morning were, in my judgment," the judge said tersely, "as anemic as the petition itself."[5]

After the hearing, despite Marshall's status, Bates did not say, "Ask my attorney." She was quoted as saying, "We knew we would win ultimately. We are very happy with the decision."[6] When Faubus stunned even his followers by saying the next day he still was not withdrawing the National Guard, Bates stated that "her forces would 'wait for the situation to clear' " and asked rhetorically, "What's the point of walking up to the National Guard line and being turned back?"[7]

On September 8 Bates was interviewed by the FBI. The affidavit is noteworthy for the consistent manner in which she minimized the threat of violence throughout the interview. Bates told the investigating agents Roy N. Osborn and Edward G. Story that she had been among a group of "Negro citizens" who met with Virgil Blossom on either August 28 or 29. The group had been told that "at that time the school authorities did not anticipate any trouble."[8] In fact, as previously noted, the group had met with Blossom on September 3 and left the meeting scared to death for the children.

This inconsistency can only be explained by Bates's unflinching determination to focus on the NAACP's mission—to get the children in school. The way to do this, she believed, was to disseminate the view that integration of Central could proceed with a minimum amount of trouble. To believe otherwise was to endanger everything she had been working for since she had become president of the State Conference of Branches in 1952. If that meant for a moment constructing a scenario that was at variance with reality, she was hardly the first person in history to do it. Was she truthful with the FBI? No, but the truth in this situation was not her paramount concern. In the same interview, she minimized the dangers to herself personally. She told the investigators that until recently "she had had no trouble since around 1956." She did not mention the paid guards and sleepless nights. Astonishingly, she told them "she did not consider the violence to her home as being any part of the school integration plan at Little Rock, Arkansas." Besides, "she had had numerous telephone calls, some from mothers at Central High School, who stated they were in sympathy with her, but could not publicly express themselves."⁹ To put it another way, Bates was an advocate, and advocates tell their side of the story. Though Bates did not give names, her last statement was true. Some whites were supportive but could not let it be known. Then there were those who were known to be sympathizers but were reluctant to go public with an announcement of the full extent of their sympathy. As federal judge George Howard Jr. remembered, there "were whites who were encouraging her . . . whites who brought in contributions to assist her . . . if [her opponents] got these records, it would bring a halt."¹⁰

By refusing again to comply with the federal court order, Faubus was heading into unknown territory as a sitting governor with troops still on the ground at Central. He had thrown down the gauntlet, literally challenging a branch of the federal government to back up its order with force. Bates was asked if the NAACP was going to request the help of the Justice Department. "The Attorney General is aware of the situation. If he is interested in giving the children protection, he will make it known." Although protecting the children would prove to be the precise issue just days later, it wasn't the question the reporter asked. Pressed for a more direct response, Bates temporized, "I really don't know whether such a request will be made. It will have to come either from the School Board or the parents of the children. It would not come from our organization."¹¹

Since the parents were being represented by the NAACP lawyers, her answer was unnecessarily disingenuous, but it reflected Bates's understanding that the legal strategy of the NAACP at the moment was to try to make the fight be between federal and state authorities. In a conversation with Current on September 9, she stated that the Department of Justice had wanted the NAACP to go back into court and ask for an "injunction" against Faubus, but "they [the lawyers] didn't fall for that. This is the job for the Department of Justice."¹²

With Bates receiving such national publicity and so prominently tied to the NAACP, it is not surprising that during this week she was elected to fill an unexpired term on the NAACP's national board. The term was only through December and could have easily gone unfilled, but Roy Wilkins surely wanted to show her his public support. What happened in Little Rock was seen by him as crucial to the success of the NAACP, and Bates was viewed as indispensable to what occurred in Little Rock. She would be elected again and again.

With no troops at his disposal, Judge Davies did the only thing possible unless he was going to relinquish authority to a state government: he requested the intervention of the Department of Justice. The attorney general of the United States, Herbert Brownell, promptly asked for an injunction requiring Faubus to comply with the court's order. Faubus and officers of the National Guard were now official parties to the litigation and were served with summonses. The court set a hearing for September 20.

Though raising his political stock in Arkansas, Faubus's actions had unleashed forces that had once stayed in the shadows. On the morning of September 9, motorcades from small towns in Arkansas, such as Blytheville and McGehee, rolled into Little Rock and headed to Central High. One man told a radio journalist, "I don't think it would take us in Eastern Arkansas over two days to raise a regiment to come over here and surround the school house to keep them Negroes out of it."[13] He had brought a .32 caliber Smith and Wesson pistol and added he had shotguns at home.

Meanwhile, Bates was perhaps experiencing a bit of an insurrection of her own. Across the river in North Little Rock, on September 9 four black ministers accompanied six students to the white high school. They were denied entry. Bates claimed that she "knew nothing of the incident today at North Little Rock High School and could not comment on it."[14] In her conversation with Current that same day, she mentioned that the "Negro students and the local ministers are now meeting with the school superintendent and the principal."[15]

Perhaps, as she told the reporter, she had not known, but that seems unlikely. Very little on the subject of school integration in the black community escaped her attention. More probably, she had known but could not have stopped it had she tried. Both nationally and locally the NAACP had all the battles it needed and was not about to sign on for another one. On the other hand, without the NAACP, blacks who tried to act independently got nowhere. Though on September 14 a group of black ministers told reporters that litigation would be resorted to in the coming "week," nothing was ever filed.[16] It had been hard enough to find one black lawyer to file suit back in 1956, and that suit had resulted in enough work for several attorneys.

As to when another attempt would be made to enter Central High, Bates told a reporter on September 8 she "knew nothing of the future plans of the Negro students to attempt to enter the schools again or whether they would ask for police protection."[17] What Bates meant was that nothing had yet been decided. The pressure was becoming intense on all sides. After her conversation with Current on September 9, she sent a letter to him that again revealed that she and L. C. were paying for part of their own police protection. "We have to have our home guarded nitely, and we have to pay $15.00 per nite for off-duty police."[18]

It was in the September 9 conversation with Current that "Mrs. Bates asked for help—either Mildred Bond or Clarence Laws for a few days."[19] Current said he would send Clarence Laws. Tony Freyer has written that "it was not until Faubus' proclamation [on September 3] made international news that the New York office virtually took over the cause in Little Rock."[20] He mentions that Clarence Laws replaced Frank Smith in Little Rock. He more accurately characterizes the relationship by saying, "by phone and letter he [Laws] kept in regular touch with the New York leadership, while directly assisting Bates, Crenshaw [*sic*], and others in local matters."[21] The recorded transcripts kept by the NAACP during this period reveal Bates was not in any sense a mere figurehead. Every day there was a new crisis, and there were many decisions of a nonlegal nature to make. As she told Current: "Mildred Bond had called to find out if the young lady student [Elizabeth Eckford] could make a speaking engagement. Mrs. Bates said they had sent her out of town for the weekend so she wouldn't be bothered by reporters etc. She didn't think it was such a good idea, but if Mr. Current will discuss it with Mr. Wilkins and she will discuss it with the girl's parents."[22] This concern for Elizabeth Eckford had not prevented Bates from having three others of the Nine (Thelma Mothershed, Gloria Ray, and Ernest Green) sit down in her living room for an interview with the *New York Times*.[23] The matter of how much the Nine should be used to generate publicity was a ticklish question for the national office, whose branches outside the South were salivating at the fund-raising possibilities. The NAACP would soon be charged with "using" the students to raise money for the organization. Yet at the same time, the Nine themselves made the best case for integrating Central. "Why should anyone want to harm us?" Thelma Mothershed asked the *New York Times* reporter. "We're not mad at anybody. Maybe they don't like us because they don't know us."[24]

This wistful naïveté in the face of the massive resistance of southerners was genuine. One finds it in the diary kept by Melba Pattillo Beals: "I longed to tell them, 'I won't hurt you, honest, give me a chance, come on. I'm an average teenager, just like yourself . . . with the same aspirations and heartaches.' "[25]

The black press ran story after story about the Nine and would continue to do so throughout the school year. On September 13 the headline of the *St. Louis Argus* read "ARKANSAS HATE!" and the paper ran the picture of Elizabeth Eckford walking away from the mob. "As mobs of baying whites daily congregate in front of Central High School here, a slender, 15 year old girl who was born with a profound respect for the law—and in fact has an intense desire to be a lawyer—sits in her grandfather's little store."[26]

Help was coming soon for Bates, both locally and nationally, but before it arrived, the country was treated to what would become a recurring spectacle—negotiations in which southern governors seeking to save face before capitulating to federal authority dealt with U.S. presidents. Arkansas congressman Brooks Hays arranged a meeting between Faubus and Eisenhower on September 14 at Newport, Rhode Island, where the president went to play golf. The meeting proved to be so embarrassing to the president that future negotiations between southern governors and presidents over the issue of integration would be conducted mostly in secret. In Roy Reed's words, "the meeting was a fiasco. Faubus, the sometime integrationist, almost persuaded Ike, the would-be segregationist, that he should order the whole process stalled. Give us a little more time. Ten days, a few weeks. The old general saw nothing wrong with that. His lawyer, Brownell, spoke up firmly and said that he couldn't give Little Rock anything. Even a president is not above a court order, he said."[27]

Eisenhower's dithering was likely due in part to his own misgivings over *Brown*.[28] Unable to sway his own attorney general, the president accepted Brownell's advice and refused to offer any compromise. Eisenhower left the meeting with Faubus certain that the governor had agreed to let the students into Central. Brownell later wrote that he and Hays were allowed to talk with both men after they had met alone for about twenty minutes. "And the President told us that Faubus had agreed to let the black children into the high school. Just as flat as that. Faubus was standing there. I can't recall Faubus said anything. And I was absolutely amazed he was capitulating."[29]

Brownell was referring to the fact that in just over a week Faubus had become a national political phenomenon for defying the federal government. To back down now would risk that and a sure third term. Just hours later, Faubus announced he had no intention of changing his position. Brownell had told Eisenhower that he could not trust Faubus. The president telephoned him the next day. "You were right," he said. "Faubus has gone back on his word."[30]

A new hearing was scheduled in Judge Davies's court in less than a week to consider the government's request to enjoin Faubus from further interference. While this was being played out, Roy Wilkins had decided that Bates was too essential to the national NAACP to let her and L. C. go under. On September 12, responding to his phone call, Bates wrote a letter that set out in some detail their financial predicament. The economic pressure had begun in 1954 after the *Brown* decision and she had been involved with having parents write "petitions" to the Little Rock School Board. The *State Press* had lost a contract worth $2,400 with the gas company. In 1955 the Southwestern Telephone and Telegraph Company canceled their yearly advertising, which had brought an annual revenue of $1,200. "Many merchants" said "plainly" they were canceling because the paper "is so foreign to the traditions in the South." In the past political season, "candidates came to us and explained that they were afraid to advertise and offered undercover money to keep the goodwill." Now even the company that sold them paper was insisting on cash. Finally, they were having tax problems, owing $1,300 to the state of Arkansas. Though they disputed the amount, they had signed an agreement to pay it. If not paid, they faced seizure and sale of their equipment. If they could get $2,000 "and if given until January to begin repaying it," she thought they could make it.[31]

During this period, the Little Rock Nine were out of school, but their schoolwork was not forgotten. Both Bates and Lee Lorch have said it was their idea for the children to be tutored during this period by college professors. Melba Pattillo Beals remembered, "Dr. Lorch and his wife, Grace . . . organized tutoring sessions and structured them along the lines of regular classes."[32] But no matter whose idea it was, it became part of the story that Bates would repeatedly tell reporters and put in her book.

On September 13 L. C. ran pictures in the *State Press* of the students being turned away by the National Guard on the fourth, including one of the famous shots of Elizabeth Eckford being taunted by the mob. Behind her in a bow tie, writing as he walked, was Benjamin Fine, the *New York Times* reporter. Along with the pictures was a brief announcement that Daisy had been elected to the national NAACP board, "making her the first person from Arkansas ever elected" to that position.[33]

The war to run the NAACP out of the state was ongoing. Attorney General Bruce Bennett wanted the organization's membership lists and financial records. This battle would be fought all the way to the Supreme Court. Thurgood Marshall and Wiley Branton prepared

Bates's responses, which were duly reported in the press. Though refusing to provide the names of individuals, the lawyers believed they had no choice but to reveal the names of the twenty-seven Arkansas communities where the NAACP had branches. Bates's response pointed out that to give up the names and addresses of members "would expose . . . [the NAACP members in those communities] to reprisals, intimidations, and unwarranted hardships solely because they have associated together for the purpose of securing the constitutional rights of Negroes."[34]

The federal court hearing on September 20 to enjoin Faubus from keeping the Nine out of school was itself anticlimactic, but it provides a window on the way Bates related to the students. It was an exciting day. "The nine of us walked up the sidewalk toward the federal building at a brisk pace. Our group included Mrs. Bates, attorneys Thurgood Marshall and Wiley Branton, and a number of people I didn't know. I was told they were community ministers, coming along to protect us," Melba Pattillo Beals wrote. As they got off the elevator in the courthouse, "Mrs. Bates touched my shoulder. 'Shhhhhh!' she said. We had been cautioned not to talk back to reporters on that day. We were to say nothing until after the NAACP attorneys made our case. 'Smile, kids,' Mrs. Bates whispered. 'Straighten your shoulders. Stand tall. . . . Melba, we're inside now. Take off those dark glasses. Please.' I was embarrassed to get singled out that way by Mrs. Bates."[35] Bates knew the world was watching. If she, as one observer noted, acted sometimes like a "drill sergeant" in dealing with the children, it was for a reason.[36]

The news that made the papers was the manner in which Faubus's team of lawyers capitulated during the hearing. After a few of their motions were denied by Judge Davies, with the court's permission, they gathered up their papers and got up and walked out of the courtroom before the hearing was over. "Now," Bates quoted Thurgood Marshall as saying, "I've *really* seen everything."[37]

Ordered to desist from further interference, Faubus went on television that evening and announced he had given instructions to remove the National Guard from Central High. The job of protecting the Little Rock Nine now fell solely on the shoulders of the Little Rock police. The presence of the National Guard had been enough to restrain the mob on September 4. The people who had participated in it had no cause to complain, since no black students had entered Central. Now southern policemen were going to assist a total of nine black children. Though none of the children (including Elizabeth Eckford) had actually been physically assaulted on September 4, the Little Rock Nine and their families did not delude themselves about the possibility of violence that now seemed all too likely.

By resisting federal authority, Faubus was reaping the political benefits, and he was not about to undermine himself by using the National Guard to protect the children. It was one thing for Faubus to take the state to the edge of federal defiance. It was quite another to abandon his responsibility to preserve the peace and "good order of the state," as he liked to call it, by choosing to attend the Southern Governors' Conference. He would be out of town on September 23, the day the students would try to enter. No single act by a governor would hurt his state more. How Faubus was able to avoid taking political responsibility for his abandonment of his obligation to preserve the peace after so much rhetoric about it is astonishing. That voters would let him get away with it was a measure of the values of white Arkansans. They refused to hold him accountable for such a calculated desertion of duty. Without the National Guard to shield them from the mob, the danger to the Little Rock Nine would obviously be far greater than it had been on September 4. Mayor Woodrow Mann's failure to request that the National Guard be called back into duty was a study in pride over good judgment (he had opposed Faubus's decision to send the National Guard to Central High). As a lame-duck mayor (the city had voted in a city manager form of government), he had no political future to consider.

Given what had happened on September 4, it was obvious how dangerous the effort to enroll the students on September 23 would be. The crowds at Central were large and ugly. Faubus had stirred the pot well. Nothing could minimize the tension felt that weekend before the students were to enter the school on Monday. Though Bates and others made repeated efforts on Sunday to get federal authorities to provide assistance, no help was forthcoming. Bates would phone Gloster Current in New York that afternoon, "We cannot get any federal help. We requested it all day yesterday."[38]

Edwin Dunaway and Harry Ashmore had spent Sunday with Bates, along with Woodrow Mann, to try to ensure protection for the children the next day. She wrote, "We worked all day yesterday with the Mayor and with Dunaway and Ashmore. They are helping us."[39] Dunaway and Ashmore had also met Sunday with "Brooks Hays, Virgil Blossom, Sid McMath . . . at Henry Woods' home to devise a strategy to protect the Black children."[40] Dunaway and Ashmore would continue during the week to assist Bates.[41] They had been in contact with the Justice Department in Little Rock and Washington, D.C., but without success.

Bates ended the conversation by telling Current, "We are not planning to go back tomorrow. I am afraid the children may be killed." She had already issued a statement to the press that the children would not go back until they had protection. Bates wrote in *The Long Shadow of Little Rock* that Chris Mercer had accompanied Rev. Bert Cartwright (whom she misidentified as a Methodist) and Will Campbell of the National Council of Churches to the offices of the *State Press* that Friday. The ministers offered to pray for her. Bates told them, "I don't need prayer. If you are really interested in doing something to help, go visit the homes of the nine children—pray with them—they are the ones who will have to face the mob."[42] This the ministers did.

The passages in *The Long Shadow of Little Rock* describing the tension that morning before the children left for school are the most effective in her book. Much of what she wrote was taken directly from a speech she made in Baltimore on October 21. The speech apparently had been recorded and later appeared in the magazine section of the *Afro-American* on November 9. The Little Rock Nine had come to the Bates's home so they could go to school in a group. Bates was not about to take a chance again of having a child show up alone at the school. In hindsight, Bates's judgment again has to be questioned as to why she allowed the Little Rock Nine to try to enter the school on September 23. She wrote that a reporter asked her that morning, "Mrs. Bates, are you really sending the children to Central? The mob there is really vicious now."[43]

Only a few days earlier, Bates had given the possibility of danger to the children as a reason for not continuing to try to enter Central High. Now, however, the police were saying they could offer sufficient protection. Perhaps it seemed she had no alternative but to make the effort to get the children into Central. On September 4 she had acted to satisfy the lawyers. This time, unless there was an attempt to enter the school, the NAACP apparently could put no meaningful pressure on Washington.

All the parents but two (the others had to leave for work) had come inside the Bates's house to wait for the police to give the word to head for school. The news was not encouraging. Live sidewalk interviews offered the following warning: "Just let those niggers show up! Just let 'em try!" The decision to go forward was one that Bates apparently made without the assistance of the field representative of the national NAACP. Clarence Laws, who had come to Little Rock to assist her, was in New Orleans making a speech.[44]

It was not as if the children had not become fully aware of what they were facing. "The children stationed themselves all over the house to listen" to the reports on radios. As she waited for the police to call her to say they were ready for them to come to the school, Bates noticed Imogene Brown and Oscar Eckford praying. "For the first time I found that I was praying, too," she wrote. The courage and resolve of the nine children proved to be decisive. Though they were "strangely silent" as they listened to the radios, "the faces of all were solemn but determined."[45] The memory of that morning would stay with her all her life. Bates wrote in an early draft of her memoir that injuries to the children, or possibly even their deaths, would be on her head. Had she said "this is too dangerous," no one in the room would have questioned her judgment. Had any of the Nine been injured or worse, no one would have trusted her again.[46]

Of course, it was not just the parents who were waiting with the children. The house was overrun with reporters. Bates's description of this scene in *The Long Shadow of Little Rock* suggests the extent to which the print media, both white and black, had become dependent on her. As newsmen (she mentions no women reporters being there on this day), they were all part of a fraternity, and Bates shrewdly managed them like an indulgent house mother. She would have her favorites among the black reporters, and among the whites as well, all according to how sympathetic they were to the NAACP's point of view.

When the call came from the police that they were ready to meet the children and escort them into the school, "the white newsmen left my home for Central High. The Negro reporters remained, seating themselves around the kitchen table drinking coffee." At the time, Bates thought she was giving them a scoop. They were not to follow her and the children, but if they were at the Sixteenth and Park entrance, "they would be able to see the Nine enter the school" and watch history being made.[47] Tragically, they would become part of the story.

This time there was no train of ministers to accompany the students. Bates, Chris Mercer (who would soon be put on the NAACP payroll), and some of the students rode in one car (she would not be able to remember who rode with whom); field secretary Frank Smith, who would be fired in December, drove another car.

As soon as the crowd saw them, the black reporters became targets for the mob waiting for the students. In particular, Alex Wilson, editor of the *Memphis Tri-State Defender*, was savagely beaten. Others, including Earl Davy, the photographer for the *State Press*, were also physically assaulted, as were white newsmen from the North, including the staff of *Life* magazine. Incredibly, three *Life* employees were briefly detained for allegedly inciting a riot. As photographer Francis Miller said bitterly, "he was evidently arrested for striking a man's fist with his head."[48]

While the mob's attention was diverted, the police, under the leadership of assistant police chief Gene Smith, were able to whisk the Nine into the school through a side entrance. Predictably, the whites, which included a healthy contingent of troublemakers from outside Little Rock, were furious that the Nine had gained entry. Bates wrote that she returned home and told Oscar Eckford and Imogene Brown the children had made it inside and then called the other parents who had left.

The reports on the radio were horrifying, full of misinformation about what was occurring to the Nine inside the school. The children were being beaten, were "hysterical," and had "locked themselves in an empty class room."[49] Bates actually was aware what was going on inside the school and knew none of this was true. In *The Long Shadow of Little Rock*, she wrote, "A young white lawyer [Edwin Dunaway], who was very close to Assistant Chief of Police Gene Smith, devised a plan by which he would keep me informed of the goings on inside the school. When I called him, he assured me that the reports were false. After each report I would check with him, then call the parents."[50] Given the fact that they could not verify the situation with their children, the parents could not be particularly confident their children were safe. What surely increased Bates's own anxiety was the fact that waiting with her that morning were the mother of Minnijean Brown and the father of Elizabeth Eckford. She told her audience in Baltimore, "White kids went in Central High then came out, went to the radio station microphone outside the building, and broadcast that the colored boys are running down the hall, they're beating them with blood all over them. Another got the mike and said, 'All nine colored children are locked in a room. They are afraid to come out even with a police escort.' My two parents stood shaking, as they listened to this on the radio."[51]

Though Arkansas state police supplemented the ranks of the city police, they had difficulty controlling the crowd as the morning wore on. Lieutenant Governor Nathan Gordon had said publicly he would call out the National Guard, but only if Mayor Woodrow Mann requested it in writing. Mann, a bitter foe of Faubus's, was not willing to acknowledge that the police could not handle the situation. They could not. The *Arkansas Democrat* described the scene at the school in its early afternoon edition as a "howling, shrieking, violent mob of more than 1,000." Shortly before noon, the crowd, which had grown steadily throughout the morning, began "hurling rocks and bottles indiscriminately at passing cars."[52]

About this time, assistant police chief Gene Smith conferred with Blossom and made the decision to remove the children. They were rushed out of a back entrance of the school. Only with the news of their departure did the crowd begin to drift away. Bates told her audience in Baltimore that when the decision was made to withdraw the children, "I wanted them to, because I didn't think the parents would last until 4 o'clock."[53]

In the *Afro-American* account, Bates prudently does not mention that a young white attorney was helping her keep informed of what was occurring in the school. She told the *Afro-American*, "I called the school—I had a direct line in the school and the principal said, 'What is happening, why are you calling over here every three minutes? We're doing fine, the children are in class. Nothing is happening in the school.'"[54]

Setting a pattern that she would follow the rest of the school year, Bates minimized any problems inside the school, and in fact there had been no major incidents directly involving the students. The memoir of assistant principal Elizabeth Huckaby, entitled *Crisis at Central High*, confirms the relatively smooth morning the Nine had at Central. However, made fearful by the rumors, a number of white parents withdrew their children from the school that day.[55]

That afternoon Bates called Gloster Current to tell him the students had been withdrawn because of the mob outside Central. She reported that inside the school, the Nine had been treated fairly well. "One boy walked out of class where a Negro student was and one girl's mother came to get her. The girl pretended she didn't want to leave class, but her mother took her anyway. The students are nice, the teachers are nice. For the most part, everyone was very nice. But the mob on the outside is building up and building up and building up." Bates described the mob as only about "three or four hundred people. They are imported from the rural areas—real red necks. The kids wanted to know why they were being brought out of school." She listed the names of the black reporters who had been assaulted. "They beat up Jimmy Hicks from New York and they beat up my photographer, Earl Davy and Wilson from the *Tri-State Defender* and Mose Newsome from the *Afro-American*." Historian Pete Daniel has noted that while Bates had "correctly identified the outsiders in the crowd," in fact "few in the crowd fit the redneck mold. Neither photographs nor television footage captured many individuals in overalls." He points out that "most of the men and women were dressed casually but neatly; it was, at its core, a respectable-looking working-class crowd."[56]

In her memoir, Bates wrote that on the night of September 23, she and L. C. experienced the most danger they would ever encounter. She drew upon much of her speech in Baltimore for this material as well. Since the National Guard had not been called out, racial incidents continued throughout Little Rock that day. But the cover of darkness emboldened the worst elements of white southerners, who had experienced the withdrawal of the Nine as a complete victory. The Bates's house had become basically a command post for reporters, who were welcome to spend the night. Daisy told her Baltimore audience that at around 10:30 P.M., while L. C. was talking to Brice Miller, a reporter for United Press International, she noticed one of his photographers in a hiding place across the street. She confirmed the rumor that a mob would be heading for her house when Miller admitted that a high school student had bragged to him earlier in the day that this "would be their first stop." Miller had called the FBI and police. At that moment, L. C., who had gone outside with his shotgun, came running back in. "Something's up! A car just passed driving slow with its lights off, and a bunch of tough-looking characters in it. And the police car outside is following it."[57] She remembered later that L. C. told her to turn out the lights and go downstairs, but she went only as far as the first step and sat down to wait. Upstairs, L. C., Alex Wilson, and the Bates's neighbor Garman Freeman waited anxiously, their weapons at the ready.

It was in the Baltimore speech (and her book) that Bates went over the edge in telling a good story about events that occurred that night. She told her appreciative listeners, "FBI men broke up this caravan and carried a lot of them to jail and took all of that dynamite and those weapons." Finally, they heard the wail of a police siren, and a policeman came running up to the house. He explained, "We just stopped a motorcade of about one hundred cars, two blocks from here. When we followed the car that passed, we ran into the mob head on. We radioed for help and a whole group of city and Federal agents showed up. We found dynamite, guns, pistols, clubs, everything, in the cars." Some of them had abandoned their vehicles and fled into the darkness. The *Arkansas Gazette* mentioned the next morning that police stopped "a caravan of about 100 cars" going east on Roosevelt Road at the intersection of High Street, but a search of "four or five" cars turned up no weapons. The drivers were ordered to go in different directions. There was no mention that any cars were abandoned.[58] Nor did the next afternoon's *Arkansas Democrat* offer any confirming details of dynamite and arrests of individuals in a caravan. The police "got the caravan stopped and searched several cars before breaking it up. No one was arrested."[59] The *New York Times* carried a similar story.[60] With the dispersal of this group, the danger, in retrospect, was over for that night, but the fear of an attack lingered. Bates wrote, "No one slept that night." The next morning at 7:30 she received a telephone call. "We didn't get you last night," a man's voice told her, "but we will. And you better not try to put those coons in our school!"[61] She also received a call from Thurgood Marshall, according to the NAACP transcribed conversation.

In her conversation with Current that morning, Bates started off by telling him about the events of the previous evening, obviously not bothering to confirm what she had been told with the account in the morning's *Arkansas Gazette*. "They stopped a caravan of about 50 to 75 cars about a block from my home. They had dynamite. We had police guard all last night. The mob had sent a car through to meet the caravan and bring it through. The police arrested some people and the police took away a bit of ammunition and dynamite. In the meantime, the children are at home where they are going to stay. We cannot subject these children to that mob violence."[62]

Still acting as field secretary for Arkansas, Frank Smith was handed the telephone to speak to Current about "office matters," but he had no further role in the conversation. Concerned about "rumors" that some Little Rock blacks were engaging in acts of retaliation, Clarence Laws took the telephone and read a statement that he and Bates had apparently prepared that morning. It alluded to unverified "reports" that "a number of Negroes" were arming themselves and "destroying property." The substance of it was that the NAACP "deplores violence or vandalism whether committed by white or Negro persons" and "called on all Negroes" to desist from any such acts. Current urged that the statement be distributed in leaflet form and suggested that Bates call a meeting of "key people" to urge blacks not to retaliate as that gave whites an excuse to "start in first with the minority group."[63]

Getting back on the telephone, Bates told Current that "we had police protection for the children last night, one car outside each home. I talked to all nine of the children last night." None had been hurt nor "even treated badly," and she again reiterated that "the teachers and students were very nice."[64] Bates, like others, repeated reports that the bulk of the mob the previous day were from towns outside Little Rock, primarily England and Lonoke. Current again encouraged her to spread the word that blacks should not retaliate.[65]

Oddly, no one raised the question of whether President Eisenhower would now intervene, though it had to be on their minds. Since he had taken no action in Mansfield, Texas, which had recently resisted school integration in similar circumstances, it was not at all clear he would take decisive action in Little Rock.

Chapter Eleven

A BATTLE EVERY DAY

The United States' enemies were having a field day. Communists had always been able to score points in the running worldwide propaganda war: the U.S. government's acceptance of the white South's "way of life" represented unmitigated hypocrisy. After September 4 and after the photographs of Elizabeth Eckford being harassed by the mob had gone around the world, Little Rock had become a major foreign policy sore spot. With the debacle on September 23, there was no doubt who had won a major battle. Did mobs rule in the United States, or did the federal government?

Before the morning of September 24 was out, President Eisenhower signed a proclamation that began, "Whereas, certain persons in the state of Arkansas . . . have willfully obstructed the enforcement of orders from the federal district court," they must "cease and desist."[1] He backed up his statement by not only federalizing the Arkansas National Guard but, in his most controversial action, ordering the deployment to Little Rock of 1,000 troopers from the famed 101st Airborne Division to ensure that the orders of the federal court would be carried out.

At 3:30 in the afternoon Bates was back on the telephone to Gloster Current. She began the conversation with obvious excitement: "I haven't been able to talk with the U.S. attorney Cobb, but I understand they have called out the troops." She was meeting with the children at 6:00 that evening. The news media were overwhelming her. "From all over they are coming here; I have all these newspaper people and no facilities for them."[2]

With the troops on the way, the eyes of the world were again on Little Rock. Understanding the public relations value to the NAACP, Current was totally sympathetic. "You will have to set up a press phone in your place there; get some emergency telephone service and the Association will take care of it. . . . I know what this is costing you, Daisy. I understand the problem. Work out what it costs with the entertainment and extra expenses and the extra help . . . and we will work it out immediately."[3]

Bates told Current she had only gotten two hours' sleep the night before. "The FBI started calling me about two o'clock this morning," but she wasn't complaining, so much as describing how busy she was. George Howard had called her about witnesses for a court hearing. She was at the center of all the activity and knew it. She blurted out to Current, "I just employed Chris Mercer for a whole week. He has been my backbone."[4] Because of all the litigation, Bates desperately needed someone who had the time to help her understand the legal hoops through which the NAACP was being forced to jump.

Current, in this conversation, okayed Mercer's employment for as long as "you will need him." With Frank Smith already on the payroll, Bates thought it necessary to discuss Smith's performance. Smith had disappeared at 11:00 in the morning during the crucial events the preceding day, and she had not seen him until today. "When I asked him where he had been," she said sarcastically, "he said he had to go home to hold his wife's hand because she was nervous."[5] Though Smith was still on the NAACP's payroll until the end of the year, he was effectively finished as an employee.

Bates's forte was public relations. She was in her element with the newsmen who were swarming the place. "I have been speaking to Jimmy Hicks [of the New York-based *Amsterdam News*]. I told him that he had not been on our side for quite some time and now that he was here in Little Rock, I wanted him to see the type of leadership we have from the Youth Council on up. I told him that when he printed his story to make sure to print what the NAACP had been doing. That we are making history and the NAACP is doing it. We have to get our story told in a manner it should be told."[6]

This was music to Current's ears. In this capacity, Bates was worth her weight in gold. Current told her that he would get her money for all the entertaining she had been doing "right away." As Current himself pointed out, "the Negro reporters . . . really have no place to go in Little Rock." She ended the conversation with Current by once again referring to her efforts to cultivate James Hicks. "I think I have done a good job with the Negro reporters down here—especially Jimmy—they are convinced." But she still wanted to have another talk with Hicks before he left Little Rock. She wanted "to find out what is on his mind and why. Sometimes it is just a misunderstanding. I want him to get off his mind what is on it."[7]

In Bates's mind, even the pose of objectivity meant something was suspicious. There was only one side, and that was the NAACP's side. Neither L. C. nor Daisy had made the slightest attempt to balance their coverage in the sixteen years the *State Press* had been in operation, and neither was going to change now. In their minds, civil rights was about advocacy. If you were not for Daisy and L. C. Bates and civil rights, you were against them. Bates was willing to educate people and along the way give them food and drink and a place to stay. She took the time to cultivate a person. She would turn on the charm. It worked. Bates got great press. James Hicks would shortly write a glowing multipart series in the *Amsterdam News* on Bates and the Nine.

From Bates's perspective, the high point of the entire ordeal that September would be the next morning (September 23) when the troops arrived to escort the Little Rock Nine into Central High. But she had to get the students to her house first, and her account of how that occurred in *The Long Shadow of Little Rock* is grimly humorous. Now that the troops were coming to escort the Little Rock Nine into the school, it would have seemed a small thing for the military to have kept Bates better informed when the students were expected to make their next attempt to enter the school. Bates wrote in her memoir that she had waited until ten o'clock that night to hear from Virgil Blossom before calling the parents. Not having received a call from him, she telephoned them all (the Eckfords had by then gotten a phone) to let them know the children would not be going to school because she "assumed the mob would still be at the school the next morning and therefore decided that the children could not be sent to Central the next day, troops or not."[8] Blossom, however, called "shortly after midnight" to tell her that the troops would be there bright and early that morning to collect the students. Blossom's account does not contradict her. He wrote that he telephoned her "late in the evening."[9]

"Oh, no," she replied, "I have told them they would not go until the following day. We had a meeting about it." What Blossom didn't write was that Bates had an agreement with the parents that she would call before midnight if she needed them. After that time, they disconnected their lines so they could avoid the harassing phone calls and get some sleep. Bates, of course, had no choice. She had been waiting for this to happen since September 4.

Daisy Bates, February 1958. M.A. Binns Studio, Little Rock, Feb. 9, 1958. Daisy Bates Papers, MC 582, box 9, photo 3. Courtesy of Special Collections, University of Arkansas Libraries.

The Little Rock Nine and Daisy Bates, after being awarded the Spingarn Medals at the forty-ninth annual NAACP convention in Cleveland, Ohio, July 1958. From left, standing: Thelma Mothershed, Elizabeth Eckford, Gloria Ray, Jefferson Thomas, Melba Pattillo, Ernest Green, Carlotta Walls, Minniejean Brown, and Terrence Roberts; sitting: Daisy Bates. Daisy Bates Papers, MC 582, box 9, photo 24. Courtesy of Special Collections, University of Arkansas Libraries.

Daisy Bates (second from right), Wiley Branton (second from left), and two unidentified people. Daisy Bates Papers, MC 582, box 9, photo 73. Courtesy of Special Collections, University of Arkansas Libraries.

Daisy Bates receiving the Diamond Cross of Malta Award, presented by the Philadelphia Cotillion Society, 1958. From right: Raymond Pace Alexander, Mayor Dilworth, Hobson R. Reynolds, Daisy Bates, George Padmore, Ray Lessly. Photo by Wert S. Hooper. Daisy Bates Papers, MC 582, box 9, photo 123. Courtesy of Special Collections, University of Arkansas Libraries.

L. C. Bates (second from right), Dr. Jerry Jewell (far right), and two unidentified men. Credit: Photo by Ralph Armstrong. Daisy Bates Papers, MC 582, box 9, photo 18. Courtesy of Special Collections, University of Arkansas Libraries.

Daisy Bates signing copies of *The Long Shadow of Little Rock* at book party, Little Rock, November 11, 1962. Daisy Bates Papers, MC 582, box 10, photo 219. Courtesy of Special Collections, University of Arkansas Libraries.

Daisy Bates (far right) with Eleanor Roosevelt (second from right) and two unidentified people. Daisy Bates Papers, MC 582, box 9, photo 60. Courtesy of Special Collections, University of Arkansas Libraries.

Daisy Bates, L. C. Bates, and two unidentified men unraveling the cross in the Bates's yard. Daisy Bates Papers, MC 582, box 11, photo 443. Courtesy of Special Collections, University of Arkansas Libraries.

Daisy Bates leaving Mitchellville City Hall, with unidentified man. Daisy Bates Papers, MC 582, box 10, photo 276. Courtesy of Special Collections, University of Arkansas Libraries.

Daisy Bates with President Lyndon Baines Johnson at the White House, April 9, 1964. Daisy Bates Papers, MC 582, box 9, photo 58. Courtesy of Special Collections, University of Arkansas Libraries.

Bates told Blossom she could not go to the parents' homes by herself, so he called Edwin Hawkins, principal of Dunbar Junior High School and L. M. Christophe, principal of Horace Mann, both black schools, to go with her. Bates's account of creeping up on each family's stoop and hoping not to be met with a shotgun blast at that time of the morning has its amusing aspects. Understandably, at that hour, the parents were not happy to see her. "What do you want now?" Gloria Ray's father demanded of her after he finally came to the door with his shotgun. "In my most pleasant, friendliest voice, and trying to look at him instead of the gun, I said that the children were to be at my house by eight thirty the next morning, and that these were the instructions of Superintendent Blossom." "I don't care if the President of the United States gave you those instructions!" he said irritably. "I won't let Gloria go. She's faced two mobs and that's enough!"[10]

Bates told Current later she had not been at all certain that more than "two or three" would show. But the Nine were there at her house the next morning, and, in truth, it was a glorious moment. Whatever one's feelings were about the military, the 101st Airborne inspired confidence. Bates re-created the scene in her memoir. She has Minnijean Brown exclaiming, "Oh, look at them, they're so-so soldierly! It gives you goose pimples to look at them!" Then Brown added solemnly, "For the first time in my life, I feel like an American citizen."[11] The government was making good on its commitment to them. After the convoy began to roll out, Bates turned to go back inside her house. "My eyes none too dry, I saw the parents with tears of happiness in their eyes as they watched the group drive off."[12]

This time the mob waiting outside Central had met its match. Instead of bullies, they quickly turned into victims, nursing a hundred-year old grudge. A small minority of the students inside the school would just as quickly revert back into bullies as soon as the soldiers' backs were turned. The soldiers were there to keep order, and even one photograph of a soldier on the school grounds with a fixed bayonet was worth a gold mine to Faubus. To men like Rev. Wesley Pruden, the fight was just beginning. That very morning he was agitating for a school closure law. A long school year for the Little Rock Nine was just starting as well.

Fearful that the NAACP would be criticized for trading on the instant fame of the Little Rock Nine, Roy Wilkins publicized the telegram he sent to Bates. "The NAACP will continue to impress students and parents that all such proposals [for public appearances] must be refused."

But Bates was available, and the invitations for her to speak at NAACP events around the country poured in. She went from being the "Women's Day" speaker at Bethel AME church in Little Rock to criss-crossing the country on the weekends for the NAACP. On the front pages of the *State Press*, L. C. would grandly announce his wife's appearances, calling her the "esteemed and fearless leader" of the state NAACP.[13] The way she was eclipsing him was an old story, but in the beginning he didn't seem to mind it. He had been her tutor, her mentor, her protector, and now he was being reduced to being just one of her several advisers while remaining her biggest cheerleader. L. C. treated Daisy's rising fame as a way to enhance the NAACP's stock in the state. His daily influence had been so great and constant that one cannot imagine Daisy Bates becoming a civil rights leader on her own without him. In retrospect, it is clear that even as she had profited from their relationship, she could not help but resent him and chafe under his guidance. Just as some children resent their parents and long for escape, Daisy had been more than ready to get away from her husband's dominating presence. Not that he had demanded the limelight that was naturally hers as the far more attractive of the two. She was the talker; he mostly listened and did his talking through the paper. L. C. always knew more about any subject than his wife, and both of them knew it. Like most people, he occasionally could be mean. Their friend Annie Abrams has said that "one of the things [L. C.] would say when he was the maddest at her was, 'Oh, shut your stupid mouth up.'"[14] Now, in October 1957, Daisy was at the beginning of a journey that would take her far from her husband.

The transcripts of the telephone conversations between New York and Little Rock clarify the roles Bates was to play in the coming months. Though the NAACP was mostly careful not to allow the Little Rock Nine to be used as fund-raisers, there was no reason why Bates could not fill that role herself. In one of two conversations on October 1 between Gloster Current, Bates, and Clarence Laws, Current explained to Bates that on the night of October 4 the national office wanted her to be available for a telephone hook-up with NAACP members who were to solicit for the NAACP's Freedom Fund. He talked about the speaking tour he was planning for her beginning around October 30. She would be hitting the road long before then.

The October 1 morning conversation with Current and Laws dwelled in part on the litigation to drive the NAACP out of business in Arkansas. Though the attorneys would ultimately make the decisions,

Bates, as the primary defendant, stayed abreast of the details, contrasting the suit against the Arkansas NAACP to a similar suit in Alabama. Though she was simply repeating what her attorneys had told her, the conversation shows she was knowledgeable and concerned about the bottom line. "In Alabama they were slapped with a fine for refusing to show the books. . . . They might slap a hundred thousand dollar fine on us too."[15]

That afternoon, Current told Bates that "Bob Allison of CBS called . . . and expressed his appreciation of the hospitality given the reporters and himself by you in your home; they don't know what they would have done without it."[16] A reporter for the *New York Herald-Tribune* also stopped by the national office to thank the NAACP for what Bates had done for him while he was in Little Rock.

Now that Laws was staying in Little Rock, he and Bates tried hard to project the image that integration in Little Rock was going to succeed. Bates had mentioned to Current that Gloria Ray was going to appear on Dave Garroway's television program on October 3. She also told him that a Little Rock black student (not one of the Nine) would be in Detroit on the weekend and would be speaking at a church rally. Bates was meeting with her to go over "an outline of things she should say." Laws followed up with more details and discussed similar matters. He also referred to two related situations that would rankle Bates in the coming months. The FBI was conducting interviews about the behavior of whites on September 23. Bates and the others fully expected the individuals who had beaten the black reporters to be indicted. Laws said, "I assume that as soon as they get a sufficient number of identifications on the photographs they will issue subpoenas against those people." Not a single white would be charged, however, a failure Bates noted bitterly in her memoir. Laws also mentioned that "the Mothers' [*sic*] League is going all out."[17] Daisy would go head to head (and invariably lose) with the Mothers League during that first year over whether the school administration would control the harassment of the Little Rock Nine. At the beginning of October, now that the children were in school, the mood was one of hope that the Nine would be accepted within the school and that opposition would lessen.

October 2 was the roughest day yet for the Nine. "The students were pushed, bumped, threatened, they were pelted with pencils, spit balls and other small objects," Laws told Current in New York. The National Guard was now on duty, and they were sympathetic to the white troublemakers, ignoring their behavior. "We drove by just after the students had entered—Daisy, I and L. C.," Laws remarked. "It was reported by the students yesterday that pressure is being placed on white students who have been friendly to Negroes."[18]

On October 2, at 3:30 P.M., Bates reported to Current that the harassment on October 1 was worse than the day before. It had gotten so bad that Minnijean Brown and Melba Pattillo had gone to the principal's office. "The Principal called me about this and begged me not to come over to the school and take the children out. . . . A few minutes later, the kids themselves called me from the Principal's office; I talked to all four of them. At 12 o'clock Carlotta Walls called me and she was o.k. . . . The guards aren't doing a doggone thing."[19]

Current then began to talk about the proposed tour he had for her in November. Bates responded by saying, "Being away that long with things the way they are, I just don't know."[20] For the most part, L. C.'s name does not appear in the conversations that took place on a routine basis between New York and Little Rock, but occasionally his name is mentioned. For example, on October 3 it was revealed by Laws that Osro Cobb, the U.S. Attorney, had called L. C. and "advised him that there was strong feeling against one of the students, Minnie Brown."[21] What was Minnijean doing that was attracting such attention? She was talking back. One wonders if L. C. influenced Daisy to keep Minnijean out of school on October 3 when some white students, inspired by the Mothers League, walked out in protest. In any event, it was, as Laws pointed out to Current, risky strategy because staying home was a sign to the group that wanted all the Nine to quit that they were succeeding.

Additionally, it appears that Minnijean and her mother were not consulted about the real reason why she was missing school. Deceiving the Little Rock Nine and their parents was also risky business. The telephone transcripts do not reveal other instances of this occurring, but the fact that it happened without criticism (except on tactical grounds) leads one to believe the NAACP was not occasionally above putting its interests ahead of other considerations. Clearly, Bates had no qualms about deceiving the media or the Central High administration if it advanced the cause, but she and Laws went further. "We told Minnie Brown's mother that the FBI wanted to talk with her and that was why she was kept out of school today. I told the Principal that she was ill and would be in either this afternoon or tomorrow morning."[22] Doubtless, Bates believed she was justified in saying to the school administration or white press whatever served the interests of the students or advanced the cause of the NAACP. On the other hand, it was essential that members of her own organization and her followers be able to trust her word completely. There would be hints later that not all of them did.

Against this backdrop, the media was demanding access to the students for interviews. On October 3 Bates told Current she got up at four o'clock "this morning with the little Ray girl to prepare her for the live interview with the Dave Garroway Show." Bates had been impressed with Gloria Ray and told Current how she had answered two different sets of questions "off the cuff." Though most of the Nine seemed to enjoy the attention, it had its downside, and Bates was sensitive to it. "Mrs. Bates said there are signs of jealousy on the part of the other Negroes not attending Central, and the white youngsters also tend to be jealous of the Negroes who are being given so much publicity."[23]

The main issue was, and would always be, how to deal with the harassment of the children. Bates reported, "I gave the children money this morning so they could call me from the school if anything happened."[24]

The attacks on nearly all the children were serious enough without the need for hype. What makes *The Long Shadow of Little Rock* generally unreliable as a historical record of this period is that Bates consistently fails to describe the collaborative nature of the fight waged by the NAACP in Little Rock. The telephone logs make clear that while he was in Little Rock, Clarence Laws was just as much involved as Bates on behalf of the Little Rock Nine.

To try to put some pressure on the Central High administration, Bates "got in touch with [Harry] Ashmore and he got in touch with General Walker and Blossom." According to Bates, "General Walker said last night that he was going to have plenty of people in that building today. I called the parents and told them what General Walker said." Bates said she "made the kids give me statement after statement to describe the students that are bothering them, physical description, description by locker number if they could."[25] The difficulty would be the unwillingness of the school administration to back the Nine and take decisive action to stop the harassment. Naturally, almost all the incidents occurred out of the sight of the teachers, and Principal Jess Matthews, backed by Blossom, refused to take action without the word of a teacher.

At this stage New York was in contact with the Little Rock situation twice a day. The feeling in New York was that it would be a disaster if the children quit, and every effort was made to give moral support to Bates so that she would continue to put pressure to ameliorate the conditions at Central High for the Nine. To this end, she was routinely praised and encouraged by the staff in these conversations. At the same time, NAACP leaders in New York wanted both Laws and Bates to talk with the national office before issuing any statements to the press. In the morning conversation on October 3, Current told Laws and Bates, "If the two of you could consult and then let us know before you follow through on announcements, it would be helpful all around."[26]

Sensitive to Bates's feelings, Laws replied, "I can understand the situation here and you can too. The ball has been carried here by one person and one person alone." Bates's feelings notwithstanding, the New York office wanted to micromanage what was occurring in Little Rock and keep the good national publicity going. Henry Moon, who directed publicity for the NAACP, got on the telephone and confronted Bates with recent complaints by the press that she had "intervened" to stop an interview of the children. "I was quite disturbed about it, and Stan [Opotosky of the *New York Post*] said there were four other reporters around at that time and they were upset, too."[27]

Bates was not averse at all to keeping everyone happy in the press and in New York, too, but she saw how the interviews were affecting the children. "Stan has been wonderful," she replied. "We have allowed them to go into the homes of the children to see the parents, but now we are trying to cut down on the publicity. This thing has been going on for months. But every time they print something about the kids, the kids have to face it the next day in school."[28]

The New York office had to walk a fine line. It was Bates who had the closest relationship with the parents and children, not Clarence Laws and, of course, not anyone in the New York office. They had to trust her. As Moon admitted, "I told Stan I couldn't make a judgment from New York on what you do down there. Thurgood feels that way, too. But I wanted to let you know he had talked to me." Bates replied that she "would have given the reporters a good story. The reporters want to quote the children, on the spot. If they would just give a general story of what happened and not put the children on the spot."[29]

On October 4 L. C. ran excerpts on the front page of the *State Press* of a letter of commendation Daisy received from Channing Tobias, president of the national NAACP board. She was praised for her "steadfast, sober, calm, courageous leadership and guidance."[30]

Other mail was not so complimentary. Letters had begun to make their way to Little Rock from everywhere, especially after the president sent the troops in. One gets a picture during October of an exhausted woman who nevertheless took great pleasure in her sudden worldwide fame. Elizabeth Oliver, a reporter for the *Afro-American*, came to Little Rock and captured the delight Bates took in the invitations to speak that began pouring in. Oliver wrote, "Proudly, she announced, 'I just got an invitation from Mrs. Lillie Mae Jackson in Baltimore and I'm to speak there on the 20th of October. I'll be there,' she said, winking an eye and nodding her head to say, 'You betcha.' " It was in this interview that Bates began to weave a story of her origins that would make writing her memoir of her early life difficult. She gave the name of her father in this interview as "Orlee Gaston."[31] The reporter misspelled his last name—it was "Gatson"—but Bates was not admitting at that point that she did not know who her birth father was.

Though the fight now was concentrated against the Little Rock Nine, Daisy and L. C. were not forgotten. On the night of October 4, "an effigy of a Negro was burned on the lawn of the home with a rope around its neck." In reporting the incident the next week in the *State Press*, L. C. labeled it the "sixth attack" against them.[32] Again, no one was arrested, though one of the guards had chased an individual away.

Well before the original plan of making fund-raising appearances in November, when things had settled down a bit, Bates hit the road. She decided she could travel on the weekends, but she needed to be home during the week. Her first trip was to speak to the Minneapolis branch of the NAACP at St. Peter's AME Church on October 13. As always, when Bates spoke outside the South, her remarks would be received warmly. No transcript of this speech survives; however, she "was given an official welcome" by the mayor of Minneapolis. In her talk, she praised President Eisenhower "for his forthright action" and related what she and the children and their parents had been through in the last six weeks.[33]

Back in Little Rock, Bates had to deal with more mundane business, such as responding to the city of Little Rock's passage on October 15 of an ordinance requiring the NAACP to divulge membership names as well as financial records. In theory, the ordinance was neutral on its face and applied to any group. In practice, it was aimed directly at the NAACP. Little Rock mayor Woodrow Mann, who had lambasted Faubus for surrounding Central High, went along with the charade that it was an appropriate response by city government. He claimed that groups such as the Capital Citizens Council and the Little Rock Central High Mothers League, as well as the NAACP, "represented the minorities that have contributed much to the disgraceful situation in which Little Rock has been dishonored." Amis Guthridge was delighted. "Now we will see the names of white people helping this group," he said, referring to the Arkansas NAACP.[34]

Other NAACP chapters in Arkansas (but not all) would be faced with the same demand for information. It was part of the plan to drive the NAACP out of the state. The branches would be meeting in Little Rock the weekend of October 18 and would need to be told how they could respond.

On October 15 the headline on the front page of the *Arkansas Gazette* read: "HALF OF U.S. TROOPS TO GO." Bates responded to this news by telling the press, "We're not concerned. I certainly think the troops that remain will be able to handle anything that might arise. The community is getting back to normal."[35]

Brave words, but the truth was that the stress from the harassment was beginning to tell. Bates reported to Current on October 17 that Elizabeth Eckford, Terrence Roberts, and Melba Pattillo were out with the flu. "I am getting physically weak. The weekend will be tiring, but I will be getting away from it for a few days."[36] She was referring to appearances in the Washington, D.C., area that Sunday.

No matter how bad things were, the illusion that all was manageable within Central had to be preserved. Melba Pattillo Beals was asked to write an account of her experiences during this time for the Associated Press. In her memoir, she remembered her "instructions" to "accentuate the positive" and not "to complain too much." She obliged but admitted in her memoir that "if I told what really happened, one of the officials might say we couldn't come back. I composed the story in a way that would make my day sound okay."[37]

It was during this week that Bates began to suspect her telephone line was being tapped, but the calls were deemed too necessary to stop them. To buoy the Nine's morale, on Friday, October 18, the national office arranged a telephone call at the Bates's home with another pioneer, the legendary baseball player Jackie Robinson, the first African American to play in the major leagues.

The state of Arkansas continued to ratchet up the pressure on Daisy and L. C. On October 24 Daisy created a small stir on the state capitol grounds when newsmen noticed she and L. C. were meeting with the state income tax authorities. Daisy passed it off as "routine," but

Orville Cheney, state revenue commissioner, could not resist smiling when he told reporters that he couldn't comment on why the Bateses had been summoned. "I can't say but I would think anybody in that room would be having income tax troubles."[38]

By the last week in October, an effort began in earnest to save the paper. Ads from NAACP chapters in different parts of the country began appearing in the *State Press*.[39] L. C. continued to spotlight his wife's role: each ad bore Daisy's name. "We Commend Mrs. L. C. Bates and the Nine Children For Unprecedented Heroism," read an advertisement from the "NAACP Central Long Island Branch. Dr. Eugene T. Reed, President."[40] Reed, a dentist, would become a leader of the so-called Young Turks on the national board of directors of the NAACP who would unsuccessfully challenge Roy Wilkins's leadership years later. As we shall see, Daisy Bates would be remembered as a "silent partner" in the effort to oust Wilkins, who in the fall of 1957 was her biggest backer.

Chapter Twelve

WOMAN OF THE YEAR

O n October 31 Clarence Laws continued his almost daily conversations with Gloster Current. Laws told Current he had attended a committee meeting of the Little Rock NAACP branch two days earlier, at which time the Lorches' name came up. Two members had wanted to pass a resolution commending the Lorches. Laws was horrified. He said "definitely not." On the other hand they should not be asked to withdraw from the NAACP either because, as Laws explained, "that wouldn't be well because Dr. Lorch has friends there."[1] The "problem," Laws explained, could be taken care of at next month's election. Clearly, the national office was worried that the NAACP's enemies might discover the depth of Lee Lorch's involvement in the Little Rock branch. On top of this, Grace Lorch had been subpoenaed to testify in Memphis before HUAC. A showdown over the Lorches was coming that would directly involve Bates, but meanwhile she was in New York.

On October 30 the deadline passed for the Arkansas State Conference of Branches and the Little Rock NAACP to list their officers in accordance with the local ordinance. Two other organizations filed their reports. The Capital Citizens Council listed a membership of 510; the Mothers League report showed 163 members. Little Rock aldermen met the next day and voted to instruct the city attorney to immediately request that a warrant be issued "against all officers of the NAACP in the city."[2]

L. C. called Daisy in New York to tell her the news. She had left for New York on Wednesday, October 29, for a round of appearances and, despite the warrant, initially responded by saying she "would probably not return to Little Rock until Monday."[3] She reversed her decision, however, and cut her trip short because she needed to come home and prepare her testimony for federal court on Monday. This hearing was to be on the NAACP's motion for a preliminary injunction to restrain the city of Little Rock from enforcing its recently passed ordinance requiring the NAACP to turn over information.

Still, Bates's visit to New York put her in the big leagues of the civil rights movement. She appeared with Jackie Robinson and Roy Wilkins at an NAACP rally, had tea with New York governor Averell Harriman and his wife, and had lunch with Dorothy Schiff, owner of the *New York Post*, in her New York City penthouse. Bates sipping tea with Harriman, one of the most respected statesman and politicians in the country, was news not only in New York, it went out over the wires all over the world.[4] She stayed in the famous Algonquin Hotel, where she held "several press conferences in her suite," and also spoke at a press conference at New York City College. There "she . . . praised the courage of the parents of the Little Rock Nine and branded the Little Rock crisis as a political scheme cooked up in the minds of unprincipled politicians who would set Arkansas back to pre–Civil War days."[5]

The words of her speech reminds one of L. C. more than Daisy, and, as mentioned, he wrote some of them. A description of Faubus as "gloating in his ill-famed glory" certainly reads like L. C. Her forte was not political rhetoric but in making concrete the experiences of the children and telling their story. When she told audiences that upon seeing the U.S. Army's escort, one of the children said, "For the first time I felt like an American," she moved people. Anyone could denounce Faubus, and his enemies did so routinely. What others could not do and Bates could was to bear witness, and she did it well in the eyes of those who were predisposed to hear her message. She was to speak in Washington, D.C., on Saturday night, November 1, and be named "Woman of the Year" by the National Council on Negro Women and then fly to St. Louis. However, she flew to Little Rock instead, where she was met by L. C., "her attorneys, three Negro photographers and a white photographer." If Daisy was going to be arrested, the NAACP wanted to make sure there was plenty of publicity. The entire group went directly to the Little Rock police station, where Daisy surrendered to the police and posted an appearance bond.[6]

While Bates had been in New York, a drama was being played out closer to home that demonstrated the ways in which the nation, and not just the South, could make it difficult for individuals willing to stand up for civil rights for blacks. Grace Lorch had refused to answer HUAC's questions. Though Lee Lorch had formerly been a member of the Communist Party (and it probably can be assumed Grace had also been a member) and the couple still ardently believed in the principles of communism, it is hard to imagine that anyone could have considered this brave and idealistic couple as threats to the national security. But given the tenor of the times, they were so regarded. Just as pressure was put on Martin Luther King Jr. to dissociate himself from those alleged to have ties to the Communist Party, so pressure would be exerted on Bates to turn her back on Lee Lorch. First, pressure was exerted on Lorch directly. Tony Freyer has noted that Clarence Laws wrote him in November: "Noting the professor's 'unauthorized' calls to members of the city council concerning actions against the NAACP, Laws sought to make a number of things crystal clear." The field secretary asserted that integration in Little Rock "could be done irreparable harm by the injection of extraneous issues." He then expressed the view that the "best contribution" Lorch "could make to the cause of full citizenship in Arkansas . . . would be to terminate, in writing," his affiliation with the Little Rock branch of the NAACP.[7]

Lorch claims he did not "lessen my involvement" with the Little Rock NAACP as a result of his talk with Clarence Laws. Bates, he said, stuck by him. "She told me not to pay any attention." When told that Bates had minimized her relationship with him, Lorch pointed out that she "was under pressure from the National . . . [office]."[8] While it does not appear that Lorch ever resigned from the Little Rock NAACP, it seems clear that his profile was lower in the remaining months he and his family lived in Arkansas.

On November 3 Bates and three other officers of the NAACP testified in a federal court proceeding challenging the ordinance that the NAACP "had been losing memberships and contributions because the ordinance had resulted in widespread apprehension." Only Bates, however, testified that she had been threatened.[9]

Her arrest for refusing to give the city of Little Rock information about the NAACP infuriated her: "Why give these segregationists, who are supported by the city administration, a direct target at which to shoot? They are harassing the Negro as a whole to the point where it is almost unbearable. . . . I don't want any Negro in Little Rock to suffer the inhuman attacks, arrests, and other harassments of which my husband and I are victims, merely because he is exercising his rights as an American citizen."[10] This was as close as Bates would ever come to admitting publicly that the harassment was getting to her personally. If there was any sense of shame expressed by the white community, it was not communicated to Bates locally. On the other hand, by this time mail was pouring in to her home from all over the United States and the world.

Her arrest did not keep her home for long. The next Saturday night she spoke at the Willard Hotel in Washington, D.C., and the following afternoon in St. Louis she had an audience of 6,000 people at Kiel Auditorium.[11] Then it was on to Atlanta the next weekend, where she was introduced by Wilkins again and addressed a meeting at the Wheat Street Baptist Church. Bates spoke in Tulsa on November 22 at the twenty-seventh annual convention of the Oklahoma NAACP.

Two decisions in the latter part of November didn't bode well for the Little Rock Nine. First, the army announced it was pulling out the troops of the 101st Airborne, and the Justice Department confirmed that it was not going to prosecute anyone for his or her behavior during the disturbances at Central High. As much as Bates had rejoiced in Eisenhower's decision to send troops into Little Rock, this failure to insist that individuals be charged for beating black newsmen was a bitter pill to swallow. It was business as usual in the white community, and that would not begin to end until blacks began to vote in sufficient numbers to make the failure to prosecute whites an issue that could not be ignored.

At home during the week there was Central High and the ongoing harassment of the Nine. As has been said, Bates liked young people, and she especially liked the Little Rock Nine. It would have taken a hard heart not to have liked them. They were all attractive, appealing youngsters. Bates did act like a parent in the sense that she provided guidance to them on how to present themselves to the media. As Bates recounted in *The Long Shadow of Little Rock*, the Nine gathered at her house on a number of occasions to go over the day's events. "Daisy opened her home to us," recalled Terrence Roberts in 2003. "We spent a lot of hours there. Just as a sanctuary. . . . Many times Daisy's basement would be where we congregated to play rock-and-roll and dance and that sort of thing."[12]

Though they would forever be thought of as the Little Rock Nine, it is easy to forget that first and foremost they were nine individuals who have been routinely lumped together. Inevitably, some became closer than others, but all were protective of each other. But how did they relate to Bates? Obviously, it depended on the individual. Terrence Roberts said, "I think she saw herself as our chief mentor." When asked if that was indeed true, he answered, "Well, I think that is open to debate whether or not she really was."[13] Although it may not be possible to answer that question, it is a crucial one, for Bates's reputation in part rests on her being considered their mentor. Certainly, Bates saw herself that way, as Roberts was quick to acknowledge.

Bates continued her close consultation with the NAACP national office in November, and in retrospect one can see that she followed its suggestions. The announced withdrawal of the troops of the 101st Airborne concerned her more than she said publicly. Gloster Current told her "that she should take the line that we expect nothing to happen with the removal of the 101st. . . . You have to exude optimism. If you take the line that the Jackson woman [Margaret Jackson of the Mothers League] . . . is taking, then you will be called a troublemaker."[14]

With respect to the internal revenue matter, Clarence Laws told Current that Bates had "paid them off and thumbed her nose at them."[15] He didn't mean publicly. Bates always kept her cool in public and exuded confidence she didn't always feel, for the noose around the state NAACP was drawing tighter. Ordinances requiring organizations to open their books to city authorities were passed in communities other than in Little Rock and North Little Rock. L. C. reported in the *State Press* on November 29 that these "anti-NAACP" ordinances had been passed in ten Arkansas towns, including the two in Pulaski County. The NAACP expected to lose its cases in the municipal and state courts in Arkansas but hoped to win on appeal in the federal appellate courts.

Toward the end of November Bates was again becoming disenchanted with the work of her Arkansas field secretary, who was now Chris Mercer. In a telephone transcript marked "Confidential," she reported to Current on November 25 that Mercer had missed a meeting on Sunday. Asked where he had been, Bates replied, "Oh, I don't know, I heard somebody say he was playing poker all night." Current warned her that if Mercer didn't work out, "you won't get a replacement, I assure you."[16]

Bates could absolutely depend on Clarence Laws, and she knew it. Laws, she told Elizabeth Jacoway, moved "in the front room" during the fall of 1957.[17] "Without Clarence I don't know what I would do," she admitted to Current. "You know Laws is strictly business and when we work together we work very well."[18] Before too much longer, Mercer would also be gone, but he later recalled that Bates had always greeted him warmly. The good feelings would outlast the bad ones. Just as Harry Bass would attend L. C.'s funeral in 1980, Daisy was not a person to take to the grave any grudges.

Interest in the Central High story by the media continued to be strong, and Bates worked hard to accommodate anyone whom she thought would report the story favorably. She went so far as to stage a pre-Thanksgiving dinner at her home on November 25, three days before the holiday. The filmed event with the Nine had been arranged by Robert Gray, who was described in the press as a "public relations man" from Toronto, Canada. Curiously, it was one event that Bates did not go over beforehand with the national office in New York. When asked by Current if she had discussed the interviews with Roy Wilkins or Henry Moon, director of public relations, she told him that "she did not know what the publicity men from the networks had done."[19] Bates was led to believe that the major networks wanted to do a filmed interview with her and the Nine that would be shown all over the country on Thanksgiving. Each child was to tell what he or she was thankful for as they ate Thanksgiving dinner at the Bates's home. Apparently the interviews were not shown nationally. The children read their statements, undoubtedly ruining the spontaneous feel the media wanted. In a photograph that has become famous, L. C. is shown in a dark suit and white shirt carving the turkey. Daisy and L. C. are seated in folding chairs around a table. "Do you kids want light or dark meat?" Daisy asked the children.

Fifteen-year-old Melba Pattillo quipped, "This is an integrated turkey."

Daisy was not amused. Melba remembered, "The annoyed expression on her face matched the one on Mother's, letting me know that maybe I should have prepared a speech. The reporters snickered as they posed a series of questions on turkeys and integration, calling on me by name to answer. I didn't want the others to think I was trying to steal the spotlight, but once I had spoken out of turn, 'integrated turkey' became the theme."

"You'll live to regret that statement," Daisy told her. "I knew she was agonizing over the consequences of my frivolity."[20]

In fact, Melba's comment was exactly what the media may have been hoping for from the students. It showed a badly needed sense of humor. While perhaps not the television event Bates planned, the staged dinner got wide coverage.

Bates had worked hard to bring this event off. She mentioned how busy she was with this "eleventh-hour deal" and had gone to the trouble of bringing one of the Nine back from Huntsville, Alabama. For L. C., her efforts should have been an early warning sign that her appetite for fame was much larger than his own.

With the national attention Bates was getting, it was hard not to have her head turned by it all. Thirty-five hundred people turned out to hear her speak at Olympic Auditorium in Los Angeles on December 1. She was introduced by actor John Carradine. As much as Bates was lionized in the black press (the *Afro-American* headlined the story "Mrs. Bates Moves Audience in Stirring Oration"), occasionally a negative view of her abilities as a speaker was recorded. Writing in the *Los Angeles Sentinel* on December 5, reporter Almena Lomax began her story by saying, "Mrs. Daisy Bates of Little Rock is no practiced speaker." Besides a sound system that did not carry her voice, "her Arkansas diction which sounds like a combination of Bob Burns and a Jews Harp would have defeated it anyway," meaning Bates delivered her message in a "high, sing-song voice." On the other hand, Lomax was quick to say that "like all of the other frontline fighters whom we have heard, she held her audience enrapt."[21] Listening to Bates's taped voice today, one wonders if the writer was not reflecting her own disdain of southerners, white or black, because Bates's voice did not carry the inflections associated with uneducated African Americans or entertainers pretending to be southern characters. Certainly, she had a southern accent, but she was careful to try always to use standard English in public.

On December 3 Daisy was convicted in municipal court and fined $100 for failing to turn over records of the NAACP to the city. This led to an appeal all the way to the U.S. Supreme Court. Rev. J. C. Crenchaw, who had been charged as well, was dismissed from the suit because the city had failed to request documents from him.[22]

During this period of time, the national NAACP undertook a project to ensure that the Little Rock Nine would be able to attend college. Bates's papers contain an unsigned trust document that gave Bates and Crenchaw, along with the students' parents, supervisory power over the terms of the trust.[23] In a letter to Wilkins on December 17, Bates referred to the scholarship fund, advising him that Thelma Mothershed's mother was serving as the trustee. Whatever the initial arrangements, Daisy, and then later L. C. when she was in New York, would dole out the money for college expenses to the Little Rock Nine.

Giving Bates an early Christmas present, the White Citizens Council published a handbill showing her arrest record, complete with her mug shots. The handbill began " 'MRS.' DAISY BATES, Little Rock's 'Lady' of the Year." The handbill's language followed the traditional pattern of ridicule and sarcasm that southerners employed when threatened by black behavior. Above her mug shot it read: "Central High's Most prominent P.T.A. member. Self-appointed protector of Nine Negro children, having received 'subpoena' powers from Jess Matthews, Central High School Principal, and also authority to cross examine white students, unofficial 'principal' in charge of lecturing white students at Central High who 'cross' any of her 'brave' students."[24] Below these words were Daisy's mug shots from her 1946 arrest when she and L. C. had been held in contempt for an article in the *State Press*. The description of her first arrest revealed that Daisy had been detained on November 16, 1934, in Monroe, Louisiana, for an investigation and then released. What made this item noteworthy was that under her photograph, Daisy's name appears as "Daisey [*sic*] Bates." Her name was not "Bates," she told the *Arkansas Democrat*. "I remember the Monroe arrest. I remember that L. C., several relatives and myself, were traveling and a service station operator spotted a gun in the car—and he had a permit to carry the gun. The only thing the police asked me was my name. I told them 'Daisy.' They were questioning L. C. and assumed my name was Bates also. I was only 14 and L. C. and I were not married at the time."[25] Of course, as stated earlier, she was born in 1913 and would have been around the age of twenty-one in 1934. In the *State Press* on December 20, L. C. provided a slightly different explanation. She "does not recall giving any name, and she most certainly did not give the name of Daisy Bates, for she was not a Bates at that time."[26]

Whether Daisy was passing herself off as L. C.'s wife in 1934 had nothing to do with the issue of school integration in 1957, but it was another weapon in the white supremacist assault on black leaders. The hypocrisy of whites raising, even indirectly, the hint of sexual impropriety was ignored, since Daisy's skin color said volumes about that issue. The idea to check her arrest record may well have come from the *Arkansas Democrat*, which was hostile to integration. Clarence Laws wrote Roy Wilkins on December 18 that "apparently the attack upon Mrs. Daisy Bates was precipitated by the fact that the Associated Press recently selected her as the "Woman of the Year" in education. . . . A reliable source said the pro-segregationist *Arkansas Democrat* hit the ceiling . . . that Daisy had been so honored and threatened such an attack." Laws explained that though this recognition for Bates had not yet been announced, the press had been made aware of it. In any event, the *Democrat* ran the story under the headline, "Daisy Bates Laughs off Police Record."[27]

As Bates's fame grew in the fall of 1957, the more tempting it became to rewrite her past to make herself seem more respectable, younger, and better educated. "She is exactly twenty years the junior . . . of her fifty-six-year-old husband," reads a line from an interview she gave the *Pittsburgh Courier* on December 7. In fact, Bates was then approximately forty-three. For the same article, Bates changed the date and place of her marriage to make it appear she and L. C. had gotten "married in February, 1941, in Memphis, Tenn." before they moved to Little Rock to begin the *State Press*. She also emphasized that "she put in two years" at Philander Smith and said her life had not prepared her for a career as a newspaperwoman. "All I knew was how to be a lady. My father had drilled that into me."[28]

The idea that a black woman in the South in 1957 would characterize herself in those terms incensed her white enemies, who assumed, correctly as it turned out, that they had evidence of a breach of moral behavior (hence the quotation marks around "Lady" in the handbill; however, by dropping seven years off her age, she made the Monroe story a bit more plausible). Her explanation of why her name was listed as "Bates," of course, rings hollow in light of L. C.'s December 1962 letter to the effect that he had taken her away from Huttig in 1932.

On January 26, 1952, L. C. and Daisy had been arrested for "gaming" after participating in a friend's penny-ante poker game. Despite their protests, they were convicted and fined $5. The last item in the handbill was Bates's recent arrest for failing to turn over documents of the NAACP to the city of Little Rock.

The bottom of the flyer, addressed to "parents," read in part as follows: "There is a vicious fear campaign in process at Central High School, whereby the white children are being told that at anytime a white child has trouble with a negro student that the white students must face Daisy Bates and be cross-examined by her." This statement must have made Bates curse under her breath. If only she had that kind of influence at Central High. All the memoirs written about this period document how limited her influence was, not that it kept her from trying repeatedly to protect the Nine. The allegation that Bates was being allowed to cross-examine white students was absurd, but Bates had been to Central in the past week at the request of Minnijean Brown's mother, Imogene, for a conference. Minnijean was not being allowed to participate in the glee club's Christmas program. Elizabeth Huckaby, in her memoir, wrote that the principal, Jess Matthews, "was upset" that Imogene Brown had brought Bates, but he went ahead with the conference.

> Mrs. Bates joined the discussion. The chief point she wished to make was that Mr. Matthews lacked control over the students; he failed to enforce discipline. Mrs. Bates and I were doing most of the talking. . . . I could see why Mrs. Bates was successful as president of the state NAACP. She was a good infighter, persistent, intelligent, unintimidated—a woman who had made a choice of this career fully aware of its dangers to her person and also its rewards in prestige and in service to her people.

As an aside, Huckaby observed that Bates doodled as she talked. Bates was unable to do anything about the Christmas program, but she took the opportunity to complain "that the treatment of the children had been getting worse in the last two weeks in the form of kicking, spitting and general abuse."[29]

Blossom's unwillingness to allow Minnijean Brown to appear in the Christmas program was news (it ran in the *New York Times*), but so was another incident at this time. Minnijean was goaded into responding to the harassment at Central and was suspended three days from school for dumping a bowl of chili on a boy's head.[30] Laws wrote Wilkins that "Mrs. Bates and I visited Minnie Brown at her home last night to hear first hand her story of the cafeteria incident, and to assure her that while we did not advocate such behavior we understood how she could have been provoked to such action." He reported that "Mrs. Bates, the children and their parents are standing up well under this vexing experience. For her it frequently means working long hours, conferring with various ones on school matters. Added to this is the matter of bolstering the morale of branch leaders here and elsewhere who fear arrest or reprisals under the city ordinance which requires the filing of confidential organization data. To date 12 cities have passed the decree."[31]

Christmas break was coming, however, and it could not come soon enough. Bates received a letter before the holidays from Kenneth Clark, the psychologist whose testimony had been quoted in *Brown* about the psychological effects of segregation on black children. With his obvious connections to the NAACP, he would have met Bates on previous occasions, and he addressed her in the letter by her first name. Clark wrote that he and his wife, Mamie, were going to Hot Springs (an hour's drive from Little Rock) for Christmas, and he had been hired by the Southern Regional Council to "make an informal study of the impact of the Little Rock crisis on the Negro community in general and particularly on the adjustment of the nine students who are directly involved." He asked Bates to arrange for him to meet the Nine and their families. Clark saw the children on December 27 and 28 and interviewed others as well. His partial findings are contained in a fourteen-page report to the Southern Regional Council. In his opinion, the ordeal of the integration crisis had

> served to mobilize and unify the [Negro community] and has increased its pride and morale significantly. . . . The present psychological health of the nine Negro children appears to be good. They are accepting their role with poise and dignity. They have been helped significantly by the wise guidance and counsel of Mrs. Bates, by the warmth and support of their families, and by the admiration and respect which they have received from the immediate community and from the nation. Of special significance also is the evidence of international concern and support which they have continually received.[32]

Four months into the first semester's ordeal, the children's parents appeared to remain solidly behind Bates. A particularly strong supporter of Bates's among the parents initially was Gloria Ray's mother, Julia Ray. She wrote Wilkins in December, "We love her for her courage, patience, endurance, and her willingness to go all the way with us inspite [sic] of insults and danger of bodily harm." Bates felt enough confidence in Julia Ray to have arranged for her to "speak on a Women's Day Program" about the travails they had all experienced.[33]

During December Bates mentioned to Wilkins that the Arkansas NAACP treasury was running on fumes and suggested that the national office send $1,000 per month to cover the mounting bonds that were being required for defending cases against the local branches in Arkansas. The "financial statement" Bates referred to in her letter showed that between September 4 and December 17, Daisy and L. C. had spent $350 on "guard service," and $500 went to the cost of the bond for Birdie Williams of the North Little Rock NAACP. The national office had sent $1,500 to Bates during this period, but it was not enough, because at the end of the period the Arkansas State Conference of Branches was running a deficit of $337. Bates estimated she had spent $400 during this period on "entertainment" and food for the newsmen.

The recognition that came with being named the Associated Press "Woman of the Year" in education and one of the top ten newsmakers in 1957 took Bates to the zenith of her prominence as a national figure. Eleanor Roosevelt, who would write the foreword to Bates's memoir, was named "Woman of the Year" in 1957 in the category of public service. Queen Elizabeth was named "Woman of the Year," so Bates was in elite company.[34] The only other African American to be named was tennis star Althea Gibson. Though Bates would make the cover of *Ebony* in 1958, this would be the peak of her fame. She sent telegrams thanking everyone from Dorothy Schiff, the *New York Post* owner who had entertained her at her penthouse; the wire services; and the three major networks, ABC, NBC, and CBS; to black publications such as the *Chicago Defender* and to Johnson Publications, which owned *Jet* and *Ebony*. The telegrams expressed her gratitude for their "fair, constructive . . . reporting of the Little Rock story."[35] Nor did she neglect the reporters who had covered the story, sending telegrams, to, among others, Benjamin Fine at the *New York Times*, Ted Posten at the *New York Post*, and Jimmy Hicks at the *Amsterdam News*. Now that her prominence had been publicly confirmed, Bates, whose formal role in the Arkansas NAACP was mostly confined to presiding over the yearly meeting of the State Conference of Branches, now thanked the media in the names of "the nine Negro students, their parents and my associates" and wished "them a happy new year."[36]

L. C. continued to spotlight Daisy in the pages of the *State Press*. A Christmas party to be given for the Nine by a national black sorority at the Dunbar Community Center on December 23 became a party "for the nine Negro children and Mrs. Daisy Bates." In the same issue, L. C. ran a story about another award in St. Louis from a black fraternity to the Little Rock Nine and Daisy. "In accepting the award, Mrs. Bates displayed the same calm serenity, and humbleness, along with an exuding Christian attitude, that she has shown throughout the ordeal."[37] Cool under fire, proud, dignified—these were all adjectives that might describe Bates, but at the end of a long and hard year the image of a Christ-like figure leading the Little Rock Nine was stretching it a bit.

In fact, with the rising star of Martin Luther King Jr., the national civil rights movement was already moving into new phases of the struggle by the end of 1957, even as local chapters of the NAACP in Arkansas were wilting under the attack of militant segregationists. Only nine of the twenty-five Arkansas chapters sent any contributions in 1957 to be forwarded to the national office.[38] The Arkansas NAACP was now a ward of the national organization.

There was too much going on to sit and meditate. Her enemies seldom rested. A December editorial titled "Our Opinion You're Wasting our time, Mr. Charley" in the *State Press* read:

> The names of three Negroes have been given to us by parents of children attending Central hi school. These Negroes, according to the parents, are trying to encourage them to withdraw their children from the former all-white hi school.
>
> This is interesting, but not at all surprising—knowing the tactics of the Negroes involved . . . it is our opinion that this advice must have come from Mr. Charley.[39]

In an early draft of *The Long Shadow of Little Rock*, Bates named I. S. McClinton, head of the Democratic (Negro) Voters League, as one of the blacks who tried to persuade the Little Rock Nine to drop out of school. She claimed that she called him and said, "Some low down bastard went over . . . and told Mr. Ray I was a drunkard, not fit to deal with the children." She then threatened to expose McClinton in the *State Press* if it happened again. She also named Harry Bass as another person who tried to get the children to withdraw. He had gone to see Minnijean Brown's mother.[40] Bates told Elizabeth Jacoway that "McClinton went to Mrs. Mothershed and said, 'Mrs. Bates is using you. I would take my kids back to the other school.' " Bates also claimed that $10,000 was offered to the person or organization that got the children out of school.[41] By the end of 1957, it must have seemed to Daisy and L. C. that their enemies were everywhere they turned.

Chapter Thirteen

HOLDING THE LINE

A new organization called the Greater Little Rock Improvement League appeared on January 9. Headed by Rev. Oliver W. Gibson, it proposed "a more moderate stand" than that taken by the NAACP. Bates went to see what it was all about. The *Arkansas Gazette* reported the group stood for resolving racial differences without going to court. Bates was invited to speak and told them, "When we go into court we are fighting for the dignity of man. I am sure that is what you will be fighting for in your new organization."[1] She obviously was not worried by them. The group had a second meeting in private two weeks later, but only about twenty attended. Though whites of all stripes, and some blacks, would have preferred it otherwise, the NAACP was still the only real game in town for the time being. Bates was determined to keep it that way.

Bates wired Roy Wilkins on January 7 that "a crude incendiary bomb was thrown in the carport of [my] home" but that no damage had been done. She continued to speak every weekend. Bates often suggested that her "co-workers"—Chris Mercer, Clarence Laws, or one of the parents—speak when she was unavailable. Sometimes groups took her up on the offer, but it was Bates people wanted to hear and see. Also in January Bates received a letter from Wilkins in which he acknowledged the NAACP was "committed to bearing the expenses in connection with the Little Rock situation and through the direct payment of legal expenses in connection with the defense of the State Conference and the Little Rock Branch from assaults by the State of Arkansas."[2] With her selection as "Woman of the Year" in education, Bates's election to a full three-year term on the national NAACP board in January was a mere formality.

Bates continued to have contact with Edwin Dunaway and asked him for his help when Minnijean Brown was in the process of being expelled from Central. During the month of February Minnijean had called a girl "white trash." There was nothing he could do. In fact, Minnijean's fate was effectively sealed as soon as the chili incident occurred in December. She had been readmitted on the totally unrealistic condition that she not respond, no matter what the provocation. Though Bates gave Minnijean's mother the telephone number of the president of the school board and asked her to call him and ask for a meeting of the school board, Bates had to believe there would be little hope in successfully appealing Blossom's recommendation that Minnijean be expelled. Having already provided for this contingency, Bates immediately got on the telephone to Tim Clark, headmaster of the New Lincoln School in New York, to see if Minnijean could be enrolled.[3] Wilkins pointed out in a telegram to school board president Wayne Upton that this basis for a permanent expulsion "is an absurdity which your board cannot accept," but the plea was ignored.[4] Under pressure from the white community and Faubus, the board had shown no backbone and was not about to now.

Bates handled the details of Minnijean's trip to New York. Gloster Current sent a memo to Wilkins, letting him know that Bates had called to tell him when Minnijean and her mother were arriving in New York. She had purchased tickets for them and was "giving the family $100 for clothes and $50.00 for incidentals connected with the trip." Current wrote, "Mrs. Bates was rather insistent that we leave Clarence there until the situation clears up." Current gave her no guarantees and in fact told Bates that Laws had "a responsibility to the region." On the other hand, he promised her that the Little Rock situation would continue to receive priority. With L. C. trying desperately to save the paper, Daisy had to have one person on whom she could rely completely. She knew immediately how disastrous Minnijean's expulsion was and told Current, "they will start on the others."[5]

"The expulsion of Minnie Jean Brown is having a reaction among the better class of white citizens who feel that it was unjust. A prominent white woman, Mrs. D. D. Terry, called [Daisy] and has agreed to get together fifty or more other prominent women to work on the school issue," Laws wrote Wilkins on February 19.[6] "Prominent" was an understatement in Adolphine Terry's case. Sister of Arkansas's Pulitzer Prize–winning poet, John Gould Fletcher, and years ahead of him on the racial issue, Terry's wealth made her invulnerable to the pressure experienced by other whites who were sympathetic to Bates and the Nine. The Terry Mansion, now a museum, is still one of the landmarks in downtown Little Rock. With her own roots deep in Arkansas soil, her husband, David Terry, was equally well connected, once having served in Congress. Though she was Episcopalian, her cousin was Catholic bishop Albert Fletcher of the Little Rock Diocese. Despite the fact that she and others, including a group of white ministers and interracial groups like the Arkansas Human Relations Council, would accomplish nothing that semester, Terry's personal involvement would be a harbinger of things to come.

Meanwhile, the "Eight" were doing their best to hold on until the end of the school year. No matter how bad the intimidation became, the authorities refused to take steps to stop it. On April 7 the *New York Post* ran an article under the headline "Eight Kids Who Walk Alone" about forty-two incidents that ranged from physical harassment to outright attacks recorded by Bates and passed along to reporter Stan Opotosky, who had reported on Central from the beginning of the school year. The article listed each incident and quoted Blossom as saying, "The segregationists are now only a hard core, and we don't intend to give them some martyrs which will enable them to spread their influence. . . . The temper of the community is such that we must be prepared to see each case through court."[7] The school board was not about to do that. In large measure, the Eight were expected to grin and bear it. Moreover, it was never just the harassment that made each day a trial. For a teenager, the constant social isolation may have been the worst part. Thelma Mothershed remembered, "There were some mornings I got up and my throat was tight. I didn't want to go because I knew I would be ignored all day for the most part."[8]

Instead of standing up to the troublemakers at Central, in February the Little Rock School Board succumbed to the pressure and asked the federal court for a delay in integrating its schools. Based on her recent experience, Bates told an audience in Washington, D.C., "The segregationists are using everything at their command, the courts, night riding, vandalism, cross burnings, and many other vicious forms of intimidation and harrassment [*sic*]. We are involved in seventeen law suits. We are in these law suits to defend ourselves against efforts to kill the NAACP in Arkansas." In this speech at the Statler Hotel in the nation's capitol, she told the tenth annual National Civil Liberties Clearinghouse Conference that Faubus "has made a mockery of the

Constitution" and was running for a third term "with the Federal Government picking up the tab."[9]

The pressure on Daisy and L. C. was almost overwhelming, and now Daisy was no longer denying it. The last week of February 1958 the *State Press* ran a story about their continuing harassment. "Young white hoodlums who are free to roam at will in Little Rock have stepped up their attacks on the home of Mr. and Mrs. L. C. Bates. Where once you looked forward to weekly attacks, now it is daily without any interference on the part of those who have taken oaths to uphold law and order. Objects were thrown thru two plate glass windows last week."[10]

Meanwhile, Faubus, who had never been silent throughout the school year, began to heat up his own rhetoric. On April 11 the *Arkansas Gazette* quoted Faubus on the subject of Lee and Grace Lorch. He "charged . . . that a white professor at Philander Smith College and his wife were among those responsible for causing the school integration crisis at Little Rock." He said that the Lorches "have been identified as members of the Communist Party. . . . Both of them were active behind the scene and then openly in the Little Rock affair." The article reported that "the Governor also charged that the Lorches had worked closely" with Bates.[11]

Yet despite the unrelenting pressure, Bates did not wilt. Of all the events that occurred in 1957–58, none was more indicative of her influence than the exchanges between her and Herbert Thomas, author of a plan introduced in April 1958 to "solve" the continuing crisis at Central. President of the First Pyramid Life Company in Little Rock, Thomas was one of the movers and shakers in the business community, and though firmly in the camp of the moderates, he was given permission by Faubus to present the plan to the State Department of Education at a meeting on April 7. The plan was that the Eight would finish the school year, but no blacks would enroll in white schools the next academic year. The State Department of Education would appoint an interracial committee to make recommendations to the federal court on how integration should proceed. African Americans would be required to admit to and accept responsibility for their moral and educational deficits. In return, "racial harmony would be restored." Though it was never spelled out, implicit in the Thomas plan was a promise to end the assault on the black community and accept *Brown* in principle. Knowing he would be asked the question, Thomas issued a statement, quoted in both the *Arkansas Democrat* and *Arkansas Gazette*, that, indeed, he was a "segregationist" but that he recognized the aspirations of blacks and their desire for participation in a just society. The *Arkansas Gazette* endorsed the plan in a front-page editorial: "yet, [Thomas] believes, as does this newspaper, that it is possible to meet the new legal conditions without any real dislocation of the social patterns under which the two races have always lived."[12]

Without ever admitting it, white moderates like Thomas expected to control the pace of any further desegregation if blacks accepted his plan, just as whites had in the years when small steps had been taken to desegregate public facilities in Little Rock. Furthermore, they fervently hoped the black community could be persuaded to go along with the plan.

Bates immediately announced her opposition and never wavered. On April 8 she was quoted in the *Arkansas Gazette* as saying that the NAACP could not endorse the plan because it "seeks to hang indefinitely in abeyance the rights to which Negro children are being denied."[13]

Daisy and L. C. met with Thomas on April 11 in a small interracial group, but the meeting did not go well. "I found the Arkansas President of the NAACP to be able and unemotional," he said about their only exchange. "Her answers were concise and clearly stated. My opinion is that she is uncompromising."[14]

Hoping to put pressure on Bates or to do an end run around her, Thomas had invited 126 blacks to a meeting on April 13 to discuss his plan. On the list were Harry Bass and publisher C. H. Jones. Ninety people showed up. There was no mention that Bates was at this meeting.[15]

Even L. C., who was desperately trying to save the *State Press* and in some ways was as conservative as the moderates, would write, "the plan does have merits" and implied it would have been acceptable "had it been proposed eight or ten years ago."[16] In fact, the Thomas plan was unacceptable to the NAACP from the beginning. When it became apparent to Thomas that few blacks were interested in it, he wrote Bates a letter on April 28, claiming that other black leaders had originally accepted the plan in "principle," but when he had talked to them later, "their whole demeanor had changed. They were aloof. They would express no opinion. Some were as men afraid. . . . There are rumors that few Negroes dare face the pressures which are brought against them if they do run counter to the stand taken by the NAACP."[17]

Thomas urged Bates to change her mind. He called the racial problems "a tangle of misunderstanding" that could be solved "only by knowing each other's viewpoints, aspirations, hopes and even prejudices." After reciting at length his efforts to engage both blacks and whites in the process of discussing the plan, he asked Bates the following questions: "I should like to know from you if the NAACP in Arkansas accepts the principle of gradualism? If you accept different approches [sic] a Negro racial responsibility of substantial improvement of education and moral standards before moving into integration in certain areas?"[18] In traditional white supremacist fashion, Thomas was proposing that blacks now trust whites to do the right thing without admitting there were reasons why they might not want to. There was no acknowledgment that whites had exploited blacks since bringing them in chains to Arkansas and had denied them an equal education at every opportunity. Would it have made a difference if Thomas had done the unthinkable and taken moral responsibility for the past? Not at this point. It was too little and too late. Bates had put her trust in the federal government, and she was unquestionably the leader. John Kirk has noted that in 1958, "twenty-two out of twenty-six black leaders interviewed" by sociologists from Arkansas AM&N identified Bates as "the most influential Negro in the community," and twenty-four out of the twenty-six described her as "the most influential Negro in determining policy on educational desegregation."[19]

The *New York Post* continued its periodic coverage of the battle being waged in Little Rock. Looking back over the school year, Bates struggled to be optimistic. "There have been three stages. . . . There was the trouble in September. There was the long period of things—I hate the word incidents, because actually they are little crimes. And now there is a little bravery among the 'moderates' who were afraid to speak before."[20]

There was nothing Bates could do about the peer pressure sympathetic white students faced. White students who attempted to be friendly to the Eight were ostracized. The *New York Post* article concluded: "For a long period even those white students who favored integration kept their distance. They feared ridicule and even attacks from the violent segregationists. Now they are venturing a smile in the halls or even a 'hello' in the classroom. But they don't go beyond that. 'If only they would,' says Melba Pattillo. 'If only someone would speak up.'"[21]

Outside Arkansas and the South, groups expressed their support. One was even willing to put Bates on the payroll. The Elks, a black fraternal organization Bates had spoken to in Detroit, offered to pay her a salary for going around the country to speak, but before she accepted, she took it up with Wilkins, who objected. Bates remained loyal to the NAACP.

The financial situation at the *State Press* was getting worse all the time. L. C. had been offered jobs as a printer in Detroit and Los Angeles. Clarence Laws recommended that Daisy be put on salary by the NAACP national office, "which would permit her to make speaking engagements in the larger cities." Like Wilkins, he believed that if they left Little Rock, it would send a signal "to other Negroes in the South who are already a little fearful about becoming" members of the NAACP.[22]

Finally, the school year was about to end, but one obstacle remained. Rumors were flying that Ernest Green was not going to be allowed to graduate. Bates told Current on May 22 that "the White Citizens Council had planned to stage a riot in order to keep Ernest Green from marching with his graduation group and to give Faubus additional ammunition to run for governor." With harassment increasing against the children, she "had called Major General Walker yesterday and told him that there were no guards around the school and had asked for four more guards." Walker had called her back and "promised . . . that their would be guards for the children this morning."[23]

Wilkins called Bates in late May to tell her the Little Rock Nine had won the Spingarn Medal, the NAACP's most prestigious award. It was the first time the award had ever gone to a group. Bates's omission caused an immediate controversy and became front-page news in the black press. The *Amsterdam News* reported that "when the nine children told their parents they would receive the prized award but that Mrs. Bates was excluded, the parents objected to separating Mrs. Bates and the children." The *News* ran a letter that Ellis Thomas, father of Jefferson Thomas, had written to Roy Wilkins in which it was disclosed that the students would not accept the medal unless Bates was included. "We have discussed this matter among ourselves and with the children. We are all of the opinion that immediate reconsideration is imperative. . . . The children have told us that they will not accept the Spingarn Medal unless Mrs. Bates is included." Wilkins had refused to make the letter public, but the *News* had no trouble getting a copy. Reached at a party at the Bates's house on the day Ernest Green graduated from Central, seven of the nine spoke with Louis Lomax of the *Afro-American*, who reported that the children "met at midnight Tuesday and voted not to accept the coveted Spingarn Medal."[24]

The Spingarn Award Committee, which included Eleanor Roosevelt, may well have thought that for this one time the Nine themselves should stand alone in the spotlight. Bates and the children had just flown to Chicago to receive the Robert S. Abbot Award from the *Chicago Defender* and spent four days there as guests of the paper. Certainly, a case could be made that only the Nine should receive the medal, or if anyone should share it with them, it should be their parents. Clearly, not everyone agreed. The committee received, among other protest mail, a long letter from NAACP supporter Pauli Murray, the remarkable black activist who combined careers as a lawyer and Episcopal priest and became a life-long friend and admirer of both L. C.'s and Daisy's, pointing out that one could not think of the New York Yankees without their manager, Casey Stengel.[25] One person who apparently did not argue that it was the children's moment to shine alone was Bates herself. In fact, Elizabeth Eckford contends that Bates contacted certain parents of the Nine. "My father and Mr. Thomas signed a letter saying that we wouldn't accept it unless she got it. That was something she put them up to do. My father cooperated. And Mr. Thomas did. It may have been the Mothersheds, too. There was nothing coming from us about that."[26] If Lomax's account is correct, this last statement by Eckford is inaccurate. Nor did Oscar Eckford confirm his daughter's allegation that Bates engineered her inclusion in the award.[27] Doubtless, Bates believed she deserved the NAACP's highest accolade along with the Nine. Daisy and L. C. had committed their lives to the work of the NAACP and were in the process of sacrificing their livelihood to advance its cause. On the other hand, the Nine's primary protectors and emotional supporters were their parents, who were there for their children every day and on the weekends while Bates was off on speaking engagements that, since October, had become as regular as clockwork.

The school year was finally over. Despite the stresses, all of the Nine had passed, and Jess Matthews said that one of them had made the Honor Roll. Bates disclosed it was Carlotta Walls, a sophomore.[28] With tight security, Ernest Green graduated on May 27 without incident. Bates's strongest supporter in the future, Green told reporter Lomax after his graduation that "Mrs. Bates is more deserving [to receive the Spingarn Medal] than the rest of us. I would not be graduating but for her."[29] His graduation and what he represented were not taken lightly.

Sitting in the stands to watch Ernest Green graduate was Martin Luther King Jr.

June was to be a whirlwind, with another trip for Bates and the Nine. They arrived in New York on June 12 to receive an award from the Hotel and Restaurant Employees Union #6, AFL-CIO. In New York for five days, they visited the NAACP headquarters, where Bates introduced them to Roy Wilkins, and they appeared at NAACP functions in Brooklyn and Long Island. Bates picked up another award given by the Utility Club as "Woman of the Year."[30]

On May 30 the headline on the front page of the *State Press* announced: "STATE PRESS CONSIDERING QUITTING BUSINESS — LACK OF SUPPORT IS CAUSE." As Wilkins noted in a letter to an anguished supporter in July, Daisy and L. C. weren't blaming the NAACP.[31] The headline of the *State Press* was aimed at "Arkansas Negro citizens." In June, with the financial situation at the *State Press* deemed critical, Wilkins hired W. O. Bryson, a business consultant from Baltimore, and flew him to Little Rock to determine how much help it would take for the paper to survive. Daisy and L. C. were thinking of moving to Detroit, where they had been offered jobs, Daisy told the *Pittsburgh Courier* in June. "They've cut the circulation of our paper to its lowest point; they've frightened most of our advertisers away from us. They've intimidated our dealers; they've done everything they can to put us out of business. . . . They feel without us and our newspaper the whole thing will be dropped." Bryson's "management report," as he termed it, was completed on July 10. He found that "the gross income of the *Arkansas State Press* must reach the level of approximately $30.790.45 if the newspaper is to survive." This included a salary to L. C. and Daisy of just over $7,500 per year. Though it came as no surprise to them, he said that they would obtain practically all their advertising revenue "from sources outside Little Rock."[32] He identified by name thirty-nine advertisers between 1954 and 1957 who no longer advertised in the *State Press*. Based on Bryson's report, on July 22 the NAACP national office continued its support, sending Daisy another $1,500 check to be used for advertising.[33]

On June 20, 1958, federal judge Harry Lemley, a southerner who had replaced Ronald Davies of North Dakota as presiding judge over the case, granted the Little Rock School District's petition to delay integration in the school district for two and a half years. Ignoring the constitutional rights of the students, Lemley exonerated all the whites who had disrupted the implementation of the Little Rock School

Board's plan. Their behavior "did not stem from mere lawlessness . . . or to injure or persecute as individuals the nine Negro students in the school. Rather, the source of the trouble was the deep seated popular opposition in Little Rock to the principle of integration, which, as is known, runs counter to the pattern of Southern life which has existed for over three hundred years."[34]

As astonishing as Lemley's reasoning was, it made perfect sense to white southerners, whose idea of constitutional rights came color-coded. Lemley, agreeing with Virgil Blossom's testimony, concluded "that a tactical delay is not the same as a surrender. . . . In the two and one-half year period involved tempers will have a chance to cool down, emotions may subside to some extent, and there may be changes in some of the personalities involved in the dispute."[35] Lemley, who had practiced law in a small town in Arkansas before being appointed to the bench by Roosevelt in 1939 and who was said to "have loved the South 'almost as a religion,' " was referring primarily to Faubus. On cross-examination, Wayne Upton flatly testified that the board had chosen the time period of two and a half years because it was hoped Faubus would not be in office any longer.[36]

On June 27 the *Arkansas Democrat* reported that Chris Mercer had been fired as the NAACP's field representative. Bates was quoted as confirming that Mercer "is not with us any more." When asked if she would take the job, she responded, "I have enough to do."[37] It is not known if she even considered the idea. She and L. C. were both hoping the paper would be given enough outside help to survive.

When Bates was introduced on May 12 to President Eisenhower, his classic grin in place, the photograph shows Bates clasping his hand with both of her hands in a heartfelt gesture. The occasion was after a luncheon speech in Washington by Eisenhower to members of the black press. Bates was reported as saying to the president, "The children of Little Rock send you their love."[38] One wonders what Eisenhower actually thought of the woman whose fight had caused him so much trouble. It could not have been very flattering. Yet it surely galled Eisenhower to see Faubus swamp his hapless opponents in the Democratic primary, which was tantamount to election. The governor called his victory over two opponents in July "a condemnation by the people of illegal Federal intervention in the affairs of the state and the horrifying use of Federal bayonets in the streets of an American city and in the halls of a public school."[39] Arguably, the primary victory was more than that. Historian Tony Freyer has noted that "blacks in

Little Rock and across the state voted overwhelmingly for Faubus."[40] In Arkansas, it was business as usual: on July 18 Bates was hung in effigy at the county courthouse in Camden in southern Arkansas.

In June L. C.'s father died in a Memphis hospital at the age of seventy-six, and "Mother Bates," as she was known, would come stay with her only son and his wife. The funeral service had contained a plea from the minister, "who virtually called the father a casualty of this integration fight" to save the *State Press*. He "called for 100,000 new subscriptions."[41]

In August Daisy and the Nine traveled to Washington, D.C., for a week, guests of the Improved Benevolent Protective Order of the Elks of the World (IBPOEW), a black fraternal organization. They were in the city on August 18 when the Eighth Circuit Court of Appeals handed down its decision, overturning Judge Lemley's decision by a vote of six to one. However, the lone dissenter, Chief Judge Gardner, delayed immediate implementation of the order reversing the decision, and Thurgood Marshall asked for a hearing before the U.S. Supreme Court. Wilkins wired Bates that the "attorneys who will argue case Thursday feel very strongly that the students should not repeat should not be in the courtroom. We are depending on you to send them home as scheduled Wednesday." He further advised her not to comment on the case "if you remain for the argument. . . . Reporters and others should be referred to Marshall."[42] The NAACP legal team apparently did not want to appear as if it was attempting to influence the courts by extrajudicial means. Bates apparently came home as scheduled with the students. Normally, an appeal would have taken months, but the Supreme Court responded by calling a special session for September 11, since Central was due to open after the Labor Day holiday.

A whole year had passed, and the issue was still the same: federal power versus state power. The difference was that Faubus had been given a full twelve months to pound in the message that he, and by extension, whites in Arkansas were victims of an oppressive federal government that was usurping their rights as a majority. It was a message that had played well. Forgotten was the "progress" between the races that he had called attention to in his Labor Day speech a year earlier. Roy Reed has written, "Now, he was sliding into the separatist rhetoric that would mark his public discourse for years."[43] In total control of the legislature, he called a special session to clear the decks for a school-closing law to prevent integration should that become necessary. Citizens of Little Rock were now being asked to take a blind leap over a cliff—all for the right to maintain the principle of white supremacy, though those involved were careful never to characterize it in those terms.

On September 12, one day after oral arguments, the U.S. Supreme Court issued a three-paragraph order upholding the circuit court's decision. With the graduation of Ernest Green, the number of black students left to "integrate" the Little Rock School District was down to six, since the family of Terrence Roberts had arranged to get him into high school in Los Angeles. In *The Long Shadow of Little Rock*, Bates claimed that the "strain" had been too much for his family.[44] In an interview in 2002, Roberts said he had finished high school in Los Angeles because the schools were closed and not because of any pressure. Likely, Bates took any defections personally.

Faubus reacted to the Supreme Court's decision by signing into law the school-closing act, and he arranged to have an election set for September 27 to decide whether to close the schools in Little Rock or keep them open on an "integrated" basis. As presented to the voters, the choice was made to seem as if the alternative was immediate and total school integration, which, of course, was not at all the case. In response, new organizations sprouted up to try to influence the outcome of the election. The Save Our Schools (SOS) committee was a watered-down version of organizations like the White Citizens Council. Pretending to be neutral in the continuing fight between Faubus and the Little Rock School Board, it tried to undermine the NAACP's influence in the upcoming election by appealing publicly to blacks thought to be influential to "counsel with those who direct the activities of the NAACP in Arkansas [and] parents of the children, [and] recommend and urge that they be tolerant and not press their position too strongly at this critical time."[45]

The public appeal to the black community (as well as to whites thought sympathetic) to isolate the NAACP and at the same time to put pressure on Bates was blatant. Numerous ads were taken out in the *Arkansas Democrat*. Headlined "A SPECIAL MESSAGE ADDRESSED TO THE FOLLOWING COLORED CITIZENS OF ARKANSAS," "Reverend Harry Bass" and other blacks thought sympathetic were mentioned by name. "The key to the present grave situation which has developed and exists at the present time, is in the hands of your race, the parents of the seven colored children and Mrs. L. C. Bates."[46] It did not work. Though the vote was overwhelming to close the Little Rock schools (19,470 to 7,561), black voters helped carry five of the wards that voted to keep the schools open.

Faubus's plan, now that the voters had expressed their wishes, was to reopen the schools in Little Rock as a private corporation, but this transparent effort to avoid desegregation would ultimately go nowhere. When lawyers for the Little Rock School Board filed a motion with the federal court asking whether the public schools could be privately leased by the Little Rock School Board without being in contempt of the court's order, Faubus charged that the Little Rock School Board was colluding with the NAACP. "I have it on good authority that Marshall prepared [the motion to be filed in court], handed it to Daisy Bates who handed it to Virgil Blossom." Faubus made this charge without presenting any evidence for his claim, and attorneys for the school board categorically denied his allegation.[47] Faubus was furious. He had wanted the Little Rock School Board to turn over the keys to the schoolhouse door to him per the legislation passed by the special session. There was no collusion between the NAACP and the Little Rock School Board, and the NAACP filed suit almost immediately, challenging the school corporation law. It would be months before it obtained a ruling, and the schools stayed closed for the entire year. The Little Rock School Board went ahead and signed a lease with the private school corporation, but this would be nullified by the federal courts.[48]

Though the margin of Faubus's victory was substantial, a coalition of white Little Rock women and their male supporters had come together to fight Faubus. Known as the Women's Emergency Committee (WEC), this group would have more success the next year. With its initial meeting at the home of Adolphine Terry, plans to enlist black women in the organization were quickly abandoned after "several women in the audience quietly left."[49] A lily-white organization was tactically necessary, though it did not set well with blacks who were initially sympathetic. Historian Laura Miller has shown that "many of the first contributions" to the WEC were from blacks, who "sharply curtailed" their donations after learning the organization was segregated. In her interview with Elizabeth Jacoway in 1976, Bates was of the opinion that Vivion Brewer, one of the WEC leaders, had wanted her "and the black community to turn over control of the movement to the white community, to these liberal members of the white community."[50] The day was coming when WEC would be victorious, but as necessary as its tactics were to its success, its failure to include black women obviously left a bad taste in Bates's mouth.

Shutting down the high schools in Little Rock hurt many children but especially African Americans who had fewer resources. Neither

L. C. nor Daisy could understand how whites were so willing to punish their own children. After the election, the *State Press* editorialized, "We never anticipated their speaking out in defense of Negro children, but we did think they would come to the defense of their own children."[51]

Of the original Little Rock Nine, six were left who would have gone to Central during 1957–58. Five of the six—Carlotta Walls, Jefferson Thomas, Thelma Mothershed, Elizabeth Eckford, and Melba Pattillo—took correspondence courses from the University of Arkansas. The lost school year was particularly frustrating for all concerned, but Bates wrote nothing in her memoir about her interaction with the remaining six. She did describe some of the retribution encountered by the parents, but if she asked for assistance from the NAACP national office for them, it is not apparent from her papers. It would not have been granted anyway. The NAACP was paying good money to try to save Daisy and L. C. as well as the state organization. During this period, Wilkins continued to keep the coffers of Bates's operation filled by maintaining a balance of $1,000 in the Arkansas State Conference of Branches account. "Their fund is down to $237 and the Little Rock situation will make further demands upon our Arkansas officials."[52] In a letter to a supporter, Wilkins revealed that payments had been made the previous fall to pay off Daisy's state tax problems and "to purchase a quantity of newsprint which was being held up by the jobber." Further, the letter showed Wilkins had committed the organization to paying $3,000 for advertising, to be spread out over a year's period.[53]

It was in this period that Faubus was mentioning Bates by name as the reason for the continuing upheaval. "If Daisy Bates would go to work and get an honest job, and if the U.S. would keep its cotton-picking hands off the Little Rock School Board's affairs, we could open the Little Rock (public) schools," Bates quoted him—as saying.[54]

One result of Faubus's singling Bates out for special attention was that it gave license to the persons who harassed her and L. C. In early October she made the news by claiming to have fired her pistol at an intruder who was not content to throw one rock at a window and then run. She told a reporter from the *Pittsburgh Courier* that when she and L. C., roused by the sound of a rock crashing into a window, came outside, she saw a man poised to throw again. In all, she said she fired five shots at him as he ran and jumped into a car and sped off.[55] As often occurred, the incident became part of her presentation for a time, and she shaped the story to fit the point she was making as well as the image she wished to project. Speaking in Washington, D.C., at the Metropolitan Baptist Church the week afterward, Bates told her audience she "saw this person with hate and bitterness on his face and a picture of Governor Faubus flashed through my mind. I realized he had said blood would flow. I told myself . . . I will have to live with myself and I will not let them make a murderer out of me."[56] Like most people, when Bates spoke at churches, she became a bit more saintly. She would say in the future that she and L. C. never aimed at anyone, knowing if they shot one of their white harassers what kind of trouble she would be buying. The story in the *Pittsburgh Courier* illustrated the differences between the Little Rock police, over which Faubus had no control, and the State Police, which was run like a gestapo. The night before Bates fired at the intruder in October, "police had provided protection" at the house "for a while," but not the night she fired her pistol. The fact that Daisy and L. C. received any protection at all from the Little Rock police said much about the Chief of Police Gene Smith, whom Bates came to respect as she did few whites in Little Rock. Because of his willingness to try to protect the Little Rock Nine and enforce the law even-handedly, Smith became almost as persecuted as Bates herself.

Making the November cover of *Ebony* in 1958 meant Bates continued to be an important symbol of social justice for blacks throughout the country. She had to like the words on the cover: "First Lady of Little Rock." Written by Lerone Bennett Jr., himself a celebrity in the black world, Bates had "become a name known around the world but few know the real woman." The article was as glowing as it was mythical. "She has the public-relations know-how of the late Walter White, the ideological nimbleness of the Rev. Martin Luther King and the biting tongue of the late Mary McLeod Bethune." No accolade was too strong. "During one of the greatest constitutional crises in American history, she wielded as much power as has been given to any woman of her time."[57]

As usual now in interviews, Bates dropped seven years from her age and gave her foster father's name as Orlee Gatson. To avoid embarrassing her and himself, L. C. was complicit in the fiction that he had first met Daisy "around 1933."[58] Always hungry for heroes, the black press was not about to probe too deeply into their past.

In an interview with the *Minneapolis Sunday Tribune* during this period, she gave a slightly different version of when and where she had met L. C. Buried in the article runs this account by Carl Rowan, then a staff writer before becoming a nationally syndicated columnist: "Daisy

Bates finished high school and became so busy trying to earn a living in Memphis, Tenn. that she gave little thought to those childhood days until she met L. C. Bates, a specialist in advertising and public relations. Shortly after marriage they moved to Little Rock."[59] In the end, it matters little where they met, but when it came time to write her book, the story of having met L. C. in Memphis where she was working had disappeared, and the romantic, sweet account of L. C. calling on her father to sell him an insurance policy, bringing her trinkets as a young girl, and gradually holding her hand in the movies had taken its place.

There are revealing glimpses of their domestic life in the *Ebony* story as Bates wanted it portrayed. Johnnie McFarlan, Daisy and L. C.'s housekeeper, is shown serving them dinner. Bates talked about the ceramics she enjoyed.[60] They liked movies but said they had not been to a single one in Little Rock, where there were no black theaters. They were not about to sit in a segregated balcony. It was almost as if Bates could not decide which aspect she wanted to emphasize the most—the well-brought-up publisher's wife or the tough civil rights advocate. Yet having the chance to reach a national black audience, Bates did not pull any punches about civil rights. "The majority of professional people . . . are making their living off the masses and they are certainly not giving enough back in return." It was in this interview that Bates appears to have first noted publicly, and would repeat more than once, the observation that a black female leader can "get away with more in the South than a Negro man."[61]

Though at least two of her "children," as she called the Nine, would later say that Bates focused much of the attention on herself, she told Bennett, "The children and parents involved must be cultivated and spotlighted. . . . The children came from good homes; they were taught how to act. The rest was easy."[62]

Though Bates had probably not started *The Long Shadow of Little Rock* by the time of the *Ebony* interview, she had already developed one of the main themes: her foster father had been the one who taught her not to hate. The story of the purchase of meat as a child appears here, as it had in other interviews. There is not one word in the six-page story about the woman who raised her. In the *Ebony* interview, the impetus to get out of Huttig comes from her foster father. Bennett wrote, "He decided to send her way for a spell. Travel would help her. It would broaden her mind. Daisy went to Memphis, and then she went up North. She visited Canada, where Orlee had friends. And she began to understand that some white people are civilized. The hurt and hate dissolved, but Daisy never did forget."[63] There is no mention here of her birth mother being raped and murdered, nor is it mentioned in any of her other interviews. When it came time to write her book, the single incident of the butcher making her wait must have seemed to her ghostwriters too garden-variety a story to support the rage against whites Bates said she felt as a child. As mentioned earlier, the story about her mother's rape and murder does not appear in the pages of the *Huttig News*. Why didn't this story surface in the in-depth interviews she gave to the black press? If one believes Bates's story that her mother was raped and murdered, a possible explanation for this omission is that in her effort to present herself as the "First Lady of Little Rock," Bates may have been loathe to admit that her birth parents were never married. Or it may never have happened.

What emerges from the story given to Carl Rowan for the *Minneapolis Sunday Tribune* is Bates's deep understanding of the resentment many whites in Little Rock felt toward her and L. C. "They'll never really forgive us. . . . They can never really forgive a Negro for doing what we have done. We have called forth pride and boldness in these youngsters who have dared to demand their constitutional rights through the courts. Negroes are supposed to be too humble to do that, so they can never forgive us." "Subservient" or "cowed" would have served equally as well as "humble." Even almost a year before the *State Press* was closed, she knew it was doomed. She told Rowan, "We know that even though the threat of violence may subside, we'll never be able to stay in Arkansas and make a living."[64]

As Bates had wanted, Roy Wilkins flew into Little Rock the first weekend in November to see her reelected as the president of the Arkansas NAACP. He told an audience of "several hundred" on November 2 that "the opposition is flopping about, but it knows it doesn't have a leg to stand on."[65] Brave words, but he might better have said that it is darkest before the dawn. Despite what the Supreme Court said, there was not a black student at Central, and Faubus was on the verge of winning his third term in the general election, with black support. In addition, the attacks on Daisy and L. C. continued. The *State Press* noted that a recent effort to set the house afire marked the seventh time someone had tried to burn it down, in addition to the scores of times the house had been attacked. Rowan's November 1958 article told readers of the condition of the house. "Its picture windows are dotted with pieces of cardboard, taped on to cover holes made by stones before the extra protection of a fine-meshed steel screen was nailed on."[66]

Despite the fact there were no headlines coming out of Arkansas, Bates was still in demand as a speaker. In November she was in Louisiana, St. Louis, Tampa, and Cincinnati. The news from Arkansas was dismal. As expected, the Arkansas Supreme Court in December upheld her conviction (as well as that of Birdie Williams, president of the North Little Rock NAACP) for not turning over NAACP records. The case was on its way to the Supreme Court. The situation in the Little Rock schools appeared hopeless. Though Virgil Blossom and the Little Rock School Board had given the people of Little Rock token desegregation of the schools, which was all their opponents could have expected, his contract was bought out on November 12, 1958, and five of the six members turned in their resignations. An election on December 6 left the board evenly divided between the radical segregationists and the so-called moderates.

No matter how optimistic Roy Wilkins sounded in public, privately he was worried, and rightly so, about the implications for the rest of the South should Daisy and L. C. be forced to close the *State Press*. The national office had "already invested more than $3,000 in advertising in the paper," he wrote supporters on December 11, but "a minimum of $15,000 a year in advertising" would be required to sustain it. If the *State Press* shut down, it would not only leave a vacuum in Arkansas, "moreover, it would discourage other Negro newspapers in the South from participating actively in the civil rights struggle. The voice of the southern Negro would then be effectively silenced to the glee of the White Citizens Councils and other segregationists."[67]

As dismal as all this was, the most glittering social event of Bates's life came on December 26 in Philadelphia, when she accepted the Diamond Cross of Malta Award at the tenth annual Christmas Cotillion, a Philadelphia society event. Bates, whose dress was made for the occasion and donated to her by a Philadelphia designer, "fought tears" and spoke in a "faltering voice" as she accepted the award from the cream of Philadelphia society. L. C. accompanied her. What he thought of the extravaganza, which featured a cast of 900 performers, is not known, but the event held at Convention Hall with 7,000 people in attendance would always remain a highlight of her life.[68] It would be a good way to end another hellish year.

Chapter Fourteen

COPING WITH DEFEAT

As the calendar turned over to 1959, Daisy Bates may have guessed what a fateful year it was to be for her and L. C. On January 29 she wrote Roy Wilkins that she would be in New York on "February 1, to address the Great Neck Branch. I will leave for Lakeville, [Conn.,] Monday. I plan to drop by the office Monday morning, and if it is at all possible, I would like to see you for a few minutes."[1] What Bates wanted to say in private to Wilkins is not known. Most likely, it was about money. Though there would be no black students in the Little Rock School District until the fall of 1959, the national office faithfully continued to underwrite the Arkansas State Conference of Branches. In actuality, Daisy and L. C. were being subsidized, for the checks were sent directly to her. She spent the money on everything from guards for the house to travel for the NAACP.

Though she was increasingly out of town for longer periods of time, Bates still needed to watch her back in the black community. Every few months Little Rock blacks outside the NAACP still continued to try to speak on behalf of the black community on school integration matters. I. S. McClinton, president of the Arkansas Democratic (Negro) Voters League, brazenly told reporters on January 22, "We would accept anything that legal counsel for both parties agreed to." The implication was that McClinton had authority to speak for the parents. Bates set the press straight. "He is simply speaking for himself as a private citizen," she said. "We already have a plan."[2] The so-called Blossom plan was hardly what the NAACP had wanted, but it was all that was on the table in Little Rock. Bates was its jealous guardian, a fact that did not make everyone in the black community happy. Ozell Sutton, who considered L. C. a mentor and would later assume a leadership role in the early 1960s, remembered, "Daisy Bates was a leader for the Negroes in the contending forces concerned with integration, but there was definite disagreement within the Negro community over her tactics and her personality. However, there was never any public disagreement because of the unanimity of commitment to desegregation. Because the community power was centered in Daisy Bates, she made arbitrary decisions."[3]

Increasingly, Bates was involved with the national board. In March she agreed to "accept membership on the special Committee of Fifty," a fund-raising project that required each member to raise $5,000. It was explained that the $250,000 the committee was to bring into the NAACP's coffers was over and above the regular fundraising goal. Given the finances of the *State Press*, taking on this responsibility seemed an arbitrary commitment to make, but Bates obviously saw no inconsistency. Similarly, she volunteered to help A. Philip Randolph in preparing for a "Youth March for integrated Schools," scheduled for April 18 in Washington, D.C. Randolph wrote her that though he knew how difficult it would be to arrange, "a small delegation from Little Rock on April 18 would have tremendous effect and would electrify everyone. For Little Rock remains at the focus of this entire struggle."[4] Bates was listed as one of the "chairman," along with such notables as Harry Belafonte, Sidney Poitier, Martin Luther King Jr., Jackie Robinson, Norman Thomas, and Walter Reuther.

Bates's attitude about money was that those who had it should feel privileged to give it to a worthy cause. Without ever quite needing to say so, she accepted contributions from others as her due. First, her foster father had provided for her, and then L. C. had done the same. Though she would make it appear that her courses at Shorter College had prepared her to cope in the business world, her behavior indicated that she was somewhat above it all. In her mind, she was serious when she said that her father had prepared her to be a "lady." As Chris Mercer said, Bates did not have any skills. She had no nose for the bottom line. This cavalier attitude toward the grubbier aspects of daily life would finally catch up with her after L. C. died and was not there to protect her from the bad advice of others, but that was almost a quarter of a century later. Bates, for all her tactical skills, was a trusting soul.

As time went on, it became apparent that Bates was not on the same wavelength with every parent of the Nine. The NAACP national office had never filled the field secretary's position in Arkansas that had been left vacant after Chris Mercer was fired. Gloria Ray's mother, Julia Ray, applied for the position. She had apparently crossed Bates by withdrawing Gloria when it appeared the Little Rock schools were going to be closed. Presumably, she wanted to enroll her daughter somewhere else, just as the parents of Terrence Roberts had done. Though she never said so, clearly Bates felt a sense of betrayal. She wrote Gloster Current that Julia Ray was "unreasonable." Bates found her to be "temperamentally unsuited, as well as impatient," and could not recommend her for the job.[5] One of the first social workers ever hired by the state of Arkansas, Julia Ray was one of the parents who lost her job as a result of her daughter being one of the Nine. These bad feelings may have rubbed off on her daughter, for, according to Elizabeth Eckford, in later years there was a time when Gloria "wouldn't even be in the same room" with Bates.[6] The NAACP was in no hurry to fill the position and left it vacant until L. C. was given the job in 1960.

The details surrounding Bates's book contract with the David McKay Company unfortunately remain a mystery, due to the policy of the publishing industry to refuse to release information without the consent of the author's estate, which was not given. However, Bates's papers reveal that she most likely signed a contract with the company in May 1959. She was advised in a letter by her new friend and admirer Pauli Murray not to represent herself.[7] It appears that David McKay wanted her to have a completed manuscript by the end of the year. Murray advised her to insist that January 1 was a "target date subject to developments in [the] Little Rock situation and the demands upon your time and energy."[8]

McKay naturally wanted a book as soon as the company could get one. It likely thought that with her journalistic background, Bates was an experienced writer who would have little difficulty in organizing an engrossing narrative of her life intertwined with her experiences with the Little Rock Nine. The book would not be published until the fall of 1962, after as many as four ghostwriters had worked on it. The effort to complete it would change her life. Her correspondence with Roy Wilkins reveals that she had met with him before she signed the book deal with McKay. "Based on our conference in April, I signed a contract to write 'The Little Rock Story,' and cancelled all but two speaking engagements." Bates had taken such a step thinking that the NAACP would continue to subsidize the *State Press* at least through the end of the year, when she expected to have the book completed. In July she would remind Wilkins that he had "promised that the organization would supplement our income of $600 per month until December 31, 1959."[9] According to Bates, he had informed her in May that "the board had authorized advertising space for May, June and July."[10] The difficulty was that the *State Press* was becoming a bottomless financial pit that almost no amount of subsidy could rescue.

An incident in the South in May 1959 that received national attention reveals that Wilkins's financial support for Bates did not come without a price. In Monroe, North Carolina, the judicial system in separate cases had allowed two white males charged with brutally assaulting two black women to go unpunished. It was too much for Robert F. Williams, president of the Monroe NAACP branch. Williams had seen black women abused one too many times. He told the press immediately afterward: "We must be willing to kill if necessary. We cannot take these people who do us injustice to the court and it becomes necessary to punish them ourselves."[11]

In New York, Wilkins understandably had a problem on his hands because of Williams's stance, which was at odds with the NAACP's traditional reliance on America's judicial system. Instead of papering over the dispute with Williams, within a day Wilkins had suspended him from his position as president and seemed intent on making an example of him. But if Wilkins thought he could snap his fingers and demand support from members to expel a branch president under these circumstances, he was badly mistaken. For example, the *State Press* did not take a position on Wilkins's action. "We do know . . . it is pretty hard to suppress certain feelings, when all around you, you see only hate."[12] After some equivocation, L. C., surely with Daisy's concurrence, suggested that this was a matter for the national NAACP board. To add insult to injury, Bates did not attend the next board meeting or send Wilkins a telegram supporting his position. She was not the only one not to support Wilkins. Bates, however, was not going to be allowed to get off the hook so easily. In his excellent *Radio Free Dixie: Robert F. Williams and the Roots of Black Power*, Timothy B. Tyson has documented the pressure brought to gain her support. Working through Kelly Alexander, a board member, Wilkins "scold[ed] her for not having attended the earlier board meeting and for failing to send a telegram of support." The letter from Alexander further "demanded her 'utmost cooperation to put a stop to Mr. Robert Williams.' " Tyson writes that Bates "cut a deal" with Wilkins.[13] In any event, not only did the board vote to sustain Wilkins's suspension of Williams, Bates took the floor at the national convention in July at a crucial moment in the debate over Williams and carried the day for Wilkins's supporters. "Mounting the podium, Bates denounced Williams for betraying the ideals of nonviolence and for endangering the success of the movement. . . . Bates turned the insurgent tide and sealed the vote against Williams."[14] Just weeks earlier she had admitted she had shot at people who had attacked her home.

Williams got the last word. Two years later at a rally in New York on the anniversary of the *Brown* decision, Williams's supporters drowned out Bates's remarks and prevented her from speaking. Roy Wilkins was hit with an egg.[15]

Despite her financial problems in 1959 and the compromises needed to deal with them, Bates stayed involved in the lives of most of the original Nine. Three of the students were to spend part of the summer in St. Louis and attend school under the supervision of the St. Louis NAACP. Bates had asked her friend Frankie Freeman "to sort of act as Big Mama" to the girls. Freeman offered to allow the girls to live in her home. Due to a board meeting in New York and "other engagements during the same week," Bates was unable to travel with them as she had originally planned.[16]

Throughout this period Bates was called upon to handle the finances of the educational trust and make the disbursements to the educational institutions. The children, some of whom were now leaving for college, were dependent on her to get the checks out to pay their expenses. Allowing for the necessity to maintain Bates's goodwill, one often encounters a genuine note of affection for her in their correspondence with her while they were in college and making the adjustment to a much less regimented life. While she remained in Little Rock, Bates faithfully discharged this responsibility, using the secretaries at the *State Press* (until it closed) to take dictation, as was her custom.

Melba Pattillo was going to Chicago to summer school, and Bates made arrangements for her, too, through the NAACP there.[17] The NAACP reached out to those of the Nine who wanted their help. Melba's mother could easily have written the letter herself, but it was Bates who had the contacts and who attended to the details. The children were still her project. She saw it as her mission to have them stick it out. The first year had been tantamount to establishing a beachhead that had to be maintained at all costs. Minnijean Brown had been a casualty and had been honorably evacuated. Summer school was a necessity for some to assure that they progressed to the next grade level when they returned to Central. To do so, Bates had arranged for tutors for those of the Nine who needed them during the "lost" year.[18]

Though Bates was naturally offended by the WEC's policy of excluding blacks from participation in its organization, that did not keep her from working in June to turn out voters at a special recall election of school board members. The "three radical segregationists" (as Roy Reed has dubbed them in his book on Faubus) on the Little Rock School Board had finally crossed the line by trying to fire forty-four teachers and employees whose sympathies for maintaining the "southern way of life" at all costs were suspect. Thus anyone believed to have shown sympathy to the Nine were on the hit list, including the school administrators at Central, Jess Matthews, Elizabeth Huckaby, and J. O. Powell.

Bates was even threatened with arrest on the streets of Little Rock on May 25 for passing out leaflets urging people to vote.[19] It was well worth the effort. The effort to recall the "three radical segregationists" on the board was successful, but just barely, with the margins in each race razor thin. Historian Tony Freyer has noted that making this "victory possible was the traditional pattern of black and high-income wards voting together. The election broke the power of the governor and his supporters over the Little Rock school system."[20] Then on June 18 a three-judge federal court overruled the Arkansas Supreme Court and held unconstitutional the school-closing law. The way was now open to move forward or at least maintain the status quo.

Bates continued to make news in the black press in 1959. In a speech to the Negro Georgia State Medical Association in Atlanta in June, which was reported by the *Afro-American*, Bates "noted that in Little Rock the doctors were not among those who could be counted upon to stand up and fight." The headline quoted part of her message that a person "can't measure human dignity by a big car." If L. C. had no qualms about instructing the black masses about how to behave with his weekly cartoon of "dos and don'ts," Bates did not hesitate to criticize wealthy African Americans who held themselves back from the struggle. She was quoted as saying, "Men who have lost their jobs in the desegregation fight have not had the professional classes behind them." "If you do not have the courage to put your name on a petition," she told the doctors, "you have the money to back those who work to make desegregation a fact in the United States."[21]

White politicians in the North continued to score points (as did black politicians) with their constituents by making sure they were photographed with Bates. Massachusetts attorney general Edward J. McCormack was shown dancing with Bates at a function sponsored by the Boston NAACP at the Sherry-Biltmore Hotel in May. The entire Massachusetts legislature honored her.[22]

In the spring of 1959, as Bates was making repeated trips to New York, she was naturally attracted to the Greenwich Village area, whose liberal residents welcomed her with open arms. At an NAACP rally in June in Washington Square, Bates shared the podium with the playwright Lorraine Hansberry (who had written *Raisin in the Sun*), and the two were to become good friends.

Bates's enemies in Little Rock had not forgotten her. On July 6 the *New York Post* reported another bomb blast on the lawn, and Bates complained loudly about the failure of the government to protect her. "We've asked the city and county and gotten no place. And of course it would do no good to ask the state. I'm tired of these hoodlums. You never know from week to week when they'll strike."[23] Actually, the Little Rock police department had occasionally watched the house but was not about to provide a permanent guard. Fed up, as a last resort, Bates wired the Department of Justice for help. It turned her down, as did the president.[24]

The publisher of the *Amsterdam News*, C. P. Powell, responding to the news of the latest bomb blast, put a $100 check in the mail to Bates, whom he had met recently when she came to the offices of the paper. More important, he said he wanted to run an editorial setting out her plight and suggesting supporters send a contribution. Bates accepted his offer. It would not be the only one. People from all over, learning of their plight, sent small amounts to her and L. C.

In June there were signs for the first time publicly that all was not well within the Bates household. L. C. told *Jet* magazine that he "estimates he now sees his wife an average of six days a month—if her schedule is not too demanding."[25] It was a tough time in a long period of tough times. The *State Press* was down to 6,000 in circulation; there were now only four employees. L. C. spent his nights alone, guarding the house with occasional help from friends, while his wife was off making speeches. It was not an ideal way to sustain a marriage. In the *Jet* article, Daisy was pictured among her awards, L. C. reading the *State Press*. The title of the article was "L. C. Bates: Little Rock's Forgotten Man."

Bates plugged away at her commitment to raise her share of the $250,000 for the NAACP. On June 26 she wrote Kivie Kaplan, the chair of the committee, "I finally returned to Little Rock last Monday, after an absence of almost one month."[26] She had sold two "life" memberships ($500), one to her new friend Lorraine Hansberry, and got another commitment later from Lionel Hampton. She was getting to the point where she was meeting herself coming and going, since the NAACP convention was being held in New York in early July. As far as her book went, by July Daisy had gotten through a draft of only her first chapter, which she had asked Benjamin Fine to read. On July 23 he wrote her that he was "much impressed" with it and tried to buck up her spirits. She must have already been having doubts about her ability to write a book. "I know you will do a magnificent job in your subsequent chapters," he wrote.[27] It was a warm, cordial letter, and he invited her to visit his family on subsequent trips to New York. Bates needed all the encouragement she could get, for on August 3 she wrote to Carolyn Anthony, then an editorial assistant at David McKay, "I have had little or no time to devote to the 'Daisy Bates Story,' much to my regret."[28] It is not known when the working title of her memoir became the "Daisy Bates Story," but that is how she would subsequently refer to her work in progress.

If people were generous to Bates, she was invariably generous to others who asked for her help. An unhappy young friend named Julia Owen apparently called her to tell her some personal problem, and Bates paid for her transportation to Little Rock for her to stay at the Bates's house.[29] One wonders how Daisy explained her generosity to L. C., who at this time was only months from closing the doors at the *State Press*. The truth was that if Daisy wanted something, he was glad to give it to her. Perhaps this was the only way he felt he was going to hold on to his glamorous wife. How long her guest stayed or what her circumstances were is not known.

The NAACP conference in New York in the middle of July could not have been easy for Bates. First, she was tired, was running a fever, and came home "with the worst cold I have had in years."[30] She had come home early because she'd received word that the Little Rock School Board was trying to outsmart Faubus by opening the schools early, and she needed to ensure that Little Rock black students would register for Central and Hall high schools.

It was believed that Faubus would try to call a session of the legislature and close the schools again. Thus, while she was ill, she had to go about seeing that black children applied to enroll in Central and Hall. In a letter to Wilkins on July 29, she explained that she and Sybil Jordan, a tenth grade student (now head of the Rockefeller Foundation in Little Rock), had contacted parents and students, and a total of fifty-six black students had registered for the fall. Once again Clarence Laws came to Little Rock to help out. He went with two board members to try to persuade "parents in person, while we continued to work on the phone."[31] Bates claimed that they had been successful in getting "our top scholastic-quality pupils to register at both Hall and Central. After much persuasion and a little pressure, we were able to get two of our leading ministers to register their children."[32]

It was in this letter that Bates reminded Wilkins of his commitment to the *State Press*. Apparently at the board meeting she had just attended, the board of directors had balked at continuing to subsidize the paper. "With the board's position, and without the earnings from the speaking engagements, it leaves us in a pretty tight spot."[33]

The schools would open in Little Rock on August 11, but only two of the original Nine, Jefferson Thomas and Carlotta Walls, were reassigned to Central under the pupil assignment law. Only three black girls (again, none of the Nine) were assigned to Hall High School. The Little Rock School District was committed to tokenism, but given the racial climate, it would be an accomplishment to open the schools at all. Since Carlotta Walls was still in summer school in St. Louis, Jefferson Thomas would have to go it alone for the first few days.

In 1959 Bates knew she would be writing about the events that were taking place. However, the portion of her book dealing with the school year of 1959–60 is truncated and reads almost like an afterthought. It lacks the high drama of those heady days when troops of the 101st Airborne had escorted the Nine, their heads held high, into Central. Still, the beginning of the school year was exciting enough. This time there were no federal troops, no National Guard, only the police force under the command of the courageous police chief, Gene Smith. He ordered fire hoses turned on the howling mob of approximately 1,000, who waved Confederate flags and raised signs that demanded, "GOVERNOR FAUBUS SAVE OUR CHRISTIAN AMERICA."[34] Bates recorded that she spent part of that morning in Jefferson Thomas's house. Present were Thomas, his mother, and visitors Elizabeth Eckford and Minnijean Brown. Bates described how she and the others watched as Jefferson Thomas's father, accompanied by Carl Rowan, the columnist for the *Minneapolis Tribune*, drove off to Central that morning with his son. Within minutes a report on the radio described an on-going battle at the school: twenty-four demonstrators were arrested. "[Jefferson's mother] ran from the room, sobbing pitifully. No one tried to console her. No one knew what to say."[35] Jefferson Thomas made it safely inside, but of course that was just the beginning of another trial by fire.

As she had done two years earlier, Bates provided a haven for sympathetic black reporters. That night she described the scene at her house. L. C. was broiling a steak while Carl Rowan was making a salad. "Ted Poston of the *New York Post* was pecking out a story in the front bedroom. . . . Ted had laid claim to the bedroom. He called it 'Ted's Post.' He virtually set up shop there and usually worked far into the night."[36] As always, Bates treated the black reporters like kings and, in turn, was rewarded with great press. After two of the volunteers guards (Jefferson Thomas's father and dentist and neighbor Garman Freeman) and a paid guard, Isaac Mullen, a special deputy sheriff, were arrested and taken into custody for carrying concealed weapons, Bates again wired President Eisenhower for help, saying in part, "Now state police have begun to arrest and harass the upstanding citizens who have provided us with volunteer protection, leaving us defenseless before those who constantly threaten our lives."[37] Probably with justification, Bates believed the men had been lured into a trap. Eisenhower, having learned his lesson the hard way, was not about to intervene in Little Rock again. Bates admitted as much, telling her reporter friend Ted Poston that night, "I have just been informed that the President will not answer my appeal." Bates was at her wit's end. Asked by Poston what help she required, she responded, "I don't care how they do it. They can set up a machine gun in my front yard if they want to. I'm just tired of all these harassments."[38]

Unlike 1957, when Bates did not make a move without the advice of the NAACP national office or her attorneys, she now made some decisions that brought her into conflict with Wiley Branton, who was still serving as local counsel. Trying to increase the number of black students at Central and Hall, Bates had advised those who had applied for admission to Central and Hall to stay out of school until they had a hearing before the school board.[39] A number of them had agreed to do so. Bates arranged a meeting for the parents with Branton on August 25. Branton surprised and irritated her by saying the children should be in school.

Bates responded by criticizing him in a letter the next day and copied Roy Wilkins, Thurgood Marshall, and Robert Carter. "I didn't appreciate your advising them [parents] to send their children to Horace Mann." According to the letter, Branton had told the group, "The children ought to be in school getting an education," to which Bates replied in the letter, "You should have discussed it with me and the committee that worked night and day getting the children interested and registered."[40]

Branton had obviously embarrassed Bates before the parents, but it was unlike her not to have worked this out with the attorneys and the NAACP in advance. Bates's reason for advising parents to keep their children out of school was that once they were enrolled at Horace Mann, "they will have a hell of a time getting a transfer." She had convinced nineteen children (and their parents) to remain out of school, but she had not walked away from them afterward. In fact, she had resumed the same activities of two years earlier and listed them for Branton:

> You are not aware of the many problems that I face daily getting tutors for the children in Hall and Central; keeping a day to day record of the intimidations, getting the information to the source that will help eliminate the intimidation, because all of the people who are involved with the safety of the children are not sympathetic; holding separate weekly meetings with children who are not in school and their parents; conference with the local, national and foreign press' [sic] meeting with interested groups from the white community, acknowledging the large volume of mail.[41]

This was vintage Bates but with a jarring difference. She was obviously freelancing, whereas before almost all her actions had been thoroughly choreographed in advance with the NAACP in New York. Whether this reflected the national office's lack of attention to Little Rock at the time or whether Bates had become so certain of her judgment that she thought she need not consult anyone in advance is not clear. Though she mentions that Clarence Laws had come to Little Rock to help her contact parents, there is no indication that he remained in town and was involved in the decision to have the students who had applied to Central or Hall stay out of school. More important, she had disregarded Branton's advice not to have students who might intervene in the litigation file appeals to the Little Rock School Board, once their requests to transfer to white schools had been denied. Two years earlier she would not have acted so boldly. Now there was no longer a local active network around her that had input into these decisions. Years earlier, members of the Little Rock chapter had solicited students and parents to set up the litigation that became *Aaron v. Cooper* and had carefully worked out each move in advance with their lawyers. The Arkansas NAACP had basically stopped functioning, according to the financial records for the second half of July through October. The Little Rock branch raised the paltry sum of $50 during this period. No other branch in the state raised any money.

The radical segregationists in Arkansas had accomplished their mission of destroying the NAACP without being aware of it. If they had been successful in forcing Bates to turn over her records, they would have realized they had reduced the organization to a shell.

The NAACP in Arkansas had taken a tremendous battering over the preceding two years. But there was another factor operating as well. Bates had been gone so much from Arkansas that it is fair to say she was neglecting the organization inside the state, when once it had been her passion. Now she had other commitments: a book to write, fund-raising chores for the national organization, constant travel. It is likely, too, that she no longer was running matters by L. C. as routinely she had in the past. Now he was mentioned in correspondence with the national office only in passing ("Mr. Thomas and I were out last night until after 10:30 P.M., much to my husband's disapproval with the recent shootings and arrests.").[42]

Her autocratic behavior earned Bates a stinging rebuke from her attorney. On August 29, making sure to copy Roy Wilkins, Thurgood Marshall, and Robert Carter, Wiley Branton referred to her letter of August 26 "in which you write a partial autobiography of Queen Daisy." He accused her of putting the NAACP "in a difficult position because of your failure to follow legal advice." Though she was doing an "outstanding job . . . you are not a lawyer and the sooner you realize that, then the sooner our work can be coordinated."[43]

It would be a while before her increasingly imperial way of doing things would fully catch up with her. Her base of support in Arkansas had always been narrow, but it had been rock solid because of the internal strength of the organization. Now she was relying on some of the parents of the Nine and students of the youth organization of the NAACP, to whom she was like a god. She no longer had a person who served as a reality check—someone who could have told her that the "boycott" was an idea that should have been fully discussed with the national office and her attorneys. When someone as responsible and judicious as Branton dared to express his opinion to the parents (she had invited him to talk to them), she rebuked him and made sure her criticism reached the ears of the national office. The old Bates never would have behaved in such a manner. Of course, the old Bates had not been chosen "Woman of the Year" or received honor after honor. Who could have resisted internalizing all the wonderful things that had been said about her week after week by some very influential people for the past two years? The attention would have turned anyone's head. Bates's response to Branton was weak in the extreme: Branton had not consulted her in advance.

The years 1958 and 1959 were a difficult period for others as well. Two years of stirring the racial pot by Faubus and the radical segregationists had emboldened that element in Little Rock, which was already prone to violence. Roy Reed has described as well as anyone the climate of fear that enveloped Little Rock during the years that Faubus rode the racial issue. He details how it transformed Faubus from a man who had been cautiously supportive of the aspirations of blacks to someone who could allow himself to believe that their efforts to vindicate their constitutional and human rights were part of a vast Communist conspiracy when there was no meaningful evidence to support this view. Reed writes, "it is clear from his actions and statements at the time that he was motivated by something deeper than cynicism. For a period of some years, he became a true believer. He had chosen sides. He fought with every weapon he could find."[44] As governor, Faubus controlled the State Police as well as a number of boards and commissions. Before he was through, he would control them all, but the State Police, through its Criminal Investigation Division (CID), allowed him to investigate anyone who might be even remotely connected with African Americans who were involved in civil rights activities. As Reed documents, "Anyone who spoke favorably of integration risked being overheard and reported to the CID." No activity seemed accidental. "Someone in a state-owned car was seen entering a store patronized by Daisy Bates," and that was reported, too.[45] The Bateses and their organization, along with the Urban League, were studied intently. The Little Rock establishment had regained control of the schools, but the radical segregationists were not going down without a fight. Bates remained a primary focus of their ire as the schools approached opening day.

With school opening early, the attacks on the Bates's house had begun to increase. In a letter to Thurgood Marshall on August 3, inviting him to speak at the State Conference of Branches meeting in November, Bates wrote, "during the past week, gangs of from four to six drive by each evening cursing and throwing rocks." Despite having received notice from the Justice Department that it would not be providing any protection, she hoped that somehow Marshall could persuade them to help her "because I don't think my nerves can hold out much longer."[46]

It was not only Bates, of course, who was under fire. On Labor Day bombs doing minimal damage exploded at the Little Rock School District office and the new mayor's private business. The fire chief's automobile was also damaged, presumably because he had obeyed orders to turn the hoses on the white demonstrators at Central. The most prominent of the bombers, E. A. Lauderdale, who owned a building supply company and was a member of the Capital Citizens Council, received a three-year sentence. Faubus saw to it that his sentence was reduced, which allowed him to serve only six months, and even managed to return his fine of $500.[47]

On October 30 the *State Press* appeared on the street for the last time. On November 19 Daisy wrote the board of directors in New York she had hoped that with a loan of $8,000 from the NAACP national office, she and L. C. could keep the paper going until the next summer. She thought *The Long Shadow of Little Rock* would be published "around convention time [and], I would have been able to pay you a substantial amount on the loan and we could start a comeback."[48] In her mind, this scenario would have coincided with the election of a "decent governor" (Winthrop Rockefeller was expected to run against Faubus, she noted). The letter reveals she never got around to asking the board for the loan. She had not been able to arrange an appointment with Wilkins before the last national board meeting and clearly believed she would not be successful without having gotten his support in advance of the meeting. In thanking the board for its past contributions to the paper, Bates noted that she knew "some of the Board members did not approve" of subsidizing the *State Press* in the first place. Bates's reluctance to ask for a loan of this magnitude was understandable. With the other demands on the NAACP's national budget and the actual prospects for repayment, she knew how difficult a decision it would have been for the board to agree to such a large amount.

Bates's letter begins with a frank and bitter admission of defeat: "There comes a time in everyone's life when one must realize that there are forces too powerful to withstand. For more than a year, L. C. and I have watched our white friends and supporters being picked off one by one for daring to stand up for what is right. Each month agents [who sold the *State Press*] grew fewer and fewer. Our friends, teachers and principals from whom we get most of our state support, reported in September that they could not support the paper any longer because of local pressures."[49]

Though she did not say how she expected she and L. C. would survive financially, she wrote the board that she had assured the "children and their parents of Central and Hall High Schools" that she "would seem [*sic*] them through the school year." Bates kept no log of the incidents at school as she had the past year, but she noted for the board, "The courage of these children is remarkable. They are constantly subject to sneak attacks," and she described an assault on two of the boys. There were three additional black children at Central besides Jefferson Thomas and Carlotta Walls and three at Hall High School. According to Bates, one of the new students at Central, "Sandra Johnson, a girl who weighs about 90 pounds, beat the h——out of a girl in her study hall a few weeks ago." Bates went on to relate that Sandra had been hit twice by a "girl, one of the trouble makers in 1957," and had "quietly put her books down and beat the devil out of her. The teacher had to separate them. They were sent down to the principal's office, who gave them a lecture and sent them back to class. Since that time, she has had no physical violence—just veiled threats." It was a far cry from how the Central High School administration had handled Minnijean Brown two years earlier. Though the tone of this letter suggests the violence against the black students was constant, she had written three days earlier to a white friend, Bill Hadley, "The children at Central and Hall have been doing okay for the last three days."[50]

Her letter to the board mentions that there was "one member of the school board [during the school year of 1959–60] on whom we can depend." She was referring to Ted Lamb, owner of a successful advertising agency in Little Rock. Bates credited him with having "led the fight to get the three additional children admitted to Central." Serving on a school board committed to tokenism, Lamb, in 1961, began calling for genuine integration. Originally elected to the Little Rock School Board on the "Businessman's Slate," which had opposed Faubus, Lamb, unlike any white elected official in Little Rock, characterized school integration as a "moral" issue. Bates noted in her November 1959 letter that after Lamb had lobbied to have three more black children admitted to Central High, "the next week he lost seven advertising accounts."[51] It would not be long before he was out of business completely.

Near the bottom of the letter, Bates wrote that she would be entering "the hospital this Sunday for four or five days for a routine check-up."[52] Physically and emotionally exhausted, she would stay ten.

Though Bates had put in thousands of hours for the paper, in every respect it had been L. C.'s from the beginning to the end. In one of the last issues, L. C. mentioned that twenty Arkansans had attended a session in September of a world peace group called Moral Re-Armament.[53] After having Rajmohan Gandhi, grandson of the Indian leader Mahatma Gandhi, as a house guest in Little Rock (Daisy had invited him to speak at the November State Conference of Branches meeting), L. C. and Daisy attended a workshop on Mackinac Island in Michigan. L. C. would mention it later as providing an antidote to the bitterness he felt in losing the *State Press*. Founded on Gandhian principles and run in part by Rajmohan Gandhi, Moral Re-Armament appealed to the moralist in L. C., who even in the last issue of the paper was still preaching to blacks in his cartoon "Loud Talking in Public Can Be Disturbing to Others." Seen as a radical by most whites and many blacks in the South during Jim Crow, he was profoundly conservative. He had no taste or interest in modernity. He was a champion of black people but never embraced "Negritude" or found any special virtues in "blackness." Yet through his advocacy for civil rights in the *State Press*, no one was a more valiant spokesperson for blacks in America during the eighteen years the paper was in operation. It was Daisy who had white friends and invited them to the house. L. C. tolerated them for her sake, but left to his own devices, one can hardly imagine him seeking them out to be his friends. True, he would say Thomas Paine was his intellectual hero, but L. C. was far more eclectic in his tastes, as demonstrated by his interest in the distinctly non-European appeal of Moral Re-Armament. Though not a student of Eastern philosophy, L. C. claimed to have taken comfort in its message. Asked if he were bitter about losing the *State Press*, he told *Jet*, "I was at first. But I talked to Rajmohan Gandhi, the son [*sic*] of the late Mahatma, and he explained that I should examine myself, realize the scope of my contribution. Now I'm not angry or sorry. I believe it was the only decent course for us to take. I will always be struggling to improve conditions, wherever I am, wherever I go."[54] In 1980 he reiterated his belief that his experience on Mackinac Island had helped him recover from the bitterness of losing the *State Press*. He told Irene Wassell, "I came back a changed man. Instead of being angry with those trying to harm me, I felt sorry for them."[55]

As her husband did on an intellectual level, somehow Daisy transcended color and race. She appeared to have had white friends all her life. In essence, people were simply people to Daisy. Unlike her husband, she responded to their personalities. Both leaders in their own ways, each would, for different reasons, soon become passé in the civil rights movement. Unashamedly, L. C. preached both racial uplift and political involvement. Some white Arkansans would realize how basically conservative L. C. had been in his approach to race relations, but that would be almost at the end of his life.

In December 1959 a bizarre picture of Daisy Bates and Orval Faubus shaking hands at the state capitol created something of a stir in both segregationist circles and the black press. Bates had been asked to arrange a Little Rock tour for a West Indies official, William Richardson, whose skin color was darker than her own. William Hadley, a white friend of Bates's then living in Washington, D.C., whose public relations business had been ruined in Little Rock as a result of his support for integration, had asked her to set up the visit. Bates tells the story in *The Long Shadow of Little Rock*. She asked that Faubus agree to see Richardson. Amazingly, the governor agreed to receive him and allowed a photograph to be made of Bates and himself (with Richardson between them), his hand in the firm grasp of hers. He was roundly criticized by his segregationist supporters. For Bates, it was something of a coup. The Associated Press photograph was picked up by newspapers throughout the country.[56]

Though Bates continued to smile in public, physically, the strain of the past two years had taken its toll. Though she joked about her test results while in the hospital, the reports were ominous, if vague. In a letter to her friend Bill Hadley, she wrote, "Patient in No. 131 O.K. from neck down—neck up, pretty bad." She reported that had lost her sense of smell. She added, "Well, after three years of Faubus, something had to give."[57] From her hospital bed she told *Jet* she had been existing on "pep pill [*sic*], tranquillizers and vitamin tablets . . . you can't live forever on that."[58] Who prescribed them for her or what she took is not known. Was Daisy being treated for drug addiction? As mentioned earlier, in an unpublished draft of her memoir, she alludes to mixing sleeping pills with scotch to help her sleep. She had to deal with stress some way. The innocent flippancy of her remark to *Jet* suggests that for a time she was psychologically dependent on pharmaceuticals—they kept her going and helped her sleep. She did not take them to get high. Bates got her highs from public attention. Nor is there is any evidence she suffered from depression. Her defense mechanisms would not let her brood on any one defeat. One sees it in the letters she wrote on the same date or even in the same letter. She switched topics with an alacrity that suggests an uncanny ability to distance herself emotionally from negative thoughts. No one needed to put some space between himself or herself and reality more than she did. For the most part, Little Rock had been a hellhole for two years, and if she had gone into an extended funk, it would have been understandable. She escaped her life by travel and basking in public acclaim.

The one area in which she would show herself to be emotionally vulnerable was in her disintegrating relationship with L. C., but that was still ahead of her. As for L. C., he had coped with stress every day by going to work at his beloved paper, on very little sleep to be sure, but now it was gone. The thing that he cared about the most, except for Daisy, had been taken away from him.

What were they living on now that they had no income from the *State Press* and a mountain of debt, including Daisy's medical bills? Daisy said she was supporting them both. She told *Jet* for the December article, "We have no income now, except for the book I'm working on, and an occasional speaking engagement. The doctors have ordered a long rest, and I might have to give up speaking for a while."[59]

Doctors' orders to the contrary, Bates was not about to give up public speaking, for any advance from the book would have been spent long ago. Actually, other sources of income were about to come into the house. Daisy and L. C. also allowed their plight to be publicized by Roy Wilkins, who on December 17 sent out an article addressed to "editors and radio program directors."[60] Individuals, both white and black, from all over the country sent small amounts of money to them. The national headquarters of "Dollars for Daisy" was in Kansas City, Kansas, where an account was set up for them at the Douglas State Bank. Daisy and L. C. were presented a cashier's check for $1,000 before Christmas. The amount collected through the bank exceeded $1,800 by January 9, 1960. Bates wrote a letter on January 21, 1960, to H. W. Sewing in Kansas City, acknowledging that she and L. C. had received a total of $2,000 from his group alone. She said they were still trying to "liquidate our indebtedness" by selling the *State Press*, so there was no thought of reviving the paper. If Bates received any more substantial sums from out-of-town supporters, her papers do not record it. She did observe that "our major creditors, thus far, have been lenient. We feel that it is more from a business standpoint than an act of mercy."[61] Her correspondence gives no indication of their total indebtedness.

Despite their situation, Bates continued to receive visitors as if the *State Press* were still successfully in operation. In the December 10 letter to Bill Hadley, she mentioned she was "entertaining dignitaries— Congressman Charles Diggs of Detroit is due in this afternoon for two days, Bob Carter of New York City will be in on the 14th for the Dollarway School Case (Pine Bluff) and Mr. Richardson from the 15th through the 17th."[62]

Daisy and L. C. continued to fight a rearguard action against blacks who resented the NAACP's stranglehold on school integration in Little Rock. Congressman Charles Diggs had written a report critical of the school situation at Central and Hall. An ad hoc committee composed of their usual black antagonists, I. S. McClinton and publisher C. H. Jones, had responded by criticizing Diggs's findings and upsetting parents of the black children at Hall and Central. L. C. wrote Gloster Current that "after several meetings with the parents," they decided to "ignore" this issue, and it went away.[63]

The upside of Daisy and L. C.'s situation for the new year was that he was to start in January as the Arkansas NAACP field secretary for $600 a month. Though it was a far cry from the $30,000 revenue the *State Press* had provided for them each year, the NAACP national board had also agreed to continue to subsidize the Arkansas State Conference of Branches at least until the end of 1960. Wilkins wrote, "Our Board of Directors regards the situation as one still warranting our interest on the same level as in the past."[64]

For his part, L. C. was about to enter the new year with a difficult job, especially for a man who was much more successful communicating in print than in person. As always, the primary mission of the field secretary was to build the chapters within the state. It would not be for lack of trying on L. C.'s part, but his personality and his natural conservatism (which perfectly reflected the conservatism of the national office) would not be conducive to bringing young people into the organization. It also meant that he would be working closely with Daisy. Hadn't they always been a team? Only time would tell.

Chapter Fifteen

THE NEW YORK YEARS

When black college and high school students in larger cities in the South began peaceful demonstrations in February 1960 at whites-only lunch counters, the civil rights movement entered an important new phase. A younger generation of African Americans who would not be intimidated by centuries-old white supremacy seemed to come into being from out of nowhere. Where did these idealistic young people come from, and who motivated them to confront white supremacy directly when their parents could not?

Daisy Bates's Emancipation Day appearance at the Second Baptist Church in Chattanooga, Tennessee, on January 1, 1960, may have seemed like a routine event to the adults in the audience, but there were young people present who would take her speech to heart. Bates's speech was mostly aimed at blacks themselves, and there was a growing militancy in her words and actions. She refused to join in the singing of the National Anthem, telling the crowd of approximately 500 that "she felt great sadness" each time she heard this song. America was not yet "the land of the free." Some of her sharpest words were aimed at ministers. She said she had often received letters from the church asking if she had "paid her pledge," but she had never gotten a letter from a minister "asking if she were a registered voter." Ministers should "demand" that their congregations register to vote. "The day is past when we need a white man to speak for us." Obviously thinking of Little Rock, she said, "We must stop the Uncle Toms from running down town saying 'we have the Negro vote in our back pocket.' "[1]

Bates made scores of speeches in her lifetime to adults and students alike and was greeted with thunderous applause at the conclusion, but she must have often wondered at their lasting impact beyond raising money for the NAACP. Concrete evidence of having made a real difference arrived in the form of a three-page letter dated February 26 from Bettye Williams, a high school senior in Chattanooga who had heard her talk almost two months earlier at the Second Baptist Church. She wrote, "I'm sure that by now you know what has happened here. Some of the students at Howard School have been conducting 'sit-down' demonstrations at different Department stores down town. It began Friday, February 20, 1960. We decided we were tired of waiting for the adults to do something about this matter. So we went to three stores Friday." After describing her participation at sit-ins at lunch counters with other students, Williams commented, "I wonder, if you hadn't given such an effective speech that day what would we have done? I have learned from different people that your speech was what gave them so much inspiration and courage to take the steps we have taken. If they do integrate schools, I will apply at the University of Chattanooga this fall."[2] The letter was dramatic proof of Bates's ability to move people when the timing was right—at least outside her home state.

Daisy and L. C. now faced the difficulty of working together since he was on the NAACP's payroll as Arkansas field secretary. How much authority was L. C. supposed to have? Did L. C. work for her, or did he only answer to Gloster Current and his superiors in New York? It had to be a problem for them. She had never felt the need to get detailed instructions about the duties of the previous Arkansas field directors, but on February 29, 1960, Current sent her a four-page letter carefully outlining L. C.'s responsibilities. L. C., of course, was sent his own copy. The first two items surely caught her eye: "In consultation with the president and under her general direction the field secretary will execute" the program of the NAACP. But at the same time, L. C. "is responsible for the development of a program based upon the objectives, program and policies of the State Conference, as outlined in the resolutions of the State Conference, National Board of Directors and the Annual Convention of the Association." Then, as if to take it all back, Current added a sentence at the end of the letter that read, "We want him to have as free a hand as possible in executing the program."[3] Obviously, a strong state conference president and a conscientious state field secretary had to be in close agreement on tactics as well as goals if they were going to work together in harmony and live together in the same house as man and wife. Time would shortly tell if that would be possible.

On February 23 the U.S. Supreme Court unanimously reversed Bates's conviction and that of Birdie Williams, the North Little Rock

NAACP chapter president. The right to "freedom of association" trumped any reason that could be given by the government for making the NAACP turn over names of its officials and members. Bates's statement to the media after the Supreme Court's decision in her favor was terse. "Today's supreme court decision should make it crystal clear that we do not have to release our membership lists to [state attorney general Bruce] Bennett or anyone else. This decision renews our faith in the strength of our democracy."[4]

In fact, she was preoccupied by an explosion that had occurred at Carlotta Walls's home on February 9. Three sticks of dynamite had been detonated, leaving a three-foot hole in the exterior wall but fortunately no injuries. What made the bombing most troubling was that two blacks were charged, seventeen-year-old Herbert Monts and Maceo Binns, an adult. It had caused a major flurry of activity by Bates because Binns first told the police he had gotten the dynamite from Carlotta Walls's father. According to Bates, the police had picked up Walls and held him "incommunicado for about eight hours."[5] She issued a statement calling the allegation that he was involved in bombing his own house "ridiculous," but she could not begin to breathe a little easier until Binns recanted his statement that Walls had been involved.[6] Her enemies in the black community had tried to make something of it. I. S. McClinton, when reached for comment, suggested in the same article that "some integrationists" had prior knowledge that the bombing would take place. The *Arkansas Democrat* pointed out that Bates admitted she knew Binns as well as members of the Monts family, thus implying that she might have set up the plot. Had the allegation that Carlotta Walls's father been involved with the dynamiting of his own house held up, it would have been a major blow to Bates's credibility and to the NAACP. Much larger issues for the civil rights movement loomed on the horizon, but Bates did not have the luxury to ignore what was immediately before her. "We have been on the alert for several days. Cars have been stopping in front of the house with hard looking occupants, but when the guard would show himself, they would speed away," she wrote Roy Wilkins on February 23. The tension was unrelenting. She said she was aware of the expense to the national office "in maintaining a guard, but now I am not sure I can sleep in this house without a guard."[7] It was a plea for more money. The treasury was down to $100.

On March 18 an event occurred in the white community that stunned many in Little Rock, including Bates. Police chief Gene Smith, whom

Bates had genuinely admired for his "great personal courage" in enforcing the law evenhandedly, shot his wife and himself in a murder-suicide. The wrath of segregationists against Smith ever since the fall of 1957 had been unrelenting, a story of persecution all its own. In the eyes of many, Smith was a traitor like no other white southerner. The pressures on him came to a head the morning of March 18 when his twenty-year-old son, Raymond, a student at Harding College in Searcy, Arkansas, pleaded guilty to theft. One can only imagine the pain Gene Smith was feeling.

Perhaps it was the lack of money in the NAACP account that made Bates react so cautiously to the beginnings of the sit-ins in Little Rock. In her February 23 letter to Wilkins, she wrote, "Some of the students from Philander Smith College contacted me Sunday—they are ready to move in on the downtown eating places. They asked for advice on how to proceed, etc. I told them to wait until we had checked and/or interpreted Arkansas' recently passed law concerning sit-down protests and crowds assembled for this purpose."[8]

It was one thing to make a speech that would rouse people to the barricades, another thing entirely to pick up the pieces afterward. The sit-ins were a defining moment in the history of the civil rights movement, but not in Little Rock, where, initially, instead of viewing the sit-ins as an opportunity to advance the cause of civil rights, Bates was almost skeptical. In fact, this letter from Daisy suggests the influence L. C. was having in his new role as field secretary. Clarence Laws had called her, saying, "that the organization was going all out to protect the children in the sit-down protests. I told him that if such a move were made in Little Rock it would have to be well organized because of the lack of police protection for Negroes. Such things as having lawyers on the scene, bondsmen ready to bail the students out of jail and briefs should be ready to be filed in Court contesting it on the same day." They were all excellent points, and Bates wanted to know what Wilkins thought about it all. "Let me have your comments on this right away." But instead of staying in Little Rock and working with the students, Daisy was "taking off for Florida tomorrow. I will speak on Thursday for the Tampa Branch and for the Miami Branch on Friday, returning home Saturday."[9]

Bates's experience had been that activist African Americans in Little Rock were lambs for the slaughter. She was understandably cautious about leading them to the sacrifice. It was quite a bit easier to speak to a well-heeled, adoring audience on the coasts of the United States than it was to exhort blacks in Arkansas who might lose their jobs or worse if they took her words seriously. It would prove to be a crisis of the first order for her leadership abilities, and, despite her own largely symbolic involvement, the failure of the NAACP in the state to rally blacks in Little Rock around the students marked the beginning of the end of her influence. The sit-ins exposed her weaknesses as nothing else had. There was no longer an effective grassroots NAACP chapter in Little Rock as had existed during the mid-1950s. The NAACP in Arkansas had become largely Daisy Bates, working through the national organization and its lawyers.

In the winter of 1960 both Daisy and L. C. were almost entirely dependent on the NAACP. Specifically, they were dependent on Roy Wilkins. He had made the decision to carry them into the 1960s. From his perspective, in Arkansas, there was nobody else. Perhaps as a team, which they had always presented themselves to be, they could rebuild the Arkansas NAACP from the bottom up. As field secretary, L. C. was supposed to be in the process of carrying out this mission, and in his earnest, didactic way, he tried. But L. C. exemplified what could happen if a person took the NAACP too seriously. Stand up for it and you lost your job or business. The unconscious message was that white supremacy won out every time. As crucial as it was to fight the good fight, what did Bates and the NAACP have to show for it in the winter of 1960 in Arkansas? Nothing but painfully few black students enrolled in two Little Rock high schools after four full years of litigating *Aaron v. Cooper*. The cost, both to them and to others involved with them was, mind-boggling. Suffice it to say, the achievements of the preceding four years were not much of a recruiting tool for L. C. as he went around the state trying to get blacks interested in the NAACP again.

With L. C. as Arkansas field secretary and Daisy as president, their working relationship had to be difficult. He was supposed to serve the president of the State Conference of Branches, but for nineteen years L. C. had been loudly voicing his own opinions about how blacks ought to go about achieving civil rights as well as about how they ought to go about improving themselves.

Though historian John Kirk has written that L. C. was a passive partner in the relationship, the evidence during this period of their lives does not bear out this conclusion. Relatively soon after L. C. became field secretary, he began to speak in the name of the organization, when previously it was Daisy who had always issued statements and fielded reporters' questions. An obvious example is how the couple responded to reporters' questions after the first sit-ins in Little Rock on March 9, when approximately fifty black students from Philander Smith College demonstrated and sat in at Woolworth's lunch counter. Eventually, five were arrested and posted bond of $100 each, which was supplied "by the local NAACP."[10] As noted earlier, Daisy (and probably L. C.) had met with the students beforehand, but it was L. C. who talked with the reporters afterward.

Obviously unwilling to have the NAACP get out in front on this issue, L. C.'s reply straddled the fence. His wife, he told reporters, had neither advocated for nor against the sit-ins (or "sit-downs" as L. C. often referred to them). He then commented that the NAACP supported any black person who took action to claim his or her legal rights. Clearly, L. C.'s words were aimed at avoiding giving Little Rock authorities an excuse to arrest Daisy or himself. Though there seems to be no record of it, this display of caution may have been prompted by the national office. Daisy had asked for help in dealing with this new tactic. It seems likely that she would have received a phone call warning her not to do anything that would give whites a chance to arrest her. Thus it was L. C. who handled the questions by the Little Rock press. Why had the students done this? He replied: "Well put it this way. You can go anywhere in any store and buy anything but when you buy food you are trespassing and the kids can't understand it and I can't understand it either."[11]

The students were not done demonstrating. The *Arkansas Gazette* reported on March 17, 1960, that "an estimated twenty-five to forty blacks peacefully sat-in at lunch counters on Main Street in Little Rock, then went to the state capitol steps and sang 'God Bless America' and 'The Star Spangled Banner.' "[12] No one was arrested. There is no mention of Daisy or L. C. participating in the demonstration in any capacity.

On April 9 James Lawson, the charismatic leader of the student sit-ins in Nashville and a fervent apostle of nonviolence, came to Little Rock and spoke at the Dunbar Community Center.[13] It appears that Lawson's visit galvanized Daisy and L. C. to become directly involved with the students. Sit-ins seemed too risky, but on April 15 Daisy led an effort to picket three downtown stores to protest segregated eating places. The *Arkansas Gazette* reported the next day: "About 20 Negroes set up picket lines in front of three Main Street stores yesterday, parading with placards protesting segregated lunchrooms. Mrs. L. C. Bates identified the students as college and high school students.

Mrs. Bates appeared at all three stores and for a brief time wore a sign. Later she turned it over to one of the students and continued to check on the demonstrations. Her husband reportedly brought five Negroes to Pfeifers Department Store."[14] When asked by an *Arkansas Democrat* reporter in front of the Blass Department Store if she was going to "sit-in," Daisy coyly replied, "You can't tell. I just might get hungry, you know. I sometimes like a cup of coffee or tea and a sandwich."[15]

While in the picket line for a short time at the Blass Department Store, Bates carried a sign that read "Jailing Our Youth Will Not Solve the Problem in Little Rock. We Are Only Asking for Full Citizenship Rights." She was wearing a lapel card that read "I'm supporting the NAACP racial self defense policy. I refuse to patronize segregated stores." Bates "divided her time between the picket lines at Pfeifers of Arkansas, McLellan's Variety Store and the Gus Blass Co. She told newsmen the picketing would continue until 5 P.M. but did not say it would be resumed tomorrow." She informed Little Rock reporters that "picketing will continue indefinitely until the conscience of the community is made to realize that Negroes are being refused service in these places."[16]

Unfortunately, the white community had no conscience, and the black community failed to support her efforts. On April 22 a letter (probably drafted by L. C.) went out under Daisy's name to NAACP members asking for donations to pay the legal expenses for the thirteen students who had been arrested. Signed also by J. C. Crenchaw, still president of the Little Rock branch, and Garman Freeman, Daisy and L. C.'s neighbor and now chairman of the Little Rock branch's executive committee, it called on blacks to boycott several Little Rock stores that had lunch counters for whites only. L. C. admitted in his annual report in December that the boycott had been a disaster. Though in the "first week," blacks had stayed away from the downtown stores where there were lunch counters, afterward, "the news media became mum, the Negro paper became critical of the policy and ministers failed to cooperate with the Branch in the campaign." Though L. C. contended that the "policy had been felt by the two department stores emphasized in the memorandum sent out by the NAACP," his report made it clear that nothing had been accomplished. Efforts to work through a "citizens group" by himself and Crenchaw "to raise funds to reimburse the NAACP" for defending the students came to nothing. "Dominated by the ministry" and composed of "leading citizens," initially the group had been supportive of the students, but "there has not been one thing accomplished by the group."[17] The efforts of the pickets collapsed, and this tactic was abandoned.

Though in the next month attempts were made to avoid arrest, the students were not always successful. Further sit-ins led to further arrests, and the municipal court trials of the initial five resulted in each receiving a fine of $250 and a thirty-day jail sentence for violations of state law.[18] The NAACP put up money to appeal and got the students out of jail, but without a unified effort from the black community, the sit-ins were an expensive and divisive proposition. Not willing to risk jail herself (it must be remembered that Martin Luther King Jr. did not go to jail until October 19, 1960, when he sat in with students in Atlanta) and unable to galvanize support for a boycott, Bates's leadership role in the civil rights movement in Arkansas ground to an abrupt halt. The failure doomed any effective collaboration with those students in the future who would go on to embrace a separate organization, SNCC, which would become a hated rival of L. C.'s in the coming years.

L. C. made clear just how expensive the sit-ins were in his year-end report to the national office. He described briefly the three sit-ins that occurred in Little Rock in the spring of 1960 and the disastrous results that followed. Thirteen students had received fines and jail sentences (some as much as a $1,000 fine and seven months in jail) for violating a trespass statute enacted by the 1958 legislature. "These demonstrators worked with the NAACP; they held periodic meetings with the State Conference President and the Secretary and planned their movements for over a month. The NAACP is handling the defense for the 13 students."[19] But unlike 1957, when Little Rock had become a national symbol of resistance and the national office of the NAACP had put its resources into the fight, the sit-ins in Little Rock received little attention. Though the national office put up the original bond money for the students, the Little Rock branch was obligated to pay it back, and no more money would be forthcoming from New York, which was dealing with a number of larger issues in other parts of the South.

Where was Daisy Bates in all of this? She was not even around to plan the one major event the Arkansas NAACP had all year—the annual meeting on November 5 and 6. Putting the best face on his wife's absence, L. C. wrote that "the major state officers were out of the state during preparation for the meeting, and the Field Secretary had to assume full responsibility for the arrangements."[20] He duly noted Daisy had been "re-elected president." He did not say the meeting had been a success.

It was not that Bates had not been moved by the students' struggle. She wrote to Lafayette Harris, the head of Philander Smith, on their behalf after he opposed their participation in civil rights activities, but the president's situation was no different than most blacks in the state.[21] Philander Smith depended on white support. Ill and in the hospital when the sit-ins began, Harris showed no sympathy publicly.

By 1960 John W. Walker, then an employee of the Arkansas Human Relations Council and later the leading civil rights attorney in Arkansas and close friend of and financial contributor to Bates, commented in a report, "Negro leadership is virtually nil."[22] What had happened? Two years earlier Bates had been able to single-handedly short circuit an effort by white businessman Herbert Thomas to pressure the Little Rock Nine and their parents to abandon court-ordered desegregation in Little Rock. There had been support for his effort within the black community, but Bates had beaten it back, and, to the dismay of many, the Thomas plan had gone no further.

As John Kirk has shown, Daisy's and L. C.'s enemies within the black community had never been vanquished; they just did not get the kind of publicity she did. Outside the NAACP, assistance for the students was not forthcoming. Typically, the publisher of the *Southern Mediator Journal*, C. H. Jones, was hostile to any kind of confrontation, including boycotts. African Americans were employed as janitors and cooks in the offending stores. If they were fired, "where else would these people get jobs?" he editorialized.[23] The average black preacher in Little Rock was not going to come to L. C. and Daisy's side either. The *State Press* had been far too critical of black preachers to make their cooperation seem worthwhile.

It is difficult today to imagine how radical these acts of protest seemed to whites, who simply could not fathom what would induce blacks to risk arrest when for generations they had been obedient to white authority. L. C. said in exasperation to a reporter, "You all aren't colored and never have been, so you have no idea what's it's like." Asked if it was hard to be a "colored person," he replied, "it's hell to be a colored person."[24] During this period, he seemed equally exasperated with both blacks and whites.

By June 1960 Bates had taken up residence at the Hotel Brittany in New York. Her stay was thought to be temporary, but she would not return to Arkansas permanently until a stroke incapacitated her in

1964. Her departure from Little Rock coinciding with L. C.'s first six months as NAACP Arkansas field secretary surely was no accident. Since the fall of 1957, Daisy had been celebrated on almost a weekly basis by some group in the country. She had finally eclipsed her older husband, who had clearly dominated the relationship in the beginning. L. C. had played a part in this glorification of his wife, and now it would come back to haunt him. Daisy began, with some justification, to believe her own press clippings, some of which he had written.

In Daisy's mind, the balance of power in the relationship had shifted as early as December 1957, when the Associated Press had crowned her "Woman of the Year" in education in the country. L. C. had played up her successes in the *State Press* for two reasons: with each honor and news story about her, the NAACP, he believed, was strengthened, and he was every bit the champion of the NAACP as she was. The second reason was more mundane: he thought it made her happy. But underneath all the glitz, she was still Daisy Lee Gatson from Huttig, whom he had rescued from a life of poverty. He had pampered her, had spoiled her, had been happy to let her play at being in the news business while he had done all the heavy lifting. He couldn't deny she had matured and had developed a real nose for the news, grabbing photographers like Earl Davy or Gelive Grice and going out and getting a story. With her election as president of the Arkansas NAACP and the crisis at Central High, increasingly she had become part of the story, and that was fine, too.

As far as Daisy was concerned, at some point she had become the story, as evidenced by her working title of the manuscript that became *The Long Shadow of Little Rock*. Now in the winter of 1960, here was L. C. again, not going off to the *State Press* every day but home meddling in her business. Actually, he was not meddling, since the NAACP had become his job, but it must have been unsettling to both of them. Again, who was whose boss? On paper, she was his boss, but everyone involved in a nonprofit organization knows that the paid employees do the actual work and run the organization. In Arkansas, there was only one paid employee, and that was L. C.

Given the size of Daisy's ego by 1960 and L. C.'s expectations about his role as field secretary and his own conservative nature, there was not room for both of them in Little Rock doing NAACP work, not in Daisy's mind. It was not a unique problem. It is a rare husband and wife who can successfully work together, and Daisy had outgrown her role as junior partner in the relationship. For his part, L. C. always saw himself as Daisy's superior—in intellect, in judgment. No matter how famous she became, he never quite believed she was capable of taking care of herself. Their difference in years, the way their relation began and developed, and then her astonishing fame and its opportunities for absence while L. C. was tied to the *State Press* created a recipe for marital problems, whether the two of them worked together or not.

Of course, Bates never publicly said she moved to New York to get away from her husband. She may not have admitted it to herself, but a person does not have to live in New York to write a book. Though L. C. was willing to let her enjoy the limelight and loved her, that love seemed increasingly to come at a heavy price, and Daisy was increasingly unwilling to pay it.

There were other considerations, too. Orval Faubus had turned Little Rock into a living hell for them. In the winter of 1960 he was still there, and things were not getting any better. Just as many others would, she blamed their troubles on Faubus, when it was the centuries-old dedication to white supremacy that allowed him to exploit it.

Another reason for leaving Little Rock, at least temporarily, was that Bates was exhausted. As mentioned earlier, the onslaught by the radical segregationists against the NAACP in Arkansas had been wildly successful. Had chapters throughout the state been required to identify their members, it would have been revealed that ten chapters were no longer active. L. C. wrote in his year-end report in 1960, "The Field Secretary feels that one of the barriers that has hindered the NAACP program will soon be removed when the Attorney General leaves his post January 1, 1961."[25] Neither Daisy nor L. C. would admit publicly how much damage Attorney General Bruce Bennett had done the organization. Though the NAACP ultimately won most every legal battle with the state of Arkansas, the cost was incalculable. Without referring to Bennett by name, L. C. wrote he "established fear" in the hearts and minds of "many" blacks throughout the state. As already discussed, the national office had kept a financial prop under Daisy, and that had been the only way she had survived in the first place.

The NAACP national office could not have been pleased with Bates's increasing absences from Little Rock. The NAACP wanted her to be involved in urging parents in Pine Bluff to register their children in the white schools there. Bob Carter wrote her a letter stressing how much work there was to be done before school was out in May. "It is very important that the kind of job which you undertook in Little Rock last fall be undertaken in . . . Pine Bluff."[26] Ultimately, only one·

black student was allowed to enroll in the schools in Pine Bluff during this time. It would be L. C. who tried to recruit students. He did not mention Daisy or the number of students whom he found to apply in his monthly reports. It was not an auspicious beginning, but Pine Bluff was Old South and by comparison made Little Rock seem like a liberal bastion.

Bates's stated reason for moving to New York was to work on her book. If she had said she was moving temporarily to New York to find someone to help her write her book, it would have been closer to the truth. By the winter of 1960 Bates's book was in trouble, and she was becoming quite preoccupied by it. She tried and failed to convince her new friend Lorraine Hansberry to help her with it.[27] Edward Muse, the treasurer of the Greenwich Village Chelsea branch of the NAACP, wrote her that he was "making a couple of exploratory contacts" on her behalf.[28] It was Chelsea and Greenwich Village where Bates felt most comfortable in New York. She was making many friends there, including Robert Nemiroff, who was married to Hansberry at the time. Nemiroff would also try to help Bates find a ghostwriter for her book, which was becoming almost impossible for her to write. In late March Bates thought she had found someone, a young African American writer by the name of William Branch, as "a possible collaborator for my book." Branch, who became a successful playwright for a time, was then a ghostwriter for Jackie Robinson, writing Robinson's New York newspaper column. Ultimately, Branch, who wanted his own name on his work, would turn Bates down, but he became her good friend.

Bates's stays in New York in the spring of 1960 were no longer just for the weekends. In a letter the third week of April to Agnes Birnbaum, who became a friend, Bates told her she had speaking engagements the weekend of the April 23 but would be available to see her. "However, I do hope we will be able to get together for dinner during my stay— Monday, if possible, if not then later in the week."[29] The Birnbaums were young, idealistic liberals who had read about Bates's plight. Agnes Birnbaum remembered that she and her husband occasionally sent small amounts of money to Little Rock. What would have attracted Bates to the young couple was that they knew writers.

Bates's first ghostwriter was Constance Pearlstien, who recalls she met Bates "toward the end of 1959 or early 1960." Who recommended her to Bates is not clear, but Pearlstien was then well known in certain circles in New York as a writer and for her sympathy to civil rights. She had been a member of the Socialist Workers Party and still considered herself "in those days a revolutionary." Once married to Trinidad native and Marxist theoretician C. L. R. James, Pearlstien counted among her friends Richard Wright, Ralph Ellison, and James Baldwin. She was particularly close to Wright and wrote a biography of him. By 1960 Pearlstien was working as a freelance writer. Pearlstien remembers that she would go to the Hotel Brittany and "sit with Daisy and question her." They would "work steadily for about five hours." Then Pearlstien would go home "and write part or all of a chapter" and show it to Bates the next day. "In the beginning," Bates was "ecstatic about seeing her story appearing in print." Bates, in Pearlstien's opinion, "could not write at all." Bates's enthusiasm for her first ghostwriter did not last. Pearlstien recalls that "after she had written a number of chapters, later she learned [Bates] had been seeing [Alex] Haley to persuade him to take on the ghosting of her book."[30]

Unfortunately, Bates never paid Pearlstien for her work. Bates's failure to do so is confirmed by an entry in her FBI file.[31] Bates felt concerned enough to consult Adlai Stevenson's law firm in New York. Ultimately, Pearlstien never filed suit. Besides being "costly, litigation would not have been good for either of our reputations." Though she has forgotten the specific amount she was owed, Pearlstien thinks "it was probably a couple thousand dollars."[32]

Despite this unpleasant episode, Bates liked New York. Or more precisely, she liked the way she was treated in New York. Audre Hanneman, who became Bates's secretary and a close friend, remembered that Bates did not "travel on crowded buses or subways. She would either take a taxicab or one of her friends would drive her wherever she wanted to go."[33] How she managed to afford to live there without a regular income remains a partially unsolved mystery. The money she made from her speaking engagements was now absolutely essential but would not have been enough to pay all of her bills. Letters between her and L. C. are few and far between, and none of their letters in Bates's papers at the State Historical Society of Wisconsin in Madison or the University of Arkansas in Fayetteville mention money. Yet it is difficult to imagine that L. C. was not contributing at least something to her support, even as their relationship became increasingly problematical and however much he disapproved of her decision to live in New York.

Liberal New Yorkers, both white and black, responded warmly to Bates. On her increasingly frequent and lengthier trips to New York, she had gravitated to Greenwich Village and the Chelsea area in particular. There she would find the writers who could help her with her memoir. She had spoken there with Lorraine Hansberry and was photographed demonstrating with Greenwich Village NAACP members. Another of Bates's good friends there was Edward Muse, the treasurer of the same organization. Muse, Hanneman remembered, "greatly admired her, and was always very willing to be at her beck and call. She treated him like a younger brother."[34]

In the second week of June 1960 Gloster Current notified the national staff that Bates was living "temporarily" at 55 East Tenth Street, the address of the Brittany Hotel, "while completing her book."[35] The Brittany Hotel later became a residence hall for New York University. Built in 1928, it housed many famous New Yorkers over the years, including Walter Winchell, Jerry Garcia, and Al Pacino. It had its own share of celebrities while Bates was living there, two of whom would become her friends. Thinking Bates's stay in New York was only a few months at most, Wilkins and his staff would have at least liked the fact that she was more available to make appearances at NAACP fund-raising functions in the New York area without the expenses previously associated with her appearance, and the staff did not hesitate to call her.

There was one instance where Bates's assertiveness got her into trouble. In August 1960 she attended an executive committee meeting of the Chelsea branch of the NAACP, which had been called to allow two members to air grievances against each other. The difficulty was that she had not been invited and must have voiced her opinion. According to the letter of protest sent to Roy Wilkins by the branch, Bates told the executive committee "that it was usual custom for National Board Members to participate in any Branch Executive meeting, even one which by its nature would warrant being considered a closed meeting." A majority of the executive committee expressed to Wilkins its "doubt . . . as to the validity of Mrs. Bates [*sic*] statement."[36]

Bates's feelings were still hurt more than a month later. Instead of backing down gracefully and admitting that she had overstepped her authority, she wrote the executive board that she had helped "organize your branch . . . and regularly assisted [its] progress." She claimed that a "formal resolution" welcoming her "participation" had been passed on August 26. The letter to Wilkins "seeks to question my integrity," and thus "I resent and protest your President's act and interference."[37]

It was this aspect of her sometimes aggressive personality that occasionally made enemies out of people who would otherwise have been her friends. Without such aggressiveness, however, she would not have been the leader she was. Bates was never a wallflower, whether she was in Little Rock or in New York. If New Yorkers needed to be straightened out, so be it.

As far as Little Rock went, Bates still felt obligated to the Nine and personally attended to many of the details of their scholarships, although L. C. began taking over this chore as early as 1960. She went home for a few days before school opened in Little Rock in the fall of 1960 but was back in New York for the national board meeting in early September. She wrote Wilkins that "the school opening at both schools [Central and Hall] was quiet and peaceful."[38] There was little reason for whites to worry. Ted Lamb, the only liberal member of the Little Rock School Board, said prophetically, "The School Board has not acted in good faith. They never intend to desegregate completely. . . . I am sure that Little Rock will finally be forced by litigation in the courts truly to desegregate."[39] Tokenism was the order of the day in the South and would remain so until the Supreme Court ordered an end to the charade years later. According to L. C.'s annual report, only one hundred black students, including eleven students in Little Rock, were attending desegregated institutions out of 104,000 children in the state's public schools. "Full integration," he noted, "can be expected in about 600 years."[40]

The Little Rock Nine were now out of school, and it is appropriate here to consider the question raised earlier: how well did Bates fulfill the role of mentor to the Little Rock Nine? Since only five of the Nine consented to be interviewed for this book, the answer can only be suggested. As stated earlier, Bates portrayed herself as their mentor and in turn was portrayed as such by the black press. Her fame today rests in part on her relationship with the first nine black students to enter Central High School.

No public criticism from the Nine in this regard surfaced until after Bates's death. In his interview with the author, Terrence Roberts offered a measured, tentative assessment of Bates's relationship with the Nine. Though unstinting in praising her commitment and courage, Roberts said, "I would have perhaps wanted her to have a more balanced perspective about that—to see herself more in a service role than the role of occupying the spotlight."[41]

In her interview, Elizabeth Eckford was even more blunt:

Q: One of the things I asked Dr. Roberts was whether he considered that [Bates] . . . provided emotional support for you and the Little Rock Nine or for him and the Little Rock Nine, and I'm curious what your response is.
Eckford: I think not.
. . . .
Q: Would you explain what you mean by that?
Eckford: Because she was a very pushy person. When we were around her it was for press purposes or it was for the purpose of explaining what was happening legally. She didn't explain it but the attorneys did. We gathered at her place. First we would go every day and report what happened but even stupid Elizabeth after awhile stopped doing that with her and stopped doing that with school officials because nothing was changing.[42]

There is no escaping the tone of bitterness that surfaces in Eckford's comments. In one instance she calls Bates "a self-promoter."[43] To dismiss Eckford's remarks because of her admitted diagnosis of post-traumatic stress disorder would be a mistake. Occasionally emotional, Eckford remained in control during the interview. Although one has the feeling that Eckford's bitterness has colored her memory of events that happened long ago, one has the nagging suspicion that perhaps some others of the Nine share at least Roberts's ambivalence toward Bates but had informally agreed not to discuss her publicly. In a vague reference to this general subject, Minnijean Brown Trickey said in 2002 that the Nine once had made a "group decision not to say what is wrong."[44]

One of the Nine who has no ambivalence is Ernest Green, who as a senior that year was generally seen by outsiders as the leader of the Nine. The tone of his interview was totally positive toward Bates in every respect. Green said, "I didn't see Daisy as a self-promoter. . . . I think she was the right person at the right time to lead the charge in Little Rock."[45] He acknowledged that he had contributed to Bates's support later when she became impoverished. On this subject, Roberts explained that it had never really occurred to him to contribute to Bates's support. "For me there was no lasting tie to the woman, so although I appreciated her efforts on our behalf, I did not connect her in any lasting way with what I was going to do in life."[46]

One suspects that Roberts's view of Bates is not unrepresentative. Though Melba Pattillo Beals did not respond to the author's request for an interview, her own memoir of the 1957–58 school year, *Warriors Don't Cry*, which contained excerpts of a diary she kept during this period, only occasionally places Bates at the center of events. In fact, *Warriors Don't Cry* almost seems as if it were written as a counter to Bates's *The Long Shadow of Little Rock*. In Beals's memoir, the support she derived from her family; her minister, Rev. Rufus King Young; and others figures much more heavily than Bates's. At one point she writes, "If I got into trouble and really needed protection, it would probably be the network of phone calls initiated by Reverend Young that would set off a rescue and construct a web of safety."[47]

Undoubtedly, one of Rev. Young's first calls would have been to Bates, who was a member of his church, along with Gloria Ray and Ernest Green. In Beals's acknowledgments, Daisy's name is listed after L. C.'s and followed by Wiley Branton "and the ministers who stood beside our parents to cheer us on."[48]

Though Ernest Green is proud to acknowledge his financial support of Bates, he "didn't organize the effort [to collect funds for Bates] among the other Nine."[49] One suspects his reason for not doing so was his knowledge that this effort would have met with resistance, and one can see why there would be some resentment. In interviews with the press and in her memoir, Bates spoke of herself as a mother figure to the Nine, which clearly was an exaggeration. From all accounts, the Nine had exceptional family support, including strong support from their own mothers. Yet in Bates's defense, her maternal instincts were aroused by the Nine. In some ways, the Nine were her children, along with other young people she cared about throughout her life.

Perhaps the proper perspective is that at least some of the Nine have lamented the fact that more attention has not been paid to their parents. Though Minnijean Brown Trickey was careful not to criticize Bates in her interview with the author, she did say that "nobody talks about the day-to-day horrific terror that our parents experienced. There was all this focus on what happened to Daisy."[50]

Trickey's comments to go to the heart of the issue: in the main, the Nine's regret seems not that Bates did not go to bat for them but that their parents' contributions have not been properly recognized. Melba Pattillo Beals's memoir contains a telling excerpt from her diary: "What will become of us if the NAACP is not strong. It feels as though segregationists are attacking from all sides. They know very well we count on Mrs. Bates and the local NAACP as well as Mr. Marshall. If they are busy defending themselves, who will see after us?"[51]

Bates's reputation has not been enhanced by an exaggerated sense of her own importance to the events in Little Rock in 1957–58. For example, in 1979 she wrote a representative of Time-Life Films that "I was the central figure in the desegregation [*sic*] of Central High."[52] Did Bates really believe this? It may well have seemed that way to her.

As 1960 wound down, L. C. noted the presence of a new student group in Little Rock that was reviving the tactic of the sit-ins. This new group called themselves, he wrote, the "Southern [*sic*] Student Non-Violent Coordinating Committee." His bare mention of SNCC, which would successfully play a role in the desegregation of the downtown businesses in Little Rock and Pine Bluff, suggests his disapproval as well as a misunderstanding of the dynamic role that students were to play in the civil rights movement.[53] In the early 1960s SNCC chapters would aggressively compete with the NAACP for members in the Arkansas Delta, causing problems for L. C. in his role as field secretary. Compared to L. C., Daisy would prove to be much more sympathetic to the younger generation's desire to confront white supremacy through marches and demonstrations.

Money continued to be a problem in 1960 for Daisy and not only because living in New York without a regular income was a challenge. In September the insurance on the house in Little Rock was canceled. One match in the right place, and Daisy and L. C. would literally have nothing. She finally got a loan for an unspecified amount from her friend Mrs. Howard Lewis Aller in Lakeville, Connecticut. On December 20, Bates wrote to her, "I am ever so grateful to you for coming to my rescue when I needed it so badly. I hope to repay you soon."[54] Instead of doing so, she apparently asked for another loan but was turned down. In a letter to Aller on January 4, 1961, Daisy revealed that Kenneth Rawson, her publisher, had given her an advance of $1,000 to cover the five-year policy that the Travellers Insurance Company was willing to write for $889.[55] This would have been in addition to an initial advance she would have received upon signing her book contract.

By the winter of 1961 Bates was in agony over the book. A consoling note from Robert Nemiroff tried to cheer her up. Humorously claiming that he had discovered the Achilles' heel of the unconquerable Daisy Bates, he wrote, "Faubus, mobs, tent cities, Generals and Presidents-nothing! But one single solitary manuscript—and you go to pieces."[56]

Writing was no easy business. For a time in 1961 Rawson himself met with her each Thursday, and Bates wrote that each conference left her "usually a nervous wreck."[57] Telling her story was a harder task than simply writing about her life and her role in Little Rock in 1957. Besides the normal though difficult decisions of what to emphasize and what to skim over, the effort of concealing certain aspects of her private life had been made more difficult by the interviews she had given in the last two years. A big problem surely was how to handle her relationship with L. C. A memoir about the 1957 crisis and her role in it need not go into the minutiae of her personal life. Yet Bates herself had called it "The Daisy Bates Story," and doubtless Rawson wanted a book whose unspoken working title was "How I Rose from Southern Poverty and Racial Hatred to Become a Heroine of the Civil Rights Movement." The words on the cover of *Ebony* in 1959 fit Bates's own image of herself: "First Lady of Little Rock." In her mind, she had solved the problem of what to do with L. C. by telling a sweet story about the moment she knew as a teenager she would marry him and then skipping over the years until she and L. C. arrived in Little Rock in 1941 to start the *State Press*. Small wonder she may have had as many as four ghostwriters. But Bates was protecting more than herself. If she had told the truth in *The Long Shadow of Little Rock*, her white enemies would have been triumphant. Had she been willing to tell the truth about her life, however, what a fascinating book her ghostwriters could have written.

Nemiroff mentioned that he was "trying to arrange for Jim Baldwin" to meet with her.[58] While that apparently never happened, Bates did get to know Alex Haley, though no details have surfaced about his specific contribution to *The Long Shadow of Little Rock*. Haley would go on to worldwide fame as the writer of *Roots*, a multi-generational epic that traced his family's journey from Africa to the United States. William Branch recalled hearing that Haley, whose first book, *The Autobiography of Malcolm X*, was collaborative, "had helped her somewhere along the line."[59] Haley, who lived at the Brittany for a time, had Bates and Audre Hanneman to lunch on one occasion, but Hanneman did not recall if Bates told her that he had helped with Bates's memoir.

The ghostwriter who probably contributed the most to the organized structure of *The Long Shadow of Little Rock* was a New Yorker named George Penty. A white southerner by birth who had worked with labor movements at one time, Penty had published articles in several national publications. At the time Penty worked with Bates, Audre Hanneman was her secretary.[60] According to Penty, Bates was "frantic" because she had missed deadline after deadline. He recalled that "Ben Fine helped write the Elizabeth Eckford chapter." The material for the book "was in boxes." Penty "worked five weeks with her almost every day," primarily organizing the material. Their work took place in Bates's apartment at the Brittany. Penty did not recall Bates writing anything in those weeks. "She would talk," and Hanneman would type it.[61]

This was consistent with the way Bates "wrote" most of her letters. She was accustomed to telling a secretary what she wanted written. In Hanneman, Bates had someone who was light years above the average secretary. Bates paid her $59 a month, which was the cost of her rent-controlled apartment in New York. Though she was far too modest to acknowledge having a role, it is likely that Hanneman contributed her own bit to the writing of *The Long Shadow of Little Rock*, and Bates acknowledged her help in her memoir. Hanneman would go on to compile two highly acclaimed bibliographies of Ernest Hemingway. Both Hanneman and Penty had memories of these sessions when they were all together. Penty claimed that Bates was so grateful for his help that she wanted to put his name on the front of the book. He said he was paid $200 for his help. It wasn't all work and no play either. Penty remembered that in the evenings Bates liked to go out. "We went to the Village Gate, and [John] Coltrane was playing. Coltrane came over to our table."[62] After their work was done, Hanneman remembered that occasionally "Alex Haley . . . would come up and the four of us would sit around and have a drink and talk, with Daisy usually picking the subject."[63]

Bates made her apartment in the Brittany all her own. Hanneman recalled Bates having a "white rabbit, who chewed the telephone cord more than once, and a bird . . . who ate sunflower seeds." She owned a television in "an attractively furnished living room, a bedroom, entrance hall, narrow kitchen and bathroom."[64]

Once in a while, Bates entertained in her apartment. William Branch recalled her hosting a baby shower for his wife. "Occasionally," said Hanneman, "Daisy cooked for us, or ordered in Chinese." She once entertained the New York staff of the NAACP in her apartment in the Brittany. Hanneman helped her with the drinks and food. Probably in 1961 Bates fixed Thanksgiving dinner for six people, including Hanneman and Dr. Otto Nathan.

Bates was entertained as well. She was invited to a Fourth of July party at the home of Cissy and Thurgood Marshall. In attendance were such luminaries as Lena Horne and Alex Haley. The Marshalls lived on the seventeenth floor of a new apartment building in Harlem, and Thurgood Marshall was famous for his parties. A neighbor and friend of the Marshalls', Marietta Dochery said, "People liked to be around Thurgood, he had lots of friends. Cissy would cook her soul food—pigs' feet, greens, spare ribs, black-eyed peas. Sometimes Thurgood would sing. Maybe he had a couple of drinks or something, and he would sing, 'Happy am I.' "[65]

Bates was friends with a number of people at the Brittany (including the staff who were eager to assist her), but there was something almost poignant about her friendship with the fiercely idealistic and embattled Otto Nathan. Hanneman recalled that perhaps half a dozen times she had dinner "downstairs" at the Brittany with Bates and Nathan, who would always pick up the tab and give Hanneman "five dollars for the doorman to get me a taxicab and then ten dollars for the cab . . . because Daisy knew I did not like to walk home alone in the dark." Hanneman recalled "Dr. Nathan as an elderly lonely little gray-haired Jewish man in a gray suit."[66]

Given his apparent generosity, Nathan may well have helped Bates out financially. As with so many other people, Bates probably expected Nathan to help her without any quid pro quo. He obviously had some money; she did not. After she became prominent, Bates frequently expected others to make her life more comfortable, and often they did, gladly and willingly. As Hanneman responded, "You asked if Daisy used people. If so, they were people, like myself, who were willing to be used because we admired her courage in confronting racism."[67]

However, the way Daisy handled her celebrity status could not have helped her relationship with L. C. Hanneman stated that around her, "he was a quiet, soft-spoken man, with a deep sadness about him. He was always kind and thoughtful where I was concerned, kind of avuncular." Hanneman recalled coming to Little Rock with Daisy and sharing a room with Mother Bates in November 1961 when Daisy had come home for the NAACP state conference. Daisy "made it quite plain she was the important one."[68]

Possibly, Daisy's motive in bringing Hanneman with her was to avoid a confrontation with L. C., who was even more circumspect about these matters than his wife. He was certainly not the type of man to fight in front of others. Hanneman stayed at their home "for several days. . . . I never noticed any dissension between them."[69]

Yet by October 1961 there were signs that Daisy and L. C. were seldom in touch with each other. Mother Bates was now living at the house in Little Rock with L. C. and Johnnie McFarlan, their housekeeper. McFarlan, who was now married, had been a faithful employee for four years before the 1957 crisis but was about to leave her employers to join her husband in California the next month. She had hoped to say good-bye to Daisy. "I have been looking to hear from you but somehow I guess you don't have time to drop us a few lines or call. . . . Nobody knows exactly when you will be home."[70]

McFarlan mentioned that "everybody here is fine Mother Bates, Skippy & L. C.," but obviously they were not. One senses that L. C. was telling his mother and housekeeper that he rarely heard from his wife any more. McFarlan ended the letter by writing, "Please let me know if you exactly when you will be home if you will [be] coming [*sic*] home."[71]

Bates did not run for reelection as president of the Arkansas State Conference of Branches at the November meeting. If any politics were involved, it was kept quiet, and Bates's papers do not refer to any conflict. However, she had been effectively gone from Arkansas for more than a year and may have been encouraged by the NAACP national office to give up the presidency since she had not finished her book. Still, her decision not to run for reelection was a major milestone in her civil rights career. She had been president since 1952.

With the public or friends, Bates was never comfortable with the thought that others might realize she had so little formal education. Hanneman assumed she had at least graduated from high school. "When she made grammatical errors or showed a lack of knowledge about American history I thought it was the fault of the Arkansas school system."[72] Of course, it was exactly that, but Bates was so insecure about her background that she spent her whole life making people believe she was much more educated than she was. The supreme irony was that she spent much of her life avoiding having to write and then signed a contract to write a book. Only Bates could have brought it off, and she did—with the help of professionals, just as so many others have done.

Almost their entire lives together, Daisy and L. C. presented a united front to outsiders, even when their relationship was at its worst. They were so successful that most people in Little Rock who knew them did not know or forgot they were ever divorced. Certainly that view of their relationship made sense, for in the long run that is how they wanted themselves to be seen. To Hanneman, Bates "never spoke of problems in her marriage, or of L. C.'s first marriage."[73]

One comment by Hanneman bears repeating. "I have to admit I thought I knew Daisy a lot better than I apparently did." Hanneman was hardly alone in this sentiment. It was another example of Bates preferring admiration to intimacy, because it was not that she did not genuinely like Hanneman or vice versa. Years later, in 1979, a lonely Bates invited Hanneman to come to Little Rock and stay with her for as long as she wanted while Hanneman was trying to write a novel. Hanneman, who was still living in New York at that time with her sister, was perfectly happy where she was and politely declined the invitation. Hurt, though she had no reason to be, Bates never wrote her again.[74]

Chapter Sixteen

GOING IN DIFFERENT DIRECTIONS

As the civil rights movement picked up steam, it would become more apparent that the differences between Daisy and L. C. were widening. First, there was the fact of their physical separation. In November 1961 L. C. was assigned to work in Louisiana for "at least the next six months."[1] His year-end report in December 1961 offers a glimpse into his conservatism. Writing in the third person, he noted that "the Secretary has not been involved with Sit-Ins or Demonstrations this year. There has been only one attempt to sit in this year and it was poorly planned by a member of SNCC. The sponsor served notice that the students didn't need the NAACP and did not want the NAACP. Seven of the students from Philander Smith College went downtown in March. The police told them to leave. They left and came back to the college. They renewed their attack on the NAACP."[2]

In fact, L. C.'s attitude was probably not too much different than the year earlier, but then he had always been more conservative than Daisy. In his view, demonstrations, sit-ins, and "freedom rides" only caused conflict that served no purpose. His reluctance to support demonstrations wasn't from a lack of courage. He had demonstrated courage far beyond his young rivals. But he couldn't bring himself to believe that white supremacy would disappear as a result of blacks going out into the streets. To L. C., protest activities seemed too much like blacks asking whites to give them something. It offended his sense of the work ethic. If African Americans wanted to change things, they had the power of the ballot. Daisy might think she could "prick" the conscience of a white supremacist; L. C. never did, at least he never stated so publicly. Soon, he would even go to Faubus for jobs for blacks, a move that would get him into trouble with his bosses at the NAACP.

Bates was now expecting her book to be published in April 1962 and once again began declining speaking engagements. Every time she turned in her manuscript to her publisher, Kenneth Rawson, she expected it to be the last time. On April 2, however, she wrote to Thelma Mothershed that "I am still working on the book."[3] No longer was she telling people when she expected it to be published. But then sometime in April, Rawson accepted it. Instead of returning to Little Rock, however, she stayed in New York. The months waiting for a book finally to appear in print are a hopeful time for many first-time authors, who, despite all the evidence to the contrary, allow themselves to dream of having a best seller. Bates had helped her chances by approaching Eleanor Roosevelt to write the foreword for the book. In 1962, seventeen years after the death of President Franklin Roosevelt, his widow was still a familiar though controversial figure in the South because of her vocal support for civil rights and the liberal wing of the Democratic Party. Though just two pages long, the foreword signaled to would-be readers, not to mention book reviewers, that Bates's memoir was to be taken seriously as an important account of the modern civil rights movement.

Given what Bates had gone through and the savagery that still awaited those most active in the civil rights movement in the South, Eleanor Roosevelt's words strike a sympathetic reader today as hopelessly naive. She wrote in part, "I wish that Mrs. Bates who suffered so much . . . had been able to keep from giving us some of the sense of her bitterness and fear in the end of her book."[4] It is an astonishing comment, but doubtless one shared by many whites who did not wish to be unduly discomforted by thoughts of anger that might be welling up in the hearts of black people. As long as Bates and her many helpers were cobbling together a heartwarming account of a plucky black woman who forgave her enemies and expressed long-lasting hope for the country's future, no one needed to feel nervous about *The Long Shadow of Little Rock.*

In retrospect, Bates's expression of the sense of frustration she felt one wintry day in Washington, D.C., after the 1957–58 school desegregation crisis, ring the truest of any of her words in her book. In the last few pages of her memoir she recounts seeing a group of foreign students gazing at the Capitol dome, one of whom remarked upon its beauty. Bates wrote, "I couldn't help but feel anger for our country. . . . I felt repulsion for the political bigots who had taken the oath of office, the likes of my own State's United States Senators John L. McClellan and J. W. Fulbright, who didn't raise their voices while Negro children were being mobbed."[5]

Watching their shining young faces, Bates suddenly asked an African student, "dressed in his native garb," what the Capitol represented to him. Startled, the young man managed a conventional answer. "It means freedom and justice." Overhearing this exchange, "a beautiful Indian girl, dressed in a colorful Sari," turned the tables on her. "You're an American Negro—what does it mean to you?" For perhaps the only time in her life, Bates says she was speechless. "I couldn't answer her. I just stood there, not uttering another word. I knew all the speeches that patriotic Americans are supposed to make at such a time, but I just stood there. Sensing my confusion, they smiled and walked away, leaving me in the swirling snowstorm with the words *freedom* and *justice* sticking in my throat."[6]

Whoever crafted the words, this was the real Daisy Bates, who in this brief passage gave eloquent voice to the feelings of ambivalence of every black person who has ever lived in this country. But whatever the real story of her life had been, she could not bear to tell it in the pages of *The Long Shadow of Little Rock*. Given the times, those who bought the book would not have wanted to hear it, any more than Eleanor Roosevelt wanted to be confronted by Bates's anger. Her publisher wanted a heroine, and Bates and her collaborators were eager to oblige. Bates was no fool. She knew that to reveal her humanity with all its messy personal tragedies was to hand a loaded gun to her detractors, and she was far too smart to do that.

Ironies abound in *The Long Shadow of Little Rock*, including the way the book ends. By the time it was finally acceptable to Rawson and turned over to a copyeditor, Daisy's marriage to L. C. was in deep trouble, but apparently she thought it was salvageable. In the last paragraph she wrote, "L. C. and I have committed our lives to this crusade. Together we continue to take an active part in the fight for the emancipation of the Negro in the South. That is why L. C. has accepted the position of Field Secretary of the NAACP in Arkansas."[7]

By stopping her personal account in December 1959, Bates would not have to deal with the stresses on her marriage during the time she spent in New York: It was as if she had never left Little Rock. With her final draft completed, Bates's stated reason for living in New York ended as well, and she intended to return to Little Rock. Speaking at an NAACP meeting at St. John's AME Church in Pine Bluff on April 17,

Bates reportedly told the group that she was back home and would be working with the Little Rock NAACP.[8]

In fact, she returned to New York. Still on the NAACP national board, she would continue to remain active. She was named to a national NAACP board committee, the Special Committee on Strategy Concerned with Expanded C.O.R.E. Program, headed by Eugene T. Reed, a dentist from New York. The Congress of Racial Equality (CORE), like other civil rights organizations that had recently come into being, was an inevitable response to the middle-class approach of the staid NAACP, whose efforts were invariably through litigation, voter registration drives, and legislative programs. CORE offered its followers an activist, grassroots agenda that called for its members to confront white supremacy directly and not merely in the South. Voter registration would always be a part of its agenda, but so were demonstrations, mass action, boycotts, and sustained picketing to challenge racial discrimination in schools, housing, employment, and other areas. Reed's committee saw CORE as being "in open competition with us for the support of people interested in civil rights." But CORE was not the only group challenging the NAACP, and Reed's committee knew it. As Reed and his committee saw it, there were two questions the national office had to address: "(1), What should our relationship be with CORE and other civil rights groups? (2) How do we go about accelerating and adjusting our program and approach to the areas listed above?"[9]

As one of its goals, the committee recommended that the NAACP mount "a frontal attack on enterprises, whether they be manufacturer, wholesaler, retailer . . . willing to sell its produce to Negroes but unwilling to hire Negroes. The method of attack should be simply: SUCCESS BY NEGOTIATION IF POSSIBLE, BUT DEMONSTRATIONS, IF NECESSARY."[10]

But there was one person in the NAACP whose voice counted the most, and that was Roy Wilkins, who, along with the "Caucus," a group of his supporters on the board, set the policies of the national organization. As much as Wilkins gave lip service to the notion that the NAACP needed to become more militant, he was not about to allow it to undergo any fundamental change. There was not anything sinister about his motives: the way he had run the organization for so many years fit his personality perfectly. A handsome, urbane, sophisticated man, he was comfortable sitting down with white sympathetic power brokers in their offices and working out the best deal possible for blacks. If there were no other alternatives available, he would give his blessing to the filing of a lawsuit to bring about needed change and skillfully raise the money to support it. But like his field secretary in Arkansas, he had major doubts about the long-term benefits of taking the civil rights movement to the streets and keeping it there. That might make blacks feel better about themselves in the short run, but would it achieve their long-term goals? This debate was to be a major battle within the NAACP, and Bates was in a delicate position as a member of a board committee that ultimately wanted its executive director to take the organization in a fundamentally different direction. Nobody owed more to Roy Wilkins than Bates. It is not too much to say that without his support she would have vanished into history as nothing more than a footnote. The resources in Arkansas had been far too meager to soldier on alone under the onslaught of the likes of Orval Faubus. But Wilkins owed Bates, too. It was not that the Central High crisis had put the NAACP on the map. Obviously, nothing had been more important than the cases that led to the decision in *Brown*. But some way or another *Brown* had to be enforced if it was going to mean anything at all, and Bates had given much to that cause when circumstances had brought the case of *Aaron v. Cooper* to the attention of the nation.

Before Bates attended the NAACP national convention in Atlanta that summer, she came home in June, now secure in the knowledge that her manuscript was finally acceptable to Rawson. On June 8 Eleanor Roosevelt had let her know she would write the foreword. There was no sign of tension in Daisy's letter to L. C. telling him what time her plane was arriving in Little Rock. She wrote, "Audre sends her love. We're both very excited about Mrs. Roosevelt doing the Foreword." She signed it, "Love, Daisy."[11] On June 27, however, Daisy and L. C. signed a seven-page legal separation agreement prepared by attorney Christopher Mercer. The document would later be incorporated into their divorce decree, which became final on February 25, 1963.

Though the details of their marital problems have not been aired in public, it is not difficult to piece together the issues that divided them. Even before Daisy left Little Rock, she had become a different person, and L. C. was someone who changed remarkably little his entire life. L. C. had always stepped aside for Daisy, but by 1962 her importance had been validated for five years by people, some rich and famous, who adored her. Waiting at home was a man who knew her every weakness and insecurity. All this could have possibly been weathered but for one fact: Daisy was widely rumored to have been having an affair so torrid and notorious that her mother-in-law wrote her and L. C. on June 21, "I heard last year that Daisy was put in for a devoice & marrin a white man."[12] Her informant may well have been her son, but the rumor had made the rounds in Little Rock, and she could have heard it from a number of sources.[13]

It seems evident that it was this letter that precipitated their formal separation; however, correspondence from Mother Bates, who had moved to Chicago, makes clear that things had been going badly for some time. Though the timing of the events leading up to the separation agreement is not clear (perhaps beginning in the winter of 1962), Daisy had already insisted that L. C. move out of their house in Little Rock. The June 21 letter provides the evidence that Daisy had made this demand but does nothing to clarify when L. C. moved out and how rigid this arrangement was. One thing is certain: Daisy's ultimatum had included Mother Bates. The letter from Mother Bates is a painful letter in more ways than one. Mother Bates apparently suffered from arthritis in her hands, which made writing difficult and her words sometimes indecipherable when combined with her spelling. She had tried to stay out of their business. "Dasie I don't no one little thang about L. C. & other women. No more than I did of you and a man."[14]

Judging from her letter, one senses that perhaps L. C. had not been candid with his mother about his domestic problems. Though it is unclear, she apparently felt her son was in trouble with his wife for not paying the bills. "That is wrong. L. C. bought food ever week & paid your girls." For her part, Mother Bates obviously would have liked to have returned to a harmonious household. "If you need me to say any thang I will come Home but I no not one thang, but I am one that is worred now & hurt so if I am in your way please tell me." But her feelings had been badly wounded by her treatment, and though her letter is addressed both to her son and daughter-in-law, one can read between the lines and figure out who the culprit was in her eyes. "See you all was separate near 18 months and I tried to stay and take care of your house the best I could with the help you had there."[15]

L. C.'s letter of December 10, 1962, provides little information about their marital difficulties but says volumes about his feelings. "I have been expecting you to ask for your divorce for several years. Especially since 1958 . . ." begins the second paragraph of the letter L. C. wrote to his wife of twenty-two years. She was in New York; he was in Little Rock. L. C. was at his wit's end. "Earlier today," he had called the Brittany Hotel. "It was not a matter of checking on you." However, he wanted her to "get this letter. It may be the last communication you will have with me. However, I do not think this will faze you any."[16]

It is hard not to suspect that a bottle of the "good scotch" L. C. and Daisy once served to their guests was at his elbow as he typed this letter. For one thing, the letter contains a number of grammatical errors, none of which L. C. ever let appear in the *State Press*. On the other hand, the cause for the errors may have been the extraordinary emotion that L. C. poured into the letter. It was totally uncharacteristic of him. Dr. Edith Irby Jones has said that L. C.'s December letter was probably the only time in his life he ever told Daisy he loved her. "Mr. Bates said more in a letter than he ever said in a lifetime."[17] Undoubtedly, the early years of their marriage had been the best: Daisy hadn't been famous then. He had let her become city editor in 1945, but any time she needed to leave and do NAACP business she was out the door with his blessing. According to L. C., "it was not until 1945 . . . before you made any attempt to help earn one dime." Not that he begrudged her this freedom so few black women enjoyed. "Do not get me wrong—I did not want you to help me earn anything. I wanted you because I loved you and I was happy trying to make you happy. However I did not know at the time that I was only making you hate me." On and on the letter goes, spewing self-pity that he never displayed elsewhere. "Although old age is getting me; health failing; vision fading fast, nerves are shattered; no future in sight because ambition is gone, I do not feel that my life has been entirely wasted. Eventhough [*sic*], I do not get any credit from the source I should—I feel I have been of a little help to you in getting where you are, and this is a consolation."[18]

At the time L. C. wrote the letter, Bates was preparing for a New York book party on the December 17, which Langston Hughes and Roy Wilkins and other notables would attend. L. C.'s letter ends as sadly as it begins. "I hope your book party is a success, and all of the other ventures will be successful. What ever you do, you can always say that you were married to a man who loved LOVED LOVED YOU." Yours (as far as I am concerned) as ever, The man you married in Arkansas."[19]

One has to wonder if L. C. was in such despair that he was contemplating taking his life. Besides the earlier reference to the letter perhaps being his last communication with her, he adds a postscript after his signature: "All I have are some insurance policies and I told you where they were—in a tin box in the left hand drawer of my desk. LCB."[20]

Concerning the specifics of what was going on between them, L. C.'s letter again raises more questions than it answers. "When I think of how you put me out of the house that you and I both slaved and sacrificed to build . . . and you turn around and let another man enjoy the comforts while I am locked out, after having me to move my own mother out, This drives me to insanity, and naturally I can only think of the easiest way out." The identity of this other man is not known, but clearly being out of the house humiliated L. C. "I am ashamed to go by the house, I can't stand for people to look at me and say here is a man who built and furnished a house and cannot even go inside." According to L. C.'s letter, it appears that there was a time Daisy wasn't exactly welcome either. "Even you were not locked out, and did not have to TELEPHONE before you came or get permission to come."[21]

What if anything L. C. did to give Daisy the power to insist that he and his mother leave the home is only a matter of speculation. A letter from an unidentified friend in Memphis in July 1962 reveals clearly that Daisy was accusing him to others of seeing another woman. "But don't throw any more of the fine dishes at L. C. But do get him to sit down and work these problems out. There just couldn't be any woman in his life that he can't give up unless his head has turned to all water. Both of you admit that you love each other."[22]

The letter suggests that her correspondent was getting only one side of the story. There is no evidence that L. C. was having an affair. It seems most unlikely he would bring a woman into the home while Mother Bates was still living there, though Daisy would accuse him of it. "When I said you have other men in the house, that sounds bad. But when you accuse me of having women in the house, that sounds bad also" he wrote in December. No one ever accused Daisy of having a sexual relationship with a man in Little Rock, but at this point nothing apparently seemed too far-fetched in the way of accusations. If L. C. ever had a relationship with any woman after his marriage to Daisy, it escaped everyone's notice. Nor was there the slightest bit of gossip to this effect. Not a single person interviewed for this book would admit to having heard even a rumor about L. C. and other women.

Forty years after the fact and hundreds of divorces later, Chris Mercer, who is still practicing law in Little Rock, remembered nothing about the case. The agreement he drew up obligated L. C. to pay Daisy $200 a month and gave her the house and all the possessions "except for one TV set . . . and one refrigerator also in the basement."[23] L. C. did get the 1960 Dodge automobile he had been driving, which was an absolute necessity for his job as field secretary with responsibility for two states. Though L. C. signed a separation agreement, he was too much in love with Daisy to stay away from her when she was in town. Frankie Jeffries, who lived across the street, recalled, "I cooked for him, and washed his clothes for him, but after he got through with dinner and picking up his clothes he would go over there."[24] He could not control what Daisy did in New York, but he continued to try to get her back. L. C. even went to the Health Department and signed his name as an informant so that Daisy could get an amended birth certificate just weeks before her book came out. Thus it was L. C. who furnished the names of Daisy's birth parents, though of course he could only repeat what Daisy was telling him. Daisy's birth date is given as November 14, 1914.

The question of with whom Bates was involved in New York has been kept a secret. In a telephone interview with the author, Ann Henry, a friend of Bates's, related that on one occasion they were having drinks at Bates's house after Daisy and L. C. had remarried. Bates had gone to her closet and brought back a full-length mink coat and said her "friend" had given it to her. This relationship had ended when she was at some event in New York, perhaps to honor her. During the evening, a young black waiter was going down the stairs and accidentally bumped her friend, who had exclaimed, "You goddamned mother-fucking nigger!" Bates turned to her friend and said, "That's what I am!" and then she had angrily ripped the white evening gown she was wearing.[25] Henry had told Arkansas journalist Ernest Dumas substantially the same account but had added the details that the man was Jewish, that the incident had occurred at the Waldorf-Astoria, and that the man had given Bates the dress. Additionally, according to Dumas, Henry had told him that Bates had also said to her that when she went to New York, L. C. promptly installed in the house "a smart little thing."[26]

Again, friends of both L. C. and Daisy reported that L. C. was never interested in another woman besides Daisy, but that did not keep Daisy from making such allegations to others. Daisy may have simply been projecting her own feelings of guilt onto L. C. It did not matter to L. C. He was going to get her back. As Frankie Jeffries said,

"They were never really divorced because when they were separated they were still together. . . . I would say what time do you want dinner? He would say, make it kind of late because I got to go with Daisy." As far as how Daisy felt about L. C., Jeffries stated emphatically, "I know she loved him." No one in the Jeffries family who gathered for this interview contradicted her. Frankie Jeffries, who moved into the neighborhood before Daisy and L. C. arrived, had reason to know. She was Daisy's witness when Daisy and L. C. got a divorce in the winter of 1963, and she was their witness when they remarried six months later.

A number of other people have had a close relationship with Daisy, but this would be after Daisy had remarried L. C. and after she had suffered her stroke and had returned to Arkansas for good. Indeed, as her fame has increased, a cottage industry has grown up of people who are said to have special knowledge of her and jealously guard her memory and their special relationship. Unlike others, Frankie Jeffries made no special claim of intimacy, but from the day Daisy and L. C. moved into the neighborhood she and her husband and children lived across the street. Garman Freeman and his wife, Evangeline Upsur, both dentists, were also neighbors and close friends who socialized with Daisy and L. C. However, it was through the Jeffries children, ten in all but especially three daughters, Ruby, Linder, and Vearlon, that a bond with the family was formed. Vearlon, age forty-seven at the time of the interview in 2002, remembered, "They ate dinner here, we ate dinner there." Linder, age forty-eight, actually spent "so many nights" at the Bates beginning when she was "eight or nine." To "both of them I was [their] godchild."[27]

When all was said and done, Daisy did love L. C. He had represented a kind of security to her from the time after her foster father died when she had been a teenager. But there would always be the wish to rebel and escape the father's heavy hand. As much as L. C. loved her, it was a love that at times was stifling. L. C. was the kind of man who seemed born old. His nature was critical and judgmental. He couldn't turn off his personality just because he was crazy about his wife. "He would say [to Daisy] 'you got no business' going up there wherever it was. . . . He wanted his wife to stay home," Frankie Jeffries said.[28] He had been like an indulgent father, but the child he had raised would not stay in the house.

The relationship between L. C. and Daisy will always spark debate. L. C.'s December 1962 letter to Daisy with its unforgettable ending, from "a man who loved LOVED LOVED you," will always endear him to all but the coldest reader.[29]

It is beyond doubt that L. C. loved Daisy, but Dr. Edith Irby Jones's view of the relationship seems plausible (that he rarely, if ever, told her he loved her), especially after L. C. and Daisy moved to Little Rock and became respectable. Even L. C.'s most ardent admirers (and there were many) did not suggest that he was the type of man who remembered that Daisy like to be wooed her entire life and not just at the beginning of their relationship. Daisy, said Jones, needed the "little nothings" that make a relationship between mates more than a partnership, but she never got them from L. C. They will be remembered as partners in the battle for civil rights by those persons in Little Rock who view it as unfair that L. C.'s contributions to the movement have never been properly recognized, but their relationship was never only a partnership. After all, as a married man, L. C. had an affair from at least 1932 until 1942 and then married the woman with whom he had the affair. He may not have said very often the words Daisy longed to hear, but surely he gets credit for persistence.

The baggage they brought to the marriage complicated their lives, and it made them partners in a conspiracy to cover it up long before L. C. began the *State Press* and started telling blacks how to act. In writing what she hoped for the longest time was going to be called "The Daisy Bates Story," Bates felt a continuing need to try to maintain the fiction that they were the perfect couple.

Whom Bates had a relationship with in New York is only a matter of speculation. Was Otto Nathan the "older Jewish man" with whom she was rumored to have been having an affair? It does not seem likely, but perhaps it was their friendship that helped fuel the rumors. For one thing, Bates always called him "Dr. Nathan," including in the one short letter to him found in her papers. For another, Hanneman saw no evidence of any kind of romantic interest on either's part and has warned against reading much into his spending money on her at Bates's request. To Hanneman, it was obvious that he "admired" Bates as many others did, and doubtless she admired him as well.

Was the relationship with her ghostwriter, George Penty? Hanneman remembered no chemistry between them on the numerous occasions they were all together, and Penty has denied having an affair with Bates.[30] Bates denied having had any extramarital relationship to her friend Frankie Jeffries, but that did not keep the rumors from spreading in the black community. Her minister, Rev. Rufus King

Young, remembered, "They put a rumor here that she quit her husband and . . . gone [*sic*] with a white man."[31]

The summer of 1962 was difficult for Bates in another way as well.
Though she was no longer president of the Arkansas State Conference of
Branches, it was hard to let go, and, in fact, Bates didn't really try. Back
home after the national NAACP conference and waiting out the final
weeks before *The Long Shadow of Little Rock* was published, Bates fired
off a letter to Wiley Branton, criticizing him for turning to Ozell Sutton,
who was at the Arkansas Council on Human Relations, to find black
children to apply to white schools. In a previous telephone conversation,
Branton had told Bates that Sutton was now his "contact" man. Sutton
was also a loyal member of the NAACP, but Bates's letter to Branton
made it sound as if he somehow had betrayed the organization by doing
what was obviously necessary to further the litigation goals of *Aaron v.
Cooper*. "You know the ground-work for the case was laid in 1956 by
the Little Rock Branch NAACP." On and on Bates went in paragraph
after paragraph, setting out the history of the litigation known far better
by Branton than she. Finally, she came to her main point: It was "a problem that concerns us greatly. It is the attitude of the people here since they
have been alerted to the fact, that they do not have to come through
NAACP channels to file suit against discrimination." To make it worse
in Bates's eyes, in the suit Branton had recently filed to desegregate public facilities in Little Rock, many of the plaintiffs were "not members of
the NAACP" and did "not feel any moral or financial responsibility
toward the NAACP, or the Legal Defense and Educational Fund judging
from the small amount raised for the support of the suit."[32]

If Bates thought she was defending the NAACP by attacking
Branton, she was wrong. Instead, she was opening the door to having
an unpleasant truth pointed out to her by Branton, who had moved to
Atlanta to head up the Voter Education Project for the Southern
Regional Council. L. C., who was copied in this exchange, must have
cringed at some of the statements in Branton's letter. "Frankly, I have
become concerned about the apparent lack of interest which the Little
Rock Branch has taken in the matter for the past several months. . . .
I know that Mr. L. C. Bates has been cooperative in some instances in
helping to [recruit students] but I am not familiar with the full extent
of his cooperation." When Daisy had been around, the "cooperation
from you was as good as any to be had; however, when you left
Arkansas and went to New York it appears that no NAACP person
could effectively assume this responsibility."[33]

Branton was far too discreet to even hint at the rumors about Bates coming out of New York, but as a valued colleague of the NAACP lawyers at the Legal Defense and Educational Fund, he would have heard them. The reference to Bates's sojourn there alone surely set everyone's teeth on edge.

Branton was clearly furious and set the record straight. He wrote that the "real trouble was the fact that I have given so freely of my time to NAACP and NAACP Legal Defense and Education[al] Fund that you perhaps think of me as being on the staff and you forget the fact that I am a private lawyer engaged in private practice."[34]

Wiley Branton was not a man to be trifled with. He could document everything he said in the letter. He had taken on *Aaron v. Cooper* when no Little Rock lawyer would touch it, and he was still involved even though he was now in Atlanta. He chose his words as carefully in this letter as he did when he was litigating his cases. He never said Bates had abandoned the fight for civil rights in Little Rock to go off to New York for purely personal reasons. He didn't need to. But he was not about to let Bates take him to task in front of people whose opinions mattered to him. Bates's letter was reminiscent of her meddling in the Chelsea branch in New York. She was totally off base, but she never had a clue, copying the letter to many of the NAACP leaders in New York, including Wilkins.

The summer of 1962 was a roller coaster ride not only for Bates but also for the organization she loved. A growing minority of the NAACP national board began to contemplate revolt. According to historian Gretchen Cassel Eick, the Young Turks, as they later came to be known, first began to flock together at the national NAACP convention in Atlanta in 1962. They found themselves commiserating over the failure of the national organization to challenge segregation in Atlanta "with some sort of demonstration."[35]

Jack Tanner, a young attorney from Tacoma, Washington, and later a federal district court judge, had been elected to the national board and made his first appearance as a board member at the annual convention in Atlanta. As a future member of the Young Turks, he recalled meeting Bates, who was assigned, like other delegates, to the broiling dormitories at Clark University. As they waited together for transportation to take them to the convention headquarters, "Daisy would complain about the heat more than anyone else." Tanner "considered Daisy in the image of my friend Medgar Evers, who I considered to be the hero of the young people in the Civil Rights Movement at that time. Both Medgar and Daisy had that most uncommon dedication, courage, bravery, and character that has been rarely shown by others, white, black, or any other color, in the history of America." Though Eick identifies Bates as one of the Young Turks, Tanner called Daisy a "silent supporter." The reason why she was "not out front with the rest of us" was obvious: "The old guard was still in control and she and her husband needed money."[36]

The festering insurgency mounted by the dissidents would come to a head in 1965. At that time, it appeared for a while as if the Young Turks, who never numbered more than thirteen of the total board members but who controlled three of the regions, might gain control of the convention.[37] They were ultimately cut down by Wilkins and the Caucus in 1968, who made certain they would not be reelected to the board. As proof that Bates was never recognized as a Young Turk, she managed to win another term while her allies went down to defeat.

Chapter Seventeen

THE LONG SHADOW OF LITTLE ROCK

The national backdrop of the publication of *The Long Shadow of Little Rock* in 1962 was the violent confrontation between the Kennedy administration and Governor Ross Barnett of Mississippi. The battle on the University of Mississippi campus in Oxford over James Meredith's admission into law school in the fall of 1962 made the crisis at Central High seem tame by comparison. Though the civil rights movement had moved well on down the road, with history being repeated so recently, *The Long Shadow of Little Rock*'s publication date of October 29 helped convince reviewers of its relevance. Bates's sketchy and vague story of her upbringing and marriage to L. C. provided just enough context for her battles at Central High, and reviewers accepted the book as a seamless account of the making of a civil rights heroine.

The *New York Times Book Review* critic praised *The Long Shadow of Little Rock* as having "a sort of journalistic integrity that makes the narrative as a whole believable and convincing." Bates's name would "almost certainly" go down in history as one of the "martyrs and fearless pioneers" of the civil rights movement. The names of the Little Rock Nine would also be enshrined, but they were almost an afterthought for reviewers. Bates had written sketches of each of the children (some longer than others but all positive and laudatory), but truly her book was taken as "The Daisy Bates Story."[1]

Some reviewers, as Eleanor Roosevelt did in the book's foreword, remarked on the bitter tone that surfaced in the book's last few pages. The great March on Washington was less than a year away, but the redemptive power of Martin Luther King Jr.'s words and deeds were already beginning to resonate in the hearts of those whites who deigned to care. A reviewer in the *Churchman* in St. Petersburg,

Florida, after remarking on Bates's "contempt" for those whites who had fought against her, wrote, "Ultimately, there must be love and forgiveness, as Martin Luther King reiterates."[2] Such words, when stripped of their context, seem too meek to fuel a movement that became as powerful as the tactics of nonviolence.[3] One had to be there to experience fully the determination and persistence that undergirded marchers and leaders alike. Nothing would be more critical than keeping the movement nonviolent. Therein lay its strength, but it was not so simple.

White Americans were becoming uneasy, and it was not just that their consciences were bothering them. Whites were already beginning to feel consciously afraid, and the term "Black Power" was not even in vogue. In what was perhaps the longest and most important review of her book, Robert E. Baker, a reporter for the *Washington Post* who remembered Bates in 1957 as a "courageous, charming, witty and sophisticated Negro leader with a deep faith in her fellow Americans and the Nation's Democratic ideals," was also disturbed by Bates's anger. He commented that those positive qualities were in evidence in the book but that her bitterness was something new. If a black leader "of Mrs. Bates's stature" could give way to "contempt and hostility," then what was ahead for the country? Did the "nation . . . face a bloody war on American soil between Americans" in the future?[4]

In retrospect, one understands that what had made Bates so appealing in 1957 to her supporters was the perception that she had infinite patience and no hatred of whites. Her ability to control her emotions in public was one of her greatest assets. In fact, only a few sentences at the end of *The Long Shadow of Little Rock* could be taken as "negative." In general, the book was an uplifting reprise of Bates's struggles against great odds, just what the American public had always enjoyed.

Her publisher and editor, Kenneth Rawson, pushed the book, as did others. Bates had a ready-made readership through the NAACP. Kivie Kaplan, a fellow board member of the national NAACP, offered to buy 250 copies "for gifts" if Bates would autograph them.[5]

Though the David McKay Company had high hopes for the book, sales were ultimately a disappointment. Because the executor of Bates's estate did not give me permission to obtain information from the company that bought McKay, it is not possible to know final sales figures. The two royalty statements in Bates's papers are for the six-month periods ending December 1963 and December 1965. The documents do not reveal the size of Bates's original advance, but it probably was no more than $1,000. As mentioned previously, Bates had received $1,000 from Rawson before publication to pay insurance on the house in Little Rock. In any event, the royalty statement showed a "debit balance" of $1,325.94 at the end of 1965. Any dreams Bates had ever entertained of being able to survive even briefly off the earnings of the book turned out to be illusory.

The David McKay publicity department did an admirable job of getting attention for the book. Bates appeared on television in New York and had television appearances in Washington, D.C., and perhaps New Orleans as well. Little Rock was not neglected either. "More than two hundred persons" showed up at the Dunbar Community Center on November 11 to have Bates sign their books. Minnijean Brown and Thelma Mothershed, both students at Southern Illinois University at Carbondale, were "guests of honor."[6] While in Arkansas, Bates also signed copies at the state NAACP convention in Pine Bluff. She would later say that sales of her book were hurt by the fact that bookstores in the South would not carry it, and doubtless that was true.

Chris Mercer filed Daisy Bates's complaint for divorce the last day of 1962. Her hopes for the book may have led her to go ahead with it. L. C.'s December letter had no effect and may have had the opposite one intended, reminding Daisy that her feelings about the marriage came as no surprise to her husband. Yet surely she must have done some soul-searching about the life she was giving up. In the fall of 1962 she received two letters from her former foster child Clyde Lee Cross, who was aware her book was about to be published. How much contact Daisy had with Clyde after she and L. C. had given him up in the fall of 1957 is not known. Curiously, there is not, in all her papers, a single letter to him. It was not as if Clyde had been a child who had come to stay for a short while. Of all the decisions in her life, surely few were more painful than giving up the child she had raised for years. Bates had successfully kept Clyde's whereabouts a secret (at least from the media and her enemies). In one of his letters to his "mother" in September 1962, Clyde, who would have been a teenager, reveals that he was living in Snow Lake, a hamlet in the Arkansas Delta. He mentions the "boys and girls," leaving one to wonder if he was in some kind of orphanage. Tragically, the two letters from Clyde in Bates's papers reveal a youngster both emotionally and educationally deprived. Bates would take in other children, and they would blossom under her attention. Though Clyde requested that a "bicycle" be sent to "snow lake ark Box 109," it is most improbable that he got his wish.[7] Bates had moved on, but it seems likely these two letters would have tugged at her heart and reminded her of a time when she and L. C. had shared the routine pleasures of a less glamorous life.

Arkansas's divorce law makes it one of the easiest and quickest states in the country in which to dissolve a marriage. Bates's complaint contained the minimum allegations necessary to obtain an Arkansas divorce. Certainly, there were no specifics, no allegations of adultery, which might have caused L. C. to hire his own lawyer and fire back. L. C.'s strategy was to act as if nothing had happened and try to see Daisy as much as possible. She might think she wanted him out of her life forever, but he had other ideas.

Daisy needed to support herself. L. C. had the only job in the state of Arkansas for which she was most qualified. Though she had written a book, she was no professional writer, and as Chris Mercer pointed out, she "had no skills." However, this was not a woman who was going to clean the houses of white people for a living. Her divorce complaint made headlines in the black papers. The closest any paper came to raising the issue of other men in Bates's life was when the *Afro-American* ran a comment she made herself. "I have no man in my life that I am interested in marrying," she told the paper.[8] With a different man, such a comment might have been a red flag, but L. C. was not going to contest the divorce. To fight Daisy meant risking losing her permanently.

Applying for a job in the North was a slightly awkward matter since in the final pages of *The Long Shadow of Little Rock* Daisy had written she and L. C. would continue the battle "for the emancipation of the Negro in the South."[9] Given her loyalty and dedication, it is not surprising that her first job after her divorce was with the NAACP. Bates was given five-weeks' work at a salary of $110 per week to serve as a special "campaign director" for a membership drive in Rochester, New York, beginning in March. It was an inspired, if obvious, choice. With her feisty personality and her fame among NAACP regulars, who better than Bates to beat the drum outside the South? Gloster Current held out the possibility that if she did well in Rochester, the NAACP could "use her in another campaign."[10] Obviously, serving as a board member, any criticism she had of the direction of the NAACP nationally would have to remain hidden.

The job had its limitations. The national office would not pay for a hotel room (she would have to stay in private homes), so she would have no privacy. In the meantime, Bates had been busy networking and had managed to get an invitation to a White House reception on Lincoln's birthday. There, along with other guests, she had her photograph taken with President Kennedy.[11]

With a national campaign on the horizon in 1964, the Democrats needed northern black votes in order to be successful. Eisenhower had managed to get through the occupation of Little Rock without the loss of the life of a single irate southerner. Kennedy had not been so lucky in Oxford, and although Lyndon Johnson would be blamed for losing the "Solid South" in future elections because of his support for civil rights, the process was already well under way. The party might as well get something in return for its support. In a close campaign, the black vote would be decisive, and nobody knew it better than Kennedy, who had nearly lost the 1960 election because of stronger than expected black support for Richard Nixon.

Obviously successful in Rochester, Bates received another assignment from Current to go to Cincinnati. But with the help of Louis Martin, an influential Kennedy operative in the White House, Bates was hired by Phil Weightman of the AFL-CIO's Committee on Political Education (COPE) to register black voters.[12] The political arm of the AFL-CIO, COPE was an important ally of the NAACP. It was a natural fit for Bates.

Sometimes it was hard to tell where COPE began and the NAACP left off. In *A Rope of Sand: The AFL-CIO Committee on Political Education, 1955–1967*, Alan Draper tells of how in Ohio, then a right-to-work state, " 'Freedom buses' were organized by the NAACP, COPE, and local ministers to take new registrants to the Board of Elections."[13] In later interviews, Bates would tell reporters she cut her teeth running voter registration campaigns in the tough neighborhoods of Chicago, but it was in places like the Firestone Local 7 Hall in Ohio that she got her start. Weightman's operation left no stone unturned. "COPE . . . paid canvassers to go door-to-door in black neighborhoods to check if occupants were registered." Weightman claimed that 40,000 blacks were "newly registered as a result" of COPE's efforts. It paid immediate dividends: "Black districts voted eight-to-one against right-to-work."[14]

Bates surely appreciated the irony of her labors. There was no doubt about how COPE or the NAACP expected a "newly registered voter" to vote—Democratic. But in her home state, Orval Faubus and the Democratic Party were still riding high. It did not keep her from going home occasionally, for, as noted earlier, Bates found time to slip down into Arkansas to remarry L. C. in the town of Benton in Saline County.

Daisy and L. C. would escape the violence of the civil rights era with their lives intact; others doing the same work would not. In neighboring Mississippi, Medgar Evers, the embattled NAACP field secretary, was murdered outside his home in 1963. A photograph of Daisy staring sorrowfully into Evers's casket has survived with her papers. Given the brutality of southern law enforcement, it was difficult for even someone as cool as Daisy to stay nonviolent. After Evers's funeral, Jackson police handled a young demonstrator roughly. Bates told the media that the Jackson police "had provoked the trouble by mistreating a Negro girl of about fourteen." The crowd got angry, she observed. "We have a tendency to condemn the freedom fighters when they show human anger . . . I'm definitely non-violent, but at that moment I was ready to throw a bottle myself."[15]

It was not that Arkansas, especially the Delta, was not a violent place. As field secretary, L. C. investigated the cold-blooded lynching of a seventeen-year-old boy in West Memphis in July. A coroner's inquest found nothing amiss, although the boy had been hunted down by whites and shot and then left to bleed to death.[16] Other blacks would continue to lose their lives in encounters with white authorities in the Arkansas Delta. The difference was that Arkansas was mostly ignored by the movement, which concentrated its resources on the Deep South states of Mississippi, Alabama, and Georgia. SNCC was active in Delta towns such as Pine Bluff, Forrest City, West Helena, Marvell, and in the south Arkansas hamlet of Gould, but Arkansas was simply not a priority. White leaders, at least in Little Rock, wanted to avoid the publicity of 1957 and peacefully negotiated desegregation of public facilities, though it took litigation as well to complete the job.

Though Bates spent most of her time outside Arkansas during 1962–63, she was in Little Rock to make the bus trip to the March on Washington in August. In L. C.'s September 1963 report to the national NAACP, he recorded that eighty people from Arkansas made the trip, taking chartered buses from Pine Bluff and Little Rock. Almost all were from Pine Bluff and Little Rock, but seven were from Crittenden County (West Memphis), where blacks had organized to protest the murder of the young teenager. According to L. C., three whites made the bus trip.[17] Ozell Sutton remembered gratefully that Bates made it possible for him to ride the bus from Little Rock.

Bates, like most Americans, was depressed by President Kennedy's murder on November 22, 1963. Then on the payroll of Democratic National Committee (DNC), the national organization of the Democratic Party, but with the same job, she wrote a friend on December 19, "I do not have to tell you how the death of the President affected me. I have not been able to decide what my future will be."[18] In another letter before Christmas, she wrote, "I haven't been doing much work since the death of the late President Kennedy. The N.D.C. [*sic*] asked if I would continue working for the Party next year. I haven't made up my mind as of now."[19]

At year's end in Little Rock, Bates did not see much to be cheerful about. The weather was atrocious. She and L. C. had been "snow-bound in 18 inches of snow in 13 below zero weather [in Memphis]." About her husband, she wrote merely, "Nothing new with L. C. and I" except the snowstorm. "Faubus is still raising hell. . . . I for one am not sad to see the year 1963 end."[20] It had been a stressful year. Divorce, remarriage, a new job—all the events psychologists warn about crowding into one time period. Another event occurred that year. Bates had turned fifty in November, and it had to have sobered her a bit. She had many years left to live, but she had made a fateful choice by remarrying L. C. Given what was to happen in 1964, it was the wisest decision she ever made, because though she had many friends, Daisy had no family but L. C. "Family" would appear magically out of the blue when she was much older and recognized and honored in Arkansas as a civil rights pioneer. Against the bright lights of New York, L. C. may no longer have excited her, but he loved her and would take care of her.

With the death of President Kennedy, Bates had good reason to question the value of what she was doing simply because of who had taken his place. Lyndon Johnson was a southerner, and Bates had already had her fill of southern politicians. It is impossible to re-create the dismay blacks must have felt when Johnson became president. They had not all fallen in love with Kennedy, but compared to what they expected from his successor, Kennedy's administration really had seemed like Camelot for a brief shining moment.

Miracles never cease in American politics. Lyndon Johnson, despite all his monumental insecurities and the heavy-handedness that, when combined with his crude arrogance, could take a person's breath away, was the genuine article when it came to civil rights for "Knee-Grows" (as he was careful to pronounce the word). As Martin Luther

King Jr. had been saying, civil rights was a moral issue for the nation, and like no other American politician could have done or would ever do again, Johnson took up the cause. African Americans would later love Bill Clinton, another southerner, but nobody went to bat for civil rights like Johnson during an era when doing so was thought to be political suicide for a southerner. "Mr. Bates was crazy about Johnson," Daisy told Elizabeth Jacoway.[21]

Daisy may have been less personally enthralled with Johnson than L. C. was, but Johnson treated her well. She told Jacoway that when Johnson became president, he asked an aide,

> "Where's Daisy Bates? They said she used to be around here." And they said, "She is at home." "Where's home?" "In Little Rock. She's staying in Little Rock." He said, "Isn't she working?" "You know she can't get a job in Arkansas." He said, "Well, get a reservation for her at the Mayflower, and call her." . . . "The President commands your presence on Thursday morning. I'm going to take you to his office at nine o'clock." And I thought he was kidding.

American Airlines called and had a ticket for her. "And he [Johnson] was one of the nicest persons to work for. And he gave me a raise in salary. I think I was making for Kennedy about ten thousand dollars. And he raised it two thousand."[22]

There is evidence she did a good job for the DNC. She would be on the road three weeks and at home a week.[23] A letter to Louis Martin from an admirer in March 1964 about her work in Chicago reads in part: "After meeting and listening to Mrs. Daisy Bates here in Chicago on several occasions, I felt that you and the Democratic National Organization should know how she inspired and motivated us here . . . meeting and seeing her in action with the people is something that anyone, who has been priviliged [sic] to have this experience, shall never forget." The letter concluded, "Keep her traveling and spreading the good word."[24]

A more objective view of Bates during this period appeared in *Jet* in April. "Her name is no longer the magic it was in 1957 . . . some political pros remain unmoved when Daisy Bates grandly announces her presence." Yet there were those who admired the way she rolled up her sleeves and got out the vote in Indianapolis. "Said one old pro who usually bites his tongue on praise: 'She worked like hell.'" Bates was part of a team of workers, but according to the *Jet* article, the results were impressive. "In just over two months, 24,000 persons—about 14,000 of them Negroes—were registered to vote."[25]

The *Jet* article provided a picture of her life on the road. "Sandwiched between her two or three speeches a day (she made more than 50 speeches in 18 days in Chicago) and her energetic work for 'the party,' she manages to return to the hotel rooms that serve as her on-the-road headquarters. There a light gin and tonic seems to persuade the soreness from her slippered feet. Still svelte, still shapely, still attractive, Mrs. Bates slips into one of the big cushioned chairs." Bates portrayed herself as still a second mother to the Little Rock Nine.[26] Bates told *Jet* she heard from each of them at least once a month, "twice, or even three times a month." Based on the letters in her papers, this was an exaggeration, and when Bates did hear from the Nine, the letters invariably were in conjunction with the financial aid that was still flowing from the NAACP for their college educations. This is not to say that the letters did not display affection for her, but it is stretching it to say the Nine actually considered Bates a "second mother." The Little Rock crisis had been her claim to fame, and she did not hesitate to remind people about it. She dismissed her marital problems "with a regal flick of the wrist and the observation: 'It was simply a misunderstanding. It happens in the best of families.' "[27]

Although Bates always got good notices from the black press, the *Jet* article captured her persona with the words "regal" and "grand." As Audre Hanneman wrote, when Bates walked into a room, she expected people to know who she was and was disappointed when she wasn't "introduced at some event to which she had been invited; although this rarely happened."[28]

A campaign speech Bates made for Lyndon Johnson in 1964 survives in her papers. Surely written or vetted by leaders at the DNC, the speech was shameless in its use of hyperbole. Unable to attack Goldwater as personally prejudiced, the speech linked his conservative approach to government with racism in a way that today seems demagogic. At one point, the text reads: "If Goldwater is elected one would probably need a passport to enter the country of Mississippi."[29]

By then Mississippi had become a daily symbol for the worst excesses of white supremacy in the country, with the infamous three murders of three civil rights workers. To get the campaign juices flowing, Bates had only to mention the words "Mississippi" and "Goldwater" in the same breath. She did the math for her audiences: A vote for Goldwater equaled a vote for states' rights, and a vote for states' rights equaled disaster for blacks. "If the ardent state right's [*sic*] advocator, Goldwater, is elected, you will see the greatest exodus of Negroes, as well as many fair minded whites, out of the state of Mississippi, this country has ever witnessed."[30]

It was a speech designed to rouse blacks by scaring them, but Johnson's presidential campaign was, of course, in many ways based on fear. What reader of a certain age can forget the ad the Democrats ran warning of a nuclear holocaust if Goldwater won? If Bates's speech was any indication, in black wards the emphasis was not on voting for Johnson because he worked so hard to pass the Civil Rights Act of 1964 (while Goldwater had voted against it) and promised more to come. Rather, the message was elect Goldwater and you protect lynching and the KKK. In fact, there were distinct political limits to federal intervention no matter who was going to be the president.

Johnson's overwhelming mandate in November pleased Bates no end. She "arrived home from the campaign trail on November 4, extremely tired but estactic [*sic*] about the results of the election."[31] However, the results of the state election for governor were not pleasing at all: Faubus, running for a fifth two-year term, garnered an astonishing 86 percent of the black vote. The facts were that no matter how antiblack his rhetoric had been, he had always gotten the black vote; now that he was toning it down, he received even more. Faubus's support by blacks was galling to L. C. and Daisy, but they were stuck with him. At the national civil rights level, Faubus still ranked high in the worst southern governor pantheon, though Ross Barnett of Mississippi and George Wallace of Alabama were far ahead. It was especially a dilemma for L. C. because of his conservative approach to the civil rights movement. Though he and Roy Wilkins were not far apart (Wilkins had called for blacks to cease almost all demonstrations until after the November election), L. C. (like Wilkins) became increasingly out of step with the growing militancy of the rest of the civil rights movement. His reports to Gloster Current show he was openly contemptuous of the organizing challenges mounted by SNCC in the Arkansas Delta and the support given to it by the NAACP regional office. In commenting on an NAACP chapter in Gould in southern Arkansas, L. C. wrote, "The past three years it has been plagued by 'Snick' . . . for some reason that has never been made entirely clear, interference from the Regional Office sprung up and gave encouragement to the 'Snick' group. The branch is at a standstill."[32]

At the end of the day, L. C. still believed marches and demonstrations accomplished very little. The approach he took sparked controversy of its own, and Daisy was eventually drawn into it. As early as 1962 or 1963, L. C. had begun to deal with Faubus through the director of the state's Employment Security Division to obtain jobs for blacks.[33] The *Arkansas Gazette* reported in December 1965 that "Daisy and L. C. Bates were advising Faubus on the appointment for blacks." The reporter found this arrangement "curious," but Daisy coolly explained, "Of course we deal with the governor. He pulls the strings. He is the governor, and we go to him to get Negroes their fair share."[34] Though this tactic was pragmatic and resulted in some employment for blacks, it caused dissension in the NAACP.

The first half of 1965 Daisy was once again working for the national NAACP in the Midwest and East on voter registration campaigns. In June she had come back to Arkansas to spearhead a statewide drive, a project dear to L. C.'s heart. To people who had known them both before 1957, it must have seemed like old times again. It appeared as if they were a team, just as they had been all those years at the *State Press* and at the beginning of the 1957 crisis, before Daisy became famous. Certainly, they presented themselves that way, and as far as carrying out the work of the NAACP, they were now working again in tandem. However, it is impossible to overlook how little time Daisy spent in Little Rock after their remarriage in 1963 until she finally retired in 1977, when she had become further debilitated by her illnesses.

At the kick-off campaign in Pine Bluff, Daisy appeared first and explained that under a new law, blacks would no longer have to continue to register each year. The poll tax was dead and gone. L. C. enthusiastically followed his wife by urging his listeners to "go to the polls in groups" and not just in "trickles." "When they see you coming, they're going to say, 'Good God Almighty.'" With the 1964 Civil Rights Act and the Voting Rights Act of 1965, L. C. saw a new day for blacks, but, typically, he warned them, "They won't come out and give you anything. They won't come out and offer you jobs. You're going to have to prepare yourselves."[35]

Daisy Bates's life changed forever on July 10, 1965. According to her neighbor Frankie Jeffries, Bates was looking at herself in a mirror in her home when she realized something was wrong. She called Jeffries and asked her to come across the street. Where L. C. was inside the house at that moment and why Daisy did not call him is not known, but Jeffries says she went across the street. She and L. C. immediately took Daisy to Baptist Hospital. On July 27 Daisy called her friend Ed Muse in New York from the hospital. He had received a letter from L. C. dated July 20 telling him that Daisy had recently been "rushed to the hospital" and had been diagnosed with "Pulmonary Thrombosis." Muse, who was then working as life membership assistant for the NAACP national office, sent an alarming memo to Henry Lee Moon, director of public relations, saying in part, "Daisy called me this morning and discussed many things, even though she was quite incoherent. I think there is real cause for concern."[36] He copied Roy Wilkins and Gloster Current. On July 31 the national office sent out a press release announcing that Bates had been "stricken while in the midst of a statewide NAACP voter registration campaign she had organized." She was reported to be "improving." It made no reference to her diagnosis.[37] In any event, Jeffries remembered that Bates "was hospitalized for almost a month." Bates's recovery was slow. Jeffries recalled taking care of her, and L. C. would "put her to bed."[38]

Without the cooperation of Bates's estate, knowledge of her maladies is limited to the memories of others and references in her papers. Clearly, her future symptoms and treatment suggest that she possibly had several small strokes over the course of her life, but the timing of these events is unclear. At some point her speech would be affected, but the Jeffries family maintained that her difficulty in speaking was not caused by a stroke but occurred as a result of a surgical procedure when "they took too much of her Adam's apple out."[39]

Bates had been scheduled to go on vacation in Europe (apparently without L. C.) in July, but that was, of course, canceled. Her recovery was still under way in December, as noted by a letter L. C. wrote to Gloster Current. "Daisy is doing fairly well. She is still under the care of her physician and getting a big thrill in working with the youth."[40] It would take a while, but Daisy Bates was gathering her strength for one final crusade.

Chapter Eighteen

MITCHELLVILLE—SELF-HELP OR MONUMENT?

It does not appear that Bates's health allowed her to return to work for the national NAACP in 1965, but she was strong enough to do what she most enjoyed, and that was work with black youngsters. By June 1966, through her influence and dedication, the NAACP Youth Council flourished in Little Rock, growing to about 137 members.

Unfortunately, early on in 1966 it was becoming apparent that L. C. was having major conflict in his role as field secretary with Dr. Jerry Jewell, a Little Rock dentist who had succeeded George Howard as Arkansas president of the State Conference of Branches. Soon Jewell's bad feelings would extend to Daisy as well. On Feb. 2 L. C. copied a letter to Jewell, among others, including Roy Wilkins, in which he answered questions addressed to him by Gloster Current about his past relationship with Orval Faubus. Faubus had finally been succeeded in January by Republican Winthrop Rockefeller. In November Rockefeller had defeated arch-racist Jim Johnson in a race in which blacks had provided the transplanted Yankee his margin of victory. After a record six terms, Faubus had not run again in 1966, which made it even more strange that L. C. would continue to deal with him. Had it appeared that Faubus would continue to be governor, L. C.'s actions would have been more understandable.

The copy to Jewell was not an afterthought. Jewell had been complaining about the actions of his field secretary in dealing with a man whom he had lambasted for years. L. C. wrote Current, "In your letter, you asked, 'How does this new posture in Little Rock, Arkansas, square with our "image" as a militant organization?' "[1]

The NAACP was, of course, along with the Urban League, the least militant civil rights organization on the national scene, and it was facing competition from SNCC, CORE, and other groups that had a broader appeal to younger blacks throughout the country. If it was not going to be militant, its leadership at least wanted to appear militant, because at that very moment it was facing a revolt by the Young Turks, which included the silent support of Daisy Bates.

L. C. pointed to the fact that he had been constructing a "militant record" since moving to Arkansas in 1941, which was "the basis for the recognition I now enjoy in helping the economic condition of the Negro."[2] Seen in that context, L. C.'s response made perfect sense, but the trouble was that by working with Faubus to get a handful of jobs for blacks, he could be compared to those old-style black leaders of the past who made deals with white politicians. Of course, there was no similarity between L. C. and the black preachers and others he had criticized in the *State Press* all those years. They had lined their own pockets; he got nothing except scorn from his own superiors and a bad taste in his own mouth.

Current's second question was harder to answer: "How do we avoid the criticism that the NAACP is now collaborating with its former enemy?" Instead of pointing out that a new day was dawning racially in Arkansas, L. C. responded by saying that "my effort is responsible for some 100 Negroes in good paying dignified jobs where federal funds are being used. Many more are slated to be employed in all branches of the state government."[3]

L. C.'s responses continued along this line and may even have elicited some sympathy from Roy Wilkins, but the problem was that L. C. had apparently not cleared any of his actions with Jewell. "You asked me to comment upon the reaction and attitude of the state president. You also stated that in conversation with him, he raised serious doubts about my working with the governor." L. C.'s reply to Current was weak but hardly apologetic. "The president was not available when the conference [with Faubus] was available." Moreover, L. C. wrote, "I will not attempt to comment on his reaction and attitude, because I am devoid of clairovoyant [*sic*] power. Since you are in touch with him, I am positive that he would feel more freely in giving it to you firsthand. Therefore, I take the liberty to suggest that you talk with him."[4]

Here was the real rub as far as L. C. was concerned. The state president had been complaining about him behind his back. Moreover, Jewell seemed to go out of his way to avoid working with L. C. In his reports to Current, L. C. refers repeatedly to Jewell being unavailable.[5]

The one example of L. C. and Jewell working together was a memo signed by each of them to Arkansas NAACP members urging them to vote in the Democratic run-off since Jim Johnson was one of the candidates.

In June an incident had occurred that sent the relationship between Daisy Bates and Jerry Jewell past the breaking point. Bates apparently had built the Youth Council around the leadership of a teenager named Gladys Huggins, with whom she was greatly impressed. Bates had spent "eight or nine months" getting to know Huggins and "found her to have the dedication, integrity, and potential leadership" that was just what the program needed.[6] For her part, Huggins attributed the growth of the Youth Council, which had functioned "like a private club," to the "moral and active support I have received from [Mrs. Bates] and Mrs. Jeffries."[7]

According to Bates, Jewell was singled-handedly responsible for the demise of the Youth Council. On September 3, 1966, she wrote Jewell of the resignation of Gloria Huggins. "I truly feel that your action at the meeting on June 19 and the subsequent meeting which you called with 10 out of approximately 137 members, at the Community Center, literally killed the Youth Council of the NAACP in Little Rock." Though she does not say what was discussed at this particular meeting, Bates became quite specific in her criticism. "Before I started to work with the Youth Council, it was considered a closed organization. It also appeared that the council was being used by certain persons to furnish summer vacations for their children by having them elected delegates to the National Convention."[8]

Bates went on to describe how she had become an adviser to the Youth Council because "SNCC had opened an office in Little Rock. I have seen the NAACP lose a number of youth to Snick [*sic*] by default." She had built the group up, but "certain persons . . . started a plan to disrupt or destroy the organization and with your help they apparently have just about succeeded." She also reminded Jewell that she had persuaded Rev. J. C. Crenchaw to step down and asked him to run for president of the Little Rock branch so "new blood" would come into the organization. However, instead of "new blood," "the attendance has fallen off to the same 8 or 10 members."[9]

Bates saved her angriest salvo at Jewell for last. According to her, "during the National Convention in Los Angeles, in a called meeting, you made a statement to the Director of Branches, Mr. Gloster Current, and others to the effect that I had stolen money from the youth council."

Bates demanded that Jewell send an apology to Current and to everybody at the meeting and accused Jewell of "deformation [*sic*] of character."[10]

Both Daisy and L. C. seemed quite embattled during this period. In August L. C. complained that the regional office had "interfered" with his work by supporting SNCC. His complaint prompted an angry response from Richard Dockery, NAACP regional field director, who took "exception to your choice of words" and of course passed his response along to Current.[11]

Yet Current was undoubtedly used to the internal disputes that are inevitable in organizations and defused some of the tension by writing Bates that he had received a copy of Gloria Huggins's letter and had "noted its contents." He concluded by saying, "It was good to see you at the Board meeting looking better and as enthusiastic as ever."[12] Bates's letter to Jewell on September 3 most likely did not elicit an apology, or she surely would have kept it with her papers.

On October 22, 1966, at the Dunbar Community Center, Bates gave the official greeting at the NAACP state Youth Council meeting. One wonders how much the average member knew of the discord between the state president and the Bateses. On December 1 L. C. wrote Jewell that he was "sorry that you refused to pay the expense I went to in furnishing supplies, programs, badges, etc. and also entertainment for program participants for the [state] conference. These items can not be charged to the National office since the State Conference has the money idle in the bank. I will have to assume the loss."[13] L. C. made sure that Current and Dockery got copies of his correspondence.

Daisy Bates was elected second vice president of the State Conference of Branches in 1966.[14] One wonders if she tried for the top spot. It is difficult to imagine she was content with such a meaningless position.[15] Jewell was reelected president. George Howard Jr. was elected chair of the Legal Redress Committee.

Tragically for L. C., his job and relations with Jewell and others in the branches went from bad to worse. The nadir of his stewardship of the NAACP in Arkansas was undoubtedly at the annual meeting of the State Conference of Branches in October 1968.

Like others in the country after the assassination of Martin Luther King Jr., black Arkansans increasingly saw the cautious approach of the NAACP as irrelevant and obsolete. Years behind the rest of the civil rights movement in the South, blacks in Arkansas had finally erupted after King's death. For the next four years there were demonstrations, marches, and boycotts (mostly peaceful, but not always) all over eastern, southern, and central Arkansas. Understandable as their reaction was, there was a certain amount of irony in this, for L. C. ultimately would be proved to have been right in his belief that voting was key to progress. In 1968 Winthrop Rockefeller eked out another win over a weak Democratic opponent, and once again the black vote had proved decisive. As L. C. had predicted, blacks had finally started on the road to getting their share of meaningful jobs in state government. The turnaround in race relations in state government was largely due to the inarticulate, well-meaning Rockefeller, who had been the black sheep of the illustrious Rockefeller brothers. After King's murder, Rockefeller and his wife, Jeanette, joined hands with blacks in a memorial service in Little Rock and sang "We Shall Overcome." One can hardly imagine any other Arkansas politician of that era making the same gesture.

None of L. C.'s predictions about jobs made much difference to the few black Arkansans attending the 1968 state conference. A memorandum L. C. sent to Gloster Current on October 23 about the meeting, held in the Delta town of Helena, noted that only ten adults and twelve teenagers attended the business meeting. L. C. leaves the impression that he knew about the meeting only as a result of it having been announced in the newspaper. "The Annual Meeting of the Arkansas State Conference was announced and publicized through the columns of Arkansas's news media by the state president, Dr. Jerry D. Jewell, for October 18–20, it did not convene until 10:20 A.M. October 19."[16] It does not appear that Daisy was present at the meeting. Eight of the adults present were selected for office by a nominating committee. Gone were the days when Daisy and L. C. welcomed delegates to their house on the first night of the annual conference. Jewell was reelected president. L. C. had apparently invited Grover Smith, "labor field director from Birmingham," to speak at a workshop that afternoon. In his memo to Current, L. C. wrote that

the president made it clear and left the impression on the labor field director that his presence was not appreciated. The president refused to put labor field director's name on [the] program. He said that he was told to program Mr. Smith but it slipped his attention. In addition to the president's antic behavior, the president of the Columbia County Branch made every effort to embarrass and harass Mr. Smith by introducing subjects irrelevant to the program. . . . And in the same breath injected an attack on the Arkansas field director.[17]

Writing in the third person, L. C. was telling Current that his work had become the focus of the session. What was being objected to was L. C.'s effort to have the conference concentrate on economic issues. He wrote Current that he had been defended in the meeting by "Mr. Charles Johnson, a representative of the Arkansas Employment Division and a participant" in the workshop on labor issues, which was attended by "30 adults and about 20 children." Johnson stood up and

highly praised the work of the Arkansas field director. Mr. Johnson explained that a few years ago, the ESD [Employment Security Division] did not have a black face in the entire state, and now they have approximately 100 and will soon have them in every county insuring the same job opportunities to the Negro that are available to others.

He was interrupted by Mrs. Erma Hendricks Welsh, who said she thought it was useless to waste time praising people for what they had done. She said that she wanted something done now.

The session ended in the midst of turmoil.[18]

L. C. also reported to Current that "one of the first official acts of the newly elected secretary [Irma Hendricks Welsh], who nominated herself, was to draft a letter in the form of a petition at a socalled [*sic*] board meeting Saturday night directed to the Executive Director. The letter-petition is a scheme to get rid of the Arkansas field director. . . . Saturday night and Sunday were spent trying to get signatures to the letter." The embarrassment to L. C. was surely considerable. He wrote Current that one hundred "convention badges" had been issued, but only "26 registered for the convention."[19]

Though Jewell tried to get the NAACP national office to fire L. C., he managed to stay in his job as Arkansas field director until he turned seventy, when the national office retired him effective July 1, 1971. As Current had explained in a letter to the regional office in Texas, "We would be glad to do something along these lines but we have no place to put L. C. and we have to make sure that his retirement will be effective in terms of the insurance funding . . . for some time the Arkansas people have been dissatisfied with L. C."[20]

It is important not to make too much of the internal disputes Daisy and L. C. had with other members of the NAACP. Their quarrels should always be put in a larger context. Despite the fighting within the organization, L. C. and Daisy obviously had much more in common with their foes inside the NAACP than they did with their principal enemies—blacks who did absolutely nothing to advance the cause of civil rights. In any event, whatever the resentments, Jewell patched things up with Daisy and presumably L. C. as well.

What Bates truly thought about her husband's difficult tenure in his job as field secretary is a matter of speculation. Publicly, she was not going to criticize the man who had stood loyally beside her. Privately, one can imagine that neither one was shy about expressing an opinion on the subject to the other. Less than a year after he was forced into retirement, L. C. gave an interview to the *Arkansas Gazette* that demonstrated the lengths to which he was willing to go in public to criticize other African Americans. Interviewed by Bill Lewis of the *Arkansas Gazette* in 1972, L. C. said,

> "The average Negro, you see, instead of trying to improve himself, is standing around begging and complaining. I have never been one to seek popularity. I'd rather be what I term right any time. That's the way it is with me."

> Bates said one his greatest difficulties, was in "facing the fact that the Negro has more prejudices than the white man. Any time a Negro makes good, he's got to be superhuman, because not only does he have to fight opposition from the other side, but opposition from his own race. That makes him pretty hard. So Negroes are jealous—and they shouldn't be."[21]

At the *State Press*, L. C. had been criticizing blacks for years, and unlike the ministers he also criticized, he did not offer blacks the grace of God if they changed their ways. In his view, the civil rights movement had accomplished practically all that it could. Lewis reported that "Bates believes now that the barriers against Negroes are largely removed. 'The barriers that are facing the Negro are practical ones; there are no more than are facing any man who is trying to go somewhere.' Money's the password, he said. 'In this state, I feel our problem is economic instead of racial.' "[22]

It was impossible to call L. C. a hypocrite on this issue. Unlike other black conservatives who have benefited by affirmative action and then opposed it later, L. C. was self-made. To make his point, L. C. told Lewis, "I'm not one to be looking for Santa Claus. I won't forget the statement that President Johnson told a group of us right after he signed the civil rights bill into law. He told us this would not make us first-class citizens, but that it would only remove the barriers where we can make ourselves first-class citizens. That's what we've got to do."[23]

Lyndon Johnson's vision of America in that era is mind boggling today. Not only did he make civil rights legislation a reality, he promised a "Great Society" that would provide the means to end poverty in the United States. "Kennedy was a fine man," Bates told the student newspaper at the University of Arkansas at Little Rock, "but Johnson got things done."[24] In addition to civil rights programs, Johnson pushed through both houses of Congress bills that created a number of programs intended to lift poor people from poverty. Many of the programs were controversial, because for the first time in over a century efforts were being made to empower African Americans. These programs were a threat to white supremacy, which still ruled in the mid-1960s in Arkansas. To appreciate the seismic shift of what was occurring as a result of federal legislation, one naturally looks for comparisons, but in important ways, the Economic Opportunity Act of 1965 went far beyond anything envisioned by Roosevelt's New Deal. Johnson's War on Poverty, despite its failures, was a bold experiment in participatory democracy that often by-passed the traditional white power structure in local communities. The country had seen nothing like the Community Action Program (CAP) component of the Economic Opportunity Act of 1965, which was conceived as the basic building block of economic (and, its critics charged, political) empowerment. Blacks in significant numbers in Arkansas not only were given white-collar jobs but, more important, actually ran the programs, which included a range of services designed to attack poverty. Regardless of the debate on whether many of these new federal programs were judged to be unsuccessful because they were not tried long enough or because they were pie-in-the-sky remedies that had no chance of success, Bates would be intimately involved with them after she recovered sufficiently from her stroke.

As Bates's health came back, her energy returned, and with her youth program derailed, it was only natural for her to find some other place to give it an outlet. For the first time in years it was not going to be the NAACP. Though she had been elected to the national board for another term, her allies on the board had not been reelected, and thus she was marginalized, both locally and nationally.

Bates got a job as a "rural training leader" for the state Office of Economic Opportunity (OEO) in Little Rock in 1966. Barbara Graves, now a member of the city board of directors in Little Rock and a successful businesswoman, once worked as a secretary in the antipoverty agency. Even after her stroke in 1965, Bates had "exceptional posture" and "an air about her," remembered Graves. "I just remember a presence," Graves recalled. When Bates walked through the room, the reaction would be, "Gosh, who is that?"[25] There was something about Bates that got your attention, whether or not you knew who she was. A newcomer to the state, Graves did not know Bates's history, but she sensed a strong personality before she ever met her.

In 1967 Bates began an intense seven-year involvement with the town of Mitchellville, an all-black community of about 600 people in south Arkansas. Located just outside the small town of Dumas in Desha County, Mitchellville's poverty had to be seen to be believed. In the words of Linda Austin, who worked in Mitchellville as Bates's secretary from 1968 to 1974, "It was a terrible looking little town. Nothing but shanties or shacks . . . raw sewage was in the ditches . . . no paved streets, not a brick house in the town."[26] With an illiteracy rate of 75 percent, a school dropout rate of more than 95 percent, and only a handful of residents bringing in a yearly income of more than $3,000, the town seemed hopeless.[27]

L. C. once said about Mitchellville that it was worse than slavery; at least the slaves were needed. Bates visited Mitchellville in the first place because of its reputation as an all-black town. Mitchellville was not the only all-black town in the state, but there has always been something of a mystique for African Americans about an all-black town. At least in an all-black town, in theory, blacks completely controlled their destiny. Of course, it was not that simple; because the past had such an impact on their lives, blacks had few options. Mitchellville was a classic study in southern black poverty, which made it all the more a challenge to Bates. In an interview with the *Arkansas Democrat* on October 27, 1968, she recalled her first visit. "On my first visit, I drove around the town and found it in horrible condition. I remember my car getting stuck in front of the church because the street was so bad. About 100 people came to our initial meeting. I think most of them were there out of curiosity."[28]

Without question, they were there to see and hear Bates. "I put my NAACP speech down and started talking to them about their town. I asked them why they wanted a town in the first place. I could see they had little hope or pride."[29] Bates said she suggested they clean up the town first. When she returned a month later, she saw some improvement and began visiting the town regularly.

Mitchellville got its start in 1944 when an association of black Baptist churches, called the Watson Association, sold individual lots, 50 by 125 feet, for as little as $50 each. The only amenity a lot owner received after building a shack was electricity. The town basically remained the same until Bates arrived. Most of the residents had agricultural backgrounds and in this way were no different from the millions of southerners, both black and white, who had struggled through the twentieth century to make their living off the land. By the 1960s, however, progress had won out. With the mechanization of farming and the capital it took to sustain it, the war was over, and some of the black losers of the economic battle surrendered in Mitchellville, scratching out an existence on Social Security and welfare benefits. By 1968, according to an FHA survey, only fifty residents in Mitchellville had employment of any kind.[30]

In today's climate of economic determinism, the first question anyone would want answered is why invest scarce economic resources on infrastructure for a town like Mitchellville when there was the viable community of Dumas almost within walking distance? Amazingly, the short answer is because Bates wanted it done. Two years after she moved into a mobile home in Mitchellville, Bates told a reporter, "You don't challenge me. . . . Tell me I can't do something and I'm going to do it. I've put my heart and soul into this project so much that my husband threatened to divorce me. But he eventually understood like everyone else here has—I just have to do it."[31] In an article published in the *Arkansas Democrat* in October 1968, a reporter wrote, "Mrs. Bates says her goal is to put Mitchellville on the national map as a model Negro community—a showcase example of what self-governed Negroes can do for themselves with federal and state government help."[32]

To its enemies, the OEO was simply a featherbed for blacks who saw the opportunity for a handout. The criticism from whites in Little Rock could at times be scathing. "The EOA [the county operation] is a salary distribution agency for blacks, many of whom would not work elsewhere even with the EOA training they have received. Many of the EOA programs are ineffective particularly in job training," a 1971 article in the *Arkansas Gazette* read.[33] This kind of candor was fast disappearing. Instead of engaging with blacks to solve problems, most whites found it easier to withdraw, even as the era of official white supremacy was winding down. With the courts finally serious about school integration, white flight and the creation of private schools began in earnest and became huge business. John W. Walker, now the premier civil rights attorney in the state, flush from school desegregation victories as well as others, told an interviewer from the *Arkansas Gazette* the same month: "The real problem is that we live apart—not only black apart from white, but rich from middle class and middle class from poor. It is necessary to reunite the city [of Little Rock] just as the schools are reunited."[34] It was not to be. Even at the height of court-sanctioned efforts to end segregation, there were limits to how much the judicial system could and would do. Well before this became obvious, Bates herself turned her attention from integration to a task that met little opposition from her former enemies—achieving black self-sufficiency in an all-black town.

From the beginning, Bates reached out to others to help her with the Mitchellville project. One of her early collaborators was Bob Riley, a political science professor at privately funded Ouachita Baptist University in Arkadelphia, about a hundred miles from Mitchellville. Riley, who became lieutenant governor of Arkansas, was a consultant to the OEO rural training program. On a rainy, cold Saturday in early December 1967 he and twenty-one "student volunteers" traveled to Mitchellville to take a systematic survey of the town and document its economic misery. Naive as it sounds today, the 1960s were truly a time when it could be believed that the problems of poverty and race were not intractable in America. Riley went so far as to have a course created at the university called Community Development to encourage a continuation of the student interest generated by this visit to Mitchellville. Student volunteers commuted regularly to the town in 1968 to teach children to read. Used playground equipment was donated, and an informal "charm school class" was established for teenaged girls.[35]

Laudable as these efforts were, volunteers were not going to make a dent in the grinding poverty of the town, and Bates decided the only effective way for her to make a difference was to move to Mitchellville and become the official salaried director of the local OEO program. This meant taking a leave of absence from her job with the state OEO, a move that became permanent. She made less than $8,000 a year in her new job. It also meant moving to Mitchellville and living there during the workweek, which she did in October 1968.

The mechanics of Bates becoming an employee meant that the city of Mitchellville had to go through the laborious paperwork to apply for a grant and actually hire the director of the local OEO program. This was a formidable task for the town's first mayor, Charles Kelly, who was then in his nineties. Actually, all the city had to do was sign on the dotted line, and Bates did the rest, dealing with the program's red tape.

Even before moving to Mitchellville, several of her efforts had already borne fruit. Through the OEO's Concentrated Employment Program, fifteen residents were "receiving training in carpentry, plumbing, house-painting, tile-setting and related fields."[36] Because so many of the residents were elderly, Bates had gotten a grant from a program called Green Thumb, which provided part-time employment (three days a week) for fourteen men over the age of sixty. As was obvious to anyone who visited Mitchellville, the biggest need was for a sewage system. Only eight homes had indoor bathrooms. Though an application for water distribution lines had been made to the Farmers Home Administration before she had arrived, the project had bogged down because "homeowners were afraid that a lien would be put on their property. But I assured them this wouldn't happen," Bates told an interviewer.[37]

It helps to be famous, or in Bates's case, to have been famous and on the right side of history. She went to the nation's capital and made the rounds, ending with a personal interview with Agricultural Secretary Orville Freeman and showing him an *Arkansas Gazette* feature on Mitchellville. According to Bates, he read it and told her, "You can bet your life we will give you full support."[38] Freeman was as good as his word. A federal grant came through for $46,000, which paved the way for a $66,000 loan. By 1970 the town had a sewer system, but Bates was not through, using her contacts on the NAACP board in New York to get a used fire truck donated to Mitchellville. When a 750-gallon-a-minute pumper arrived on a freight car in Little Rock in 1971, the city of Little Rock traded it for a smaller truck and equipment and clothes, including helmets.

At first working out of a storefront, Bates needed a space that could be used for a number of purposes, but primarily for education. Again using her prestige and contacts, Bates's OEO "Self-Help" project eventually received over $200,000 to build a center that included a swimming pool, facilities for day care, a recreational area, a doctor's office, and three classrooms. Employing local labor from her Green

Thumb program, the "Center" was finished in 1970. Other projects were in full swing by that year: a man came from Little Rock on Tuesdays to teach upholstery classes; a credit union had been started with 143 members; classes were being offered in sewing and hat making; residents were able to get home repair loans in amounts up to $1,500. Bates dreamed of a day when residents could pull down their shacks and replace them with brick homes. Though that proved beyond reach for most residents during her stay in Mitchellville, a number of brick homes would eventually be constructed.

Although reporters writing about Mitchellville wrote puff pieces about Bates's work, there is reason to believe that initially it was not as easy as Bates made it sound. Richard McCarrell, a successful plumber in Mitchellville, agreed that there had been some suspicion and resentment in the beginning. After a while "people began to understand that she could help."[39] As everywhere, politics in a small town like Mitchellville are murky to the outsider, but it appears that Bates tried to put together a slate of candidates from the Center (including herself as recorder) to run for city offices in 1970. McCarrell remembered that J. D. Gray, one of his co-workers at the Center, ran for mayor but lost, and Bates apparently lost as well. The reason that Bates may have thought it necessary to put together a group of candidates was possibly the attitude of the mayor, Arthur Bowens. According to Linda Austin, Bowens "didn't think you had to go through a process for applying for stuff. Whatever God had for him, he would get it."[40] However, both Austin and McCarrell believed that Bates had been able to work with Bowens. Bowens's widow, who later became mayor after her husband's death, professed not to know Bates well during those years, saying she was working in Dumas. However, it is likely she got an earful from her husband and was being circumspect. One has the impression that contested elections were not appreciated in Mitchellville. Bates had to be somewhat threatening to the locals; it was their town, after all. It was essential that she be able to work with the mayor and aldermen, because improving Mitchellville's infrastructure had to come through the town's corporate structure.

As could be expected, the health care needs of the residents of Mitchellville were not insignificant. Bates made up with Jewell and with his help established a dental clinic at the Center in Mitchellville in 1973. At one point a physician and three dentists, including Jewell, were volunteering time in Mitchellville thanks to Bates.

In retrospect, Chris Mercer saw Bates's efforts in Mitchellville as an opportunity to "build a monument . . . there was no Central High Museum [then]."[41] Rev. Rufus King Young, Bates's pastor in Little Rock, agreed with this assessment. When told that Mercer had said that Mitchellville "was a monument to herself," he replied, "I think he gave a fair appraisal of her actions. . . . I think she was trying to recover some of her . . . glory."[42] Perhaps this was true: if the true test for helping others is hiding one's light under a bushel, Bates flunks with flying colors. Ego was part and parcel of her decision. The 1970 article in the *Arkansas Gazette* ended with this exchange: "Mrs. Bates said that 'right now the Project is my life. That's why I'm able to talk all the people in Washington into giving us money.'" Asked how long she planned on staying,

> she turned to an elderly man and asked, "What would you do if I left? What would happen?"
> He replied, "We're not going to let you go."[43]

It comes as no surprise that Bates was not shy about taking credit. She was transparent when it comes to one of the main reasons why some people sacrifice themselves for others. Bates would have been hypocritical had she affected an "aw, shucks" attitude. In one sense it was all about Daisy Bates—see what Bates can do when she decides to tackle a project. Her lifelong ability to focus the spotlight on herself is vulnerable to criticism. One can argue that if she had truly wanted to help people, she would have nurtured their egos instead of her own and allowed them to be reinforced by a sense of accomplishment. They would then develop leadership skills, thus following the maxim in community development that if you want to help people, don't give them a fish, teach them how to catch one and become self-sufficient. There seems no doubt that Bates reveled in the attention, that her name still meant something even more than a decade after her fifteen minutes of fame. Bates's remarks about Mitchellville typically say more about herself than about the people themselves. She is open to the charge that her attitude showed a lack of sensitivity to the dignity of the person she was helping. No one, whatever his or her station in life, appreciates hearing how pathetic his or her situation is and how badly he or she needs rescuing, whether it is his or her fault or not. This brand of heavy-handed paternalism was, after all, a staple of white supremacy for centuries, but neither Daisy nor L. C. displayed much patience for those who worried about the sensibilities of the underprivileged. Mitchellville was a cause for shame, and it no longer mattered the cause could be traced to the psychology of dependency that white supremacy had instilled since the town's inception. What Daisy found in Mitchellville appalled her. Victimhood did not appeal to her. One did not acquire dignity just by being born; it had to be earned. Linda Austin said that "at first some of the residents kind of got upset. She's trying to make us look like a bunch of illiterate poor people and you know they kind of took offense at that. The truth of the matter was that it was the truth."[44] Tact was never Bates's long suit. "And sometimes I'd bless them out, so they'd bless me out," Bates recalled, laughing, in her interview with Elizabeth Jacoway.[45]

Six months after the NAACP had retired him, L. C. told *Arkansas Gazette* reporter Bill Lewis, "It's a funny thing. Back in those days for telling it like it was, I was called the most radical man in the state. For doing that now, the Negroes call me an Uncle Tom—but I haven't changed at all."[46] There was much truth in that statement, but it would be some time before others recognized it. Daisy moved with the times more easily than her husband. Economic opportunity and the vote were the two issues L. C. had emphasized since 1941. Black Arkansans could march and protest only so long. At the beginning, middle, and end, they would always need economic opportunity and political power.

Children were always Daisy Bates's soft spot. Before moving to Mitchellville, for a number of years Bates had virtually raised Linder Jeffries, her neighbors' child.[47] For four of the six years she spent in Mitchellville, Bates repeated this pattern with Linda Mitchell. In the beginning, Linda and her brother Jimmy were just two of the children who hung around Bates's mobile home. Jimmy, who was older than his sister by three years, was a "slow learner." When she had time, Bates would take Jimmy in hand and teach him "how to groom himself." Linda's father and mother had a total of eight children. Her father worked construction, and her mother took what jobs she could get to bring money into the house. Of all the children enrolled in Bates's programs, Bates favored Linda the most. Forty years later it was easy to see why, if Mitchell's personality as an adult is any indication of her manner as a child. Interviewed in her home in Grady, not many miles from Mitchellville, Mitchell exuded perceptible warmth and good humor. Almost four decades later she had vivid memories of the four years she lived with Bates, beginning when she was "between seven and eight." Mitchell recalled that she first got to know

Bates when she was one of the children enrolled in an after-school program. The children would get a snack and then receive help with basic educational needs. Along with the certified teachers, Bates would occasionally come to the classroom and help the children herself. Soon, Mitchell was going over to Bates's mobile home, and Bates would continue to work with her. As a result of the Supreme Court's insistence, finally, that all southern schools be run on a unitary basis, the schools in nearby Dumas had become fully integrated, although basically in name only. "Tracking" left almost all the blacks in one classroom and whites in another. Mitchell recalled the time Bates went to bat for her. Convinced that Mitchell should be moved to a different track, Bates went into Dumas and "had it out because she knew my abilities."[48] Mitchell was moved.

Mitchell's parents, scraping by in their efforts to provide for eight children, had no difficulty with Bates's request that Linda move in with her.[49] Linda could see her family any time she wanted and did so, but at Bates's trailer she got special attention and thrived under it. For four years Linda Mitchell was as much Bates's child as Clyde Lee Cross had been. Daisy and L. C.'s 1972 joint tax return shows they claimed her as a dependent, paying all her expenses.

Asked why Bates had taken her in, Mitchell replied, "She knew that we were real poor and she saw that I wanted to learn. She asked me one day how would I like to live [with her], and I shouted 'sure,' but my mom wouldn't let me do it, and she said 'How 'bout if I asked her. Would you like it then?' Yeah, yeah. She did that and told my mom she would take care of me." Of course, it was more than Bates feeling sorry for a poor child. Mitchell, who was such a willing and obviously winsome tyke, allowed Bates to once again satisfy her maternal instincts, but Bates rarely coddled her. "She'd be in the bathroom putting on her makeup, getting ready to go to a meeting. I would sit on the commode with the top down," and she would have Mitchell go through her multiplication tables. If Mitchell missed one, she'd have to start all over again. Bates meant business. "She would say 'You are not going outside to play; you're not going to watch television.' Oh, she was strict. I loved her to death."[50] Bates did let Mitchell watch some television, but it was always channel 2, Little Rock's educational channel.

Bates had Mitchell's teeth fixed, which were "horrible." She had some of the Center's employees make clothes for her. The only thing that Bates did wrong as far as Mitchell was concerned was styling her hair. Laughing, Mitchell demonstrated how Bates ran a comb through it.

"I will never forget it. I never liked her hair styles." Bates let Mitchell join the Brownies, but Mitchell remembered her dress was too long. Bates, always so stylish herself, apparently did not believe in short skirts, even for preadolescent girls. Bates, who to Mitchell always seemed to be working, believed that children needed to do chores, and Mitchell remembered she did her share, though she had no sense of being exploited by Bates. On the weekends Mitchell and Bates, who apparently did not have a washer and dryer in the trailer, would load all the dirty clothes in Bates's green Chevrolet and head home for Little Rock. "She taught me how to wash, all the house chores, we would do all of that there." Bates did all the cooking, but Mitchell would "wash the dishes." She also "made her bed, made their bed, dust[ed]."[51]

Apparently, L. C. took it easy on the weekends. "All I remember him doing is laying [*sic*] on the bed. He would put something black around his eyes." Mitchell had never seen an eye mask, but what fascinated her most was that L. C. had a pierced ear. "He never had an earring in it," and told her he had "bit his earlobe." Mitchell had warm memories of L. C., too. For one thing, he was not as strict as his wife. Mitchell wanted a bicycle, but Daisy told her, "No, you don't need a bicycle. Bicycles are dangerous." L. C., however, came to her rescue. One Christmas "it was just sitting there . . . and I got on the bike I just rode up and down and I went back in and . . . thanked him." She called Daisy "Mother Bates." As for L. C., "I would call him Daddy sometimes, but sometimes I would call him Mr. Bates."[52]

It was apparent even to a child that there wasn't much affection displayed by Daisy toward L. C., at least in front of her. Daisy would allow him to hug her when they came in from Mitchellville, but "there was no affection at all. It was all just strictly business."[53] Whatever their physical relationship or lack thereof, Mitchell did not notice any particular friction between them. Others from Mitchellville commented that L. C. came down often to visit. If Bates's comment that L. C. had threatened to divorce her was other than a throwaway line, there was no evidence to prove it. L. C. loved her too much to divorce her.

With her eye for detail, Mitchell mentioned a charming scene that occurred on the weekend in Little Rock: Bates would wake her up by singing scales. "She would be real loud." Bates stayed trim by "getting on the [exercise] bike." She also "ate a lot of vegetables." She and L. C. did go out to eat at inexpensive places, and Mitchell went, too (she remembered eating at Bonanza). Bates made sure Mitchell kept her hand in her lap and ate with a knife and a fork. With children Daisy was always the teacher, so it is easy to forget she enjoyed and took time to read. "She was always in books . . . and she wanted me to do that."[54]

Linda Mitchell surely disappointed Bates by not going to college. Bates was also disappointed when the Mitchells decided not to allow her to adopt Linda. Things became awkward after they refused Bates's request. Mitchell did not want to be adopted, and undoubtedly Bates's feelings were hurt. Mitchell's parents came to the trailer and picked up Linda right after that. Her mother "got kind of nervous" over Bates's request, perhaps thinking Bates might take Linda anyway. That must have hurt Bates, too. In any event, she never called Mitchell again. Mitchell would call her, and they would have a good talk, but Bates never picked up the phone and called the child she had raised four years.[55] Bates's feelings could be hurt, no question about it. Her stubborn refusal was a matter of pride and very much a part of her personality. Like many people, Bates responded to having her feelings hurt by shutting people out. Even though she knew the child adored her and as an adult continued to love her, Bates felt rejected. In turn, Bates punished her by not calling her, as she never again called Audre Hanneman, who had nothing but the warmest feelings for her.

If one measures Mitchellville in purely economic terms, what Bates brought to the community has to be counted as significant for those whose lives were touched, but her impact was greater than can be measured in dollars and cents. Her work gave both men and women opportunities they had never dreamed of before she arrived. Alice Love, a teacher at Dumas High School at the time of her interview with the author, had moved away from Arkansas but moved back to take care of her ninety-year-old father, Dave Love. Her mother, Betty, was still alive as well, though suffering from Alzheimer's and living in a nursing home. Betty Love, born in 1915 and who had never worked at a skilled job, benefited greatly by Bates's programs. In addition to becoming an employee (driving the van for the Green Thumb and senior citizen programs and working as an aide in Head Start), she went through the adult education program and obtained a tenth grade education. She had only gone through the eighth grade as a child. In addition, she took the upholstery class and became so proficient she taught others. Alice Love explained that these experiences raised her mother's expectations. All six of her children, who had been home during these years, went to college. No longer was the wood home good enough; it was replaced by a brick structure. Her mother eventually was able to get a job in Dumas and worked until she was in her seventies. Alice Love attributed all of these accomplishments to Bates's influence. Though Bates perhaps would not have understood herself to be a feminist, in fact she became one in this period by empowering women to work and to shape their own futures. Of course, her goal was empowering the entire community through self-help principles. She would stop teenage "boys on the street: 'Why are you here? Why aren't you in school?' "[56] Bates would bring them to the Center, where she would find them summer work through her programs. Love remembered that her brother was employed at Townsend Park in Pine Bluff one summer thanks to Bates.

Though she was in Mitchellville seven years, Bates always held herself somewhat apart. Alice Love, who was a teenager in those years, remembered that her mother always called Daisy "Mrs. Bates," though she was only two years younger. Bates called her mother by her first name. One might imagine that as small as Mitchellville was, an air of informality might have been the rule, but Bates always preserved the distinction that she was the boss. Even in tiny Mitchellville, she dressed the part: Alice Love never recalled seeing Bates wear slacks. She wore suits or dresses that had a jacket—"business attire." By this time, Bates, probably tired of taking time with her hair, had started wearing a wig. "It was always well kept, but there were moments you knew it was a wig," remembered Alice Love.[57] Nor did Bates appear to have been a social butterfly in Mitchellville. Linda Mitchell remembered Bates doing "paperwork" at night, and "she'd always be on that telephone and she was always writing." Richard McCarrell worked for Bates along with his father in the Green Thumb program. He called Bates a "workaholic."[58]

At the same time, however, Bates fit into the community. Linda Austin recalled eating Bates's "greens" and that Bates got together with her friends to eat. Poignantly, when many years later Bates returned for a weekend visit at the home of Linda Austin, who was living in Dumas, Bates asked about her friends. Sadly, each person she asked about had already died. "Why am I still here?" Bates mused aloud. Austin met Bates for the first time right out of high school. She had been first in her typing class, and Bates was looking for a new secretary. Austin remembered that she had been told that "she was hard to work for," but in fact Austin got along well with her. Bates "wanted things done right," and Austin apparently caught on quickly how to compose the letters that Bates needed to send in her quest for funds for the town.[59]

Bates was friendly but probably a bit formidable in such an impoverished environment, even with the permanent disabilities of a stroke.
Alice Love recalled that "when she spoke there were times when she
would slow or stutter."[60] In the early years at Mitchellville, Bates's
health did not get in her way, but there is evidence that in her last year,
her condition began to worsen. Isabel Griswold, a teacher who was
given her first job by Bates, recalled that last year she could understand
Bates "most of the time but if she got upset . . . you really couldn't understand her." Griswold also noticed that Bates walked with a "little
limp." It appeared to her that "her health was getting worse."[61] Linda
Austin agreed. "Sometimes she would kind of stumble." Austin believed
"she decided to curtail her work so she wouldn't have another
stroke."[62]

In retirement, L. C. spent more time in Mitchellville. Daisy still had
a car but was no longer making the drive herself. Driving in Little
Rock on Roosevelt Road with her used to terrify Linda Mitchell. "I
had been in accidents with her where she run up on the curb and hit a
post." L. C. had been having problems with his eyesight for years, and
with Daisy's stroke, they must have made quite a pair on the road.
Austin was crazy about L. C., then in his seventies. L. C. could be a bit
formidable if he chose, but apparently rarely was. "I loved him . . .
because he was very soft spoken. He had so much knowledge. I enjoyed
talking to him. He was so abreast of everything. I really liked him a
lot." Asked if he took an interest in Mitchellville, Austin laughed and
explained it this way. "Whatever Mrs. Bates wanted to do, he was
behind her. He just really, really loved Daisy."[63]

As a boss, Bates was exacting but generous. She let Austin work
part-time and go to college at what was then Arkansas A&M, the pre-
dominantly black college in Pine Bluff. Not only that, Bates "paid my
tuition, herself." Working so few hours and coming from a family with
six children did not leave Austin with much money to buy clothes.
Bates would buy fabric and have Austin's clothes made by the women
in the sewing program she ran.

Another person in Mitchellville who benefited from Bates's presence still lives there. At the time of his interview in 2002, Richard
McCarrell was a fifty-nine-year-old hardworking plumber. He met
Bates through his father, who supervised the Green Thumb project.
Bates arranged for a grant for McCarrell to go through a plumbing
apprenticeship course at nearby Great River Technical School, and he
also took an adult education class. He worked on various programs

for Bates, including a city sewer project and remodeling houses in Mitchellville. McCarrell eventually obtained a master plumber's license and credited Bates for it. "No, it would not have happened without Mrs. Bates." McCarrell remembered that while he was working in Green Thumb, approximately fifteen homes in Mitchellville were remodeled. Although his father had worked for Bates and would have been about her age, he also called her "Mrs. Bates." As McCarrell said, "Some people you call by first names and some people you don't."[64]

Eventually, probably fearful of another major stroke, Bates returned to Little Rock to live. Though in 1977 her name was still listed as project director on letterhead stationary, Bates had been only a consultant for the Mitchellville project since around 1974. One of her last and best projects was obtaining Head Start funds for Mitchellville.

After moving back to Little Rock, Bates clearly missed the challenges and attention and admitted to being a little bored without them. In 1975 she wrote a young admirer and friend that her summer had been "routine." It was "difficult for one accustom [sic] to action," to adjust to the "absence of the stress and strain."[65]

Mitchellville missed Bates as well. In the summer of 2002 a visitor to Mitchellville would discover that the swimming pool had not been open for the preceding two summers, nor was there a compelling reason for its lack of use. Though since her departure the town had acquired a city hall and some apartments and some of the programs remained, it appeared to lack the energy that Bates had once brought to it, or maybe it was just the heat of a torrid Arkansas summer.

Chapter Nineteen

FIGHTING OVER A LEGEND

During the years that Daisy Bates spent in Mitchellville, a profound change was occurring in Arkansas politics, as it was throughout the South. It wasn't just the politics of expediency that produced a new breed of Arkansas Democrats in the late 1960s who turned their backs on white supremacy as a governing principle. The civil rights movement had a cumulative effect that today is taken for granted. Thanks to the success of Republican Winthrop Rockefeller, the politics of racial inclusion was now acceptable. It was a moment in Arkansas like no other. Democratic racial progressives such as Dale Bumpers and David Pryor would occupy the governor's chair and then go on to the U.S. Senate, replacing racial mossbacks J. William Fulbright, who despite his liberal reputation in foreign policy was no friend to blacks, and John McClellan.

Locally, too, roughly in this time period, there began a transformation within Little Rock in the attitudes of some of its most powerful movers and shakers. For example, the *Arkansas Gazette* relatively quickly transformed its editorial stance from that of "Southern Moderate" to that of "Liberal Queen" and became a stalwart defender of racial integration within the Little Rock schools and elsewhere. Both L. C. and Daisy felt this sea change in attitude, though among whites it was patchy at best. In doing interviews for her master's thesis on L. C. in 1980, Irene Wassell discovered that it was "difficult to find a public official who will speak ill of him, but in the private sector it is a different story." "Many of us who were here during the crisis do not think kindly of the Bateses and did not appreciate what they did to the community during the 1950s," one individual told her.[1]

Within the black community, it was a given that Daisy Bates's name would always be sacrosanct in the halls of the NAACP. She had owed too much to Roy Wilkins to do anything but complain about him in private, hence her status as a silent member of the Young Turks. If one wants to view it this way, Bates's growing acclaim was a vindication of Wilkins's leadership, even as she once gave her tacit approval to those who would overthrow him.

According to Annie Abrams, however, even as Bates was gradually becoming a civil rights icon after her return to Little Rock, she felt lonely and isolated from the black community. "The only time she would get called is the Democratic connection during an election season. She was not called in Little Rock to do a lot of speaking . . . because people were very elitist. She was a Delta [sorority member] at the national level because Dorothy Height and Lena Horne and all those folks were the ones who made her a Delta. . . . She was honorary. The Deltas here in Little Rock didn't accept her. They resented her and therefore she didn't have a lot of speaking engagements in Little Rock or in Arkansas."[2]

However some blacks in Little Rock privately felt about her, officially there was no doubt about her status. Because she stayed true to nonviolence and the mainstream principles of American democracy, Bates gradually became in Arkansas what Martin Luther King Jr. became in death to the rest of the nation: an icon to genuinely revere, or at least to give lip service to.

An irony in the 1970s was that blacks on a national level did not know what to do with their new-found political clout. In March 1974 blacks were so fragmented about the direction they should take that about the only thing those attending the National Black Political Convention could really find to agree on was how to honor the principals of the Little Rock Crisis. Though the convention was primarily notable for its absence of big-name politicians, with the exception of Jesse Jackson of Chicago, who was viewed by the others as a shark circling a school of smaller fish, the events of 1957 in Little Rock provided the delegates a unifying symbol. Though the parents and L. C. were honored as well, it was Daisy who received wave after wave of sustained applause from the frustrated delegates, who got to their feet to acknowledge her.[3]

Deeply moved, Bates could not stop herself from crying, a response that would have been unthinkable back in the days when she was a regular on the banquet circle. Out of the national limelight for so long, the warmth of the response proved that black people not only remembered but cared. Her health probably had something to do with her inability to conceal her emotions as she once had been able to do. On February 8, 1975, Bates wrote Audre Hanneman, "I am not working any place now. I've been ill about a year. The doctor said I am completely exhausted, but I am getting better." She was recovering some strength, but there were signs of further impairment. In this same letter, Bates, who now had no secretary, twice typed "Audra" instead of "Audre" to her friend in New York.[4] Earlier in her life, Bates would never have made a mistake like that.

In December Bates spent twenty-one days in "Edgewater Hospital in Chicago taking special treatments," but was unable to travel to Boston in April the next year to receive an award from the Martin Luther King, Jr. Afro-American Center.

Regardless of the therapy, any relief was temporary. "For a month after I returned home, I felt fine. My gait was almost perfect. . . . I am convinced that there is no miracle."[5] In 1975 she received a letter from Kivie Kaplan informing her of her reelection to the NAACP's Board of Trustees Special Contribution Fund for a four-year term, but health problems prevented her from completing it.

Bates persevered even as her health deteriorated. An interview with an Associated Press reporter in June, picked up by a number of papers, noted her impaired speech, hearing aid, and glasses, but it also captured her feistiness. Like the days of old, Bates criticized those blacks who had made it but who had forgotten those people left behind. "The Negroes who have made it as professionals and businessmen are too afraid to lose what they have to do anything for civil rights today."[6]

Discrimination had not disappeared—far from it—but it was increasingly hard to attack. Bates told the journalist, "We still have racism today—very much so. But the people who can do something about it are not concerned about the black boy on the street." The "black boy on the street" was becoming a major problem for the nation and for Little Rock as well. Whites often had the resources to privatize their drug problems, blacks usually did not. Whites reacted to the problems of blacks by moving away. Daisy told the reporter, "As Mr. Bates always says, 'We've changed the practice of segregation, but we don't have integration. We've changed the laws, now we have to change hearts.' "[7]

One does not hear the words "changing hearts" applied to problems of race anymore. The "black boy on the street" has become an insoluble problem for America, whose solution as a society is to put him in prison and keep him there for longer and longer periods of time. Soon it would no longer be just the "black boys" but "black girls" who would turn on to crack cocaine and drop out. Bates could see what was happening, and she had done what she could—taking children into her home and teaching them the values of education and discipline.

There had been something tangible to fight against in 1957—twenty years later it seemed like the battle had become indifference. The overarching symbol of the civil rights movement was gone, and there was nobody to take his place. Here, Bates lashed out. The civil rights movement "died the day Martin Luther King was shot. All the so-called leaders who were affiliated with King just gave up after that," she asserted but refused to discuss specific people. "If they'd really been dedicated to the movement, they wouldn't have given up that easily. It seems they just associated with King to get money and prestige."[8]

Bates knew about the jockeying and pettiness that had surrounded King, but this analysis of what had happened could not take anyone very far. Movements, by definition, only last a few years. King's murder did not kill the civil rights movement, and in her heart Bates knew that, but she had that old dream of activists everywhere: if someone stepped up and became a leader, things would be so different.

In 1977 L. C. finally got some recognition of his own. On February 20 a banquet was held in his honor at the Camelot Inn in Little Rock by the Theta Sigma chapter of Sigma Gamma Rho Sorority. The featured speaker was Hugh B. Patterson, the publisher of the *Arkansas Gazette*, who told his audience that "all of us in Arkansas are in debt of this man."[9] Recognition of L. C.'s contribution was long overdue, and at least for one night he was shown the respect and love that had come his wife's way as a matter of course. Old friend Ozell Sutton flew in from out of state and served as master of ceremonies. The list of patrons for the party included old enemies, too. I. S. McClinton was on the guest list.

In a letter to William Branch in 1978, Bates wrote that she had not been to New York during the past two years. "On the advice of my doctor, I resigned my membership [in 1978] from the national trustee board. . . . Neither one [of us] is as active as we have been."[10] The aging process was taking its toll, especially on L. C. Before his death, he was quoted on February 14, 1979, in the *Arkansas Democrat* as saying, "In race relations, Little Rock is second to none. It leads." It was a valentine to the city that not every black person in Little Rock would have sent. Old age had a lot to do with L. C.'s statement. Had he been nineteen instead of an old man, it is extremely doubtful he would have made such a statement. Daisy echoed her husband's sentiments. She was quoted as saying, "We feel race relations here are better than any other city in the country."[11]

Yet police brutality against blacks was still a problem, as it had been when L. C. and Daisy were campaigning against it. In December 1974 a number of blacks had brought suit in federal court alleging excessive use of force. Several white officers took the Fifth Amendment in response to the question of whether any of them had any firsthand knowledge of any instance of physical or verbal abuse of blacks. Numerous blacks testified they had been the victims of abuse by the police. Although federal judge Thomas Eisele ruled that he had found no "pattern or practice" that would have implicated the city, he found "considerable merit" in as many as a third of the thirty-five alleged instances of police misconduct. One white member of the city of board of directors, A. M. "Sandy" Keith, said candidly about Little Rock police chief Gail Weeks: "There is no question he is a racist. I am, too, about half-way."[12]

In 1981, a year after L. C.'s death, the *Arkansas Gazette* ran a three-part series entitled "Turmoil in the Schools," in which it examined the reasons for white flight. In 1963–64 the number of whites attending public schools in Little Rock had been 17,654. In 1981–82 the number had dropped to 6,740. The so-called tipping point had been reached, and the race out the schoolhouse door was on, as the percentage of black students in the district reached 66 percent. In the series, one unidentified black parent complained: "It seems that we have come full circle and are back where we started, still having to fight for something as basic as an education for our children, still hassling over something so trivial as the color of one's skin."[13]

Whites, however, did not see the issue so simply. In 1975 Harold D. Algee, the white principal of Dunbar Junior High School, gave "as the major reason for leaving the District and taking another job in Mountain View the inability to demand and expect discipline from black students who composed fifty-six percent of the enrollment." Algee said, "It seems that black students don't respect the limits that you can verbally request of them." In discussing the number of blacks who were suspended from Dunbar, Algee stated the students had not been attending classes and then added: "But there have been quite a few suspensions for either threatening or striking another student, or making threatening remarks to students or teachers. Student relationships between blacks and whites did improve this year, but there still are too many instances where blacks have intimidated whites or asking for money." Algee said that in his four-year tenure at Dunbar, he could cite no instances where whites had been accused of intimidating blacks or asking for money.[14] Instead of working together with black parents to deal with the problems in public education, whites in Little Rock, like whites elsewhere, increasingly voted with their feet. The black underclass was perceived as being out of control. Increasingly, one encountered the phenomenon of black professionals enrolling their children in private schools and buying homes in once exclusive neighborhoods in west Little Rock to escape the "turmoil" in the schools.

Meanwhile, frustrated blacks who could not afford to put their children in private schools perceived white flight as simple racism. An unidentified black woman in the *Gazette* series in 1981, a divorced mother of three, explained, "as she was fighting back tears that she viewed the movement of white students out of the district as another way of telling blacks 'you're not good enough to associate with us. It doesn't matter if you're a doctor, lawyer or garbage man, whites still view you as some inferior being with animalistic tendencies.' "[15]

Had L. C. been interviewed for this series, one wonders what he would have said, but he never lived to see it. His death on August 22, 1980, brought many friends to Daisy's side. Dr. Edith Irby Jones flew in from Houston to sit next to her during L. C.'s memorial service. As a number of others would, Jones contributed to Daisy's support, but she also remembered who else had helped her. She gave $500 to the L. C. Bates Educational Enrichment Fund at the University of Arkansas for Medical Sciences. As she stated, "I serve humanity better because he helped me in becoming prepared to do so."[16] As old age had closed in, L. C. suffered from a number of ailments, including problems with his vision, but it was his heart that finally gave out. The cause of death was an "acute coronary occlusion."[17] As he had wanted, his body was taken to the anatomy department at the University of Arkansas for Medical Sciences for use by the future doctors of the state.

L. C.'s memorial service at the Union AME Church on August 27 was like a kaleidoscope of Daisy and his civil rights past: 150 people attended, including Harold Flowers, W. Harry Bass, Edwin Dunaway, Fred Darragh, and Lois Pattillo. The honorary pallbearers included Dr. Jerry Jewell, W. H. Townsend, and John W. Walker. Ernest Green, who of the Little Rock Nine remained closest to Daisy and who had become an assistant secretary at the U.S. Department of Labor, was one of those chosen to give a three-minute tribute. Also speaking was Jesse Jackson. Among other whites attending were Daisy's friends Ann and Orville Henry. Daisy heard from hundreds of people, including Wiley Branton, Earl Davy, Lee Lorch, Thelma Mothershed, Harry Ashmore, and Benjamin Hooks, who had become head of the national NAACP. Nor did the White House let L. C.'s death pass by unnoticed. "Both of you played a critical role in advancing the cause of equal education in Little Rock and across the nation, and we in America are indebted to you," wrote Jimmy Carter.[18]

As the years slipped by, Bates was of two minds in dealing with those who wanted to trade on her name as a famous person. She wrote William Branch in New York, who made part of his living as an agent, "I am tired of people sticking cameras in my face, and most of the time, it is strictly exploitation. So, from now on every time I am asked to face a camera, unless it is a news story, I am referring them to you."[19] If others were going to capitalize financially on her name as a civil rights heroine, she understandably wanted a piece of the action. Thus when in 1979 Time-Life Films in New York approached her about a proposed "dramatization" of the 1957–58 school year and sent her a consent form to use her name, she offered to put its representative in touch "with my agent in your city."[20] Of course, the entertainment business has other ways achieving its purposes. When Elizabeth Huckaby's diary became the basis for an HBO movie, *Crisis at Central High*, in 1981, with Joanne Woodward playing Huckaby, Bates's character was "fictionalized," as were most of the Little Rock Nine. At the same time, Bates encouraged people she knew who were writing scripts about her life and tried to help them. She went so far as to write her friend, the writer and former fellow Arkansan Maya Angelou, for help.[21] However, nothing on a national level came of this effort.

Bates increasingly had mixed feelings about her marriage to L. C., but she missed him. Thanksgiving and Christmas were both especially hard. After she attended a dinner party during the holidays, she wrote Brynda Pappas in Washington, D.C., "I was very lonely."[22] Though L. C. was old and had been in the hospital as recently as the month before he died, his death still came as a surprise. His daughter, Loretta, wrote Daisy in September that she was "still in a state of shock." It had been a shock to Daisy, too. She wrote a friend later that he had only been ill for about four or five days. Loretta's letter was quite affectionate, beginning with "Dear Mom" and expressing concern for Daisy's health. She reminded Daisy to take her medicine.[23] It was not the only time Loretta came through for her. For Thanksgiving, she sent her a small gift.[24] Still, Loretta hurt Daisy's feelings terribly by not remembering Mother's Day. Daisy wrote her, "I thought that when we adopted you we would be a family. Evidently, I was wrong. . . . Had it not been for my friends it would have been a lonely day for me."[25]

In 1981 the National Newspapers Publishers Association brought Daisy to Washington, D.C., to honor her and L. C.'s contribution in journalism. The black press had long provided a crucial function for African Americans everywhere, but particularly in the South, where for years white newspapers had treated them as either invisible or as criminals. Perhaps it was this recognition that helped rekindle her desire to start up the *State Press*. There were many reasons why reviving the *State Press* was a bad idea financially, but Bates was determined to do it. In an interview in 1992, she revealed that her greatest weakness was "trusting too many people." She may have had in mind her venture to revive the *State Press*. In theory, it must have seemed like the old days could be made to come to life again when black entertainers and athletes made the *State Press* offices on Ninth Street one of their first stops in Little Rock. After a certain age, perhaps it is nostalgia that is the greatest aphrodisiac. One of the difficulties was that by this time Ninth Street was nothing more than the name of a street. Black businesses along that historic corridor had been obliterated when the white power structure that ran Little Rock solicited the help of Congressman Wilbur Mills and obtained the funding for a connecting strip of the interstate highway system that today runs through the heart of downtown Little Rock. A revenue stream was gone, but Bates and her business partner, Ari Merretazon, apparently believed that the official goodwill that was now being manifested by the white power structure could be converted into advertising revenue to sustain a revival of the paper. L. C. would always claim that whites constituted almost half his readership, but that had been a different era, when people depended on newspapers for information they could not get any other place. Many of the reasons for the *State Press* had vanished with the end of the civil rights era. By the 1980s discrimination had become more subtle and, frankly, less sexy than in the old days, when all L. C. had to do to get his readers' blood boiling was to stand on the sidewalk, watch black people get on street cars, and then go back inside and write about it.

None of this would have mattered if this ill-fated venture had been launched using funds from outside investors. Bates's near-fatal mistake was to put up the money for reviving the *State Press* by mortgaging her house. Had L. C. been alive, he would have nixed that move instantly.

As she grew older and more enfeebled, Bates quite understandably depended more on the kindness of strangers. Of course, they weren't strangers to her. As Bates said in her 1992 interview in the *Democrat-Gazette*, she was most comfortable with people who "have an outgoing personality." Ari Merretazon had personality to burn.[26] A handsome young man with a wife and family, it appears that Bates had complete faith in him. Given the title of "managing editor," his relationship with Bates was more than just a business relationship. According to Annie Abrams, Bates considered Merretazon part of her unofficial family; he even lived in the house for a while until his family moved to Little Rock. Frankie Jeffries recalled that Merretazon once took Bates to Huttig to look for her biological family.

The first issue of the new *State Press* was published on April 11, 1984, on borrowed money. James McDougal and his savings and loan business, Madison Guaranty, with his business connections with Bill and Hillary Clinton, are rapidly becoming a mere footnote in the Clintons' legacy. Though their enemies made much of their failed real estate venture called "Whitewater," there was no scandal unearthed. The scandal was in McDougal's business practices, and he paid dearly for them. The *State Press* was one of his bad loans. By the time Bates started up the *State Press*, the day was past when the paper could primarily depend on a readership to carry the financial burden, as L. C. had largely done when the white power structure had rammed into place the first boycott by advertisers in the 1940s.

It was a new market in Little Rock, and it would not be too many years before weekly publications such as the *Arkansas Times* simply gave away their product because to do so was cheaper than trying to distribute and sell each issue. The advertising dollar was essential. Two years into the operation, Merretazon put together an awards ceremony, ostensibly to thank the *State Press*'s main advertisers but rather transparently to encourage them and others to continue to support the paper. Receiving "publisher's awards" for "most consistent advertisement by a major corporation" were Arkansas Power & Light Company, Safeway, Arkansas Louisiana Gas Company, Kroger, and Southwestern Bell Telephone Company. Dr. Edith Irby Jones, John Walker, and Dr. Archie Hearne were recognized for their support of the *State Press*. Despite their support, the paper continued to lose money.

By January 1988 Bates had sold the *State Press* to Darryl and Janis Kearney Lunon. She had become the paper's managing editor in 1987.

Ari Merretazon was already gone by then. The *State Press* "was not in great financial shape," Lunon, who had become Janis Kearney Nash at the time of her interview by the author, remembered.[27] Bates came into the office every day, no small feat for a woman in her physical condition. Nash was told that Bates had suffered two strokes. At the time the paper was sold, Bates remarked, "I have looked forward to retiring and leaving the paper in someone else's hands for a while now." She added, "I get tired a lot easier now." Carrol Hicks, who had been Bates's personal attorney and later the attorney for her estate, has said that she thought Bates was supposed to have received $14,000 or $15,000 for the *State Press*. According to Nash, Bates mostly deferred to her decisions regarding the paper's content. The *State Press*, which had begun as a crusade for civil rights, was now about the black community. Nash left in 1993, and the paper was operated by her sister. It closed for good in 1997, a victim, like so many others, to changing times as much as anything.

As the 1990s came to a close, Bates's political attitudes mirrored those of the few whites in Little Rock who identified themselves as liberals. By 1984 white flight had become such a problem in Pulaski County that federal judge Henry Woods (who had aided the WEC's fight to reopen the Little Rock schools in 1959) ordered consolidation of the three school districts that comprised Pulaski County. While the case was being appealed to the Eighth Circuit Court of Appeals, Bates was called by a reporter for the *Arkansas Democrat* for her opinion about Woods's order. Nothing was more controversial than the issue of busing children all over the city to achieve racial balance in the schools. Now it appeared that even more busing would be part of the desegregation plans. It was hard for anyone who supported busing not to sound defensive during this era, and Bates was no exception. "They keep asking, 'Do you want your 6-year-old child riding the bus before day[light] and riding 10 miles?' . . . Of course I don't want it. But if they didn't have busing (as an excuse) they'd have some other reason."[28] This was the twenty-eighth year of the litigation originally known as *Aaron v. Cooper*.

In 1986 the University of Arkansas Press issued a reprint of *The Long Shadow of Little Rock* with considerable fanfare. The president of the university, Ray Thornton, penned a brief introduction, and University of Arkansas professor Willard B. Gatewood Jr. wrote in a new foreword that Bates "occupies a place along with Frederick Douglass, W. E. B. Du Bois, Mary Church Terrell, Rosa Parks, Martin

Luther King, Jr., and others in the vanguard of movements to transform American ideals into reality."[29] With this imprimatur, *The Long Shadow of Little Rock* two years later won the prestigious Columbia Award for reprints. Historians writing about this era would grab on to incidents in Bates's memoir and present them as fact.

In her interview by the author in 2002, Annie Abrams remembered that L. C. once referred to "those lies" in *The Long Shadow of Little Rock*.[30] In Bates's defense, she was obviously not asked to verify what she wrote. As mentioned, her publisher wanted a heroine, and Bates delivered one. In reprinting the book, the University of Arkansas Press surely wanted the same, and so did those individuals who awarded it a prize. Today it remains as one of the University of Arkansas Press's best sellers.

For Bates's High Profile article in the *Arkansas Democrat-Gazette* in 1992, she could not avoid being photographed in a wheelchair. Still, Bates, despite her health problems, at the age of seventy-eight looked quite attractive and vital. "If I could just get rid of this arthritis, I'd feel fine," she told reporter Linda Caillouet. There, of course, was no getting rid of that pain, but Bates wasn't complaining. Caillouet wrote, "Her body may be weak but her spirit seems strong. Behind the glasses, fire still burns in her ebony eyes—it surfaces when she speaks of racial injustices of the past and present."[31]

In her long decline, Bates continued to depend on others. Since her death in 1999, a debate has raged over whether in fact she was taken care of or exploited or perhaps both. Sometime in the 1980s Cleodis Gatson and his wife, Sharon, became part of Bates's life. Cleodis Gatson claimed to be Bates's nephew. As has been asked repeatedly by those who had known Bates since she had moved to Little Rock in 1941, where had they been before she became a civil rights icon? Why hadn't Gatson announced his relationship before then? Why did he wait until Bates was famous to become close to her? Why hadn't Bates ever mentioned him before to anyone in Little Rock? No one seems to dispute that Gatson, whom Bates accepted as her nephew, cared about Bates or that Bates cared about Gatson. Annie Abrams said that Bates "loved Cleodis," and Bates accepted Cleodis as her blood relative. According to Abrams, "When Cleodis came into her life, Mrs. Bates was experiencing such emptiness. . . . Cleodis represented youth, he represented strength. He represented dignity of an extended family member . . . and so this boy filled a lot of the emptiness in that house. . . . She became very, very close to him."[32]

Frankie Jeffries recalled that Gatson would cut the grass and take Bates about in her wheelchair while "Mia" (Sharon) did light cleaning in the house. Was Sharon Gatson also close to Bates? Abrams said Bates "never knew [how] she truly felt about his wife."[33] Despite repeated requests, neither the Gatsons nor any other member of the Gatson family consented to be interviewed for this book.

One thing is certain: a number of persons who were close to Bates believe that the Gatsons have quite a bit of explaining to do concerning a number of incidents involving Bates, who, as the 1990s wore on, increasingly needed assistance. First, there was the matter of her house, which had been mortgaged to secure the loan for the publication of the new *State Press*. Bates was about to be turned out of her house after years of being in default. Were that to happen, it would have been a severe embarrassment to the city, which now embraced her as a civil rights heroine. Had it been left up to Madison Guaranty in 1998, Bates could have lived in her house for as long as she liked; however, the federal government had by then created the Resolution Trust Corporation (RTC). The RTC was created precisely to clean up the likes of Madison Guaranty and salvage what it could from the financial messes of the savings and loan industry, which had been pyramiding one bad loan after another during an era of rising real estate values. As it always does, the bubble burst, and people like Jim McDougal went to jail. It was ironic that a beneficiary of this national orgy of greed would be Bates. Coming to her rescue was an unusual coalition of anonymous white Little Rock businessmen and the Christian Ministerial Alliance (CMA), a group of black ministers in the Little Rock area at one time headed by Bates's long-time pastor, Rufus King Young. A remarkably young ninety-one years old at the time of his interview by the author in 2002, Rev. Young still preached one service a month at a church in North Little Rock. When asked why the businessmen preferred anonymity, Rev. Young replied that they were composed of the same businessmen who had at one time withheld advertising in the *State Press*.[34] Whatever their motives, the businessmen transferred $29,315 to the ministers, who signed a contract with Bates to pay off the rest of her debt, which had totaled $67,000. In return, Bates gave the CMA the deed to her house, retaining a life estate in it. The CMA planned to turn the house into a museum after Bates's death. According to Rev. Young, Cleodis Gatson "was trying to get possession" of Bates's home. Like others in Little Rock, the CMA "had never heard of him."[35]

The showdown between the Gatsons and the ministers occurred after a tornado struck Little Rock and severely damaged the house. Fortunately, Bates was not in it at the time (she was then in a nursing home), but the neighborhood was treated to the spectacle of the Gatsons emptying the house of its possessions while the members of the CMA documented the events with video and tape recorders. Rev. Young recalled that after the tornado damaged the house, the "nephew went in and took all of her artifacts, pictures, honors and recognition."[36]

The Gatsons' side of the story is told by their attorney, Carrol Hicks, who cast the actions of her clients in a much different light. After the tornado hit, Cleodis and Sharon went over to the house and parked in "the driveway to make sure no one looted the place." To protect the house, "they spent the rest of the night there." The next morning they called her and reported that part of the roof was off and some of the furniture was outside. Hicks said her office then called the office of George Ivory, the CMA's attorney, to let him know what had happened. Hicks said she and her partners went to the house and invited members of the CMA to come inside. "They refused. We stayed there, my partners and I, probably three or four hours, just helping Cleodis and Sharon lifting and toting, trying to salvage as much as could be salvaged."[37] The contents of the house—what belonged to the CMA and what belonged to Gatsons after Bates's death—would become a fierce bone of contention. Hicks claimed that Bates had signed a durable power of attorney giving Cleodis Gatson the authority to handle her affairs. Whether this was valid at the time of the tornado will never be known. The CMA let the statute of limitations run without filing a lawsuit.

What is certain is that Daisy and L. C.'s beloved "dream house" will be of much less interest to tourists without the vast memorabilia she preserved over the years. The furniture, photographs, paintings, awards, and citations were taken by the Gatsons "to preserve" them, according to Hicks. What furniture was rightfully owned by the CMA was returned, again according to Hicks. As the sole heir of Daisy Bates's estate, Cleodis Gatson now owns all of her personal property outright. What is unfortunate is that there is little doubt that Bates herself would have loved the notion of the house becoming a major tourist spot with all of her awards on display. Perhaps that will come to pass. As Rev. Young said in his interview: black people are the most forgiving people on earth.[38]

There is also the matter of the various wills Bates was said to have made. Though reportedly Bates had previously signed a number of wills, the will that is being probated in Pulaski County was drafted by Carrol Hicks. It leaves all of Bates's property to Cleodis Gatson. Given the racial distrust that continues to exist in Little Rock (despite all the optimistic pronouncements about race relations), the selection of a white attorney to represent Bates raised eyebrows in the black community. Hicks said, "I know that after I was hired, people in town, including prominent black attorneys . . . called [Cleodis and Sharon] up and asked why they were hiring a white woman—which, I don't think it even mattered to Mrs. Bates." Hicks added a telling comment. "I don't think race was as big a deal to her as it's been to people around her."[39]

According to Hicks, the only will she drafted for Bates was the one admitted to Pulaski County Probate Court. Hicks remembered that Bates had become her client in "about '98." Hicks and her then-partner Diana Turner "went to her house. Her physical condition was frail. She was in bed when we talked to her." Hicks said that Cleodis Gatson introduced them to Bates and explained how he knew Hicks. With Gatson out of the room, Hicks talked to Bates about a will and to whom she wanted to leave her property after her death. "Did she want me to represent her? Was she sure? . . . She was real clear about it." Asked about her knowledge of Bates's actual kinship with Cleodis Gatson, Hicks admitted she had no information other than his word. "It never occurred to me to question it, because Mrs. Bates called him her nephew." Hicks was quick to acknowledge that she didn't "know if any evidence of the relationship exists." She mentioned the names of two persons who were considered "cousins" of Bates—Betty Moore and Georgia Jones.[40] I explained, as I had in letters to the Gatsons, that I had no vested interest in whether others were or were not related to Bates, but as someone trying to write her biography, I was obligated to document her family, if possible. No evidence, anecdotal or otherwise, was ever offered by anyone in the Gatson family or anyone else to prove the relationship. Obviously, a number of persons are related to her through her marriage to L. C. but are her not blood relations.

On behalf of the Gatsons, Hicks pointed out that the CMA had agreed with the committee of businessmen to keep the house in repair, including the "exterior walls, roof of the house and make other structural repairs that may be required to keep the premises in good condition."[41] She felt that had not been done.

If one believes Carrol Hicks, the Gatsons had no interest in exploiting Bates's fame for financial gain. A number of people in Little Rock disagree. Hicks believes the exploitation was the other way around. Bates's likeness was showing up on T-shirts, and the estate was receiving nothing. Actually, there was not much in Bates's estate as a potential moneymaker. Other issues involved various organizations set up in Bates's name after her death.

Indeed, Bates's last few months were marked by hostility between these two factions. Those once close to Bates maintained that Bates had been virtually hidden from them by the Gatsons. They couldn't find her. Whether the Gatsons misled anyone about Bates's whereabouts is not clear, but Bates was in three nursing homes and the Baptist Rehabilitation Institute during this period, which undoubtedly made it difficult to keep up with her. Bates's financial position was so dire that she was eligible for Medicaid. Cleodis Gatson, through the power of attorney given to him by Bates, used the last of her assets to qualify her for Medicaid by prepaying for her funeral, according to Hicks.

Daisy Bates took her last breath at 1:13 A.M. on Thursday, November 4, 1999, at the Baptist Hospital in Little Rock. Like L. C., the cause of death was listed as a heart attack. Her passing was a page-one event in Arkansas, but the articles streaming from the press and statements from politicians were peppered with a lifetime of misinformation. For example, the front-page story in the *Arkansas Democrat-Gazette* the next day reported that Daisy had married L. C. when she was fifteen and that she and L. C. had been divorced for two years before they remarried.[42] City flags were lowered to half-staff in Little Rock. Her body was to lie in state in the rotunda of the Arkansas state capitol on Monday. Republican governor Mike Huckabee announced that the state flag would fly at half-staff the day of her funeral, which was scheduled for Tuesday. In Washington, D.C., President Bill Clinton issued a statement: "Hillary and I were very saddened to learn of Daisy Bates' death this morning. She was a dear friend and a heroine. She was known chiefly as a leader during the crisis of Central High School in 1957 and a mentor of the Little Rock Nine. But she was so much more."[43]

Behind the long faces, all hell was breaking loose. The Gatsons had scheduled the funeral for Tuesday, the same day the Little Rock Nine were to be in Washington receiving the Congressional Gold Medal, the country's highest civilian award given by Congress. This was no ordinary event. Previous recipients included George Washington, the

Wright Brothers, and Mother Teresa. Normally presented to the recipient at a ceremony held at the Capitol, President Clinton was given permission to make the awards at the White House because of the Arkansas ties. Retiring senator Dale Bumpers had used all his considerable prestige and clout to get this award for the Little Rock Nine. It was an appropriate swan song for Bumpers, who, as a young city attorney for the town of Charleston near the Oklahoma border, had successfully urged acceptance of integration of the handful of blacks into the white school system after the *Brown* decision.

Despite entreaties from the White House, the Gatsons refused to delay the funeral by a single day so that the president of the United States and the Little Rock Nine and their families and others could attend. When queried about why the Gatsons had refused what appeared to be an obviously appropriate request, which would have added enormous significance to the funeral, Carrol Hicks had no answer on behalf of the Gatsons.

The only plausible answer is that the Gatsons wanted the focus of the funeral to be on themselves. On the front of the funeral program, Bates's name was listed as "Daisy L. Gatson-Bates." In neither collection of Bates's papers had she ever hyphenated her name, invariably signing her letters "Daisy Bates," sometimes adding afterward ("Mrs."). The service was held in North Little Rock at the Full Counsel Christian Fellowship Shirley A. Barnes Family Life Center, where Sharon Gatson was one of the ministers. The eight-page program, obviously written by members of the Gatson family, claims that Bates was the daughter of the "late Hezekiah 'Babe' Gatson and the late Millie Riley." According to this document, Bates had four brothers: Emmitt, Lucas, Lovell, and Leo. Cleodis is mentioned as a "very special nephew as care taker" along with "three very special relatives, who weathered the storm during her last illness": Cleandrea (Mia) Gatson Barnum, Betty Williams Morgan, and Melenda Gatson Hunter (who later visited the Wisconsin State Historical Society in Madison). Repeated efforts by the author to speak to a number of these alleged relatives proved fruitless. The *Arkansas Democrat-Gazette* reported that approximately 1,000 people attended the funeral, which was held in the "gymnasium" of the Family Life Center. Honorary pallbearers included John H. Johnson, an Arkansan by birth who went on to found *Jet* and *Ebony*; attorney John Walker; and dentist Jerry Jewell. Tracy Steele, a state representative and executive director of the Martin Luther King Commission, spoke briefly, as did Bates's attorney,

Carrol Hicks. Rodney Slater, President Clinton's charismatic secretary of transportation and a native of Marianna in the Arkansas Delta, was the president's representative at the funeral and read a letter from Clinton. Letters were also read from Coretta Scott King and Rosa Parks, who wrote that Bates had been "a sister in the [civil rights] movement."[44] The national offices of the NAACP, for which Bates labored for so long, paid its respects. Julian Bond, chairman of the board of the directors of the national NAACP, and Kweisi Mfume, executive director, sent a "resolution" praising Bates for her work. Dale Charles, president of the Arkansas State Conference of Branches, also read a letter. A page and a half of the funeral program included a poem by Cleandrea "Mia" Gatson-Barnum and a "tribute to Aunt Daisy" by "Minister Sharon Gatson," in which she stated that she saw in the departed's face "strength that the world seems to have forgotten about."[45]

Not exactly. In May 2000 a crowed of approximately 2,000, including President Bill Clinton, Governor Mike Huckabee, Little Rock mayor Jim Daily, and others, paid tribute to Bates at a memorial service at Robinson Auditorium in Little Rock. Acknowledging her longevity, Clinton compared her to a "diamond" that gets "chipped away in form and shines more brightly."[46]

Clinton had made the issue of race one of his major initiatives in his second term. His extraordinary rapport with blacks led him to try to engage the American people in a dialogue on the issues dividing black and white. The unwillingness of the public at large to grapple with racial problems was not the fault of the president, who returned again and again to the theme of racial harmony and how it could be achieved in the United States. His words largely went unheard. The country had no particular interest in grappling with the wounds of race, and Clinton reluctantly moved on, but his own commitment to the process of racial conciliation never wavered. Even after he left the presidency, he returned to Little Rock to help raise money for a proposed museum to be made of Daisy and L. C.'s home.

In 2005 Bates's legacy endures as a symbol of courage and dignity, but the outcome of her work to integrate Central High School is in doubt. At one time she and L. C. had believed that integration of the schools would be the key to racial progress, not its battleground. At the beginning of the 2004–5 school year, most of Little Rock's schools were substantially black. Though genuine friendships between African Americans and whites are evident in the state of Arkansas, there remains deep distrust between the races, but it is not a subject that attracts a great deal of public discussion. The percentage of children in private schools in Little Rock in the 2003–4 school year was "probably" over 50 percent, according to a study conducted by the *Arkansas Democrat-Gazette*.[47] Northwest Arkansas has become the mecca for growth in the state as white flight continues.

As for Daisy Bates, one perceives something of a backlash against her in the present era, as the contributions of her husband, the Little Rock Nine, and their families and others begin to be better understood and appreciated. Still, her memory endures. What she accomplished— the insistence that she, at great personal cost and sacrifice, be accorded the dignity that all humans seek—will always be her true legacy, whatever happens in the future.

NOTES

INTRODUCTION

1. Ted Ownby, ed., *The Role of Ideas in the Civil Rights Movement* (Jackson: University Press of Mississippi, 2002); David L. Chappell, *A Stone of Hope: Prophecy, Religion and the Death of Jim Crow* (Chapel Hill: University of North Carolina Press, 2004).

2. Thomas Gentile, *March on Washington, August 28, 1963* (Washington, D.C.: New Day Publications, 1983), 229.

3. Taylor Branch, *Parting the Waters: America in the King Years, 1954–1963* (New York: Touchstone, 1989) 882–86.

4. Ibid.

5. Ibid., 880.

6. One of the ironies of the period was A. Philip Randolph's appearance at the all-male Press Club in Washington just days before the march. Women, white or black, were not permitted but could observe the proceedings from the balcony. Gentile, *March on Washington*, 140.

7. Douglas Brinkley, *Rosa Parks* (New York: Viking Penguin, 2000), 185.

8. Ibid., 186. There is much recent discussion in the literature about the role of women in the civil rights movement. See particularly Anne Standley, "The Role of Black Women in the Civil Rights Movement," in *Women in the Civil Rights Movement: Trailblazers and Torchbearers 1941–1965*, (Bloomington: Indiana University Press 1993), 183–201; Bettye Collier-Thomas and V. P. Franklin, eds, *Sisters in the Struggle: African American Women in the Civil Rights–Black Power Movement* (New York: New York University Press, 2001); Belinda Robnett, *How Long? How Long? African American Women in the Struggle for Civil Rights* (New York: Oxford University Press, 1997).

9. Michael Eric Dyson, *I May Not Get There with You: The True Martin Luther King, Jr.* (New York: Free Press, 2000), 199.

Notes

10. Clayborne Carson, *In Struggle: SNCC and the Black Awakening of the 1960s*, quoted in Dyson, *I May Not Get There*, 207.

11. In his review of the civil rights career of Modeska Simpkins in *Stone of Hope*, 63–66, David L. Chappell whets the reader's appetite for more information about this powerfully outspoken and talented woman.

12. Ibid., 206.

13. John Andrew Kirk, "Black Activism in Arkansas, 1940–1970" (Ph.D. diss., Newcastle University, 1997), 21. Kirk's book on this subject is *Redefining the Color Line: Black Activism in Little Rock, Arkansas 1940–1970* (Gainesville: University Press of Florida, 2002).

14. *American Legacy*, Spring 2004, 37. Height was undoubtedly remembering that no woman was scheduled to speak.

15. Gentile, *March on Washington*, 141.

16. Gentile records that A. Philip Randolph made the first speech (all the main speakers were limited to seven minutes and remarkably stayed on time) at 1:15 and followed it with the "the tribute to women" with his introductions of the women mentioned above, though Myrlie Evers, the widow of Medgar Evers, was absent. Gentile, *March on Washington*, 225. It would have been here that Daisy Bates made her brief remarks, though her own memory of the events had her speaking after Martin Luther King Jr., whose speech was undeniably the last on the program. It is likely that Roy Wilkins prevailed upon the others to allow Bates to speak.

17. Sound recording of excerpts of speeches at the March on Washington, August 28, 1963, Exhibit 15, National Civil Rights Museum, Memphis, Tennessee.

18. Daisy Bates to Roy Wilkins, Oct. 19, 1962, Box 1, File 1, Daisy Bates Papers, Special Collections, University of Arkansas Libraries, Fayetteville (hereafter cited as Fayetteville).

19. Gender issues as they affect racial history are finally becoming part of the intellectual landscape. Jeannie M. Whayne has summarized the often sharp differences among historians, primarily women historians, who have written within the last thirty years on women's roles within the family and the gender issues facing black and white Southern women as the Civil War ended. See Jeannie M. Whayne, "Southern Women in the Age of Emancipation," in *The Blackwell Companion to the Civil War and Reconstruction*, ed. Lacy Ford (Malden, Mass.: Blackwell, 2005).

20. Tony Freyer, *The Little Rock Crisis: A Constitutional Interpretation* (Westport, Conn.: Greenwood Press, 1984), 54.

21. *Arkansas Gazette*, May 5, 1956.

22. *State Press*, May 11, 1956.

23. In commenting on the legacy of white supremacy for a conference commemorating the fortieth anniversary of the Central High Crisis, historian David R. Goldfield has written, "The damage all of this did to black southerners is incalculable and, in

Notes

fact, historians have scarcely begun to assess the impact of segregation on blacks, whites, and the South." David R. Goldfield, "Segregation and Racism: Taking up the Dream Again," in *Understanding the Little Rock Crisis, an Exercise in Remembrance and Reconciliation*, ed. Elizabeth Jacoway and C. Fred Williams, 37 (Fayetteville: University of Arkansas Press, 1999).

24. Kenneth M. Stampp, *The Era of Reconstruction, 1865–1867* (New York: Knopf 1965), 55.

25. John Gould Fletcher, "Letter to the Editor," *Nation*, December 17, 1933, 734.

CHAPTER ONE

1. "Huttig," General File, Arkansas History Commission, Little Rock.

2. *Huttig News*, Mar. 6, 1915.

3. Daisy Bates, *The Long Shadow of Little Rock: A Memoir* (New York: David McKay, 1962; reprint, Fayetteville: University of Arkansas Press, 1986), 8.

4. Jelynn Little, interview by author, Feb. 4, 2002.

5. Bates, *Long* Shadow, 8.

6. Ibid., 9.

7. Grif Stockley, *Blood in Their Eyes: The Elaine Massacres of 1919* (Fayetteville: University of Arkansas Press, 2001), 20.

8. Ibid. Estimates of the blacks murdered in Phillips County range from 20 to 856. Whites falsely accused blacks of having attempted an "insurrection." See ibid., xxv, chap. 4.

9. Daisy Bates was well aware of the actual events in Elaine due to the fact that L. C. Bates had previously worked in Helena at a black newspaper shortly after the massacres occurred. In a draft of *The Long Shadow of Little Rock*, Bates wrote with deadly accuracy, "in 1919 mobs of white men from many counties in Arkansas and Mississippi shot down Negro men and women in the cotton fields and in their church. . . . Negro tenant farmers had organized societies to pool their moral and financial resources against the landowners." "Faubus" section of draft of *The Long Shadow of Little Rock*, 3, Ms. 523, n.d., microfilm, Daisy Bates Papers, State Historical Society of Wisconsin, Madison (hereafter cited as Madison).

10. Ibid.

11. *Huttig News*, Oct. 24, Nov. 12, 1914.

12. Census record of Lapilo Township, Union County, Arkansas, Feb. 17, 1920, U.S. Department of Commerce, Census Office, Fourteenth Census of the United States: 1920—Population, 228.

13. Delayed birth certificate issued by state of Arkansas, Aug. 10, 1962, Box 3, File 3, Madison.

14. Bates, *Long Shadow*, 12.

15. Ibid., 15.

16. Ibid., 22.

17. Daisy Bates's death certificate lists her mother's name as "Mary Riley" and her father as "H. C. Gatson." See chapter 19.

18. *Huttig News*, Aug. 12, 1916.

19. Tommie Mae Pearson, interview by author, Mar. 28, 2002.

20. Note from Harry Miller, reference archivist, to users of Daisy Bates Papers, July 2, 2001, Box 3, File 3, Madison.

21. Clifton Broughton, interview by author, Mar. 27, 2001.

22. Bates, *Long Shadow*, 12.

23. Ibid., 29.

24. Ibid., 15.

25. Fragment of draft of *Long Shadow*, Madison.

26. Bates, *Long Shadow*, 25.

27. Ethel Smith, interview by author, Mar. 26, 2002.

28. Daisy Bates, interview by Elizabeth Jacoway, Oct. 11, 1976, 2, Southern Oral History Program, Library of University of North Carolina at Chapel Hill.

29. Leroy Matthew Christophe, *The Arkansas African-American Hall of Fame* (Little Rock: National Dunbar Alumni Association of Little Rock, 1993), 71.

30. *Huttig News*, Feb. 20, 1915.

31. Bates, *Long* Shadow, 7.

32. Ibid.

33. L. C. Bates told historian C. Calvin Smith that he and Daisy moved to Little Rock in the "late 1930s" and sold insurance. C. Calvin Smith, "From 'Separate but Equal' to Desegregation: The Changing Philosophy of L. C. Bates," *Arkansas Historical Quarterly* (Autumn 1983): 254–70. L. C. Bates was still listed in the Memphis city directory in 1939.

CHAPTER TWO

1. Lerone Bennett Jr., "First Lady of Little Rock," *Ebony*, September 1958, 17, 21.

2. Irene Wassell, "L. C. Bates, Editor of the *Arkansas State Press*" (master's thesis, University of Arkansas at Little Rock, 1983), 5.

3. Smith, "From 'Separate but Equal,'" 254–70.

4. Wassell, "L. C. Bates," 6.

5. Ibid., 9, 10.

6. In correspondence to Loretta, Daisy acknowledged on one occasion that she and L. C. had adopted her. Christopher Mercer, who served as L. C. and Daisy's

attorney for many years, said he could not recall whether he had completed the papers for an adoption. Loretta is specifically mentioned in Daisy Bates's will but was not left her estate (a common procedure to prevent heirs from claiming they have been "forgotten" by the person making the will). I was unable to interview members of the immediate family.

7. Wassell, "L. C. Bates," 10.

8. Bates, *Long Shadow*, 33.

9. Broughton, interview.

10. Lottie Neely, interview by author, Apr. 20, 2002; Wassell, "L. C. Bates," 12.

11. Wassell, "L. C. Bates," 12, n. 3. In various interviews, L. C. Bates was equally complicit in the fiction that the couple was not having a relationship until they moved to Little Rock in 1941.

12. Entries in Memphis City directories during the period, Jim Cole to author, e-mail, Mar. 18, 2002.

13. Federal Bureau of Investigation, Daisy Bates File, Butler Center for Arkansas Studies, Little Rock (hereafter cited as Daisy Bates, FBI Files).

14. L. C. Bates to Daisy Bates, Dec. 10, 1963, Box 1, Folder 4, Madison.

15. Ibid.

16. Ibid.

17. L. C.'s letter contains uncharacteristic grammatical errors.

18. Bates, *Long Shadow*, 33.

19. Wassell, "L. C. Bates," 12.

20. Ibid., 11.

21. Ibid., 7.

22. Ibid., 76.

23. Dallas County Marriage Index 1845–1959, 1:16, Dallas County Courthouse, Fordyce, Arkansas.

24. Wassell, "L. C. Bates," 7.

25. Edith Irby Jones, interview by author, Mar. 23, 2002.

26. Wassell, "L. C. Bates," 16.

27. Jones, interview.

28. Wassell, "L. C. Bates," 14.

29. Though the *Southern Mediator Journal* would last, historian John Kirk has noted the rapid turnover in the black press. Kirk, *Redefining the Color Line*, 13, 14.

30. C. Calvin Smith has written that the Bateses bought out the *Twin City Press* and renamed it the *Arkansas State Press*, which may certainly be correct; however, in an interview, L. C. Bates gave a more detailed version that his offers had been refused. Wassell, "L. C. Bates," 15.

31. Ibid.

32. *State Press*, Feb. 13, July 17, 1953.

Notes

33. Ibid., May 9, 1941.

34. Ibid., Mar. 17, 1944.

35. Ibid., Aug. 27, 1943.

36. Wassell, "L. C. Bates," 44.

37. Ibid., 40.

CHAPTER THREE

1. George P. Rawick, *The American Slave: A Composite Autobiography*, vol. 10B, *Arkansas Slave Narratives*, Charlotte Stephens (Westport, Conn.: Greenwood Press, 1972), 226–33.

2. Adolphine Fletcher Terry, *Charlotte Stephens: Little Rock's First Black Teacher* (Little Rock: Academic Press of Arkansas, 1973), 126.

3. Fon Louise Gordon, *Caste and Class: The Black Experience in Arkansas* (Athens: University of Georgia Press, 1995) 111, 112.

4. Kirk, "Black Activism," 19.

5. In the 1920s Scipio Jones had represented the twelve black sharecroppers charged in Elaine in tandem with former Arkansas attorney general George Murphy, a former colonel in the Confederate army who had been hired by the national NAACP. Besides the twelve men sentenced to death, sixty-five others had entered into plea bargains and were sentenced from one to twenty-one years in prison. After Murphy died, Jones worked for a time with Edgar McHaney of the colonel's law firm. By 1925 all of the men, including the Elaine Twelve, were out of prison, due in large part to the untiring work of Jones, who was the ultimate pragmatist in obtaining their freedom. The services to his people in the Elaine litigation was but one of many instances during his career of how he manipulated the system of white supremacy to obtain concessions for blacks who had no such advantages. To African Americans in Jim Crow Arkansas, he was a genuine hero and an effective advocate for those who had no other recourse.

6. At the age of forty, Jones ran for the Little Rock School Board in 1902. He received only 181 votes out of over 2,000 cast in his ward. Though in 1909 he had been recommended for a patronage job in Washington as recorder of deeds, he didn't get it. When blacks, including Jones, were shut out of the Pulaski County Republican Party convention in 1920, for the first and only time they ran their own candidate for governor. While this got the Republican Party's attention, the politics of white supremacy ruled the roost in both parties.

7. Kirk, "Black Activism," 16.

8. John William Graves, *Town and Country Race Relations in an Urban-Rural Context, Arkansas, 1865–1905* (Fayetteville: University of Arkansas Press, 1990,) 151–63, 219–22.

9. Kirk, "Black Activism," 25–29.

10. Ben Johnson III, *Arkansas in Modern America 1930–1999* (Fayetteville: University of Arkansas Press, 2000), 50.

11. *State Press*, Mar. 6, 1942.

12. Preston Toombs, interview by author, May 9, 2002.

13. Kirk, "Black Activism," 40.

14. Ibid., 117.

15. Ibid., 71–73, citing the investigation conducted by Frank H. Patton, special assistant to the attorney general of the United States, before the federal grand jury for the Eastern District of Arkansas, Western Division, covering the death of Sergeant Thomas B. Foster, June 10, 1942.

16. *State Press*, Mar. 27, 1942.

17. Ibid., Apr. 3, 1942.

18. *Arkansas Gazette*, Jan. 22, 1972.

19. Bates, *Long Shadow*, 37.

20. Kirk, "Black Activism," 78.

21. *Arkansas Gazette*, June 11, 1942.

22. Bates, *Long Shadow*, 38.

23. Quoted in Kirk, "Black Activism," 65.

24. Ibid., 68.

25. Ibid. 31.

26. Juan Williams, *Thurgood Marshall: American Revolutionary* (New York: Times Books, 1998).

CHAPTER FOUR

1. Neely, interview.

2. Ibid.

3. Toombs, interview.

4. Bates, *Long Shadow*, 39.

5. Toombs, interview.

6. *State Press*, Nov. 30, 1945.

7. Bates, *Long Shadow*, 40.

8. Ibid., 41.

9. Ibid.

10. Ibid., 43, quoting *Bates v. Auten*.

11. Ernest Dumas, interview by author, Feb. 19, 2002.

12. Jones, interview.

13. Ibid.

Notes

14. Theodosia Cooper, interview by author, Apr. 28, 2002.

15. Draft of *Long Shadow*, "Daisy," 3, Madison.

16. Audre Hanneman to author, Apr. 26, 2002.

17. *Chicago Defender*, Sept. 4, 1960.

18. Toombs, interview.

19. Ibid.

20. Ibid.

21. Christopher Mercer, interview by author, Jan. 17, 2002.

22. Ibid.

23. Fred Darraugh, interview by author, Dec. 11, 2001.

24. Toombs, interview.

25. John Kirk, "Daisy Bates, the National Association for the Advancement of Colored People, and the 1957 Little Rock School Crisis: A Gendered Perspective," in *Gender in the Civil Rights Movement*, ed. Peter J. Ling and Sharon Monteith, 28 (New York: Garland, 1999).

26. Mercer, interview, Jan. 17, 2002.

27. Kirk, "Black Activism," 111.

28. Quoted in ibid., 109. A pool was eventually built at Gillam Park, but L. C. remarked in an editorial that its dedication in 1950 was hardly a cause for rejoicing.

29. Kirk, "Daisy Bates," 31.

30. Bates, interview by Jacoway, 5.

CHAPTER FIVE

1. Though southern blacks read about the injustices perpetrated against blacks in publications such as the *Chicago Defender*, which also made their way South, the NAACP's magazine, the *Crisis*, edited by W. E. B. Du Bois, held out the hope that its organization could do something about it.

2. During its effort to provide representation by a white attorney for blacks sentenced to die in the electric chair, the national office, in effect, deceived its local chapter in Little Rock before finally cooperating with black attorney Scipio Africanus Jones. Stockley, *Blood in Their Eyes*, 143. John Kirk has shown that in 1928 the NAACP was "reluctant to lend support" to the Arkansas Negro Democratic Association, which sought to challenge the legality of the white primary. Basically, the rule of the national organization was that its support of local efforts "was carefully weighed against support offered" to NAACP headquarters in New York. Kirk, "Black Activism," 27.

3. Mark Tushnet, *The NAACP's Legal Strategy against Segregated Education, 1925–1950* (Chapel Hill: University of North Carolina Press, 1957).

4. Kirk, "Black Activism," 116, 117.

5. Ibid., 117.

6. Ibid., 118.

7. Gloster Current to Daisy Bates, Jan. 19, 1949, Group 2, C10, Folder "Little Rock, Ark., 1948–1955," Papers of the National Association for the Advancement of Colored People, Manuscript Division, Library of Congress, Washington, D.C. (hereafter cited as Papers of the NAACP).

8. Kirk, "Black Activism," 120.

9. Daisy Bates, FBI Files.

10. Williams, *Thurgood Marshall*, 168.

11. See Jeff Woods, "Designed to Harass: The Act 10 Controversy in Arkansas," *Arkansas Historical Quarterly* (Winter 1997): 443–60.

12. Daisy Bates, FBI Files.

13. Ibid.

14. Kirk, "Black Activism," 114.

15. Ibid., 114, 115.

16. Ibid., 36.

17. Bates, *Long Shadow*, 47.

18. U. Simpson Tate to Gloster Current, Aug. 20, 1952, Group 2, Series C, Container 11, Folder "Arkansas State Conference 1951–52," Papers of the NAACP.

19. Ibid.

20. Mercer, interview, Jan. 17, 2002.

21. "An Autobiographical Approach to the German-Jewish Legacy," 122, 123, November 1988, Georg Iggers File, Special Collections, University of Arkansas Libraries, University of Arkansas at Little Rock (UALR).

22. Georg Iggers to Tony Freyer, Sept. 17, 1980, Georg Iggers File, UALR.

23. Freyer, *Little Rock Crisis*, 27, 28.

24. Lee Lorch, interview by author, August 18, 2002.

25. *Chicago Defender*, Mar. 15, 1952.

26. Williams, *Thurgood Marshall*, 188.

27. Kirk has noted that of the three groups, the NAACP, with its almost all-black membership, "sought an immediate end to segregation by pursuing civil rights in the courts." Kirk, *Redefining the Color Line*, 91. The point is well taken but should not obscure the fact that the Little Rock NAACP in 1952 was willing to continue the old tradition of having a white person act as intermediary with other whites and settle for much less than immediate desegregation of the schools.

28. Black students had their own print shop at Dunbar, but typically the equipment was not as advanced as that available to white students.

29. E-mail from Georg Iggers to author, Aug. 7, 2002, Georg Iggers File, UALR.

30. *Brown v. Board of Education*, 349 U.S. 294 (1954).

31. Branch, *Parting the Waters*, 144.

32. The "white sympathizers" at this point in Little Rock were generally members of religious organizations.

33. *State Press*, Mar. 18, June 10, 1955.

CHAPTER SIX

1. Kirk, "Black Activism," 98. Historians have cited the following work in noting the racial changes in Little Rock during this era: Griffin Smith Jr. "Localism and Segregation: Racial Patterns in Little Rock, Arkansas, 1945–1954" (master's thesis, Columbia University, 1965), 52–53, 80, 94–95.

2. *Brown v. Board of Education*.

3. *State Press*, May 21, 1954.

4. Virgil T. Blossom, *It HAS Happened Here* (New York: Harper and Brothers, 1959), 11.

5. Ibid.

6. Books and articles on the 1957 Little Rock crisis continue to appear as the fiftieth anniversary approaches. For a recent comprehensive civil rights bibliography that captures a thirty-year period surrounding this era, see Kirk, *Redefining the Color Line*. Elizabeth Jacoway's long-anticipated history of the 1957 Little Rock crisis coinciding with the fiftieth anniversary in 2007 is expected to be the definitive work on this period in Arkansas. Researchers of this period should also consult the bibliography detailing the "more than 40 manuscript collections" in Jacoway and Williams, *Understanding the Little Rock Crisis*, 152–61.

7. Blossom, *It HAS Happened Here*, 13.

8. Bates, interview by Jacoway, 12.

9. Ibid., 15.

10. Roy Reed, *Faubus: The Life and Times of an American Prodigal* (Fayetteville: University of Arkansas Press, 1997), 184.

11. Elizabeth Jacoway, "Taken by Surprise: Little Rock Business Leaders and Desegregation," in *Southern Businessmen and Desegregation*, ed. Elizabeth Jacoway and David Colburn, 21 n. 9 (Baton Rouge: Louisiana State University Press, 1982).

12. Blossom, *It HAS Happened Here*, 23.

13. Freyer, *Little Rock Crisis*, 46, 47.

14. Kirk, "Black Activism," 127.

15. Johnson, *Arkansas in Modern America*.

16. Irving J. Spitzberg Jr., *Racial Politics in Little Rock, 1954–1964* (New York: Garland, 1987).

17. Kirk, "Black Activism," 126.

18. For example, "As you move west through the state, this attitude [toward relaxation of segregation] changes." Blossom, *It HAS Happened Here*, 6. But as Roy Reed (and others) has pointed out, some Arkansans' "high-minded[ness] on race" had to do with the relatively few blacks in their area. Reed, *Faubus*, 168.

19. Jacqueline Froelich and David Zimmerman, "Total Eclipse: The Destruction of the African American Community of Harrison, Arkansas, in 1905 and 1909," *Arkansas Historical Quarterly* (Autumn 1999): 158.

20. Branch, *Parting the Waters*, 213.

21. Wilson Record, ed., *Little Rock, U.S.A.* (San Francisco: Chandler, 1960), 11.

22. Wiley Branton to H. R. Weaver, Sept. 30, 1955, Box 4, Folder 10, Madison.

23. As unique as Kunkel's private statement appears, research conducted by David Chappell shows that as a religious issue, Jim Crow had begun to trouble southerners, including Arkansans in the middle of the Delta. He quotes a letter from the "mildly segregationist pastor of the Earle, Arkansas First Baptist Church," who wrote that "we are divided on the issue of integration. Many of our brethren are moderate integrationist and others moderate segregationist, brethren that love the Lord." Chappell, *Stone of Hope*, 150.

24. For a unique view of Jim Johnson in the present era, see Elizabeth Jacoway, "Jim Johnson of Arkansas Segregationist Prototype," in Ownby, *The Role of Ideas in the Civil Rights Movement*, 137–55. Historians such as Jacoway seem to be implicitly suggesting, especially in light of recent conservative rulings by the Supreme Court, that there was legal merit to Johnson's states' rights position and that, given the racial quagmire of the present era, he, as a representative of die-hard racial conservatives who refuse to bow to present notions of political correctness, deserves a respectful hearing. So long as one discounts the right of African Americans (and other disfavored minorities) to the protection (as currently understood) of the Fourteenth Amendment to the Constitution, it may well be an idea whose time is coming again and indeed is already here.

25. *Arkansas Faith*, May 1956, 3, Box 4, File 1, Fayetteville.

26. Orville Taylor, *Negro Slavery in Arkansas* (Fayetteville: University of Arkansas Press, 2000), 198–99.

27. White America, Inc. formally merged with the White Citizens Council of Arkansas in October 1956. *Southern School News*, October 1956. Arkansans did not invent these groups. White Mississippians, among others, appeared regularly in the state to help their neighbors form these organizations. See, for example, *Southern School News*, April 7, 1955.

28. Mildred Bond, interview by author, Feb. 7, 2002. Bond, now Mildred Roxborough, was still working for the national NAACP office at the time of her interview.

29. Reed, *Faubus*, 173.

30. Bates, *Long Shadow*, 172.

31. Fragment of early draft of *Long Shadow*, Madison.

32. Bates, interview by Jacoway, 36, 37.

33. *Afro-American*, Oct. 12, 1957.

34. As prosecutor in 1919 Miller had been under considerable pressure, but no one forced him to rewrite history as a federal judge. Stockley, *Blood in Their Eyes*, 186–87.

35. Kirk, "Black Activism," 138.

36. Letter from Mildred Bond on national NAACP stationary written from Little Rock to Dr. H. A. Powell, August 28, 1956, Papers of the NAACP.

37. Daisy Bates to Gloster Current, Jan. 30, 1956, Papers of the NAACP.

38. Lorch, interview.

39. E-mail from Georg Iggers to author, Aug. 7, 2002.

40. *Southern School News*, Feb. 1956.

41. *Arkansas Democrat*, Jan. 23, 1956.

CHAPTER SEVEN

1. *Arkansas Gazette*, Jan. 24, 1956.

2. Benjamin Muse, *Ten Years of Prelude: The Story of Integration since the Supreme Court's 1954 Decision* (New York: Viking, 1964), 84–85, quoted in Kirk, "Black Activism" 150.

3. Georg Iggers to Tony Freyer, UALR.

4. J. C. Crenchaw to Wiley Branton, Apr. 20, 1956.

5. Wiley Branton, interview, African-American Oral History Project, Howard University, Washington, D.C.

6. Freyer, *Little Rock Crisis*, 49.

7. *State Press*, June 22, 1956.

8. Ibid., July 20, 1956.

9. Ibid.

10. Reed, *Faubus*, 166.

11. Ibid., 169.

12. Ibid., 168, 169.

13. Ibid.

14. Ibid., 188.

15. *State Press*, June 8, 1956.

16. Ibid., June 22, 1956.

17. Freyer, *Little Rock Crisis*, 56–57.

18. Kirk, "Black Activism," 150 n. 58, According to Muse, "The Arkansas suit was unique at the time in that, unlike the other sixty-five school suits being conducted with NAACP support in the upper South, it asked for existing desegregation plans to be implemented rather than suing for complete integration." Muse, *Ten Years of Prelude*, 84–85.

19. Tony Freyer has written that Judge Miller "honestly applied [the *Brown* decision], because it was the law of the land." Freyer, *Little Rock Crisis*, 55. Given Miller's actions in the past and his willingness to engage in ex parte communications with the white power structure, this author is not persuaded.

20. *Arkansas Gazette*, Aug. 29, 1956.

21. Daisy Bates to Roy Wilkins, Sept. 25, 1956, in author's possession.

22. Daisy Bates to Roy Wilkins, Nov. 8, 1956, in author's possession.

23. Ibid.

24. Roy Wilkins to Daisy Bates, Nov. 19, 1956, in author's possession.

25. Reed, *Faubus*, xii.

CHAPTER EIGHT

1. *State Press*, Jan. 4, 1957.

2. Blossom, *It HAS Happened Here*, 3.

3. *State Press*, Feb. 15, 1957.

4. Bates, *Long Shadow*, 54.

5. Ibid.

6. Ibid.

7. Ibid., 54, 55.

8. Blossom, *It HAS Happened Here*, 2.

9. Roy Wilkins to Daisy Bates, Feb. 25, 1957, Group 3, Container 4, Folder 5, "Geographical File," Papers of the NAACP.

10. Daisy Bates to Gloster Current, Mar. 23, 1957, Papers of the NAACP.

11. *State Press*, Mar. 15, 1957.

12. Ibid., Apr. 19, 1957

13. Ibid., Mar. 15, 1957.

14. Ibid., June 7, 1957.

15. Kirk, "Black Activism," 181.

16. Elizabeth Eckford, interview by author, Sept. 4, 2002.

17. Ibid.

18. Melba Pattillo Beals, *Warriors Don't Cry: A Searing Memoir of the Battle to Integrate Little Rock's Central High* (New York: Washington Square Books, 1994), 55.

Notes

19. Bates, interview by Jacoway, 11.

20. Terrence Roberts, interview by author, Aug. 22, 2002.

21. Mary Henry, interview by author, (?) 2000.

22. Bates, interview by Jacoway, 11.

23. Smith's report of the meeting (in author's possession) contained a paragraph stating that Blossom had responded to a question by saying that "Negro pupils with low I.Q.s, poor scholarship, low citizenship ranking and questionable character who are eligible and desire to attend Central High school would be discouraged if possible, but if they persisted of their own for enrollment in Central, they would be admitted." Of course, Blossom had no intention of permitting that to happen, nor did Bates.

24. According to Smith's report, Blossom told the group he had talked to the judge, which, if true, was an impermissible and unethical ex parte communication with the court by the defendants, but certainly not uncommon in this litigation.

25. According to Smith's report, Blossom opened the meeting by saying that if it had not been for Jackie Robinson with his "personality traits, citizenship ability, high intelligence, etc., Negroes would not today be enjoying the same privileges in organized baseball." Blossom was then reported to have said that "I feel that for this transition from segregation to integration in the Little Rock school system, we should select and encourage only the best Negro students to attend Central High School—so that no criticism of the integration process could be attributed to inefficiency, poor scholarship, low morals, or poor citizenship." Nothing in Smith's report indicated any disagreement with Blossom on this point.

26. Smith's account said in part, "It was reported from reliable sources that nine out of a possible seventy pupils have been encouraged to use the privilege of attending Central High." Though the number "encouraged" to attend Central would be slightly higher, it is ironic that nine turned out to be the actual number.

27. Reed, *Faubus*, 182.

28. Ibid., 186.

29. Ibid., 187.

30. Blossom, *It HAS Happened Here*, 41.

31. Phoebe Godfrey has written that during the crisis, Orval Faubus "spoke in a language that his chief constituency, Little Rock's working class segregationists, well understood—a racialized language with powerful sexual overtones." Phoebe Godfrey, "Bayonets, Brainwashing, and Bathrooms: The Discourse of Race, Gender, and Sexuality in the Desegregation of Little Rock's Central High," *Arkansas Historical Quarterly* (Spring 2001): 42. It is difficult to re-create today the power of white supremacy, particularly because it has become politically incorrect to point out that its tenets thrive just below the surface of polite discourse about race. Americans have solved America's racial problem by not discussing it. However, in the academic literature much has been written about it. Godfrey writes, "Anti-miscegenation was a legal and ideological means of

Notes

constructing racial identity, giving all 'whites' who upheld its doctrine (if not necessarily its practice) a claim to whiteness, regardless of their social class, gender or sexuality. Whiteness, as a social construction that evolved over time and crossed social class divisions, gave those 'owned' it privileges and benefits like "holders of other types of property. Whiteness was and had always been something worth defending, especially by those who had little else in terms of 'property.' " Ibid., 53.

32. Reed, *Faubus*, 188. A number of writers, including Reed, have commented upon the class distinctions present at the time. Guthridge had to supplement his law practice by "refinishing furniture in his wife's antique shop." Pruden was the pastor of "a second-tier Baptist Church." Ibid., 189.

33. *State Press*, May 3, 1957.

34. Ibid., Aug. 2, 1957.

35. Blossom, *It HAS Happened Here*, 48.

36. Ibid., 55, 56.

37. Reed, *Faubus*, 197.

38. *State Press*, Aug. 30, 1957.

39. Reed, *Faubus*, 190.

40. Ibid., 192.

41. Blossom, *It HAS Happened Here*, 52.

42. Freyer, *Little Rock Crisis*, 99.

43. Reed, *Faubus*, 198.

44. Ibid., 199.

45. Ibid.

46. Ibid., 212, 213.

47. Ibid., 199.

48. Blossom, *It HAS Happened Here*, 59.

49. Bates, *Long Shadow*, 57.

50. Reed, *Faubus*, 203–4. Historian C. Fred Williams has written that "the Little Rock School Crisis was more about class than race." C. Fred Williams, "Class: The Central Issue in the 1957 Little Rock School Crisis," *Arkansas Historical Quarterly* (Autumn 1997): 341.

51. Reed, *Faubus*, 205.

52. Ibid., 204.

53. Stockley, *Blood in Their Eyes*, 86.

54. Reed, *Faubus*, 205.

55. Harry S. Ashmore, *Epitaph for Dixie* (New York: W. W. Norton, 1957) 56, 181.

56. Bates, interview by Jacoway, 18.

57. Ibid. 12.

58. Reed, *Faubus*, 122.

59. Emmanuel West was eventually convicted and executed. In contrast to the minimal defense efforts by white attorneys in that era, the defense called twenty witnesses to say that West had been in a real estate office in North Little Rock when the rape had been committed.

60. Draft of *Long Shadow*, III, 26–27, Madison. Though it did no good, "J. O. [Powell] did not agree with Jess's policy of not suspending students for racial incidents that were not authenticated by adult witnesses. From now on, all his reports to the superintendent recommended permanent suspension for those students reported by the Nine for repeated harassment." Elizabeth Huckaby, *Crisis at Central High Little Rock 1957–58* (Baton Rouge: Louisiana State University Press, 1980), 144.

61. Huckaby, *Crisis at Central High*.

62. Bates, interview by Jacoway, 18.

63. David L. Chappell, *Inside Agitators: White Southerners in the Civil Rights Movement* (Baltimore: Johns Hopkins University Press, 1996), xxii.

CHAPTER NINE

1. Daisy Bates to Robert Carter, Aug. 31, 1957, Papers of the NAACP.

2. Though this suit did not result in striking down the State Sovereignty Commission, it did hold that persons could not required to register and report to it. *Smith v. Faubus*, 230 Ark. 831 (1959).

3. Bates to Carter, Aug. 31, 1957, Papers of the NAACP.

4. Ibid.

5. Bates, *Long Shadow*, 60.

6. Fragment of draft of *Long Shadow*, Madison. Though apparently only a portion of the early drafts has survived, its gives an idea of Bates's writing ability.

7. *Arkansas Democrat-Gazette*, Jan. 12, 1992.

8. Fragment of draft of *Long Shadow*, Madison.

9. Bates, *Long Shadow*, 61.

10. "Speech by Governor Orval E. Faubus calling out the National Guard, Sept. 2, 1957," FBI Investigation Papers, "The 1957 Little Rock School Desegregation Crisis," Special Collections, University of Arkansas Libraries, UALR.

11. Ibid.

12. Bates, *Long Shadow*, 61.

13. "Speech by Governor Orval E. Faubus calling out the National Guard, Sept. 2, 1957."

14. Ibid.

15. Reed, *Faubus*, xii.

16. Ibid., 207

17. *Arkansas Democrat*, Sept. 3, 1957.

18. Ibid.

19. Bates, *Long Shadow, 65; Arkansas Democrat*, Sept. 3, 1957.

20. Bates, *Long Shadow*, 62.

21. *Arkansas Gazette*, Sept. 4, 1957.

22. Bates, *Long Shadow*, 63.

23. Ibid.

24. Reed, *Faubus*, 200. At another time, Blossom was so agitated that Smith thought Blossom would attack him.

25. *Arkansas Gazette*, Sept. 4, 1957.

26. Bates, interview by Jacoway, 13.

27. Bates, *Long Shadow*, 63, 64.

28. Ibid., 64.

29. Ibid.

30. *Arkansas Gazette*, Sept. 4, 1957.

31. Bates, *Long Shadow*, 65.

32. Ibid.

33. Fragment of draft of *Long Shadow*, Madison.

34. Elizabeth Eckford, interview; Oscar Eckford, interview by author, Nov. 21, 2002. Much has been written about Elizabeth Eckford's encounter with the mob (the picture of her being followed by the cursing, screaming crowd of whites is one of the enduring photographs of the civil rights movement), but what is not generally realized outside of Little Rock is the emotional cost to Eckford that endures to this day. In own her words, she was "an extremely shy person" and has suffered psychological difficulties throughout her life. Though she has been able to work, it was only after many years that she was diagnosed with posttraumatic stress syndrome as a result of the trauma suffered that day. During the interview, when she realized it was an anniversary date of her encounter with the mob, Eckford became quite agitated before recovering her composure.

35. Transcript of telephone conversation between Gloster Current and Daisy Bates, Sept. 4, 1957, Papers of the NAACP.

36. Ibid.

37. Ibid.

38. Ibid.

39. Bates, *Long Shadow*, 66.

40. Ibid., 67.

41. *Arkansas Gazette*, Sept. 5, 1957.

42. Rev. W. H. Bass statement, Sept. 4, 1957, FBI Papers, Special Collections, University of Arkansas Libraries, UALR. "We proceeded to 13th and Park where we met the students. We met the students at approximately 8:20 A.M. and decided to

accompany them to the High School grounds because of the presence of the National Guard and felt the students needed our moral support. At about 8:24 A.M. we proceeded down Park St., towards the school."

43. Bates, *Long Shadow*, 67.

44. Bass statement, UALR.

45. Special Collections, University of Arkansas Libraries, UALR.

46. *Arkansas Gazette*, Sept. 5, 1957.

47. Bates, *Long Shadow*, 75. As her FBI affidavit makes clear, Elizabeth Eckford, probably in shock, could remember very few of the actual details of her attempt to enter Central. In his account for the *New York Times*, following the journalistic tradition of the times, Benjamin Fine left himself out of the story. In the author's interview with Elizabeth Eckford, she recognized that Bates's account of that morning was given to her by Benjamin Fine.

48. Bates, *Long Shadow*, 67.

49. Ibid.

50. Affidavit of Minnijean Brown, FBI Investigation, Sept. 3, 1957, UALR.

51. Affidavit of Harry Bass, FBI Investigation, Sept. 3, 1957, UALR.

52. Bates, *Long Shadow*, 67.

53. Rev. Colbert S. Cartwright statement, FBI Papers, UALR.

54. For example, when Melba Pattillio's mother lost her job as a public school teacher in North Little Rock, Lois Pattillo turned to Bishop Sherman, not Bates or the NAACP, for help. It was through the bishop's influence that her teaching contract was renewed. Beals, *Warriors Don't Cry*, 293, 294.

55. Bates, interview by Jacoway, 13.

56. Ibid.

57. *Arkansas Democrat*, Sept. 5, 1957.

58. Blossom, *It HAS Happened Here*, 27.

59. E-mail from Georg Iggers to author, Aug. 7, 2002.

CHAPTER TEN

1. Transcript of telephone conversation between Daisy Bates and Gloster Current, Sept. 6, 1957, Box 5, Folder 2, Madison.

2. Ibid.

3. Christopher Mercer, interview by author; Carutha Braden, interview by author, Aug. 2, 2004.

4. Williams, *Thurgood Marshall*, 264, 265

5. *Arkansas Gazette*, Sept. 8, 1957.

6. *Arkansas Democrat*, Sept. 7, 1957.

7. Ibid., Sept. 8, 1957.

8. Affidavit of Daisy Bates, FBI Investigation, Sept. 8, 1957, UALR.

9. Ibid.

10. George Howard Jr., interview by author, Jan. 9, 2002.

11. *Arkansas Democrat*, Sept. 8, 1957.

12. Transcript of telephone conversation between Daisy Bates and Gloster Current, Sept. 9, 1957, microfilm, Part 3, Reel 1, NAACP Administration, 1956–65, General Office File "Little Rock, Central High, 1956–57," Papers of the NAACP.

13. Reed, *Faubus*, 217.

14. *Arkansas Democrat*, Sept. 9, 1957.

15. Transcript of telephone conversation between Daisy Bates and Gloster Current, Sept. 9, 1957, Papers of the NAACP.

16. *Arkansas Gazette*, Sept. 15, 1957.

17. *Arkansas Democrat*, Sept. 9, 1957.

18. Transcript of telephone conversation between Daisy Bates and Gloster Current, Sept. 9, 1957, Papers of the NAACP.

19. Ibid.

20. Freyer, *Little Rock Crisis*, 130.

21. Ibid.

22. Transcript of telephone conversation between Gloster Current and Daisy Bates, Sept. 9, 1957, Papers of the NAACP.

23. Though the interview carried no byline, it was surely done by Benjamin Fine, who was winning Bates's trust.

24. Thelma Mothershed, interview, *New York Times*, Sept. 10, 1957.

25. Beals, *Warriors Don't Cry*, 122.

26. *St. Louis Argus*, Sept. 13, 1957.

27. Reed, *Faubus*, 217.

28. Roy Reed has pointed out the president's ambivalence in his public reaction to *Brown*. Though the Court's decision was "probably" correct, he could "understand the strong emotions on the other side." Ibid., 209.

29. Ibid., 220, 221.

30. Ibid., 221.

31. Transcript of telephone conversation between Daisy Bates and Gloster Current, Sept. 9, 1957, Papers of the NAACP.

32. Beals, *Warriors Don't Cry*, 86.

33. *State Press*, Sept. 13, 1957.

34. Ibid., Sept. 20, 1957.

35. Beals, *Warriors Don't Cry*, 93, 94, 95.

36. E-mail from Constance Pearlstien to author, Jan. 29, 2004.

37. Bates, *Long Shadow*, 83.

Notes

38. Transcript of telephone conversation between Gloster Current and Daisy Bates, Sept. 23, 1957, Group 3, Series A, Container 98, Folder "Desegregation of Schools, Arkansas, Little Rock, Central High, 1956–1957," Papers of the NAACP.

39. Ibid.

40. Spitzberg, *Racial Politics in Little Rock*, 68.

41. As evidence of this, Bates mentions their names again. According to the national NAACP transcript of the telephone conversation on September 24, Bates told Current the following: "I gave the kids instructions not to go in today until 5 to 12. That was just a general decision by Dunaway and Ashmore." In reality, there was no "decision" made by either of the two men, since they had no authority in the matter, but this statement does reveal that Bates occasionally continued to rely on them for advice. Throughout *Long Shadow*, Bates protected the identities of some whites who had been sympathetic to her, but in later interviews, when it would have been safe to acknowledge their assistance, she sometimes tended to dismiss them.

42. Bates, *Long Shadow*, 87.

43. Ibid., 88.

44. Transcript of telephone conversation between Daisy Bates and Gloster Current, Sept. 24, 1957, Papers of the NAACP.

45. Bates, *Long Shadow*, 88, 89.

46. Draft of *Long Shadow*, III, Madison. As adults, the Nine would look back and question what their parents and Daisy had risked. Melba Pattillo Beals wrote, "When on that ominous date, Mob Monday, September 23, 1957, the NAACP officials and ministers dropped us off to go to Central for the second time under court order, I wonder how in their minds they justified such an act. As an adult, I believe had it been me driving, I would have kept going rather than allow my children to face that rampaging mob. And yet had we students not gone to school that day, perhaps the integration of Central, and of a whole string of other Southern schools that eventually followed, would never have taken place." Beals, *Warriors Don't Cry*, 309.

47. Bates, *Long Shadow*, 89, 90.

48. Ibid., 93.

49. Ibid., 90.

50. Ibid., 91; Kirk, *Redefining the Color Line*, 91.

51. *Afro-American*, Nov. 9, 1959.

52. *Arkansas Democrat*, Sept. 23, 1957.

53. *Afro-American* (magazine section), Nov. 9, 1957, 7.

54. Ibid., 9.

55. Huckaby, *Crisis at Central High*, 35–39.

56. Pete Daniel, *Lost Revolutions: The South in the 1950s* (Chapel Hill: University of North Carolina Press for Smithsonian National Museum of American History, Washington, D.C., 2000), 265.

57. Bates, *Long Shadow*, 95.

58. *Arkansas Gazette*, Sept. 24, 1957.

59. *Arkansas Democrat*, Sept. 24, 1957.

60. *New York Times*, Sept. 24, 1957.

61. Bates, *Long Shadow*, 96.

62. Transcript of telephone conversation between Clarence Laws and Gloster Current, Sept. 23, 1957, Papers of the NAACP.

63. Ibid.

64. Ibid.

65. Laws told Current on the morning that the children went into the school on September 23, "18 leaders . . . signed the statement it was published in the morning paper and will be in the afternoon paper. . . . The leaflets will be printed and placed in restaurants and cab stands so that our views on this matter will be known." Ibid.

CHAPTER ELEVEN

1. Record, *Little Rock*, 64.

2. Transcript of telephone conversation between Daisy Bates and Gloster Current, Sept. 22, 1957, Papers of the NAACP.

3. Ibid.

4. Ibid.

5. Ibid.

6. Ibid.

7. Ibid.

8. Bates, *Long Shadow*, 101.

9. Blossom, It *HAS Happened Here*, 118.

10. Ibid., 101, 102.

11. Ibid., 104.

12. Ibid., 23.

13. *State Press*, Sept. 27, 1957.

14. Annie Abrams, interview by author, Apr. 12, 2002.

15. Transcript of conversation between Gloster Current, Clarence Laws, and Daisy Bates, Oct. 3, 1957, 9:30 P.M., Box 5, File 2, Madison.

16. Ibid.

17. Ibid.

18. Transcript of telephone conversation between Gloster Current and Clarence Laws, Oct. 2, 1957, Box 5, File 2, Madison.

19. Ibid.

20. Ibid.

Notes

21. Transcript of telephone conversation between Gloster Current and Clarence Laws, Oct. 3, 1957, Madison.

22. Ibid.

23. Transcript of conversation between Gloster Current, Clarence Laws, and Daisy Bates, Oct. 3, 1957, Madison.

24. Ibid.

25. Ibid.

26. Transcript of telephone conversation between Daisy Bates and Gloster Current, Oct. 3, 1957, Box 5, File 2, Madison.

27. Transcript of conversation between Gloster Current, Clarence Laws, and Daisy Bates, Oct. 3, 1957, Madison.

28. Ibid.

29. Ibid.

30. *State Press*, Oct. 4, 1957.

31. *Afro-American*, Oct. 12, 1957.

32. *State Press*, Oct. 11, 1957.

33. *Arkansas State Press*, Oct. 18, 1957.

34. *Arkansas Gazette*, Oct. 16, 1957.

35. Ibid., Oct. 15, 1957.

36. Transcript of conversation between Daisy Bates and Gloster Current, Oct. 17, 1957, in author's possession.

37. Beals, *Warriors Don't Cry*, 122, 123.

38. *Arkansas Gazette*, Oct. 24, 1957.

39. Occasionally labor unions ran ads, too. See, for example, *State Press*, Oct. 25, 1957, the ad of ILWU Local 6, San Francisco.

40. *State Press*, Oct. 25, 1957.

CHAPTER TWELVE

1. Transcript of telephone conversation between Clarence Laws and Gloster Current, Oct. 31, 1957, in author's possession.

2. *Arkansas Democrat*, Nov. 1, 1957.

3. Ibid.

4. *World Wide Photo*, Nov. 1, 1957.

5. *State Press*, Nov. 8, 1957.

6. *Arkansas Democrat*, Nov. 3, 1957.

7. Freyer, *Little Rock Crisis*, 131.

8. Lorch, interview.

9. *Arkansas Gazette*, Nov. 5, 1957.

10. *State Press*, Nov. 8, 1957.

11. Ibid., Nov. 15, 1957.

12. Roberts, interview.

13. Ibid.

14. Margaret Jackson was an outspoken member of the Mothers League.

15. Transcript of telephone conversation between Clarence Laws and Gloster Current, Nov. 25, 1957, Papers of the NAACP.

16. Transcript of telephone conversation between Daisy Bates and Gloster Current, Nov. 25, 1957, Papers of the NAACP.

17. Bates, interview by Jacoway, 29.

18. Transcript of telephone conversation between Daisy Bates and Gloster Current, Nov. 25, 1957, Papers of the NAACP.

19. Ibid.

20. Beals, *Warriors Don't Cry*, 201. Melba Pattillo Beals wrote in her diary, "When Mother and I arrived at Mrs. Bates's home for the Thanksgiving dinner, I knew even more people than usual were there, because we couldn't find a place to park. When I entered the spacious liking room, there was standing room only. I had never seen so many people, most of them reporters, squeezed into that space under hot glaring lights. . . . At the center of the room, some of the other nine students, dressed in Sunday best, were sitting at a table."

21. *Los Angeles Sentinel*, Dec. 5, 1957.

22. *Arkansas Democrat*, Dec. 3, 1957.

23. "Trust Agreement," n.d., Papers of the NAACP.

24. "Daisy Bates" handbill, in author's possession.

25. *Arkansas Democrat*, Dec. 17, 1957.

26. *State Press*, Dec. 20, 1957.

27. Clarence Laws to Roy Wilkins, Dec. 18, 1957, Box 4, Folder 10, Madison.

28. *Pittsburgh Courier*, Dec. 7, 1957.

29. Huckaby, *Crisis at Central High*, 94.

30. In an early version of *Long Shadow*, Bates wrote, "Minnijean Brown is a very high strung girl and shows her emotions on her face. She has a lot of personality and is the kind of girl one notices when she walks into a room. She carries her head high and gives an impression of great independence. . . . She had spirit and temper and would not take as much as the other children so she was always on the carpet in the principal's office." Draft of *Long Shadow*, III, 16, Madison.

31. Clarence Laws to Roy Wilkins, Dec. 18, 1957, Papers of the NAACP.

32. Report written for Southern Regional Council by Kenneth Clark, Dec. 11, 1957, Papers of the NAACP.

33. Daisy Bates to Roy Wilkins, Dec. (?), 1957, in author's possession.

34. *Arkansas Democrat*, Dec. 26, 1957.

35. Daisy Bates to news organizations, telegram, Dec. 31, 1957, Papers of the NAACP.

36. Daisy Bates to Dorothy Schiff et al., telegram, Dec. 31, 1957, Box 4, File 10, Madison.

37. *State Press*, Jan. 3, 1958.

38. "Total 1957 memberships & Freedom Fund Contributions received from Branches in Arkansas," Box 4, File 10, Madison.

39. *State Press*, Dec. (?) 1957.

40. Draft of *Long Shadow*, III, 42, 43, Madison.

41. Bates, interview by Jacoway, 30, 31.

CHAPTER THIRTEEN

1. *Arkansas Gazette*, Jan. 9, 1958.

2. Roy Wilkins to Daisy Bates, Jan. 24, 1958, Papers of the NAACP.

3. Transcript of telephone conversation between Gloster Current, Clarence Laws, Christopher Mercer, and Daisy Bates, Feb. 12, 1958, Papers of the NAACP.

4. NAACP press release, Feb. 13, 1958, Papers of the NAACP.

5. Transcript of telephone conversation between Gloster Current, Clarence Laws, and Daisy Bates, Feb. 13, 1958, Papers of the NAACP.

6. Memorandum from Clarence Laws to Roy Wilkins, Feb. 19, 1958, Re: Minnijean Brown, Folder Arkansas Schools, Papers of the NAACP.

7. *New York Post*, Apr. 7, 1958.

8. Thelma Mothershed Wair, interview by author. Nov. 13, 2004.

9. Speech to tenth annual National Civil Liberties Clearinghouse Conference, May 7, 1958, Madison.

10. *State Press*, Feb. 28, 1958.

11. *Arkansas Gazette*, Apr. 11, 1958.

12. Ibid., Apr. 8, 1958; *Arkansas Democrat*, Apr. 7, 1958.

13. *Arkansas Gazette*, Apr 8, 1958.

14. Ibid., Apr. 22, 1958.

15. Ibid., Apr. 13, 1958.

16. *State Press*, Apr. 18, 1958.

17. Herbert Thomas to Daisy Bates, Apr. 28, 1958, Madison.

18. Ibid.

19. Kirk, "Black Activism," 180.

20. *New York Post*, Apr. 9, 1958.

21. Ibid.

22. Memorandum to Mr. Current from Ruth Yelville, May 16, 1958, Papers of the NAACP.

23. In an early draft of her book, Bates wrote about the difficulty she had in contacting General Walker directly, who was supposed to be getting information through a liaison. "After I made about four calls General Walker called me himself. We had been trying to talk to him since early September and this was in October or early November. . . . I told Walker what had been happening to the children and that there was no liaison between Blossom and the school. . . . I went down the list and told him all the things that had happened and he said he did not know any of it." As she did in the final version, Bates did not write about the daily calls to the NAACP national office. She made it sound as if she only reported to Thurgood Marshall. She said she had not been able to catch up with General Walker. She wrote that Marshall told her, " 'Daisy Bates, you cannot run the United States Army, the NAACP and the whole damn country. It is army regulation that someone is selected as liaison officer—the army does not talk to civilians.' I said, 'How in hell can he find . . .' Thurgood hung up in my ear." Draft of *Long Shadow*, III, 25, Madison.

24. *Afro-American*, June 7, 1958.

25. Pauli Murray to Roy Wilkins, May 28, 1958, Box 1, Folder 7, Madison.

26. Elizabeth Eckford, interview.

27. Oscar Eckford, interview.

28. Record, *Little Rock*, 98.

29. *Afro-American*, June 7, 1958.

30. Press release "Little Rock Students Honored in New York," June 19, 1958, Papers of the NAACP.

31. Roy Wilkins to Gus Herndon, July 1, 1958, Group 3, A44, Papers of the NAACP.

32. "Management Report on the Arkansas State Press," July 10, 1958, Papers of the NAACP.

33. Roy Wilkins to Daisy Bates, July 22, 1958, Papers of the NAACP.

34. Record, *Little Rock*, 98.

35. Ibid., 103.

36. Freyer, *Little Rock Crisis*, 145, 146.

37. *Arkansas Democrat*, June 27, 1958.

38. Daisy Bates, FBI file; *Washington Star*, May 13, 1958.

39. Record, *Little Rock*, 105.

40. Freyer, *Little Rock Crisis*, 147.

41. Charles P. Howard to Roy Wilkins, July 28, 1958, Group 3, A44, Papers of the NAACP.

42. Roy Wilkins to Daisy Bates, telegram, Aug. 26, 1958, Papers of the NAACP.

43. Reed, *Faubus*, 240.

44. Bates, *Long Shadow*, 159.

Notes

45. *Arkansas Democrat*, Sept. 17, 1958.

46. Bates, *Long Shadow*, 156, 157.

47. *Arkansas Democrat*, Sept. 24, 1958.

48. Freyer, *Little Rock Crisis*, 157.

49. Laura A. Miller, *Fearless: Irene Gaston Samuel and the Life of a Southern Liberal* (Little Rock: University of Arkansas Press, 2002), 36.

50. Bates, interview by Jacoway, 65.

51. *State Press*, Oct. 17, 1958.

52. "Memorandum from Mr. Wilkins to Mr. McClain," Sept. 8, 1958, Papers of the NAACP.

53. Roy Wilkins to Charles Howard, Aug. 22, 1958, Group 3, A44, Papers of the NAACP.

54. Bates, *Long Shadow*, 155.

55. *Pittsburgh Courier*, Oct. 11, 1958.

56. *Afro-American*, Oct. 18, 1958.

57. *Ebony*, November 1958, 17, 18.

58. Ibid., 20.

59. *Minneapolis Sunday Tribune*, Nov. 16, 1958.

60. Meyers appeared to spell her first name with an "h," but her handwriting is unclear on this point.

61. *Ebony*, Nov. 1958, 22.

62. Ibid.

63. Ibid.

64. *Minneapolis Sunday Tribune*, Nov. 16, 1958.

65. Record, *Little Rock*, 127.

66. *Minneapolis Sunday Tribune*, Nov. 16, 1958.

67. Roy Wilkins to "Dear Friend," Dec. 11, 1958, Papers of the NAACP.

68. *Pittsburgh Courier*, Jan. 10, 1959.

CHAPTER FOURTEEN

1. Daisy Bates to Roy Wilkins, Jan. 29, 1959, Papers of the NAACP.

2. *Arkansas Democrat*, Jan. 22, 1959.

3. Spitzberg, *Racial Politics in Little Rock*, 129.

4. A. Phillip Randolph to Daisy Bates, Mar. 14, 1959, Box 2, Folder 1, Madison.

5. Daisy Bates to Gloster Current, Mar. 5, 1959, Group 3, C4, Papers of the NAACP.

6. Elizabeth Eckford, interview.

7. Pauli Murray to Daisy Bates, May 21, 1959, in author's possession.

8. Ibid.

9. Daisy Bates to Roy Wilkins, July 29, 1959, Box 2, Folder 1, Madison.

10. Ibid.

11. Timothy B. Tyson, *Radio Free Dixie: Robert F. Williams and the Roots of Black Power* (Chapel Hill: University of North Carolina Press), 149.

12. Ibid., 154.

13. Ibid.

14. Ibid., 164.

15. Ibid., 243.

16. Daisy Bates to Margaret Wilson, May 25, 1959, Box 2, File 1, Madison.

17. Daisy Bates to Theodore A. Jones, May 1959, Box 2, File 1, Madison.

18. Gloster Current to Daisy Bates, Jan. 21, 1959, Group 3, C4, Folder 5, Papers of the NAACP. Current mentions drafting a letter thanking the tutors for Wilkins to sign.

19. *Amsterdam News*, May 30, 1959.

20. Freyer, *Little Rock Crisis*, 162.

21. *Afro-American*, June 6, 1959.

22. Ibid., July 6, 1959.

23. *New York Post*, July 6, 1959.

24. W. Wilson, assistant attorney general for civil rights, to Daisy Bates, July 10, 1959, Box 4, Folder 10, Madison.

25. *Jet*, June 4, 1959, 13.

26. Daisy Bates to Kivie Kaplan, June 26, 1959, in author's possession.

27. Benjamin Fine to Daisy Bates, July 23, 1959, in author's possession.

28. Daisy Bates to Carolyn Anthony, Aug. 3, 1959, in author's possession.

29. Daisy Bates to Julia Owen, July 23 1959, Box 2, Folder 1, Madison.

30. Daisy Bates to Thelma Mothershed, July 29, 1959, Madison; Daisy Bates to Mrs. Howard Aller, July 23, 1959, Box 2, Folder 1, Madison.

31. Daisy Bates to Roy Wilkins, July 29, 1959, Madison.

32. Ibid.

33. Ibid.

34. Bates, *Long Shadow*, 164.

35. Ibid., 165.

36. Ibid.

37. Daisy Bates to President Eisenhower, telegram, n.d., Box 2, Folder 2, Madison.

38. *New York Post*, Aug. 14, 1959.

39. Estella Johnson, one of the first black students to attend Hall High School, recalled in an oral interview with Tom Dillard and the author on Jan. 20, 2004, at the Butler Center for Arkansas Studies in Little Rock that it was future civil rights attorney John Walker who, while still an employee for the Arkansas Council on Human Relations, solicited her to go to Hall.

40. Daisy Bates to Wiley A. Branton, Aug. 26, 1959, Group 3, A99, Folder 2, Papers of the NAACP.

41. Ibid.

42. Ibid.

43. Wiley Branton to Daisy Bates, Aug. 29, 1959, Group 3, A99, Folder 2, Papers of the NAACP.

44. Reed, *Faubus*, 274.

45. Ibid., 277.

46. Daisy Bates to Thurgood Marshall, Aug. 3, 1959, Box 2, Folder 2, Madison.

47. Reed, *Faubus*, 257.

48. Daisy Bates to NAACP Board of Directors, Nov. 19, 1959, Folder "Student files, incidents, general reports, memos, 1957–1960," Papers of the NAACP.

49. Ibid.

50. Daisy Bates to William Hadley, Nov. 16, 1959, Box 2, File 2, Madison.

51. Daisy Bates to NAACP Board of Directors, Nov. 19, 1959, Papers of the NAACP.

52. Ibid.

53. In an interview with Irene Wassell, L. C. "jokingly" referred to Moral Re-Armament as a "high-faluting [sic] group," whose purpose it was to provide "retired capitalists" the chance to "get rid of their guilt by doing good." Wassell, "L. C. Bates," 68.

54. *Jet*, Dec. 10, 1959, 15.

55. Wassell, "L. C. Bates," 69.

56. *New York Times*, Dec. 15, 1959.

57. Daisy Bates to William Hadley, Dec. 10, 1959, Madison.

58. *Jet*, Dec. 10, 1959, 14.

59. Ibid.

60. Memorandum, Roy Wilkins to Editors and Radio Program Directors, Dec. 17, 1959, Group 3, A44, Papers of the NAACP.

61. Daisy Bates to H. W. Sewing, Jan. 21, 1960, Fayetteville.

62. Daisy Bates to William Hadley, Dec. 10, 1959, Box 2, File 2, Madison.

63. "Field Secretary's Report for Period Ending Jan. 25, 1960," by L. C. Bates for Gloster Current, Papers of the NAACP.

64. Roy Wilkins to Daisy Bates, Dec. 17, 1959, in author's possession.

CHAPTER FIFTEEN

1. *Chattanooga Free Press*, Jan. 2, 1960.

2. Bettye Williams to Daisy Bates, Feb. 26, 1960, Box 2, File 3, Madison.

3. Gloster Current to Daisy Bates, Feb. 29, 1960, Group 3, C223, Papers of the NAACP.

4. "Statement of Mrs. L. C. Bates Regarding the U.S. Supreme Court Ruling on Tuesday, Feb. 23, 1960," Group 3, A99, Folder 1, Papers of the NAACP.

5. *Arkansas Democrat*, Feb. 23, 1960.

6. Ibid., Feb. 19, 1960.

7. Daisy Bates to Roy Wilkins, Feb. 10, 1960, Papers of the NAACP.

8. Daisy Bates to Roy Wilkins, Feb. 23, 1960, Papers of the NAACP.

9. Ibid.

10. *Arkansas Democrat*, Mar. 10, 1960; *Arkansas Gazette*, Mar. 11, 1960.

11. *Arkansas Democrat*, Mar. 10, 1960.

12. Grif Stockley, "Thank God for Mississippi: Race Relations in Arkansas," 114, unpublished ms., Butler Center for Arkansas Studies, Little Rock.

13. "December 1960 Annual Report" by L. C. Bates for Gloster Current, Dec. 3, 1960, Box 4, Folder 10, Madison.

14. *Arkansas Gazette*, Apr. 16, 1960.

15. *Arkansas Democrat*, Apr. 15, 1960.

16. "December 1960 Annual Report" by L. C. Bates for Gloster Current, Madison.

17. Ibid.

18. Ibid.

19. Ibid.

20. Ibid.

21. Daisy Bates to Lafayette Harris, Box 2, Folder 3, Madison.

22. Kirk, "Black Activism," 210.

23. Ibid., 221.

24. *Arkansas Democrat*, Mar. 10, 1960.

25. "December 1960 Annual Report" by L. C. Bates for Gloster Current, Madison.

26. Robert L Carter to Daisy Bates, Apr. 4, 1960, Group 3, Box A98, Folder "School Desegregation, Ark. '56–64," Papers of the NAACP.

27. Edward Muse to Daisy Bates, Mar. 7, 1960, Box 2, Folder 3, Madison.

28. Ibid.

29. Daisy Bates to Mrs. H. D. Birnbaum, Apr. 5, 1960, Box 2, File 3, Madison. The couple's last name in the acknowledgments of *The Long Shadow of Little Rock* is misspelled as "Birnbaun."

30. E-mail from Constance Pearlstien to author, Jan. 29, 2004.

31. Daisy Bates, FBI File. According to Audre Hanneman, Bates had met Adlai Stevenson at a dinner party at the townhouse of Marietta Tree, a Democratic Party benefactor in the 1950s and 1960s. Audre Hanneman to author, Dec. 10, 2002.

32. E-mail from Constance Pearlstien to author, Jan. 29, 2004.

33. Audre Hanneman to author, May 8, 2002.

34. Ibid.

35. Memo to Executive Staff from Gloster Current, June 9, 1960, Papers of the NAACP.

36. Jeanne Nyilas to Roy Wilkins, Sept. 1, 1960, Papers of the NAACP.

37. Daisy Bates to Officers and Members of the Executive Board, Greenwich Village, Chelsea Branch, Oct. 12, 1960, Papers of the NAACP.

38. Daisy Bates to Roy Wilkins, Sept. 7, 1960, Box 2, Folder 4, Madison.

39. Spitzberg, "Racial Politics," 158.

40. "December 1960 Annual Report" by L. C. Bates for Gloster Current, Madison.

41. Roberts, interview.

42. Elizabeth Eckford, interview.

43. Ibid.

44. Minnijean Brown Trickey, interview by author, June 15, 2002.

45. Ernest Green, interview by author, Oct. 25, 2002.

46. Roberts, interview.

47. Beals, *Warriors Don't Cry*, 84.

48. Ibid., xiii.

49. Green, interview.

50. Trickey, interview.

51. Ibid., 191.

52. Daisy Bates to Freyda Rothstein, June 12, 1979, Box 2, Folder 8, Fayetteville.

53. "December 1960 Annual Report" by L. C. Bates for Gloster Current, Madison.

54. Daisy Bates to Mrs. Howard Lewis Aller, Dec. 20, 1960, Box 2, File 5, Madison.

55. Daisy Bates to Mrs. Howard Lewis Aller, Jan. 4, 1961, Box 2, File 5, Madison.

56. Robert Nemiroff to Daisy Bates, Feb. 11, 1961, Box 2, Folder 5, Madison.

57. Daisy Bates to Mrs. Howard Lewis Aller, July 24, 1961, Box 2, Folder 6, Madison.

58. Robert Nemiroff to Daisy Bates, Feb. 11, 1961, Madison.

59. William Branch to author, June 7, 2002.

60. Hanneman recalls that Bates had employed others before herself as a "secretary and researcher," but Hanneman did not know who those persons were. Audre Hanneman to author, Apr. 26, 2002.

61. George Pentry, interview by author, May 9, 2002.

62. Ibid.
63. Audre Hanneman to author, May 3, 2004.
64. Audre Hanneman to author, Apr. 26, 2002.
65. Williams, *Thurgood Marshall*, 273.
66. Audre Hanneman to author, Apr. 26, 2002.
67. Ibid.
68. Ibid.
69. Ibid.
70. Johnnie Meyers to Daisy Bates, Oct. 16, 1961, Box 2, File 6, Madison.
71. Ibid.
72. Audre Hanneman to author, Apr. 26, 2002.
73. Ibid.
74. Ibid.

CHAPTER SIXTEEN

1. "1961 Annual Report," L. C. Bates, Dec. 6, 1961, Group 3, C222, Folder 4, Papers of the NAACP.
2. Ibid.
3. Daisy Bates to Thelma Mothershed, Apr. 2, 1962, Box 3, Folder 1, Madison.
4. Bates, *Long Shadow*, xv.
5. Ibid., 212.
6. Ibid.
7. Ibid., 225.
8. Daisy Bates, FBI File, summarizing article in *Pine Bluff Commercial*, Apr. 18, 1962.
9. "National Association for the Advancement of Colored People Draft March 28, 1962, Second Report—Special Committee on Strategy Concerned with Expanded C.O.R.E. program," 1, Madison.
10. Ibid., 2.
11. Daisy Bates to L. C. Bates, June 9, 1962, Box 3, Folder 1, Madison.
12. Mother Bates to Daisy and L. C. Bates, June 21, 1962, Box 3, File 1, Madison.
13. A number of individuals (including Bates's minister in Little Rock) reported to the author that they had heard rumors of an affair.
14. Mother Bates to Daisy and L. C. Bates, June 21, 1962, Madison.
15. Ibid.
16. L. C. Bates to Daisy Bates, Dec. 10, 1962, Madison.
17. Jones, interview.

Notes

18. L. C. Bates to Daisy Bates, Dec. 10, 1962, Madison.

19. Ibid.

20. Ibid.

21. Ibid.

22. Letter from Ethyl (?) to Daisy Bates, July 27, 1962, Box 3, File 1, Madison.

23. *Daisy G. Bates v. L. C. Bates*, Pul. Chan. Ct. 122421, Divorce Decree incorporating Separation Agreement, Feb. 25, 1963.

24. Frankie Jeffries family, interview by author, May 22, 2002.

25. Ann Henry, interview by author, Feb. 20, 2002. Henry later refused to sit for a recorded interview, insisting that that Daisy's and L. C.'s privacy should be respected.

26. Dumas, interview.

27. Jeffries family (Linder Jeffries), interview.

28. Ibid.

29. L. C. Bates to Daisy Bates, Dec. 10, 1962, Madison.

30. Penty, interview.

31. Rev. Rufus King Young, interview by author, Feb. 8, 2002.

32. Daisy Bates to Wiley Branton, Aug. 28, 1962, Box 1, File 2, Fayetteville.

33. Wiley Branton to Daisy Bates, Sept. 12, 1962, Group 3, A99, Papers of the NAACP.

34. Ibid.

35. Gretchen Eick, *Dissent in Wichita: The Civil Rights Movement in the Midwest* (Urbana: University of Illinois Press, 2001), 91.

36. Jack E. Tanner to author, July 18, 2002.

37. Ibid.

CHAPTER SEVENTEEN

1. *New York Times*, Book Section, Nov. 4, 1962.

2. *Churchman*, Dec. 1962.

3. In *A Stone of Hope*, David Chappel has shown that historians of the civil rights movement have minimized the role that fundamentalist faith played in its success. Black Americans found in their religion the determination to press forward. Conversely, he writes, segregationists were disappointed by their own religious leaders who generally had no appetite for making religion the cornerstone of the opposition to ending Jim Crow.

4. *Washington Post*, Book Section, Oct. 28, 1962.

5. Kivie Kaplan to Daisy Bates, Oct. 26, 1962, Box 4, Folder 4, Madison.

6. *Arkansas Gazette*, Nov. 12, 1962.

7. Clyde Lee Cross to Daisy Bates, Sept. (?), 1962, and Dec. (?), 1962, Box 1, File 2, Fayetteville.

8. *Afro-American*, Jan. 12, 1963.

9. Bates, *Long Shadow*, 225.

10. Gloster Current to Daisy Bates, Mar. 14, 1963, Papers of the NAACP.

11. *Amsterdam News*, Feb. 16, 1963.

12. Daisy Bates to Louis Martin, May 8, 1963, Box 1, File 7, Fayetteville.

13. Alan Draper, *A Rope of Sand: The AFL-CIO Committee on Political Action 1955–1967* (New York: Praeger, 1989), 71.

14. Ibid.

15. *Akron Beacon Journal*, July 15, 1963.

16. Stockley, "Thank God for Mississippi," 121.

17. Other whites made the trip. Ernest Dumas made the trip by himself.

18. Daisy Bates to Archibald Carey, Dec. 21, 1963, Box 3, Folder 2, Madison.

19. Daisy Bates to Helen Young, Dec. 19, 1963, Box 3, Folder 2, Madison.

20. Daisy Bates to Jean Hadley, Dec. 30, 1963, Box 3, Folder 2, Madison.

21. Bates, interview by Jacoway, 40.

22. Ibid., 40, 41.

23. Ibid., 39.

24. Mercedier Goodwin to Louis Martin, Mar. 26, 1964, Box 1, File 8, Fayetteville.

25. *Ebony*, Apr. 1964, 18.

26. *Jet*, Apr. 1964, 18.

27. Ibid., 20.

28. Audre Hanneman to Daisy Bates, Apr. 26, 2002, in author's possession.

29. "The Responsibility of Citizenship in a Changing Society," Box 3, Folder 6, Madison.

30. Ibid.

31. Daisy Bates to Roy Wilkins, Nov. 6, 1964, Group 3, A99, Folder 1, Papers of the NAACP.

32. Monthly report from L. C. Bates to Gloster Current, June 11, 1965–Aug. 30, 1965, Group 6, C27, Papers of the NAACP.

33. Monthly report from L. C. Bates to Gloster Current, Mar. 14–Apr. 14, 1965, Group 6, C27, Papers of the NAACP.

34. *Arkansas Gazette*, Dec. 9, 1965.

35. *Pine Bluff Commercial*, June 22, 1965.

36. Edward Muse to Henry Lee Moon, July 27, 1965, Papers of the NAACP.

37. Press release, "In Little Rock, Ar. July 31," Papers of the NAACP.

38. Jeffries family (Frankie Jeffries), interview.

39. Ibid.

40. L. C. Bates to Gloster Current, Dec. 10, 1965, Group 3, C223, Folder 4, Papers of the NAACP.

CHAPTER EIGHTEEN

1. L. C. Bates to Gloster Current, Feb. 2, 1966, Group 4, C2, Folder 8, Papers of the NAACP.

2. Ibid.

3. Ibid.

4. Ibid.

5. L. C. Bates to Dr. Jerry Jewell, Dec. 1, 1966, Group 4, C2, Folder 8, Papers of the NAACP.

6. Daisy Bates to Dr. Jerry Jewell, Sept. 3, 1966, Papers of the NAACP.

7. L. C. Bates to Gloster Current, Feb. 2, 1966, Papers of the NAACP.

8. Daisy Bates to Dr. Jerry Jewell, Sept. 3, 1966, Papers of the NAACP.

9. Ibid.

10. Ibid.

11. Richard Dockery to L. C. Bates, Aug. 31, 1966, Folder "Arkansas State Conference," Papers of the NAACP.

12. Gloster Current to Daisy Bates, Sept. 27, 1966, Folder "Little Rock, Arkansas," Papers of the NAACP.

13. L. C. Bates to Dr. Jerry Jewell, Dec. 1, 1966, Papers of the NAACP.

14. "Report to Gloster Current from L. C. Bates," Re: Arkansas State Conference Oct. 22–23, 1966, Papers of the NAACP.

15. Efforts to obtain the records of the State Conference of Branches or the records of the Little Rock branch by historians have not been successful.

16. L. C. Bates to Gloster Current, Oct. 23, 1968, Papers of the NAACP.

17. L. C. Bates to Gloster Current, Feb. 2, 1966, Papers of the NAACP.

18. Ibid.

19. Ibid.

20. Gloster Current to George D. Flemings, Jan. 7, 1969, Papers of the NAACP.

21. *Arkansas Gazette*, Jan. 22, 1972.

22. Ibid.

23. Ibid.

24. *Echo*, Apr. 12, 1978.

25. Barbara Graves, interview by author, Aug. 7, 2002.

26. Linda Austin, interview by author, Aug. 1, 2002.

Notes

27. "Mitchellville OEA Self-Help Project," by Leo Collins of Arkansas AM&N (now the University of Arkansas at Pine Bluff), n.d., Box 6, File 5, Fayetteville.

28. *Arkansas Gazette*, Oct. 12, 1970.

29. *Arkansas Democrat*, Oct. 27, 1968.

30. "Inquiry into conditions at Mitchellville, Arkansas," undertaken at the request of Assistant Agricultural Secretary John A. Baker, n.d., Box 6, Fayetteville.

31. *Arkansas Gazette*, Oct. 12, 1970.

32. *Arkansas Democrat*, Oct. 27, 1968.

33. *Arkansas Gazette*, Oct. 5, 1971.

34. Ibid., Oct. 21, 1971.

35. "Considerations of the Mitchellville, Arkansas Project," n.d., Box 6, Fayetteville.

36. *Arkansas Democrat*, Oct. 27, 1968.

37. "Mrs. Bates Takes Plea to Capital, U.S. Comes to Aid of Mitchellville," *Arkansas Gazette*, n.d.

38. Ibid.

39. Richard McCarrell, interview by author, Aug. 17, 2002.

40. Austin, interview.

41. Mercer, interview, Jan. 17, 2002.

42. Young, interview.

43. *Arkansas Gazette*, Oct. 12, 1970.

44. Austin, interview.

45. Bates, interview by Jacoway, 45.

46. *Arkansas Gazette*, Jan. 22, 1972.

47. Jeffries family, interview.

48. Linda Mitchell, interview by author, Aug. 26, 2002.

49. Ibid.

50. Ibid.

51. Ibid.

52. Alice Love and Dave Love, interview by author, June 30, 2002.

53. Mitchell, interview.

54. Ibid.

55. Alice Love and Dave Love, interview.

56. Ibid.

57. Ibid.

58. McCarrell, interview.

59. Austin, interview.

60. Alice Love and David Love, interview.

61. Isabel Griswold, interview by author, Aug. 3, 2002.

62. Austin, interview.

63. Ibid.

64. McCarrell, interview.

65. Daisy Bates to Jennie B. Bates, Oct. 29, 1975, Box 1, Folder 9, Fayetteville.

CHAPTER NINETEEN

1. Wassell, "L. C. Bates," 66 n.2.

2. Abrams, interview.

3. *Arkansas Gazette*, Mar. 17, 1974.

4. Daisy Bates to Audre Hanneman, Feb. 8, 1975, Box 1, Folder 9, Fayetteville.

5. Daisy Bates to Elizabeth Olson, Mar. 3, 1976, Box 4, File 2, Fayetteville.

6. Associated Press, June 6, 1976, in author's possession.

7. Ibid.

8. Ibid.

9. *Arkansas Gazette*, Feb. 20, 1977.

10. Daisy Bates to William Branch, Sept. 23, 1978, Box 2, Folder 7, Fayetteville.

11. Jacqueline Trescott, "Update", *Arkansas Gazette*, n.d., Box 2, Folder 6, Fayetteville.

12. Stockley, "Thank God for Mississippi," 171.

13. Ibid., 172.

14. Ibid., 173.

15. Ibid.

16. Dr. Edith Irby Jones to John F. Coffin, Sept. 4, 1980, Box 2, File 9, Fayetteville.

17. Death Certificate, Box 5, File 5, Fayetteville.

18. President Jimmy Carter to Daisy Bates, Aug. 27, 1980, Box 5, Fayetteville.

19. Daisy Bates to William Branch, May 8, 1979, Box 2, Folder 8, Fayetteville.

20. Freyda Rothstein to Daisy Bates, May 29, 1979, Box 2, Folder 8, Fayetteville; Daisy Bates to Freyda Rothstein, June 12, 1979, Fayetteville.

21. Daisy Bates to Maya Angelou, Sept. 28, 1978, Box 2, Folder 7, Fayetteville.

22. Daisy Bates to Brynda Pappas, n.d., Box 2, File 2, Fayetteville.

23. Loretta Carter to Daisy Bates, Sept. 14, 1980, Box 2, File 9, Fayetteville.

24. Daisy Bates to Loretta Carter, n.d., Box 2, File 10, Fayetteville.

25. Ibid.

26. For a short time Merretazon was employed in the same office as the author.

27. Janice Kearney Nash, interview by author, Mar. 24, 2002. See Janis F. Kearney, *Cotton Field of Dreams: A Memoir* (Chicago: Writing Our World Press, 2004), 284–88.

28. *Arkansas Democrat*, Feb. 28, 1985.

29. Bates, *Long Shadow*, xvi.

30. Abrams, interview.

31. *Arkansas Democrat-Gazette*, Jan. 12, 1992.

Notes

32. Abrams, interview.

33. Ibid.

34. Young, interview.

35. Ibid.

36. Ibid.

37. Hicks, interview.

38. Ibid.

39. Ibid.

40. Ibid.

41. Ibid.

42. *Arkansas Democrat-Gazette*, Nov. 5, 1999.

43. Ibid.

44. Ibid., Nov. 10, 1999.

45. Daisy Bates is buried in Haven of Rest Cemetery in Little Rock.

46. *"Jet,"* May 15, 2000, 36.

47. *Arkansas Democrat-Gazette*, Oct. 28, 2003.

INDEX

Index

Index

Index

Index